Over the Wall/After the Fall

Over the Wall/After the Fall

Post-Communist Cultures through an East-West Gaze

Edited by
Sibelan Forrester,
Magdalena J. Zaborowska,
 and
Elena Gapova

Indiana
University
Press

BLOOMINGTON AND INDIANAPOLIS

This book is a publication of

Indiana University Press
601 North Morton Street
Bloomington, IN 47404-3797 USA

http://iupress.indiana.edu
Telephone orders   800-842-6796
Fax orders   812-855-7931
Orders by e-mail   iuporder@indiana.edu

Library of Congress Cataloging-in-Publication Data
Over the wall/after the fall : post-communist cultures through an East-West gaze / edited by Sibelan Forrester, Magdalena J. Zaborowska, and Elena Gapova.
    p. cm.
    Includes bibliographical references and index.
    ISBN 0-253-34432-8 (cloth : alk. paper) — ISBN 0-253-21696-6 (pbk. : alk. paper)
1. Social change—Europe, Eastern. 2. Social change—Former Soviet republics. 3. Post-communism—Europe, Eastern. 4. Post-communism—Former Soviet republics. 5. Europe, Eastern—Civilization. 6. Former Soviet republics—Civilization. I. Forrester, Sibelan E. S. (Sibelan Elizabeth S.) II. Zaborowska, Magdalena J. III. Gapova, Elena.
HN380.7.A8O9 2004
303.4'0947—dc22
                                                                    2004006411

1 2 3 4 5 09 08 07 06 05 04

This volume is dedicated to our children:
Yelena, Mislav, Nastya, Raian, and Cazmir,
who also live in between two worlds.
S. F., M. Z., E. G.

Contents

Contents

Preface

Over a decade has passed since the "fall" of communism in Eastern Europe, the surprising flowering of glasnost in the Soviet Union, the free elections in Poland that started the visible process of change, and the picturesque dismantling of the Berlin Wall. To great hurrah, various societies, formerly more-or-less closed toward the West, have opened to all the excesses of Western-style multinational capitalism, as well as to new freedoms and re-definitions of self and nationality. Here and there, the changes have been defined as good and bad, victory and defeat, gain and loss; for many of the people who actually are living through them, they have been a combination of those things. The millennium has turned, and several former Warsaw Pact nations are now part of the North Atlantic Treaty Organization—something that would once have been unimaginable.

The greater freedom of public discourse in Eastern Europe has allowed shifts in values and cultural alliances to emerge clearly, and the interchanges between East and West, once cramped by diplomatic stiffness or the finalities of emigration, have grown more fluid. North American and West European— or simply, "Western"—culture had a seductive attraction in the late Soviet and immediate post-communist period, since it offered a liberating alternative to Soviet-style socialism and responded to consumer and pop culture fantasies. The Eastern European cultural intelligentsia is now in a position more like that of artists, writers, and thinkers in the anti-intellectual climate of the United States, and to the extent that it still exists it has moved into a more sober evaluation of cultural models along with the growth of new local options in music, art, and literature. A 20-year-old Bulgarian who began her education at a Russian school is now more fluent in German and English, though she is still quite friendly toward Russians and their culture. The differences between countries that once appeared homogeneous to Western eyes have been highlighted by the variety of political fortunes, from the Czech and Slovak "velvet divorce" to war and violence in former Yugoslavia, moving from Slovenia through Croatia, Bosnia and Hercegovina, and Kosovo.

We live in that space between the end of the old order, which we welcomed as young adults, and the present, with its ever-growing residue of experience After. The first days of delight and disbelief have become the foundation for a different perspective. In this space many former misreadings of the region shift into clearer focus. With greater possibilities for openness on both sides of the traditional geographical polarization, scholars of and from Eastern Europe have struggled both to escape former distortions and to analyze those distortions.

Of course, misunderstandings between Eastern and Western Europe are nothing new: diaries of travelers from earlier centuries record all manner of surprise and prejudicial reaction to unfamiliar customs. Before the Second World War, Neville Chamberlain could call the democratic republic of Czechoslovakia a faraway state of which British citizens knew little. Still, the decades behind the Iron Curtain fed a spectacular growth in misunderstandings between East and West, especially misunderstandings of the East by Westerners, whose greater access to uncensored discourse and whose unquestioning assumption of a central position could reduce an Eastern visitor (or emigrant) to the margins, or to a condition of ironic silence:

> "*La Pologne? La Pologne?* Isn't it terribly cold there?" she asked, and then sighed with relief. So many countries have been turning up lately that the safest thing to talk about is climate.
>
> "Madame," I want to reply, "my people's poets do all their writing in mittens. I don't mean to imply that they never remove them; they do, indeed, if the moon is warm enough. In stanzas composed of raucous whooping, for only such can drown the windstorm's constant roar, they glorify the simple lives of our walrus herders. Our Classicists engrave their odes with inky icicles on trampled snowdrifts. The rest, our Decadents, bewail their fate with snowflakes instead of tears. He who wishes to drown himself must have an ax at hand to cut the ice." . . .
>
> That's what I mean to say. But I've forgotten the word for walrus in French. (Wisława Szymborska, "Vocabulary," in *Sol* [*Salt*, 1962])

The Frenchwoman feels that she must say something about the country from which Szymborska's speaker comes, and the Polish interlocutor's internal monologue leaps from a single cliché to a bouquet of exaggeration. Forgetting a key term, the word for "walrus," means that her reply must remain internal, a monologue rather than part of a dialogue, until its reproduction in writing much later. Because Szymborska's speaker must perform on the West's terms, in a Western language, she cannot communicate as she wishes to change or inform the Western other. Before she can speak, she has been relegated—and has retired of her own will—to the icy isolation of internal exile.

We approach this volume with a number of questions: How can we better know and study this field? Eastern Europe has been a province of secondary status vis-à-vis Russia in Western academic studies—therefore, we offer a collection of studies devoted to Eastern European literatures and cultures and to their relationships with the readers and cultures of North America and Western Europe. In public discourse, Eastern Europe has tended to appear through a veil of inherited clichés, reinforced by hazy journalism, unquestioned assumptions, and sometimes the nostalgia of diasporic communities. Even within scholarship, traditional approaches inherited from the era of Cold War polarization have limited discursive freedom and the resulting patterns of defensive nationalism. Can we introduce some of the theoretical sophistication that has grown up over the past several decades through tensions between "First" and

"Third" world into a study of the "Second" world? How odd that this collection of nations and subjectivities is so rarely listed by its "number," though the assumption of its continuing geographical and cultural opposition to Western Europe and the rest of the "First" world problematizes both whiteness and a generalized European identity. Scholars of postcolonial and African American studies have a particularly rich set of tools to offer to the examination of Eastern Europe—just as Eastern Europe can offer vital correctives to theories or opinions whose assumption of universal binarisms proceeds only from lack of information about the "second world."

To use Szymborska's vocabulary, can we write with our mittens off—with our mitts off—to integrate something of our own personal experiences into the dryer tones of scholarship, following the lead of colleagues in such fields as anthropology, literary studies, and women's studies who have already embraced autobiography as a useful tool of inquiry? Can we bring into the realm of literature, culture, and travelogue the sharp and troubling questions demanded by developing theories of literary and cultural studies? To put it in Szymborska's terms yet again, can we turn the "walrus" syndrome into a challenge for all our audiences and contribute to a meaningful discourse?

The editors would like to acknowledge the help and support that contributed to the creation of this volume. Our academic institutions, Furman University, Swarthmore College, Aarhus University in Denmark, and the University of Michigan offered administrative, technical, and library support. Gratitude and appreciation to friends and colleagues who made useful comments and suggestions as the volume took shape: N. B., Jiří Borský, John K. Cox, Gordana Crnković, Jerzy Durczak, Zenon Feszczak, Mikhail Gnedovsky, Bruce Grant, William Gorski, coleman a. jordan (ebo), Michael Kennedy, Yonka Krasteva, Hasso Krull, Jadwiga Maurer, Vesa Niinikangas, Ileana Orlich, Prem Poddar, Brian Porter, Nicholas Radel, Petar Ramadanovic, Leena-Maija Rossi, Bożena Shallcross, Joanna Zach-Błonska, and Barbara Zaczek. Willard Pate offered her original photographs, and Professor of Art History Michael Cothran provided invaluable expert help with slide images. Tatiana Bajuk's informative writing on the economic transition in Slovenia offered us a clear picture of contested authority and the reproduction of economic privilege in the "Wild East." Wisława Szymborska kindly allowed us to use Joanna Trzeciak's translation of her poem "Psalm" for our introduction. Marko Andryczyk shared with us the work of Yeezhak and generously gave us a copy of Jurko Koch's wonderful postcard advertising the extravaganza of Vy-Vykh.

Last but not least, we want to thank all those who inhabit the in-between spaces of the East-West whom we have encountered while working on this book and whose presence and often-anonymous anecdotal experiences, opinions, and appearances enlightened us and enriched this project.

Over the Wall/After the Fall

Psalm

How leaky are the borders of man-made states!
How many clouds float over them scot-free,
how many desert sands sift from country to country,
how many mountain pebbles roll onto foreign turf
in provocative leaps!

Need I cite each and every bird as it flies,
or alights, as now, on the lowered gate?
Even if it be a sparrow—its tail is abroad,
though its beak is still home. As if that weren't enough—it keeps fidgeting!

Out of countless insects I will single out the ant,
who, between the guard's left and right boots,
feels unobliged to answer questions of origin and destination.

If only this whole mess could be seen at once in detail
on every continent!
Isn't that a privet on the opposite bank
smuggling its hundred-thousandth leaf across the river?
Who else but the squid, brazenly long-armed,
would violate the sacred territorial waters?

How can we speak of any semblance of order
when we can't rearrange the stars,
to know which one shines for whom?

Not to mention the reprehensible spreading of fog!
Or the dusting of the steppe over its entire range
as though it weren't split in two!
Or voices carried over accommodating air waves:
summoning squeals and suggestive gurgles!

Only what's human can be truly alien.
The rest is mixed forest, undermining moles, and wind.

—Wisława Szymborska
—translated from the Polish by Joanna Trzeciak

Introduction: Mapping Postsocialist Cultural Studies

Magdalena J. Zaborowska, Sibelan Forrester,
and Elena Gapova

"How leaky are the borders of man-made states!"

Wisława Szymborska's lyric "Psalm" raises many of the issues central to this collection, describing play and motion across borders in space, time, thought, and discipline. The poem's appearance in English translation also embodies the zone that interests us: contact between the ubiquitous "West," particularly North America and Western Europe, and the cultures, literatures, and individuals of Eastern Europe, or the "East," in the years since the collapse of the socialist and communist systems that dominated the region for decades. Before we comment more extensively on its theoretical underpinnings and contents, we offer our reading of "Psalm" to open a post–Cold War[1] meditation on the themes, terms, and personal insights that emerge from the essays gathered in this volume.

Szymborska's poem crossed the border from Polish into English after the 1996 Nobel Prize for Literature made the poet's hushing, resonant name pronounceable in the West for the first time. What does this poem tell us about the nature of boundaries and of discourses that would dare to cross them? What does it mean for a Polish woman to win the Nobel Prize, joining such esteemed Eastern male dissidents as Czesław Miłosz and Joseph Brodsky, such gifted Western "outsiders" as Toni Morrison and Seamus Heaney? The poet inhabits a precise location on the map of the New Europe, a nation and tradition of considerable antiquity. What happens in the new post-1989, post-colonial, "global," and hypothetically liberated transcultural space when a voice such as Szymborska's echoes there?

Szymborska was never an émigrée or celebrated in the West: born in 1923, she remained in Poland after the Second World War in a strange and un-glamorous "internal exile" while the Cold War redrew the world map. Both the poet and most of her readers at home wrote and lived in the shadow of censorship, free to travel only inward; to them, the prize that signals a poet's or a literature's "arrival" on the world scene may suggest the arrival of new art judges, if not of a new artistic justice. No matter who guards the borders today or how their names have changed, this poet reminds readers outside Eastern Europe of a place filled with living bodies, desires, and troubles much like their own. Szymborska redefines the location of her country and calls from a subterranean landscape of excellent writing by Polish women, writing that was largely ignored in a world preoccupied with the macho struggle of superpowers.[2]

Just as Szymborska describes animals and plants that by their very nature cross the borders that humans pretend to guard, we emphasize the createdness of geography and maps of nations and cultures. Entangled in human states and human languages, we adopt and adapt the relative terms "East" and "West" in order to connote past and present divisions, a history useful in human terms.[3] Geography is, after all, "a series of erasures and over-writings," and "[t]he map functions as a mirror of the world, not because the representation of the earth has the status of a natural sign, but because it aims to invoke a simulacrum of an always inaccessible totality by means of an arrangement of symbols" (Rabasa 1995, 358).[4] Animals, plants, and soil ignore these divisions. It is the human strife for hierarchy through analysis, discovery, and establishment of difference that engenders borders and their representation, arbitrary and man-made lines separating East and West, self and other. Borders reflect not only power and acquisition but also an emergence from solipsism into awareness of the other. Knowledge too is an empire, with more-or-less sacrosanct aesthetic and intellectual borders accepted by convention but permeable in their nature.

Szymborska's speaker wisely suggests what it means to ignore the map, to "decolonize one's mind," as bell hooks might put it. Unassuming in her speech but asserting a vision of fluidity across boundaries, she tacitly defies the borders she was expected to respect. From the margins of Europe, she "writes back" against divisions: the booted human's opposition to the animal and vegetable, the thick red lines and iron curtains of Cold War Europe, and even the "proper" political subjects of a poet who "should" be treating the conditions of life under socialism, expressing the point of view of one or another polar-ized political orthodoxy.[5] The poet's vision asserts her creative freedom from imposed narratives, her engagement in a process as natural as plant and ani-mal life. "Psalm" acknowledges "the relationship between power and culture,

The Palace of Culture in Warsaw. 1997. Photograph by Willard Pate. Used by permission.

domination and the imaginary" (Pieterse and Parekh 1995, 4) and yet also evades it.

Like many messages with a religious subtext, this one draws on a variety of contexts: it is a psalm, addressing or expressing divinity, a form of wor(d)ship and questioning. A psalm originates in the contemplation or trouble of a single person but is intended to be sung or recited as often as it is read silently; the word suggests both its use in communal ritual and its identity with a larger body of texts. Integral to Christian liturgy as well as to its original Judaic context, the psalm is a hybridic form and enters the most elevated realm of discourse, the divinely inspired language of sacred books. The poet's human voice brings the sacred down to earth literally as she both addresses the divine and models the melody of prayer for other human readers or listeners. The title's associations recall borders other than the political ones: Eastern Europe is lined like a palm with religious boundaries and overlaps that are often taken as pretexts for genocide, war, and oppression. Religions can be as antagonistic or competitive as political entities, claiming the right to carve up territories and to privileged access not only to resources and discourse but to salvation itself. Like maps written over many times, the verses or personages of Torah, Bible, or Qur'an run into and over one another, paradoxically recalling the natural world the poet contemplates beyond the divisions and codifications of human believers. The poem's title aligns the poet with David, elevating artistry over political power and gift over ancestry. It is free mastery of language that forms Szymborska's relationship, if any, to temporal rule and any kingdom's borders: "O to see this whole chaos in detail, all at once, on every continent!"

All the King's Horses

Inspired by Szymborska, the editors of this volume intend it to interrogate boundaries in multiple ways. The geographic and cultural emphasis of the articles included is on Eastern Europe and the West, especially North America, as they have (re)discovered one another in the decade and a half since the Change. Russia has been privileged in the West, especially in the United States, as an object of more frequent study because of the influence of politics on the production of knowledge, and thus it has overshadowed the rest of Eastern Europe—therefore, we choose to concentrate on the other countries of the region. Since Eastern European studies in particular have until recently tended to be more traditional in their scholarly approaches than almost any comparable field, we wish to introduce more of recent interdisciplinary theory, particularly from Cultural Studies, African American Studies, and Postcolonial Studies. Each of these fields resonates with some of the cultural constructs and historical narratives of Eastern Europe while interrogating race, ethnicity, gender, sexuality, nationhood, dominance, resistance, and oppositional culture. In some cases, however, the exercise of applying theory to a new case offers a useful corrective to the theory, which so far may have focused exclusively on the "global" binary of the First versus the Third World. Because most of the many books that have appeared in recent years to make sense of the Second World in rapidly altering circumstances have dealt with sociology, political science, or economics—fields that are almost solely oriented toward the present to the exclusion of even the recent past—this volume offers articles on broadly understood approaches to culture.

We see culture as a mix of high and low academic and popular productions and discourses reflecting social and historical change and as a realm where diversity and hybridity have always provided a constant, though often unacknowledged, undercurrent for more "traditional" paradigms of thinking. To a certain extent, our collective definition echoes Raymond Williams's, especially his emphasis on engaging relationships rather than contrasts between the anthropological approach and its focus on "material production" and the historic and cultural studies approach that privileges "signifying or symbolic systems." Our volume brings together many scholars with multilinguistic and multigeographic backgrounds, all with their own understandings of culture which must not be allowed to coalesce into a uniform definition. Therefore we offer this collection as an invitation to engage, from the decentered vantage point of the Second World, the complexity of the term itself, which as Williams claims "is not finally in the word but in the problems which its variations of use significantly indicate."[6] Following Stuart Hall, we see our theorizing about "culture" in this volume as "an open horizon, moving within the magnetic fields of some basic concepts, but constantly being applied afresh to what is genuinely original and novel in new forms of cultural practice, and recognizing the capacity of subjects to reposition themselves differently."[7]

At the same time, the editors of and the majority of contributors to this volume are East-West academics and intellectuals whose heterogeneous takes on culture tend to privilege its "higher" forms: art, literature, material culture, and the interweaving patterns of interpretation that result from contacts between East and West in this era of change and realignment. The cultural work this volume sets out to perform in interpreting the cultural difference of the Second World and recording its complex dialogues with the First World, and to a certain extent with the Third, can be best summarized in the words of Homi K. Bhabha: "[W]e are faced with the challenge of reading, into the present of a specific cultural performance, the traces of all those diverse disciplinary discourses and institutions of knowledge that constitute the condition and contexts of culture. . . . [S]uch a critical process requires a cultural temporality that is both disjunctive and capable of articulating, in Lévi-Strauss's words, 'forms of activity which are both at once ours and other.'"[8]

While acknowledging the theory, we want to stress the primacy of cultural productions and subjects—artifacts, texts, and people—that made this book possible. The depth and richness of writing such as Szymborska's inspired us to seek more artistic texts by Paul Krainak or "Benni Goodman" along with "properly" scholarly pieces. Nonverbal or nondenotative means of expression, such as satire and coded humor, have held tremendous importance in Eastern European cultures. Decades or even centuries of official censorship encouraged an ironic, detached attitude and sensitized speakers to subdenotative realms, spheres of expression available for use when the verbal surface became too perilous. So-called Aesopic language invoked artistic rather than political authority—according to tradition, Aesop was a slave, one who enjoyed only discursive power. The urge to speak truth in the face of danger has packed the writing of East Europeans with the kinds of sophisticated and layered meaning that make any literature rich and rewarding to the attentive reader. Under communism, it also provided the artist and intellectual with a moral authority writers in the West could only dream of. Now the ones who win out against borders and guns in Szymborska's poem are those who have the least apparent power to affect them: "mixed forest, undermining moles, and wind."

(When we told one of our esteemed contributors that we planned to call this volume *Over the Wall/After the Fall*, she said, "Oh, no, like Humpty Dumpty!" The words do suggest a broken egg or political boundaries and changes understood in the over(t)ly simple terms of a children's rhyme. After all, Mother Goose rhymes too have their roots in long-ago plagues and political intrigues.)

If the increasingly dislocated and "globalized" cool humor of North America's MTV generation works to protect viewers from uncomfortably intense feelings, the satire of the new post-communist era, largely inherited from the past, works against numbness in the face of economic trauma or political outrage. We have yet to develop a full understanding and vocabulary to express and theorize the crises of post–Cold War representation, which can be identified using Julia Kristeva's term "new maladies of the soul" (Kristeva 1995, 9–10) or what Serguei Oushakine defines as the phenomenon of "post-Soviet aphasia," regression and disintegration of collective discursive behavior caused by society's inability to find proper verbal signifiers for new reality and practices.[9] To such serious theoretical musings on national, social, and individual psychoanalysis, homegrown Polish jesters respond with the slogan of each sociopolitical earthquake under communism: "The 'new' is back again!" (Nowakowski 1993, 53).[10]

Beyond the excitement of mapping new discourses, the academic marketplace may also tempt us to milk historic events for new theoretical concepts and professional perks. Jean Baudrillard's millennial cry—"Hooray, history is back from the dead!"—repeats rather than "revisions," as he would have it, explication of Eastern Europe as a glacially stunted and backward region (Baudrillard 1994, 28). Theorists' gestures and appropriations of rhetorical territory often mirror political feints and parries; the superpowers could slash through maps without regard for the actual inhabitants. As Graham Huggan stresses, the "map no longer features as a visual paradigm for the ontological anxiety arising from frustrated attempts to define a national culture" (Huggan 1994, 408). In Homi Bhabha's words, "the nation, as a form of cultural *elaboration* (in the Gramscian sense), is an agency of ambivalent narration that holds culture at its most productive position, as a force for 'subordination, fracturing, diffusing, reproducing, as much as producing, creating, forcing, guiding'" (Bhabha 1991, 3–4). Applying these insights to Eastern Europe (as well as to the West) creates space both for a more nuanced appreciation of local realities and for less-narrow possibilities of imagining a nation's identity—perhaps one that can embrace greater variation among individuals. The power structures of East and West, after all, have tended to construct race, ethnicity, gender, sexuality, and power with a depressing sameness, as chapters by Andaluna Borcila, Anca Rosu, and Carol Silverman demonstrate in these pages.

The struggle against resurgent racism and xenophobia in the former Soviet-bloc countries entails nothing less than a revolutionary remapping of the post-communist mind,[11] an "unlearning" of what the "White Judge" has taught us, as Toni Morrison might say. In the post-1989 era, reassessing the Atlantic (which is crisscrossed with the centuries-old routes of slave ships and ships carrying immigrants to the New World) means, too, that East and West must recognize each other in the former opponent's image; they must think of shared legacies of racism and discrimination but also of constructed "whiteness" and its legacy in a world where nothing happens in isolation and without far-reaching historic, cultural, and social consequences. The sole African player on the Polish national soccer team, Nigerian Emmanuel Olisadebe, who is a Polish citizen and married to a Pole, has had such a hard time coping with discrimination in his adopted country that he welcomed a temporary transfer to Greece; perhaps spectators there will refrain from throwing bananas at him during matches.[12] As members of "nationally defined cultures," late-twentieth-century societies and individuals have already shown what Edward W. Said calls the "oddly hybridic historical and cultural experiences" that "partake of many often contradictory experiences and domains" (Said 1993, 15). Such theory and its ironic fulfillment in everyday symbologies comes to mind when I see a Confederate flag streaming over a house in a Polish village: Haven't we been oppressed long enough to know any better? (MZ). The rhetorical nature of this question confirms the nature of walls erected in individuals' and whole nations' minds to keep out the other—we haven't learned any better than anyone else in the world: from the Pale of Settlement in Russia to the Warsaw Jewish Ghetto, from Katyń to Jedwabne to Kosovo to Armenia and Turkey to the American South. . . . And all this in just one century, the same one that saw the fall of colonial empires and the end of the Cold War. The concept of postcoloniality should be approached critically, as it can "disguis[e] the ongoing asymmetries of global power" (Pieterse and Parekh 1995, 10). So too the post-1989 moment must be interrogated within and without inherited binary oppositions so that we can struggle toward more genuinely expressive discourses.

Over the Wall / After the Fall

The metaphors for the borders between East and West have been quite expressive. One well-known landmark, the Berlin Wall, shaped the consciousness of a generation—my pregnant mother wrote as it was being built that it made her wonder what sort of world I, her child, would be born to live in (SF). More than anything else, the artificial division of a city and the deaths or sensational ingenuity of East Germans who tried to escape to a West that was also their "own" country expressed the violent absurdity of a divided Europe.[13] Of course, that division was always blamed on the East (in the West) or on the West (in the East). The "Fall" of the Berlin Wall was hugely evocative, with extensive media coverage, newspaper photos of dancers on the Wall, and shortly thereafter ads in upscale North American mail-order catalogues for "a piece of history"—small imported chunks of the wall itself, bright with spray-painted graffiti. The Wall that divided the separate houses of East and West became first a tourist attraction, then almost right away a commodity, at once history and kitsch, like the East German "people's auto," the Trabant. And yet, as both artifact and metaphor—"concrete" proof of the binary opposition sustaining both empires' identities—the Wall's fall overshadowed the beginning of the end of communist dominance in the wake of the relaxation of glasnost and perestroika in the USSR. That already-forgotten step occurred farther to the East, less glamorously (without rock concerts or mail-order goods), and without Western help—in Poland. The first truly free democratic elections there in spring of 1989 were harbingers of other "revolutions" in the region, though they offered less of a spectacle than the visuals and relics from "our own" NATO ally.

The staging of the Wall's fall nevertheless serves well to mark the new era's beginning. My student silk-screened a newspaper image of dancers atop the wall onto a T-shirt and added the words of Emma Goldman: "If I can't dance, I don't want to be part of your revolution" (SF). That juxtaposition of image and text, like some of those analyzed in this volume, suggests the complexity of a real human being's political position, the cramped possibilities offered when we insist on simple binaries. Strict and puritanical socialism is as constricting an idea as the decadence of capitalist flappers.

The Wall embodied the abstract border with a manifestly arbitrary physical barrier, cutting off traffic along what were once busy streets. To the global metropolis, it meant a shift of continents, a freezing of the compass. After all, Denmark is Britain's East, Poland is Ukraine's West. Even Alaska is East for residents of Kamchatka, that far-flung province of the "European" Russian republic. The Wall took this fluid and relative relationship and fixed it in cement, declaring an immovable meridian of division.[14] Still, for complex reasons some Eastern Europeans regret the overzealous post-communist cleanup of the landscape that erased the concrete markers of their painful past. Slavenka Drakulić expresses this sentiment quite poignantly: "It is not that I mind the demolition of the Wall—I am delighted about that—but [I mind] the way it was done, the obvious haste with which this tumor was removed not only from the face of the city, but from the memory of the people . . . as if the past, the division of that nation, doesn't count at all any more and should be instantly forgotten. . . . [T]he sooner we forget it, the more we'll have to fear" (1993, 40).

Europe's Own Local East

What could have been more artificial than the line between Eastern and Western Europe, maintained through violence and threats of more violence at the expense of so many individual human destinies? The East outfitted border guards with rifles, while the West collaborated to maintain that boundary, even while criticizing and decrying it. Novelist Maria Kuncewicz reminded an American friend, speaking openly because she wrote and mailed her letter in the United States, that "Poland is ruled by communists and nationalists,—but above all by Russia, and this is not, as everybody knows, the fault of the Polish people so much as of the Yalta agreement" (Kuncewicz 1969).[15] Like the period of colonialism for the First and Third Worlds, the Cold War produced for them and for the Second World a "political division of reality whose structure promoted the difference between the familiar (Europe, USA, the West, 'us') and the strange (the Orient, the East, 'them')" (Said 1995, 43). Eastern Europe's position reflects post–Second World War brokering in economics and geopolitics as much as geographic location: it is too close to Western Europe to excise from the map's right-hand edge, but even without Yalta it has "colors" or "flavors" unlike the ones that produced Goethe, Jean-Paul Sartre, or Virginia Woolf.

In *Inventing Eastern Europe*, Larry Wolff stresses that this region came to be the West's other during the Age of Reason, or the Enlightenment, in an "intellectual project of demi-Orientalization." It was "produced as a work of cultural creation, of intellectual artifice, of ideological self-interest and self-promotion." Like Russia, the other countries in the region were subjected to a process of "discovery, alignment, condescension, and intellectual mastery, located and identified by the same formulas: between Europe and Asia, between civilization and barbarism." It is interesting that Wolff's own deliberation on the post-1989 future of the region rings with a sense of necessary otherness that seems to be the irreversible legacy of the ways of thinking French eighteenth-century philosophers bequeathed to us: "That Eastern Europe [of the Cold War] has ceased to exist since 1989, along with the iron curtain. Either we will find new associations to mark its difference, or we will rediscover old ones from before the Cold War. Or else we may take the extraordinary revolution of 1989 as an incitement and opportunity to reconsider our mental mapping of Europe."[16] Such a remapping is already happening—several former Soviet-bloc member countries have entered the European Union—but it is not clear that the discourse of inclusion and individual mental models can shake off centuries-long habits of the mind.

Maria Todorova analyzes a particular variety of oversimplification and agglomeration of clichés in her book *Imagining the Balkans*. Part of her scholarly qualifications, she makes clear, is the position of marginality vis-à-vis both the country of her birth and early education (Bulgaria) and the country where she now lives and teaches (the United States). Not moving to America would have had intellectual consequences as well:

> Had I remained in Bulgaria, I would not have written this particular book, although its ideas and empirical material would have informed my teaching and my behavior. I would have felt compelled to write a different one, one that would have explored and exposed the internal orientalisms within the region, that would have centered on the destruction and impoverishing effects of ethnic nationalism (without necessarily passing dogmatic strictures on nationalism as such), and that, far from exhibiting nostalgia for imperial formations, would have rescued from the Ottoman and the more recent Balkan past these possibilities for alternative development that would have enriched our common human culture. Maybe I will still write it. (Todorova 1997, x)

Todorova defines "balkanism" as a complex set of stereotyping practices, including both political and everyday assumptions about the Balkans and their inhabitants on the part of Western Europeans and the self-definitions of inhabitants of the Balkans, which are often developed in opposition to an imagined orientalized or occidentalized other (ibid., 18–20). Balkanism, as one complex historical set of images and assumptions, is distinct from Orientalism and offers, in Todorova's detailed study, an example of the ways the peoples of Eastern Europe have been imagined, and have imagined themselves, in distinction to the nations farther west or farther east.

For Western Europe, Eastern Europe has formed a local East since at least the eighteenth century, an other "whiteness," viewed through a particular Orientalization that was shaped by the eras of conquest and by what often amounted to occupation or colonialism, though most recently by the Iron Curtain.[17] This Orientalization resembles the well-known paradigm theorized by Edward Said that sheds additional light on the sustenance of "intellectual *authority* over the Orient within Western culture" (Said 1995, 19). After the breakdown of the colonial empires, as "a locale [also] requiring Western attention, reconstruction, even redemption" (ibid., 206), Eastern Europe has supplied the West with a badly needed other, safely "Orientalizable" while seemingly racially unmarked. The nations and peoples of Eastern Europe could be imagined as a faceless (though almost entirely white) bloc and unproblematically used by the West both to justify Cold War ideology (See how they are oppressed by the Soviets!) and to idealize Western ideals of capitalist richness and variety (See how they crave our political system and lifestyle!). As Eva Hoffman puts it, during the Cold War,

> Eastern Europe once again became a Rorschach test for Western wishes, dreads, and misunderstandings. To some it was a repository of utopian ideological hopes; to others, a heroic region struggling against a demonic dystopia; but to most, I would hazard, "Eastern Europe" had become a lifeless, monochrome realm where people walked bent under the leaden weight of an awful System (Hoffman 1994, xii).[18]

Like Said's concept, Orientalized Eastern European "whiteness" is "better grasped as a set of constraints upon and limitations of thought" (Said 1995, 42). Wolff's study confirms this racial dimension of the region's otherness. These limitations cannot be understood without deconstructing the East-West binary in a racialized postauthoritarian context that examines equally past and present, all the players and their complicated histories. As Michael Kennedy stresses, "the formation of [new] ideologies and identities is more complicated than most discourses of transition or revolution allow" (Kennedy 1994, 1), and thus "the visions shaping and identities characterizing Eastern Europe need clarification and elaboration as much as their explanations" (ibid., 9). Wolff argues that the invention of Eastern Europe as a geographically and culturally remote and barbaric location was necessary for creation of the West as the "'more refined European lands'" (1996, 340), so it brought about a "conceptual reorientation of Europe" along the west to east rather than south to north axis, one whose effects we can see today:

> Just as the new centers of the Enlightenment superseded the old centers of the Renaissance, the old lands of barbarism and backwardness in the north were correspondingly displaced to the east. The Enlightenment had to invent Eastern Europe and Western Europe together, as complementary concepts, defining each other by opposition and adjacency. (ibid., 5)

The historical consequences of this active shifting of paradigms confirmed once again the complete subordination of geography to bipolar ideological discourse and the economic and military hegemony of the map-writers. The new paradigms were subsequently poured in concrete as the Wall in the former northern "barbaric" land of Germany or, as is less well known, as a million military pillboxes keeping guard over isolated Albania, which the East-to-West Croatian Slavenka Drakulić sees, with the condescension of a "more western" former Yugoslav, as a "dormant dreaming country, a child that has not yet learned how to take care of itself."[19]

During the Cold War, the "bloc" countries were all supposed to look the same ("Soviet") when viewed from Washington or Paris. Seen from the Kremlin, they could be *both* the same *and* different ("multicultural"), depending on how the powers gazing from Moscow chose to construct them. Identically ugly towering Stalinist skyscrapers, "palaces of culture," parade grounds in city centers, and "homes of X-Soviet friendship" in the region's satellite capitals gave, and still give, obvious architectural signs of communist sameness. There is also a great deal to be said for the socialist landscape, with its obligatory creation of standardized but habitable communal spaces, and for people's ability to make them their own. As Magdalena J. Zaborowska outlines in a chapter in this collection, the most politically charged or aesthetically impoverished elements of a city quickly become intertwined with and overwritten by the personal experience and memories of the people who live there. Recognition of individual cultures by Soviet leaders marked the "diversity" approach, which was ironically proven by pitching Poles against Czechs in 1968, when Warsaw Pact forces crushed the Prague Spring. This "difference" approach was perhaps meant to erase the memory of Soviet/"Russian" tanks in Hungary in 1956. The ability to adopt either vision—"proletarians unite" (universality) versus "international socialism" (for each nation)—proved Big Brother's power in the region and the rhetorical or political flexibility of that pole of the East/West opposition.

The satellites themselves never ceased to feel distinct from one another, despite some similarities in day-to-day existence within the bloc and clear internalization of the cultural and geographical hierarchies received from the West. Popular lore disregarded Orient-Occident axes to locate a country between East and West according to its personal freedoms and economic pros-

perity. Regardless of geography, Hungary was more "Western" than Czechoslovakia, while Albania, just across the Adriatic from Italy, was most "Eastern"
of all. Many Poles who considered themselves to be "Western" resented being
lumped together with the "peasant" Bulgarians and saw Russians as even
worse, with no taste and fashion sense at all. According to Robert Kaplan, just a
few years ago, Romanians felt that they were completely "Western"; they loved
America and hoped that President Clinton would help them get into NATO
(Kaplan 1998, 28–36). Andaluna Borcila's essay in this volume ponders similar possibilities from the perspective of living between cultures, reading Western representations of an Orientalized Romania, and realizing the imbalance
of power on the visual marketplace, no matter how fantastically Occidentalized Romanian notions of the West might be. The discourse on modernity
has rarely included the fact that socialism, as a particular form of modernity,
produced the world's most educated population in the region of its dominance. Such recognition would interfere with the accepted distribution of
global power and knowledge. Instead, Eastern Europe is represented, and is
still invited to think of itself, as premodern, a drag on the continent's progress.

A Romanian refugee in Denmark spoke to me (MZ) of the ways Westerners still see everyone from the former communist countries as the "same." It
is true that when some Danish acquaintances learn where we are from, they
assume that we lived in a uniform cross-cultural enclave ("Oh, you both must
have suffered so!"). We did and we didn't. I knew that "they over there" [in
Romania] had it even worse than we did under martial law, but I never knew
much about that country's ethnic and cultural diversity, much less about the
persecution of ethnic Hungarians in Transylvania under Ceauşescu. Writing
seventeen years after the publication of *Orientalism*, Said points out, "Even
though the Soviet Union has been dismembered and the East European
countries have attained political independence, patterns of power and dominance remain unsettlingly in evidence" (Said 1995, 348).[20] Todorova observes
with wry curiosity the persistent careless use of the words "balkanize" and
"balkanization," not only in the mass media but even by otherwise cautious
and semantically precise academics (1997, 36–37). The ghosts of the past
cannot be banished so easily, the legacies of colonialism and totalitarianism
still haunt us in all *three* worlds, and invisible Walls and Falls still cast shadows
amid the New World Order.

Hot Flashes

The words "After the Fall" evoke the final season, the annual fading of
nature, and the penultimate moment in a millennial drama: events and cultural artifacts after 1989 were colored by the end of the twentieth century and
fear of rapid social change in a coming cultural winter. The Fall (and the fall)
of communism inaugurated the post-Soviet and post-Empire millennial moment in a "globalized" era without clear-cut enemies, a period of change and
flux that affects whole nations as well as gendered, sexed, and racially and

ethnically marked bodies. It has also marked a profound redefinition of the space in which these bodies and their representations are constructed and articulated.

In addition to the Wall and the Fall, another famous description of the division between East and West was "the Iron Curtain." The combination of words, first uttered by Winston Churchill in a Missouri town in the United States, effectively conveys a pejorative judgment: iron is harsh (the iron fist, unsoftened by velvet), technological (calling up factories and polluting heavy industry), immovable, and impenetrable to sound and light as well as to human bodies. An iron curtain is all but a wall, but at the same time the curtain is resonantly semiotic: the theater curtain distinguishes stage from audience, representation from observer. A curtained window or door emphasizes the division of inside and outside, public and private. An iron curtain is more protective than cloth, hiding the inside from prying glares, preserving the innocence of those it protects as potential historical actors. As Andaluna Borcila shows, in media coverage of Romania after the Fall, the West saw and still sees the peoples of the East as immature, childish. Or they may be seen as residents of a harem, women whose virtue and traditional femininity were protected from Western consumerism and feminism (the iron chastity belt?), "true" women who now wait to be rescued from economic troubles by valiant men from the West—as can be seen in the condescending postings that advertise East European female bodies for sale on the World Wide Web.

The booming East-West marriage market and the demand for "white" "Eastern" e-mail-order brides prove beyond a doubt that the post-1989 era is gendered and sexualized. Reading it interweaves individual and collective perspectives on asymmetries of power that impact every narrative of socially constructed identity. In *Strangers to Ourselves*, Julia Kristeva remarks about one woman's situation in France:

> I wonder if Wanda's husband would have dared to act as brazenly like a Don Juan, to discover libertine bents in himself, to flaunt the girlfriends she, alas, did not have the sense of humor to appreciate—if his wife had not come from Poland, that is from nowhere, without the family or friends that constitute . . . a shelter against narcissism and a rampart against paranoid persecutions. (Kristeva 1991, 14)[21]

The fallen curtain coyly reveals erotic trafficking between the East and West into geographies previously uncharted by sociology and studies of gender and sexuality.[22] We hear more about "sex tourism" in Asia, but driving along an international thoroughfare in the New Europe reveals much about recent sexual politics and economics. East of Berlin, women walk on the side of the road with handwritten signs proclaiming their services and prices in a mixture of Slavic languages; their location bespeaks their status in the new Europe, as young girls (often underage) from Belarus, Ukraine, Romania, and Bulgaria who work the highways seem to be the lowest on the trade's totem pole in

Poland.[23] A recent program on Danish television showed women from the former Soviet Bloc fighting hard for a chance to come to the country of Hans Christian Andersen to pursue careers as "erotic dancers."[24] They usually enter Denmark legally and obtain visas and temporary work permits as "artists," but their life is no fairy tale; they rarely make the money they were promised and are often forced into prostitution, though it is illegal. According to the same program, there are as many as a thousand documented cases of "Eastern" women sold into prostitution in the West annually for about 1,000 German marks each. Despite warnings, women and girls still accept offers of "jobs" in the West to improve their family's situation back home.[25]

Like the Wall, the Iron Curtain did at last fall on the final act of the Soviet period. That Fall, of course, is the fall of communism, the [Evil] Empire; we have entered the era "After the Fall." This phrase resonates with the biblical primal scene of lost innocence. The East, fallen and finally "known," is now adrift in a world of economic dislocation and moral relativism. The system that denied its citizens political or moral adulthood was blamed for forcing an artificial childhood on the polities of Eastern Europe. Now the child-maiden of the East has bitten the apple of knowledge and has been cast into the world of market capitalism. The East is itself a long-forbidden fruit "ripe" with potential profits, sometimes portrayed as ready to drop into the hands of the canny investor. For the Easterner herself, the apple of knowledge may be a consumer good, a political idea, or access at last to the Western intellectual market. This last is essential despite its dangers: no one makes more incisive observations about the West and its relationships with the East than the Eastern Europeans themselves.

The change in Eastern Europe is also commonly described as precisely that: "the Change," wording used in English as a euphemism for menopause. This lends events in Eastern Europe since 1989 a hormonal flush, if not outright hot flashes—nationalism, misogyny, resurgent racism, anti-Semitism—name your poison! On the other hand, the climactic nature of the Change promises that the nations of the East will cease to shed blood as they join *pax Europeana*. The Orientalized sexual plaything, whose attractiveness still makes her somewhat threatening, matures into a plump, red-cheeked babushka. This image prolongs Cold War clichés of Eastern European womanhood at the height of socialism as drably dressed portly peasants with little, if any, knowledge of the subtleties of hair dye and makeup. An extreme example of this iconography accompanied the 1997 article "Fighting Corporate Flab: A Survey of Capital Markets" in a magazine devoted to business in Central Europe (Nicholls et al. 1997). A middle-aged woman is sunning herself dressed only in sunglasses and earrings. She is grossly obese, and her full-page image emphasizes the many folds of her body; smaller square images of her headless grotesque torso punctuate subsections of the article. The image says it all—she has let herself go, she is a Bakhtinian spectacle, and, like the economies of the newly capitalist East, she would be more attractive if better concealed. Thank goodness *Business Central Europe* has exposed her shape to us! The West, of course, prefers slender, shapely beauties, though "we" are shocked to hear that young women in economically depressed nations of the East have begun to suffer from anorexia or to consider prostitution an attractive career option.

At stake here is the discursive production of "East European woman" and post–Cold War Eastern Europe in general. When Eastern Europe "encountered" the West in the early 1990s, women's issues in particular became—and still remain—a point of East-West cultural clash. While former socialist countries considered the question mostly "solved," feminists in Western societies have at times believed that East European women must immediately be rescued from their subordinate status.[26] This has led to paradoxes: for example (EG), if an "Eastern" interlocutor questions the position of the "woman question" on the transformation agenda or even just asks why some women's issues should be prioritized over others (e.g., sexual harassment over paid maternity leave) by international agencies, a "Western" listener may respond as if the question is equal to attacking Western democracy. Věra Sokolová's outline of the recent legal and social ramifications of sex and sexuality in the Czech Republic in this volume demonstrates how a country often considered "Western and progressive" in local terms experiences issues in ways very unlike the standard debates in the United States or West European countries.

The very notion of "women's experience" as a basis for discourse on human rights should be subject to reconsideration: clearly, a Western urban professional and an East European prostitute have markedly different lives. What laws could make them equal, not only with regard to "their" men, but to each other? Any talk of gender equality isolated from issues of race, class, and globalization would be hypocritical, as many feminists have already pointed out. Arguing over which view of women's concerns, Western or Eastern, is "right" often misses the point, but Western feminists are still no more immune than any other collective to slipping into comfortable acceptance of their own perspective as if it were universal. Imbalances in financial and educational support have made it more likely that decisions about which gender issues are worthy of political organization will be decided by Western standards; those in the West carelessly assume that the gender issues they have defined as crucial are given the same priority throughout the world. This once again posits the West as the norm and others as deviations, producing in turn further ironies. It becomes "normal" to reprimand the Czech Republic, Poland, or Russia for the absence of special legislation on domestic violence but unthinkable to demand that the U.S. government should introduce paid maternity leave for all women. Remembering her studies in France and first contacts with Western feminism in a recent interview, current Polish secretary of state Barbara Labuda stresses that Polish women paradoxically enjoyed more rights than the French in the 1960s precisely because a socialist state deemed them more "equal" at the time than capitalist France did.[27] After the Fall, however, bourgeois gender essentialisms revived in a nostalgic reevaluation of pre–Second World War national cultures, while reproductive rights were rejected as a communist atrocity by the Catholic church, which demands that women return to their "natural" roles as wives and mothers. Poland is now closer to France in the 1960s and still awaits its de Beauvoir.

Allies in Theory

Almost half a century ago, at the Conference of Negro-African Writers and Artists in 1956, James Baldwin remarked that "[h]anging in the air, as real as the heat from which we suffered, were the great specters of America and Russia, of the battle going on between them for the domination of the world." Musing that the resolution of the ghostly East-West battle might depend largely on the world's non-European population, Baldwin admitted that "with the best will in the world, no one now living could undo what past generations had accomplished" (Baldwin, "Princes and Powers," 27). The fall of the Wall may signify the greatest geopolitical shift since the breakdown of the colonial empires in Asia and Africa. As the Other Europe comes to terms with its ambivalent past, it must learn from the experience of Third World peoples and from excluded groups in the First World—as well, ideally, as from its own racial, ethnic, religious, gender and sexual minorities. The Third and Second Worlds face similar decisions and negotiations over what to keep and what to discard from an era when external oppression may nonetheless have stimulated the creation of vibrant oppositional cultures. This does not mean drawing simplistic parallels about suffering similar fates under "colonialism." Similarities can indeed be found in the ways both regions were seen as disposable "spheres of influence" and their populations racialized or stereotyped, but perhaps the most unsettling proximities can be found at the present moment, when "the West" faces its own economic decline and is busy taking over new markets *both* east and south of its own borders. In this context, yet again, economics is the force behind the gaze and proves to be a dividing and othering force in the New World: a sweatshop set up in Ukraine may pay lower wages than one in Poland, but a young woman is still happy to have a job there; a Polish professional is glad to employ a better-educated but desperate Ph.D. from Belarus to clean his apartment; all three may now find solace in being white and better off than the people they see on their globalized televisions as they watch coverage of events in the Third World.

With NATO as the "ultimate totemic symbol of Western civilization" in Eastern and Central Europe (Kaplan 1998, 34), the globalized new millennium looks rather bleak: Is membership in a new military pact the highest aspiration of former Soviet satellites? The real challenge of East-West discourse lies in finding a common point of reference: rather than suggesting that the East should learn Western norms, can we make the post–Cold War dialogue more truly mutual, with former adversaries learning from one another as more equal partners?

The habit or assumption of the usefulness of binary categories persists over a decade and a half after the end of the Soviet Union—we ourselves appreciate the shorthand of "West" and "East" even as we discuss the frequent reductivism of the terms. Terms such as "former Soviet," "former Yugoslav," and, of course, "former communist" are still widely used in the West, not just by journalists in popular media or ordinary citizens but even by scholars who know what the terms convey and could be more suspicious of the longing for lost stabilities. This is not to deny the impact of imposed socialism on the "former Soviet Bloc"—the terms prove how important the Soviet bloc or communism were in broad perceptions of identity. The point is that the West still relies on its perceived or imagined distinction from the East—which does the same in turn, having internalized its inferiority and still lacking a new vocabulary to inscribe its new identity. The vicious circle continues despite the changes. As with so-called postcolonial states, the terms used to refer to Eastern Europe reflect a certain time lag inherent in their identities—as the "former" this and that, they appear permanently marked by their past, at best struggling to embrace a new image and fully enter the post–Cold War world. It is no wonder that image-making for countries is becoming a big agenda in East Europe: public relations remains one of the fastest-growing and most lucrative businesses there.

These changes make the term "Europe" acquire different meanings when uttered by a Bulgarian scholar naturalized in France, by a Christian Coalition member in the United States, or by my Polish mother (MZ), whose reaction to ethnic sculpture and the proliferation of "diversity" in American culture was that as a "European," she surely knew "what made art great or mediocre." Strict socialist censorship kept racist and other divisive speech out of public discourse in Eastern Europe, though ethnocentrism and anti-Semitism reigned freely along with sexism and racism in jokes and private conversations. Writing against the notion of a resurgent *Volksgeist* in Western Europe, Kristeva is "perplexed by the nationalistic boom among Eastern European peoples today; a boom that expresses itself through the same laudatory phrases such as eternal memory, linguistic genius, ethnic purity, and an identifying superego, all the more aggressive as these peoples were humiliated" (Kristeva 1993, 54). Everyone has his or her "they"—to the West "they" were communists, and some of "them" still vote for the Evil Empire's return. Now "they" may be undesirable economic migrants—or worse yet, terrorists or criminal groups who traffic in drugs, women's bodies, or weapons. By displacing anxieties and frustrations onto other "white" cultures that are politically or historically rather than racially distinct, the West can attempt to avert its eyes from that greater boundary between North and South, so painful to acknowledge, reflecting global economic exploitation and histories of violence and slavery or colonization. It feels more "civilized" to maintain a simple us-and-them of political difference within Europe with its assumed, mythical, racial homogeneity.

Strange bedfellows during the long Cold War night, East and West predicated similar self-definitions upon carefully or crudely constructed negative images of the other. Thus, the Soviet bloc opposed the myth of its identity as friend of the oppressed working class worldwide to the "imperialistic, greedy, and savage" West. The existence of the "bloc" flattered the Soviet self-image and simplified division of Europe into "us" and "them," both for us and for them. Soviet culture, at least by the time of high Stalinism, for many was in practice Russification. Even after Stalin's death in 1953, children in the satellite countries hated their mandatory Russian classes and often even their innocent and timid teachers. One of us felt ashamed to have had an "A" in Russian in high school, which was considered very uncool if not unpatriotic; now the former nerd regrets that her Russian has suffered from misuse, as it often is the only common language we have inherited to communicate with non-English-speaking colleagues from the former bloc (MZ). As war began in Croatia in 1991, my colleagues in the United States didn't want to hear that Yugoslavs were not a single ethnicity, had not as a whole transcended ethnic identification during the decades of socialist "brotherhood and unity" (SF). The idea of a nationhood that had subsumed ethnicity in less than fifty years so flatteringly resembled the homegrown theory of the "melting pot," despite the dubious historic and political origins of that term. The flood of information, unfamiliar names, and "new" nations made understanding complex and difficult. Buying new maps, after all, requires both monetary investment and a willingness to accept change.

The recent history of Eastern Europe has included a fragmentation of nationalities and nationalisms that recalls the ghettoes and separatist compounds of the United States. Ukrainians declare they are not Russians, Ruthenians claim their distinctness from Ukrainians, a group of Roma in the Republic of Macedonia argue that they are really Egyptians, not Gypsies, to the derision of Roma organizations elsewhere. Wilsonian self-determination on linguistic and national bases underlies Eastern Europe's experience of separate nationhood in the twentieth century—so it was tested on the skins of residents of Hungary, interwar Czechoslovakia, Lithuania, and Poland. Groups are quick to demand freedom but predictably reluctant to grant autonomy or recognition to their own minorities. Self-determination, always a compromise between competing interests, reacts to memories of oppression that first reinforce a sense of separate culture and then give license to nationalism and nativism.

My hometown in Poland, Kielce (MZ), is clumsily coming to terms with the facts of a cold-blooded massacre of forty-two Jews by the local population— a pogrom that took place on July 4, 1946, and was encouraged and partially conducted by local military and police forces. Rumors were that it "must have been" a provocateur, but the mob still jumped at the opportunity to "kill the Jew!"[28] In fall of 1998, defenders of "national identity" from right-wing Catholic organizations were staging yet another anti-Semitic campaign around the grounds of the concentration camp in Auschwitz.[29] An activist in Jewish-

Catholic organizations, Stanisław Krajewski, reminds us, in his important study, of Polish-Jewish solidarity under nineteenth-century Russian occupation. Krajewski is an optimist who believes in development of a Polish Catholic-Jewish dialogue: "[T]hinking of the [last] war, Poles still tend to see their shared suffering with the Jews rather than the shared Church with the Nazis" (Krajewski 1997, 195, trans. MZ). I would love to agree, and I do hope for a dialogue that goes beyond religious boundaries, despite the recent actions of my country's population that seem to prove him wrong. I can be hopeful as long as there is at least an ongoing discussion of these issues, as evidenced by a long-term exchange in the media following the publication of Jan Tomasz Gross's controversial book on Polish participation in the Holocaust, *Sąsiedzi* (*Neighbors*, 2000). Is it possible to undo decades of deliberate and furious erasure of the remnants of Jewish culture in postwar Poland if we do not speak openly about the fact that *both* "evil communists" *and* ordinary citizens participated, and still participate, in that "ethnic cleansing?" Not to mention that such cleansing can only be stopped by "ordinary citizens."

James Baldwin writes about the fine connection between individual freedom in a political sense and claiming an identity separate from one's national culture, a condition that seems necessary for building new identities in the New Europe: "Freedom is not something that anybody can be given; freedom is something people take and people are as free as they want to be" (Baldwin, "Notes from a Hypothetical Novel," 125). Poetic license such as Szymborska's clearly did not recognize boundaries even under censorship. Can art and literature, scholarship and public debate work toward a conversation in post-Wall Eastern Europe and the postcolonial world after decades of enforced mutual mistrust and profound tongue-tied evasions? What power do we have in the face of mass media and manipulated popular culture?

Pietistic surveillance of the media by the church in Poland has already resulted in a kind of "newspeak" replacing the "old" control of the media. These days, instead of Marxism, a publication is gauged by its "true Catholic morality and ethics."[30] All nonbelievers and any issues the conservative church and right-wing nationalists disapprove of—women's rights, birth control, liberal education, separation of church and state, respect for human difference in all forms—are lumped together as "forces of secularism." Thus, a new, dangerous "them" emerges, and the church which worked largely as a force for liberation and moral value under late Socialism jockeys for discursive and political power amid new social formations. These barriers should make us ask, Who benefits from them, and why do others let themselves be led? In the meantime, my nonreligious sister decided, against her husband's wishes, to baptize their son "just in case, so he won't face discrimination in school" (MZ).

The sharp distinction of East and West was set up and discursively supported not only by political and ethnocentric self-interest. Many academics whose lives or work brought us over the border found positive and negative associations on both sides (SF). The "gray" external sameness and shoddy goods of the Soviet period made the intensity of kitchen conversation and freedom from the rat race more vivid: the East was easily idealized to offer the romance or (with more sophistication) the community and cultural values neglected in Western capitalist democracies. We had the luxury of criticizing our own culture and government to East European friends who might idealize it without feeling disloyal to our homes or supporting the Soviet state or the governments of any of its satellites.

For all the real experiential differences between East and West, both sides upheld an economy of discourse, an official symmetry of binaries and borders both on the map and in the imaginary, if not in the heart. That such an economy shaped individual viewpoints and gendered perceptions of reality is not surprising. The post-Wall 1990s saw an unprecedented rise in consumption of mass-produced images, especially pornography and violence, which reached the East, previously circumspect in such "matters," as fast as Coca Cola and Pizza Hut. Like racism, xenophobia, and homophobia, sexism (or at least discourse about sex) was banned from public discourse under communism, but it has come back with a vengeance in a free market economy. One can find unabashed job ads in Warsaw or Moscow dailies: "no women need apply" or "candidates must be male and under 35 years of age." As Eastern Europe has moved from "bloc" to individual states, economies of discourse and power become entangled with issues of gender, reproduction, xenophobia, racism, and anti-Semitism.[31]

The differences between communist bloc and post-communist state should not obscure the fact that many of the same individuals who profited under communism and socialism now form a new "capitalist" economic elite. Plus ça change. . . . Many former apparatchiks have managed to exploit resources to which they had access and to build fortunes of Western dimensions, suggesting that the totalitarian era's paradoxes and black marketeering might have been good training for Wall Street. Many former dissidents in East and Central Europe bemoan the rapid "Westernization" of their cultures, an "Americanization" that leaves even scholars who have devoted their careers to American Studies ambivalent and disappointed. The proudly named "globalization" means precisely another attempt at cultural and market colonization of countries with few economic means to defend themselves. At the same time, canny survivors of Soviet-era censorship and underground cultural production may know exactly what they want and can get from American-style popular culture. In this volume Mark Andryczyk describes the Lviv Bohema, that western Ukrainian city's artistic "underground," and shows how young Ukrainian artists have used cars or soft drinks from the West in creatively ironic gestures. Socialist experience prepared these people to take corporate sponsorship with a grain of salt, and they can appreciate the relative freedom it allows after the official censorship of Soviet public culture.

The New World Order

In May of 2003, as I pondered the complex task of cultural translation that we envisaged for this volume as we were revising it for the last time, I ventured into a café in downtown Copenhagen (MZ). Its name was Europe 1989. Nothing on the menu gave any clue as to why that name had been chosen, although the interior décor sported a few artsy postcards and a "Solidarity" logo on one wall. If not for these easily overlooked touches, it looked just like hundreds of cafés in Western Europe's well-off cities and in aspiring East European capitals; I could have been anywhere—as Slavenka Drakulić has pointed out.[32] If the Café Europa blandness bespeaks the fact that the so-called New World Order establishes equality through open access to consumerism and a dislocated aesthetics signifying generic Europeanness, such blasé acceptance of the caesura of 1989 may cover up efforts to obscure the true significance of changes that may not be pleasant or easy to swallow on either side of the phantom Iron Curtain. While we would not mind it at all if this book inspired a tasteful chain of coffee shops or bistros named Over the Wall/After the Fall to upstage Starbucks or the Hard Rock Café, we tend to agree with Homi Bhabha's insistence on the importance of cultural translation as a "staging of cultural difference" (1994, 227). While engaging Benjamin's theory on the "foreignness of languages," Bhabha stresses something very important for our project: "Cultural translation desacralizes the transparent assumptions of cultural supremacy, and in that very act, demands a contextual specificity, a historical differentiation *within* minority positions" (ibid., 228). Turning Eastern Europe into a replica of the West would mean the end of cultural translation, an ultimate colonization of the "uncivilized" Other rather than the escape from essentialism and post-communist Orientalism that it sometimes pretends to be. The New World Order this volume would propose calls for a new idiom to engage the " 'foreign' element that reveals the interstitial; insists in the textile superfluity of folds and wrinkles . . . the indeterminate temporality of the in-between" (ibid., 227).

In the semiotic fallout of old codes, language changes too, and suddenly there are more countries than some U.S. politicians can easily remember in place of the good old Soviet bloc. "Czechoslovakia" no longer exists in the present tense; "Yugoslavia" has left its third and much reduced incarnation behind and now exists only as "former"; Ukraine's rejection of the definite article ("the") to preface its name in English seems at last to influence English-speaking media practice; there is only one Germany with no qualifying adjective. Cities and provinces in newly independent countries insist on different (and, from their point of view, correct) translations or transliterations into Western languages that once accepted the version of the dominant nationality, if they did not write over local names with their own. Boundaries are redrawn and national identities interrogated. Bulgarian scholars debate whether or not to reject the metaphor of the bridge that has historically been used to depict their positioning between Europe—or, as Tsvetana Gueorguieva stresses, "an entity, a civilisation (in the singular and with a definite article—*the* civilisation," and the "Ottoman Empire and, in the past few years, the former Soviet Union, i.e., barbarity."[33] Nationalistic and conservative coalitions in Poland dread the imminent loss of sovereignty, moral values, and "true faith" once the country enters the European Union, which event is painted in virtually apocalyptic colors by the ultranationalistic Radio Virgin Mary of Father Rydzyk, while other forces hope that that entry into the European Union will enable Poland to convert that secular and relativist cluster of cultures to Catholicism.

If the former "communist countries" indeed still suffer from an excess of history—from "too much past," as some critics have claimed—then this avid attention to geography, cultural translation, signification, and lexical revision also implies a desire to rewrite and retell history from a "subaltern" perspective.[34] István Rév reminds us that because "memory constitutes identity," the "writing of history . . . establishes and reestablishes identity" through new narratives (Rév 1995, 8–9). Maybe those who rename streets and topple statues of former heroes attempt not only to renarrate history but also—impossibly—to erase it, along with undesirable or uncomfortable elements of their own "excessive" past. The improvisatory essay by "Benni Goodman" in this volume cleverly unpacks the discursive potential of this desire and reveals how "great" and small narratives flip polarities and feed one another over a decade of recent Bulgarian history. The post-communist desire to change a past written by the state or by foreign powers can be usefully explained in postcolonial terms, at the same time offering an interesting new context for that field of study. Speaking of the legacy of colonialism in India, Partha Chatterjee comments on the impact of history on communal imagination, which he sees as continuously "overwhelmed and swamped by the history of the postcolonial state." He could be speaking of the former Soviet bloc members when he stresses that the real issue is not so much "our inability to think out new forms of the modern community but in our surrender to the old forms of the modern state" (Chatterjee 1993, 11) rather than embracing an alternative narrative of the community (ibid., 237).[35]

If Humpty Dumpty has fallen and shattered, along with the many bronze, marble, and granite Lenins, we already know that no political authority can reassemble the pieces. The egg is broken ("To make an omelet, you have to break eggs," as Stalin's comment that chips fly when you cut down trees is usually translated); the Cold War's prophylactic refrigeration is turned off. The monstrous something that was ripening inside has emerged. Perhaps, as in recent Hollywood dinosaur and reptile fantasies,[36] what hatched should never have been allowed to revive: violent nationalism, ethnic strife, archaic or primitive customs, debates no longer dampened by fear of censorship but not (yet?) smoothed over by Western conventions of polite discourse. Eva Hoffman observes about this uneasy transition that "if story is closer to history [in the new Eastern Europe], it's also closer to moral drama—for it was another of the system's accomplishments that it forced people to make difficult, risky, ethical choices often and under considerable pressure" (Hoffman 1994, xiv).

But the risks and drama that are quickly becoming stuff of legend, fiction, cinema, and scholarship, if not of interior décor, were also real; their consequences for individuals and nations should be constant reminders about the everyday hardship, poverty, and deprivation that came to define the region in the past century as well as the violence and suffering that accompanied its wars. The Yalta agreement came in the wake of a war that was supposed to be the last in the century, if not "a war to end all wars." Europe was supposed to have learned from that conflict, based on racism, to let such a thing happen Never Again. The most recent "New World Order" that Western leaders congratulate themselves for having brought to the blighted East has thus been paid for with death, devastation, poverty, long-lasting trauma, and a new population of "former Yugoslav" refugees spread throughout Western Europe and North America. This is the hard price of transition; it is seductively easy to shirk collective geopolitical and economic responsibility, if not for the conflict itself then for not preventing or arresting it, and to blame whatever went wrong on religion, ethnicity, class, past feuds, or the corruption of the former system.

Today's foreign-policy makers may still long for the old orders of bygone political eras, their illusion of stability. Post-1989 achievements of democracy in the former satellites are treated as brilliant victories of the West, rewards for Western "investment" in the former minions of the Evil Empire. This discourse mixes the vocabulary of myth with clear-cut "poli-sci" lingo, bouncing old symmetries back at the powerless: "It will serve no one's interests in the West now, anymore than it would have served the interests of the victorious allies after World War II, to allow despair, demoralization, and disintegration to prevail in the territories of our defeated Cold War adversaries" (Gaddis 1992, 210). It is still clear who is in power and who dictates which specific "interests in the West" are referred to. U.S. president George W. Bush's recent invitation to have Poland administer reconstruction of part of post–Saddam Hussein Iraq is a clearly calculated political gesture to strengthen ties with a country that will soon be a voice in the European Union. Given its population, Poland should command voting powers ranking just behind those of France or Germany; now its choice as a watchdog over Iraq's transformation may be a subtle rebuttal to those arrogant Western governments who opposed Bush's war.

Maintaining a continued division of Europe—if not on the map then in the minds and eyes of Europeans themselves—may be important as much to Washington as to Paris or London. Until our ways of thinking change, until acts of cultural translation reach beyond academe, that proverbial passport control officer at an international airport somewhere in the West will continue asking questions of East Europeans, considering them with much greater suspicions than a Swede or a German. The second-class citizen status could be justified for economic reasons (Wouldn't you want to emigrate if you lived there?) but also seems to go hand in hand with the tragic history of the region, whose dwellers have a very important and badly needed chance to teach a lesson about survival, resilience, and compassion to their Western counterparts. One thing the Other Europeans have learned from their wars, resurgent racism, and ethnic conflicts is that suffering doesn't make anybody better than anybody else. We are all in this together.

Post-Socialist Studies; or, the Delights of the Day After

What do we mean by citing "postsocialist studies" as a field? What role could it play? The power of changing paradigms makes Eastern Europe a fertile locale for scholarship, commanding attention with examples of postfascism, comparable to postcolonialism and the more recent phenomena of postcommunism, postsocialism, even post-totalitarianism.[37] What does it mean to recombine and interrogate the now unified or unifiable "Europe?" Many realms of discourse can be rethought if we complicate the single central binary of East/West, if we address local ways of playing out race or economic advantage that so often boil down to black/white, colony/home, alien/ours. Lisa Whitmore described to us an (East) German, former samizdat journal whose title suggests that either/or (*entweder/oder*), the mutually exclusive binary, is the rhetorical core of modern thought, but wittily deconstructs it with a postmodern twist: *Entwerter/Oder*, which Whitmore translates adequately as "Eater/Or." Embedded within the "other whiteness" that is the flip side of the myth of European homogeneity in political systems containing the same binaries in miniature, postsocialist studies poses a test case for deconstruction that makes the constructedness of walls completely obvious. Recognizing Belarus as the geographical center of Europe, which it is with responsible geometry, would mean an end to many self-serving mapping strategies and theoretical moves. Such recognition, though, would demand a reconfiguration beyond the symbolic realm. The Other Europe, the Second World, has been missing from the First/Third World dichotomy that shapes much recent academic discourse, and it can effectively problematize both the European "center" and Western hegemony in inventing and naming academic disciplines. One temptation of the "New World Order" is to shake everyone into a new "us" and "them," a hasty replacement set of binaries where "we" have won and "they" become just like "us." If the Second World ceases to exist, if it is assimilated to the First World in some economic advisor's fantasy, or if it "slips" into the Third World, as many of its citizens dread, what risks attend the new oversimplification? For the West, and especially for the United States as presumptive "winner" of the Cold War, loss of the monolithic Other could be taken to provoke negotiation of other dualisms: gender, race, and sexuality.

Stuart Hall is right to warn that "institutionalization [of theory is] a moment of profound danger" (1992, 285), but we nevertheless wish to sketch the parameters of an emerging field of postsocialist studies. Two streams may be stressed in the European East's scholarly and intellectual life: first, "theory" that struggles with the same set of issues now dominant in the West, and second, a growing body of work on Eastern Europe from a variety of disciplines that seeks to explain and interrogate accepted ways of knowing these societies. The latter seeks both to present these societies to the Western reader from a more informed, "thickly described," perspective and to bring local intellectual currents into dialogue with those of the West. This emerging field of post-socialist studies draws on cultural studies and engages some elements of post-colonial theory, together with Western scholarship, to approach culture and human subjects in a historical and social context. In the process, it discovers some of the inherent biases and limitations of these theories and thus enriches the process of scholarly inquiry.

Promoting dialogic encounters across disciplines, regions, and linguistic traditions, postsocialist cultural studies imagines a nonbinary critical location—a space for inquiry that deconstructs the East-West divide while exploring and exploding its origins. As Bhabha stresses, "It is the trope of our times to locate the question of culture in the realm of the *beyond*" because the "borderline work of culture demands an encounter with 'newness' that is not part of the continuum of past and present" (Bhabha 1994, 1, 7). Postsocialist studies shuttles between and around past and present, Cold War and aftermath, East and West, reconstructing history, geography, politics, and cross-cultural translation around the issues at the core of how identities are constructed and negotiated.[38] At the same time, its proponents are very much aware of their own unstable discursive location. Study of the "new" demands that the process of inquiry include constant self-interrogation—discourse and critic must be suspicious and self-reflective. As we go about complicating dichotomies and revisioning the past and its theories, we remap the shifting grounds of the discipline to prevent—quoting Nowakowski again—that "old" kind of "new," the recalcitrant inflexible binary perspective, from "coming back" more than is rhetorically useful.

As "no production of knowledge in the human sciences can ignore or disclaim its author's involvement as a human subject in his or her own circumstances,"[39] who are the people currently shaping the field of postsocialist studies? Many of the agents deconstructing the disciplinary boundaries of more traditional Slavic Studies through self-interrogation and self-reflection are East European scholars of the generation that was intellectually formed under communism. In his *Two Cities: On Exile, History, and the Imagination*, Adam Zagajewski ponders the meaning of the "new" for an intellectual while referring to hyperbolic dichotomies of "totalitarianism" in Poland:

> For me totalitarianism was both a nightmare and a literary theme, an oppressor and a toy, the policeman watching me and the ecstasy of political humor. I am now pretending to be a skeptical, wise, mature person, but I do not really know at all what the enormous changes in the East signify or what

> will change in me, in my manner of writing, thinking, living. A repugnant
> civilization is in decline; but it shaped me, I revolted against it, I tried to
> flee it; whether I like it or not, I am almost certainly marked by it. It will be
> a while before I find out what has really happened for me. (Zagajewski
> 1995, 223)

Traveling among categories, theories, and discourses, many of those, who "after the Fall" found themselves Kristevan "strangers to ourselves," now live postmodern lives between continents, cultures, and academic realms. Even émigrés who have been in the West for some time or children of émigrés with a strong cultural heritage must renegotiate their relationships to the Old Country, and perhaps to the new as well. A state of being unanchored, freed from the clear borders and geopolitical divisions of old has tremendous advantages. Yet the question arises immediately: Is such a discursive space tolerable in practice, habitable by real bodies and minds? Kristeva's "happy cosmopolitan" in *Nations without Nationalism* (1993) might occupy, or emerge from, such a "creative jostling" space: "When I say that I have chosen cosmopolitanism, this means that I have, against origins and starting from them, chosen a transnational or international position situated at the crossing of boundaries" (ibid., 16). In an era of ongoing racial and ethnic strife and religious warfare, Kristeva's utopian vision may be accessible only to a privileged few like herself, whose Western passports open international borders. Yet her vision compellingly links individual freedom to the movement of bodies and ideas across man-made borders and political systems, and it has enabled some of the recent debate about post-communist cultures.[40] In nineteenth-century America, Henry David Thoreau advocated walking toward frontiers and imaginary "Wests" because his "East"—the Old World of Europe, both across the Atlantic and in New England—loomed as antiquated, overconstructed, and uninspiring. Today, the plants and animals in Szymborska's "Psalm" show us that perhaps the act of migration, shifting into the place or discursive space that suits us, matters more than ideological compasses we can never fully trust.

The editors of this volume also invoke Susan Rubin Suleiman's "autobiographic imperative" as a trope that emphasizes connection between private and political critical practice. It engages with what Rosi Braidotti calls "nomadic feminist criticism"—attention to gender resides at the unstable core of postsocialist studies. Like Braidotti, who has migrated personally and professionally across many borders, Suleiman bases her concept of autobiographical criticism on her life story as a female Hungarian Jewish expatriate, currently living and working in the United Sates, whose specialties include French studies and visual culture.

This volume stresses the voices of the "native" witnesses of various theoretical migrations. After all, deconstructionist discourse could strike people from Eastern Europe as very funny, it so closely mimics what was once lived in practice. In 1990, I met a Russian on his way home from his first conference in the West who complained bitterly (to me, the American) of the immorality of literary theorists in the U.S. (SF). In 1990, the Soviet Union was on the verge of economic and environmental shambles, the rhetoric of communism and "advanced socialism" utterly discredited—but Western academics continued to advance the Marxist position, unwilling to accept that his personal experience might be a valid contribution to the debate. Admitting that would threaten their place in the Western academy's own complex system of signs and values and shake up the perceived safety zones in the halls of academic discourse.

Two of us could also say "I drank deconstruction with my mother's milk." Growing up in socialist Poland or Belarus was far from the innocence imagined "before the Fall." Every child became aware of competing and self-interested spheres of discourse as an essential element for survival in that time and place. That everydayness could be theorized in dazzling deconstructionist terms; no one can fully say what she is living until she has learned the terms—perhaps, in fact, learned them from people who have had no such personal experience. Of course, imagining the East as childish and innocent, with all the attendant Orientalized associations, including internalization of inferiority and eroticism by the Easterners, was a self-serving strategy of the West to justify exploitation of people, resources, or discourses, a way to cover up more painful facts. The West in turn appeared evil and out of control in the propaganda of the East; as such, paradoxically, it was even more attractive and seductive: if the newspapers are trumpeting about unemployment in the U.S. and Canada, then the truth must be just the opposite, and the streets there are paved with gold.

We cannot overestimate the role of autobiography in the work of theoretical writers today, as well as in many of the pieces in this book.[41] The authors' lives cross boundaries: some are Westerners who visit, study, and have come to feel a profound attachment to places or people in the East. In a sense we are poisoned by this Easternness, as our identities come to depend on our studies and understanding of this part of the world. Others of us are Easterners who moved west to work or study or whose work and study requires ongoing contact with the West that ignores, entertains, misreads, appropriates, and sometimes delights us. This is true of the editors as well, a Polish-born specialist in American studies, an American-born specialist in Russian literature, and a Belarusian-born specialist in gender studies. If we argue that theory must be rooted in practice, in *life*, then the body of writers living "in between" has a particular set of qualifications to describe, interrogate, and reconfigure the space between East and West. The combination of personal experience and theoretical preparation characterizes many of the authors in our bibliography as well.

Interdisciplinary and dialogic, postsocialist studies should have much in common with postcolonial theory, cultural, gender and identity studies—what Susan Stanford Friedman calls the "new geographies of identity" (Friedman

1996). Like Friedman's notion of the vitality and applicability of post–sexual-difference feminist critique in practice, methodological and discursive post–Cold War practice involves political imperatives. It aims to produce a "thick description" of lesser-known cultures and thinkers to increase understanding and intellectual exchange about and with the people who inhabit those cultures. The descriptions and ensuing cross-disciplinary dialogues must also aim to tear down what Paul Gilroy identifies as the "ethnocentric dimensions" of early cultural studies: "striving to analyse culture within neat, homogenous national units reflecting the 'lived relations' involved" (Gilroy 1991, 12). Eastern Europe as a scholarly locale could inspire affirmation of models of multivalent culture and subject as well as prompt a rejection of Cold War homogeneities of "race" and ethnicity. Gilroy, writing about "representing black presence" in Britain, claims that "expressive cultures affirm while they protest" (ibid., 155). Postsocialist studies would engage in a dialogic examination of cultural expressions under and after the period of Soviet domination. It must also take stock of racist, nationalist, and other hate-related discourses of "protest" against diversity that have sprung up all over the region since 1989—perhaps inevitable by-products of cultural and economic (re)construction amid "globalized" images of race and ethnicity. It must be responsive and confront issues that often escape the radar of academic discourse though they are of central concern to the often separate realm of "activism": genocide (more recently dubbed "ethnic cleansing"), family violence, rape and torture, ecological exploitation and devastation. It must be critical of ethnocentrism and exclusionary politics of identity and must regularly interrogate its own approaches.

Aware of the trajectories of theory in the increasingly transcultural academy, we might approach Tzvetan Todorov's study *On Human Diversity: Nationalism, Racism, and Exoticism in French Thought* (1993) from a postsocialist perspective as we address specific sets of textual/political issues. Todorov's autobiographical introduction emphasizes his youthful "discovery . . . of the vacuity of the official discourse . . . encountered daily" (ibid., vii) as he was growing up in a family of communist sympathizers in Bulgaria and presents the exclusively French focus of his volume as the "obligation" (ibid., xii) of a naturalized foreigner. Todorov's Europe still cleaves along the East-West axis of his own migration, and yet he sees it as united by the same lack of "ethical sense" (ibid., viii) about the "diversity of human populations and the unity of human race" (ibid., xi). In this, however, his analysis of champions of democracy, enlightenment, and scientific racism such as Montaigne, La Bruyère, Diderot, Tocqueville, Gobineau, Montesquieu, Rousseau and others limits its scope to white male thinkers and privileges a single selected European cultural tradition. Oddly undiverse, *On Human Diversity* is thus as much a story about Todorov himself, a former "fervent pioneer" (in the most junior organization in socialist societies; ibid., vii) who openly follows a moral and ethical compulsion to seek truth in the West (ibid., xiii). It also seems to privilege, provocatively and engagingly, certain subjects, critical discourses, and authorial "location(s)" that deal with "diversity."[42] Because "discourses are also events, driving forces of history, and not merely representations" (ibid., xiii), Todorov's partly troubling "critical humanism" (ibid., 390) has also its post-binary appeal:

> Let us break down simplistic associations: demanding equality as the right of all human beings does not in any way imply renouncing the hierarchy of values; cherishing the autonomy and freedom of individuals does not oblige us to repudiate all solidarity; the recognition of a public morality does not inevitably entail a regression to the time of religious intolerance and the Inquisition; nor does the search for contact with nature necessarily take us back to the Stone Age. (ibid., 399)

Like capital and foreign investments in search of cheap labor, theoretical concerns and their subjects have migrated ever more widely since the end of the Cold War. Clearly, postsocialist studies brings the cultures and issues identified with the former Soviet bloc into thematic and theoretical focus: it is more than a plea to be admitted into the fellowship of disciplines that study marginalized "Other" voices in academe. It offers new insights in the ongoing discussion of millennial anxieties: ethnicity, national identity, postcoloniality, "whiteness," gender, class, critical identity and anxiety, and (omnipresent) "globalization." Thus, it is instructive to take Rainer Gries's reading of East German cola in a larger context of the "Coca-Colization" of the world— especially the Second and Third Worlds. Gries shows how advertisements not only manipulate memory and cultural anxiety but also offer a playful opportunity to assess an East German subjectivity, appreciate this recognition of specific identity, and vote for the product with one's own purchasing power. Reading nationality and gender together against a "recentered" map of Europe with Belarus at its heart lets Elena Gapova draw invaluable insights from the paradigm.

Theories of identity reflect the experiences of masses of people, and today's deconstructionist theories recognize the nomadic experience of the world's populations. Europe, like the rest of the world, is full of refugees, émigrés, and individuals with identities too complex to express without hyphens or subordinate clauses. Western countries such as Australia, Canada and the United States would do well to recall their own immigrant past (even their "whiteness" is the result of multiple cultural and ethnic strands, somewhat concealed by the dominant Anglophone linguistic varnish)—after all, the world's second largest ethnically Polish population is in Chicago, not Kraków. Western Europe will soon have similar components where it does not already. A semantic/semiotic breakdown parallels actual (biographical, economic, political) dislocation in the lives of individuals and whole masses of people. Theory arises to investigate

Introduction

and account for the facts of experience and to expose the logic that structures (or destroys) terms of identity. No matter how "high" the theory, it must not lose sight of its human subjects.

Obviously, postsocialist studies complements work on ethnic and cultural identity within American multicultural studies and the transcultural work of the social sciences. We hope to contribute to mapping the post-communist condition in the "increasingly polycentric world" that, in the words of Henry Louis Gates, Jr., must learn to escape "misreadings of history" (1994, 213). As Gates claims, "spatial dichotomies through which our oppositional criticism has defined itself prove increasingly inadequate to a cultural complex of traveling culture" (ibid., 214). The articles in this volume show that postauthoritarian criticism lends invaluable support to a "globalized" and traveling cultural project that aims to foster agency through education in critical thinking—what Gates prescribes for post–Cold War multicultural studies. We second Gates's project: "Perhaps we can begin to forgo the pleasures of ethnicist affirmation and routinized resentment in favor of rethinking the larger structures that constrain and enable our agency" (ibid., 215).

We intend this volume to contribute to the development of the nuanced historical sense in discussions reaching beyond the primitive opposition East/West, both within and without academe, and we offer it as a hybrid and dialogic project. In Cornel West's definition:

> Every culture that we know is a result of the weaving of antecedent cultures. Elements of antecedent cultures create something new based on that which came before. . . . So when we talk about Europe, we are not talking about anything monolithic or homogeneous. When we talk about multiculturalism we are talking about a particular critique of something which is already multicultural. (West 1993, 1:4)

Like other scholars in African-American studies whose work has inspired us, West advances a widely conceived educational project that cannot be accomplished without serious international cooperation and an equally serious reevaluation of the racialized power relationships in educational institutions themselves. The pedagogical project we face in postcolonial and postsocialist hybridic cultures is a risky business, "transformation of consciousness—a changing mind set," as Gayatri Chakravorty Spivak terms it.

Vaulting over the Wall in transcultural and interdisciplinary leaps, hoping to demonstrate and make more tangible the pleasures that post-Fall intellectual inquiry, art, and popular culture can offer, we make this invitation to discussion, exchange, and collaborative educational enterprise. Our introduction closes with the hope that our colleagues, students, and readers outside of the academy will find this work inspiring and worth talking about, that they will learn from it and laugh over it, that it will lead toward new, exciting cultural spaces.

NOTES

1. We also use the following terms, often interchangeably, to refer to the historic period under study in this volume: "post-communist," "post-1989," "postauthoritarian," "post–Cold War." We are aware of the complex semantics and emotive content of terms used to describe the transitional era following the collapse of socialist and communist political and economic systems in the geographic region formerly known as the "Soviet bloc." The word "totalitarian" has also often been used to describe economic and political systems in the region, even though, following Hannah Arendt's definition, it would be a stretch to apply it to Poland or Hungary, or even to the Soviet Union after 1953. While aware of social science scholarship on "totalitarianism," which falls outside the scope of this volume, and of the ways the term has been used more loosely in literary and cultural studies to denote a "state of mind," in the wake of Czesław Miłosz's *The Captive Mind* (see also Jeffrey Goldfarb, *Beyond Glasnost: The Post-Totalitarian Mind* [Chicago: University of Chicago Press, 1989]), rather than devising a detailed etymology, we have chosen to use the term "postsocialist" as the best reflection of the diversity of our contributors' perspectives and approaches.

2. Some of these writers include Anna Bojarska, Izabela Filipiak, Małgorzata Saramonowicz, Manuela Gretkowska, Natasza Goerke, Anna Nasiłowska, Olga Tokarczuk, Magdalena Tulli. As scholars such as Cynthia Enloe, Julia Kristeva, and some featured in this volume show, the post-Yalta political division of the world affected not only actual women's bodies and minds but also the ways femininity and masculinity were constructed, performed, and represented on both sides of the Wall. (We discuss some of the gendered dimensions of the East-West divide later on in this essay.)

3. We discuss these terms at greater length in a subsequent section of the introduction.

4. Here and elsewhere we refer to terminology and concepts from the disciplines and discourses referred to as postcolonial in order to signal points of connection, common areas of interest, and themes that our work may share across academic fields.

5. Like many artists of her generation, Szymborska, too, flirted with socialist-realist writing in her postwar poems.

6. Raymond Williams, *Keywords: A Vocabulary of Culture and Society* (New York: Oxford University Press, 1983), 91–92.

7. Stuart Hall, *Critical Dialogues in Cultural Studies*, ed. David Morley and Kuan-Hsing Chen (London and New York: Routledge, 1996), 138.

8. Homi K. Bhabha, *The Location of Culture* (New York: Routledge, 1994), 163.

9. Serguei Oushakine, "In the State of Post-Soviet Aphasia: Symbolic Development in Contemporary Russia," *Europe-Asia Studies* 52, no. 6 (2000): 994.

10. In the original: "Nowe wraca!"

11. In his 1989 study of the "post-totalitarian mind," Jeffrey Goldfarb locates antiauthoritarian and oppositional thinking in Polish cultural productions years before its independence.

12. For more information about this player, see a Web site in Polish, which has been marked as "a Web site against racism": http://www.olisadebe.com.

13. See the moving chapter on the Wall, seen through a female escapee's story, in

Slavenka Drakulić, *How We Survived Communism and Even Laughed* (New York: Harper Perennial, 1993), 33–42.

14. Sławomir Mrożek made the dividing wall central in his 1967 play *Dom na granicy* (*House on the Border*).

15. See also Magdalena Zaborowska, *How We Found America: Reading Gender through East European Immigrant Narratives* (Chapel Hill: University of North Carolina Press, 1995), 213.

16. Larry Wolff, *Inventing Eastern Europe: The Map of Civilization on the Mind of the Enlightenment* (Stanford, Calif.: Stanford University Press, 1994), 7, 4, 15, 14.

17. The term "Other Europe" was used for the Penguin series edited by Philip Roth, "Writers from the Other Europe." The authors chosen—all of whom were male— and the way the series was advertised confirm the construction of East/Central European Otherness in Western cultural representation that we address here.

18. It is worth noting that certain kinds of "Orientalization" flourished inside Eastern Europe. Just as one example, Poland had a long affair with the East, including cultural and political contacts with the Ottoman Empire, not to mention imitations of Turkish fashions, cuisine, and warfare. (This is splendidly illustrated in Jan K. Ostrowski's *Land of the Winged Horsemen: Art in Poland, 1572–1764* [New Haven, Conn.: Yale University Press, 1999]). During the Cold War, one could often hear derisive remarks about "brother" inhabitants of Poland's "Oriental"/Balkan neighbors—"peasant" Bulgarians or "uncouth" Romanians.

19. Slavenka Drakulić, *Café Europa: Life after Communism* (New York: Penguin, 1996), 59.

20. Said, "Afterward to the 1995 Printing," in *Orientalism: Western Conceptions of the Orient* (New York: Penguin, 1995), 329–354.

21. Biographical notes on Kristeva's books more often than not omit her place of birth, concentrating rather on her academic honors and position in Western academe, tacitly suggesting that her pre-immigration identity had nothing to do with her present accomplishments.

22. For a provocative inquiry into the new economies of the East-West erotic "ga(y)ze," see Nicholas F. Radel, "The Transnational Ga(y)ze: Constructing the East European Object of Desire in Gay Film and Pornography after the Fall of the Wall," *Cinema Journal* 41 no. 1 (2001): 40–62.

23. A female Polish student at Aarhus University, where I taught in 1996–200 (MZ), told me that her Danish husband's friends occasionally joked that he had "bought" himself a wife in Poland. The jokes were concerned less with the idea that East European countries supply truly "feminine" women for men in Western Europe— that's a well-known fact in Denmark, where the idiom "to live the Polish way" ("at live på polsk") means "to shack up"—than with how much money the woman might have cost. Bus services between Denmark and Eastern European countries deliver (picture) "brides" on a timetable; wife-tourism between the United States and the former Soviet satellites is well known and widely developed. Sites on the Internet, such as "From Russia with . . . Wife," "Czech Partners for Life," "Riga Exxpres," "Ukraine Girls International," and others invite one to browse, order, book, visit, and sample images of women, request their addresses (for a small fee), and set up meetings at a click of a button.

24. The program *Kvinder til salg* (*Women for Sale*) was produced by Henrik Grunnet and Charlotte Bartholdy and aired on Danish TV2 on May 3, 1998. Its main

character is "Natasha," a 32-year-old married mother of two from Estonia who works as a nurse and wants to make "real" money in the West. She trains as an erotic dancer at a local school set up to prepare women for the "trade" and then leaves to work in Denmark. Warned about the danger of being forced into prostitution there, she claims that this would never happen to her. At the end of the program, the crew revisits Copenhagen and finds out that Natasha has moved up—from a nightclub dancer to highly paid hooker; she sends her child nice toys.

25. The fascination with East European bodies can also be analyzed within the paradigm of the "primitive" developed by Marianna Torgovnick, who claims, "We imagine ourselves through the primitive in other, equally devious ways . . . that challenge the border between the psychological and the political. . . . Western thinking frequently substitutes versions of the primitive for some of its deepest obsessions." One might productively apply Torgovnik's theory to read the "whiteness" of the post-communist hooker. The "primitive" Other European woman is forced into her trade but also "chooses" it as a relatively advantageous economic option. She is exploited as a site where Western fantasies of dominance and superiority can be played out carefree and without the visible presence of "race" that usually underlies, even in repressed form, such gendered transcultural transactions. See Marianna Torgovnick, *Gone Primitive: Savage Intellects, Modern Lives* (Chicago: University of Chicago Press, 1990), 18.

26. This tendency is outlined in Laura Busheikin, "Is Sisterhood Really Global? Western Feminism in Eastern Europe," in *Ana's Land: Sisterhood in Eastern Europe*, ed. Tanya Renne (Boulder, Colo.: Westview Press, 1997), 12–21.

27. Interview conducted by Sławka Wałczewska from the Center for Women (eFka) in Kraków in April 2003. This interview is still being edited for the University of Michigan's Institute for Research on Women and Gender oral history project "Global Feminisms."

28. See Wiącek, *Zabić Żyda!*, especially pp. 6–16, for a calendar of those events. As Wiącek claims, available documents and statements from witnesses are often contradictory and require further investigation. Some facts are clear: forty-two people were murdered by a mob with help from soldiers and militia members present (Wiącek lists names of the victims on p. 139), and other incidents of violence all over Poland preceded this pogrom. The trial took place quickly and with minimal media coverage; twelve people were tried out of over a hundred arrested. Nine received death sentences and were promptly executed, as there was still a death penalty in Poland at that time.

29. International agreements assign Auschwitz/Oświecim the status of an international monument to martyrs, making it an interfaith terrain that is to be free from any explicit religious symbols. Despite that, the grounds around the death camp have been staked with crosses by openly nativist and anti-Semitic groups. Along with such ideologically charged programs as Radio Maryja (Radio [Virgin] Mary), the conservative Polish church hierarchy emerges as a silent supporter of divisive actions and continued populist anti-Semitism. See also a recent article on deliberate erasure of Jewish martyrdom from discourse on Auschwitz and World War II under communism; Marcin Zaremba, "Urząd zapomnienia," *Polityka* 41, no. 2319 (13 October 2001).

30. I recall a program for drivers a few years ago in which a priest proclaimed St. Christopher the patron saint of correctly religiously identified people behind the wheel. With all due respect for religious expression, we wonder whether that saint, known for transporting Christ over dangerous waters, is really thrilled to take on this new task in post-communist Poland (MZ).

31. Of course, looking at race, nationality, and gender together yields not only responsible but interesting results. When Eurocentric whiteness is interrogated across post-communist boundaries and through the lens of gender and sexuality, it reveals in the heart of Europe what scholars such as Fred Pfeil, Rowena Chapman, and Jonathan Rutherford define as the "contemporary crisis of white straight masculinity" (Fred Pfeil, *White Guys: Studies in Postmodern Domination and Difference* [London: Verso, 1995], ix). There may as yet be no full-scale men's movement or "Iron (Curtain) John" East of the Elbe, but scholars of both whiteness and gender would do well to turn their attention to East European versions of what Pfeil terms "the modalities of white straight masculinity . . . [as] multiple, and/or riven by contradictions and fissures, and/or subject to flux and change" (ibid., x). For a thought-provoking treatment of this issue in a different area, that of early Soviet Russian literary discourse, see Eliot Borenstein, *Men without Women: Masculinity and Revolution in Russian Fiction, 1917–1929* (Durham, N.C., and London: Duke University Press, 2000).

And why, we might ask, would Kristeva, a Bulgarian woman who writes that she considers herself French thanks to de Gaulle (*Nations without Nationalism*, trans. Leon S. Roudiez [New York: Columbia University Press, 1993], 65), call her novel *The Samurai*?

"Only what's human can be truly alien," Szymborska reminds us.

32. Drakulić, *Café Europa*, 6–13.

33. Tsvetana Gueorguieva, "Bulgarians between East and West," in *The Balkans: National Identities in a Historical Perspective*, ed. Stafano Bianchini and Marco Dogo (Ravenna: Longo Editore, 1998), 153–160.

34. See also Esbenshade on the West's "temptation to view history and memory in Eastern Europe as 'out of control,' with tribal passions, blood feuds, and 'primitive' ethnic strife 'threatening stability in Europe' "; Richard S. Esbenshade, "Remembering to Forget: Memory, History, National Identity in Postwar East-Central Europe," *Representations* (Winter 1995): 73.

35. Partha Chatterjee, *The Nation and Its Fragments: Colonial and Postcolonial Histories* (Princeton, N.J.: Princeton University Press, 1993).

36. A sign of emerging nostalgia for the bygone East can be seen even in the monstrously unsuccessful 1998 movie *Godzilla*, which opens with a view of the "sarcophagus" in Chernobyl, Ukraine, and hints at the Cold War arms race as the root of all present evil. Of course, the monster herself—for it is a *she*—also comes from the East, whether located in the nuclear clumsiness of Eastern Europe or her origins in Japan.

37. See note 1.

38. See also Said's much earlier point on literary criticism's obligation to "reveal" and engage with other discourses: "Criticism cannot assume that its province is merely the text, not even the great literary text. It must see itself, with other discourse, inhabiting a much contested cultural space, in which what has counted in the continuity and transmission of knowledge has been the signifier, as an event that has left lasting traces upon the human subject" (Said, *The World, the Text, and the Critic* [London: Vintage, 1983], 225).

39. Edward Said, *Orientalism* (New York: Vintage Books, 1979), 11.

40. "Beyond the *origins* that have assigned to us biological identity papers and a linguistic, religious, social, political, historical place, the freedom of contemporary individuals may be gauged according to their ability to *choose* their membership, while

the democratic capability of a nation and social group is revealed by the right it affords individuals to exercise that choice" (Kristeva, *Nations without Nationalism*, 16).

41. To mention only a few prominent names among autobiographical critics and writers: bell hooks; Henry Louis Gates, Jr.; Susan Rubin Suleiman; Sidonie Smith; Cornel West; Eva Hoffman; Slavenka Drakulić; Maria Kuncewicz; Dubravka Ugrešić; Adam Zagajewski; and Andre Codrescu.

42. See also Henry Louis Gates, Jr.'s polemic with Todorov's "neo-colonial recuperation of the sense of difference upon which a truly new criticism of world literature must be granted," in *"Race," Writing, and Difference*, ed. Henry Louis Gates, Jr. (Chicago and London: University of Chicago Press, 1986), 403–408.

Part One

(Re-)Visitations

A true fragment of dialogue between an American and a Bosnian, recorded in spring of 1987, "before anyone had heard of" Bosnia:

"You're so exotic!"
"Oh, no. *You* are the one who's exotic." (SF)

A roadside snack bar on the main road between Kraków and Zakopane. 1997.
Photograph by Willard Pate. Used by permission.

The authors in this collection stress the need for persistent scholarly and political attention to past and future, for returns to history as well as leaps forward—but not in simple mechanical repetition. Rather, they emphasize cyclicality, the ebb and flow of patterns of discourse and historical analyses. Hence the title of this section, which emphasizes (uneasy) returns and hints at less-obvious meanings of "visitation" or repeated onsets of disorder in the body and mind. In the postsocialist moment, cross-cultural social calls are indeed often made with physical and mental dis-ease: identities cannot be studied without violating boundaries, disturbing ethnicist notions, and forging disruptive academic discourses. The increasing fluidity between East and West has tended to complicate that crucial boundary, increasing the importance of other categories of identity—gender, race, ethnicity, sexuality, plus that classic Second World term of analysis: class.

The seven contributors to this section share the experience of multiple locations and complex loyalties: we are all a bit like Rosi Braidotti's nomadic feminist, striving to draw wisdom from our discomfort. There is particular value in the questions raised by change over time, in the fertile moment before issues and priorities settle into a new order. It is no surprise that several articles in this section engage recent literary theory, which also often springs from lived experience: the fragmentation of former colonial empires, loss or abandonment of modernist discourses, and the economic and ontological dislocations of increasing global mobility, both voluntary and enforced—factors that have impacted Eastern and Central Europe heavily in the past decade. Willard Pate's photographs, four of which punctuate the collection, illustrate the juxtaposition and even clashes of Western (sometimes "Western" made in China) imports with the slower-changing material and cultural fabric of Eastern Europe, especially Poland, where Pate traveled in the late 1990s.

Like all the factors that shape identity in this "Second World," the topics of the essays cross the boundaries of real-world geographies to create unexpected points of contact with one another. They could well have been arranged in very different ways, and we encourage readers to stay open to the other connections they may note.

In "How I Found Eastern Europe: Televisual Geography, Travel Sites, and Museum Installations," Romanian-American scholar Andaluna Borcila borrows a title from Anzia Yezierska's 1920s narrative of immigrant life, "How I Found America." Borcila examines the depictions and configurations of Eastern Europe, focusing on Romania in particular, in the Western media and their overlaps into the now "globalized" realm of Romanian public discourse. Suspicious in origin and problematic in their influence, images of Romania abroad in the West impact both Western viewers and East Europeans living anywhere in the world; they heighten the contemporary tension between lived and "merely" viewed fact and experience. Elena Gapova, director of the Center for Gender Studies at the European Humanities University in Minsk, Belarus, writes in "The Nation in Between, or Why Intellectuals Do Things with Words" about both the recent history of the status of the Belarusan language and the "class or corporate" interests of the intellectuals who would impose their vision of language and culture on the "people" they propose to represent. Lisa Whitmore's "Prenzlauer Berg Connections: The Trajectory of East German Samizdat Culture from Socialism to Capitalism" traces the path since reunification of writers and artists who began work in the East German underground literary and samizdat culture, suggesting the complexities of both local situation and the global literary and intellectual market.

Polish Americanist Magdalena Zaborowska elaborates the significance of the shifting shapes of Poland's capital city in "Reading Transparent 'Constructions of History,' or Three Passages through (In)Visible Warsaw." The complexity of Polish culture, especially in the twentieth century, emerges through visible and invisible layers of history, constructed on the rubble of a city largely destroyed in the Second World War. Zaborowska stresses the erasure and more recent partial recovery in memorials and museums of once-vibrant Jewish neighborhoods, the architectural impositions and rhetorical fanfares of the socialist period, and some of the possibilities that exist amid rampant construction of new capitalist objects. David Houston's article "Can Prague Learn from L.A.? Frank Gehry's Netherlands National Building in Prague," devotes its attention to a single landmark structure in the heart of the Czech capital, tracing its origins and offering a nuanced reading of its presence and import in a very particular urban fabric.

Polonist, pedagogue, and translator Bill Johnston examines another type of post-Soviet capitalist incursion in his "Heteroglossia and Linguistic Neo-colonialism: English Teaching in Post-1989 Poland." Basing his analysis partly in scholarship and partly on field interviews with Polish teachers of English as a foreign language, Johnston draws attention to distortions caused by the wholesale rush to make English the dominant foreign language taught in Poland. Anca Rosu, a Romanian-born specialist in American literature, dissects Robert Kaplan's successful travelogue *Balkan Ghosts* from a critical and scholarly vantage point to show how the book's imperialistic tendencies reflect not only many continuing tendencies in travel writing but also a distinct set of anxieties about the "Western" identity of its author.

The essays here make clear that the region under study in this volume is not only worth revisiting but also invites a careful and thorough examination, which in turn may lead us to look behind the gaze and the observer. Localities, languages, discourses, and disciplines cross-pollinate in an exchange that envisages not so much the New World Order (we learn not only from postsocialist, but also from postcolonial and ethnic studies critics that it is neither new nor an order!) as a Second World in a new world context.

After I moved to Greenville, South Carolina, I didn't expect to run into other émigrés from Poland. When I met an older woman with that familiar accent at a restaurant, I happily started up a conversation. She asked where I was from, and when I said Kielce she started crying. Not out of homesickness, but recalling the pogrom shortly after World War II against the Jews in Kielce, which she had survived.

I had heard about the pogrom, but not until I was an adult. It was mentioned in whispers, part of unofficial history. Poles wanted badly to blame all violence and inhumanity on the Nazis, and the socialist state could not admit discussion of such recent anti-Semitism. The issue was officially dead, part of prehistory, excluded from public discourse and polite conversation.

How much of Eastern Europe's relationship with the West depends on those who left for the West, admired friends, enterprising relatives—or the Others we drove from our communities because we could not accept their difference? Perhaps carrying with them a vision of liberty that "we" could not tolerate. (MZ)

one
How I Found Eastern Europe

Televisual Geography, Travel Sites,
and Museum Installations

Andaluna Borcila

In the fall of 1995 the Museum of Contemporary Art in Chicago hosted the first (traveling) exhibit of "Eastern European" art in the United States after 1989. The question of how to respond to the interpellation of being "Eastern European" drove me to the exhibit; the same question troubles this essay. As a Romanian and an academic in the United States,[1] I access "Eastern Europe" in the media from my home in the Midwest; I enter arguments about these representations as an "Eastern European." I thus provisionally accept the fiction of "Eastern Europe," a territory and a cultural landscape with identifiable characteristics to which I have a special claim, and I find myself responding to images/representations of "Eastern Europe" produced in the media as partial, simplistic, or erroneous. The fiction of "Eastern Europe," which generates and is reproduced by these representations of "Eastern Europe," interpellates me and allows me to enter a dialogue on unequal terms. "Eastern Europe" is, it would seem, a necessary fiction. Yet I am very much aware that I never really go home to "Eastern Europe" and that I am never closer to and farther away from "Eastern Europe" than I am here, watching television.

The exhibit *Beyond Belief: Contemporary Art from East Central Europe* was one symptomatic instance of the rhetorical power and flexibility of this fiction of "Eastern Europe." The exhibit was one in a series of "regional" exhibits of "Eastern European" art, organized and housed by museums and art galleries outside "Eastern Europe." As curator Laura J. Hoptman acknowledges in the notes to the introduction of the exhibit catalogue, although curators and experts from this "region" participated in organizing the *Beyond Belief* exhibit, "the shows were not seen in East and Central Europe, making the concept of grouping the contemporary art of these cultures a decidedly foreign idea" (1995, 12). Hoptman also acknowledges the problem with grouping together such diverse artists—fourteen different artists and groups from six different countries: Poland, the Czech Republic, Hungary, Slovakia, Romania, and Bulgaria—under the fiction of an Eastern European Zeitgeist. Although acknowledged as a fiction, the fiction of the region overdetermines the exhibit. Born as a foreign idea, it is reproduced by the exhibit, the Western art critic, and the "Eastern European" artists.

Focusing on televisual sites, traveling texts, and a museum installation featured in the *Beyond Belief* exhibit, this essay traces the circulation of representations of "Eastern Europe" and the solidification of the fiction of "Eastern Europe" across discursive lines during the 1990s. It examines the ways this fiction positions subjects—viewers and readers—in unequal discursive configurations, and it considers the ways representations of "Eastern Europe" participate in the production of narratives of "Eastern European identity" and of "Western," specifically "American," identity.

Before and after 1989, the territory and shared community of "Eastern Europe" existed, and still exists, primarily in rhetoric that describes it as a "world" beyond Europe.[2] It was and still is spoken about as an area that cannot represent itself, and it appears as a spectacle of crisis and difference reinforcing the normative ideas of "Europe," "America," "Western values," "capitalism." During the Cold War, "Eastern Europe" designated a world inhabited homogeneously by communism, which was conceived of as monolithic, backward, and underdeveloped. It is a commonplace in present-day journalistic and political discourses to speak of the demise of the Cold War and of the disappearance of Cold War discourses. Academic discourses also speak of the replacement of the Cold War Other by Others in the American imaginary and U.S. international relations. Yet as we have clearly seen, Cold War discourses persist and played a crucial role in the demonization of the "communist/fascist" Yugoslavia. It is the dying communism/fascism in the former Yugoslavia that was reported as cause for the devastating crisis there; the scars of communism are similarly held responsible for the economic difficulties in countries of the former Soviet bloc.

Starting with the revolutionary events of 1989 in East and Central Europe, "Eastern Europe," the once-monochrome Cold War Other, has become an assemblage of sites in the geography of global television: it has entered the spatial distribution of what John Hartley calls "Theydom," with its specific global/Orientalist strains, while maintaining its Cold War inflections. My reading of televisual representations of "Eastern Europe" in the 1990s focuses on the images of Romanian orphans, which constitute a nodal trope in the economy of the "Eastern European" symbolic. I follow the circulation of "the Romanian orphans" from U.S. media—news, the TV movie *Nobody's Children*, and the NBC coverage of the 1996 Atlanta Olympics—to debates about Romanian and "Eastern European" identity articulated around images of the orphans in Romanian living rooms. My reading of the circulation of this site means to offer, more generally, an account of the spectral encounter between "Romania" (East) and "America" (West) in the 1990s as one produced by/ along the media vector, and it suggests that this global televisual site is a symptom of both the bankruptcy and the persistence of a Cold War symbolic.

I move from televisual sites to traveling texts in order to explore symptomatically "Eastern Europe's" apparent consistency across discursive lines. My discussion emphasizes that representations of "Eastern Europe" are produced along the coordinates of a telesthetic and spectacular bringing forth of a completely incomprehensible territory/space outside a normative Europe and United States. Eva Hoffman's *Exit into History* (1993) tells the story of an "Eastern European's" return to the territory of her childhood. Hoffman's impulse to travel to "Eastern Europe" comes from a televisual fascination with "Eastern Europe" and the nostalgic remembrance of childhood. I trace here a very particular enactment of the dynamics between "Eastern European" and "Western"/American identity. Not only does Hoffman go to the space of her childhood, she goes there as a televisually informed, mature Western viewer/ tourist to evaluate the state of things.

The concluding part of this essay returns to the *Beyond Belief* exhibit via an installation by the Romanian group subReal and poses the following question: If this fiction of "Eastern Europe" has also, arguably, become a way for people to represent themselves or to produce themselves as they find a legitimate identity, can it become a space for resignifying practices?

"Romanian Orphans": Televisual Remembering

The Romanian AIDS "scandal" first received coverage in the United States in 1990. Starting with the images aired in January 1990, "Romania" *was* "orphans" on television—in the news, in documentaries, and in a made-for-TV movie. The images of orphans attest to the undeniable harsh reality of orphanages in socialist Romania, but what else do they speak of? Along what narrative lines does this recurrent trope of Romanian orphans move, and how is Romania, as a significant site in the economy of tropes of "Eastern Europe," produced in relation to a certain way of watching Romania—that is, watching orphans—on television?

Romania's orphans were at first dubbed "Ceaușescu's little victims" and "the darkest secrets" in the mountains of Romania/Transylvania. Making Romania visible along the trope of the Romanian orphans meant revealing the core of communist reality through a palpable vision of violence, inhumanity, and poverty. The "orphans of Romania" were read in a Cold War configuration as symptoms of the decaying body of communism. Communism did not simply go away, and we witnessed in the 1990s what some journalists called "the return of the reds"[3] and others the phenomenon of Dracula-like "undead."[4] In this context the "Romanian orphans" are also symptoms of a crisis in narrative that television reproduces.

On July 2, 1996, CNN presented images of Hillary Clinton's important visit (from a Romanian perspective!) to Bucharest on a trip to Central Europe that was intended, in part, to influence perspectives in the West about whether or not to admit Romania into NATO and the Western European economic community. CNN showed images of happy little children from a "cheerful AIDS pediatric center" and of children from Primary School 57 in Bucharest surrounding the First Lady. The *New York Times*, however, pointed to Clinton's avoidance of "the harsh orphanages," dubbed it a political strategy, and criticized Clinton for praising progress in Romania rather than "scolding the government," then led by President Ion Iliescu (Perlez 1996, 45). From images of children, the media moves to larger pedocratic configurations of Romania and the Romanian government. The "communists"—the Romanian government or Romanians in general—couldn't and can't take care of the orphan children. The orphans stand in for all Romanian children but also for the idea of Romanians as children who must be monitored, evaluated, and perhaps scolded by the Western media observer as they take their first steps toward democracy.

The images of harsher orphanages did not appear in television coverage of Hillary Clinton's visit, but it has become common knowledge that Romania is a land of children with AIDS, of children sleeping on the streets in Bucharest, "the fleabag capital of Romania."[5] Images of "real" orphanages need not be shown to be seen. Adults from the United States have traveled to adopt orphans from Romania, television has run interviews with these parents when they return with reruns of scenes from orphanages, and the interviews were recycled into a made-for-TV movie, *Nobody's Children*. Hillary Clinton's visit to the orphanages in June 1996 was contextualized by this archival pool of televisual memory. In this way, viewers were part of the self-referential dynamics of meaning-production around the site of "Romania" on television. Around this process of televisual remembering, "we," the constructed audience, come together.

There is enough stored in the memory of a television viewer, Romanian or American, to read the little sequences devoted to the Romanian gymnastics team at the 1996 Olympic Summer Games, which were broadcast by NBC. Peculiar to the NBC coverage of the Atlanta Olympics, as distinct from the Barcelona or Lillehammer Olympics, were the short biographical sketches or team stories that compensated for the absence of other nationals in coverage of the actual competition.[6] Through their focus on children, and by recycling soap-opera codes, the stories speak of the emotion and concerns that other national children provoke in a constructed sentimental—that is, feminized—American subject.

The story covering the Romanian women's gymnastics team, who were constantly referred to as "sharing one father," is about broken/displaced families. Images of the little gymnasts, singing softly and laughing, playing in the grass of a medieval castle from which they appear one by one from the shadows, appear juxtaposed in this story about the nation of Romania with the different reality of "other less fortunate children." The voice-over reminds us that the gymnasts come from a country whose regime was violently overthrown and that other children in Romania are not as happy as these little girls. Then come images of a dark street with children sleeping in cardboard boxes and "darker" visions of little faces with sad eyes and contorted bodies—the same circulating footage of Romanian orphanages. These images bring the drama of recognition, a "remembrance" of how we have seen Romania before and recognition of how "they" differ from "us." The orphans are symptoms of a brutal past and of the decaying body of communism. The sketch continues with a brief overview of the Romanian gymnastics team that emphasizes the faces of the gymnasts and the sadness in their eyes. Romanian identity is produced for us in the coverage around the faces and bodies of children with "sad eyes" and around a foregrounded way of watching Romania. While the "sadness" of these other children contaminates the viewer, it also differentiates viewers from the much-less-fortunate children. This representation of others is what Judith Butler would call a "site of abjection," from which "our nation" and "our" relationship to children are differentiated throughout the coverage.[7] The trope of the orphans is indicative of what "we" are not.

"Watching the Babies Die"

I remember watching, in my home city of Cluj-Napoca, the gruesome, horrifying scenes from Romanian orphanages on a videotape that an Englishman brought to a friend's house at the end of January 1990, returning to us our own reality. The video brought home to me the palpable truth of a regime that had exceeded our worst nightmares, and it brought home "our" complicity with it. I understood then that the orphans of Romania were, like the violence on the streets and on television, the way that "they" (the West) saw "us."

The English acquaintance told us he had shown the film to other Romanians and that he did not understand how "you people" didn't do anything about the orphan problem. Later he would write to me, saying that even though Romanians would not address their own problem, *he* had *done something about it*. He had become one of dozens of Western reporters who returned to Romania to film more of the suffering, considering this a generous and humanitarian act.

Years later, as a graduate student in Indiana, I visited Romanian immigrant friends who had watched coverage of the Romanian revolution on American television day and night and therefore felt they had lived through it. They produced a videotaped program that began with a brief recounting of life in Romania under Ceauşescu, specifically Romanian Labor Day parades. These were images of small bodies in the stands of the soccer stadium that formed the letters of Ceauşescu's name from an aerial perspective. (I seem to remember being part of one of the "E's.") The tape continued with images of struggle for control over Romanian television on December 22, 1989. It concluded with black-and-white footage from Romanian orphanages. The images of the orphanages retroactively attached themselves both to the docile bodies in the soccer stadium (the concealed other side of the "festivities" in which Romanians supposedly participated willingly) and to the revolutionary bodies, signifying residues of the Ceauşescu regime and the lack of change in Romania.

Around these images my conversation with my friends reiterated the basic debate during the first free elections in 1990 in Romania between those who lived in Romania through 1989 and those who had "managed to leave" and had "only watched" Romania on television. The debate involved and produced two sides, two "others." The émigrés, according to the one side, didn't know what it was like "to suffer through the regime," had not really lived through events in '89. Returning Romanian immigrants therefore had no right to advise, lead, or criticize "us." From the other side's perspective, those who stayed in Romania had lived in cowardice, or had just stood there watching, for forty-five years. Consequently, this argument goes, those who lived under the regime are not only complicit, they are also forever scarred; they must "purge" communist residues, assisted by political exiles and Westerners. This latter perspective has also been a persistent view of Romanians in U.S. media,[8] and it is present in Eva Hoffman's *Exit into History.*

At the end of the conversation, my friends invoked the images they had seen on television as proof that Romanians like myself had "just stood there watching": while before '89 "we" had not done anything about our situation, since '89 "we" have been just sitting there in Romania, "watching the babies die."

I suggest that this trope of the orphans was one in a series of post-1989 global televisual sites which, flowing from West to East, have sown clusters of noncommunication. From the Romanian side, it brought home the horror and pleasure of seeing what was invisible during the Ceauşescu regime and of being seen by the West. Lines between those who lived through the regime/ revolution and those who just watched on TV, between Romanian identity and Romanian-American immigrant identity blur and are redrawn.

Detour: "Just Watching" the Romanian Revolution

According to McKenzie Wark, the terrain created and mapped by television vectors produces in us a new kind of experience, an experience of telesthesia, or perception at a distance. This virtual geography of experience, "a different kind of perception, of things not bounded by rules of proximity, of 'being there' " is in no way less real than our firsthand acquired geography of experience, and it "doubles, troubles and generally permeates our experience of the space we experience firsthand" (Wark 1994, vii). The images my friends and I watched in the living room in the United States validated my friends' claim that they had, to some extent, "lived" the revolution just as I had lived it. My friends saw the infamous videotape of the execution of Nicolae and Elena Ceauşescu and the images of orphans before I did in Romania. However, they never wrote Ceauşescu's name with their bodies on the grass—in other words, they could only plug into televisual memory or experience, while I had an excess of lived experience. Their claim brings forth crucial questions about the spectral/televisual encounter between East and West and the relation between telesthesia and lived experience.

Slavoj Žižek's account of the spectral dynamics between the interlocking gazes of East and West, an account that enables and informs my project, starts with a question: "Why was the West so fascinated by the disintegration of Communism in Eastern Europe?" (1993, 200). According to Žižek, the West sought in Eastern Europe its lost origins, the reinvention of democracy. The real object of fascination is "the supposedly naïve gaze by means of which Eastern Europe stares back at the West, fascinated by its democracy" (ibid., 200). McKenzie Wark turns to a global televisual event, the fall of the Berlin Wall, and unfolds the main narratives of how change happened in East and Central Europe in 1989. In Wark's account of the revolutionary movement in 1989 East and Central Europe, his rereading of Žižek via television, the East misrecognized the West's spectral/televisual images as the reality of the West.

I want to argue for a reconsideration of the fascination between East and West along the promises/illusions of post–Cold War global television by turning, first, very briefly to the role of television and the gaze of the West in the Romanian revolution. The televised revolution of December '89 in Romania is one exceptional moment in the emerging world of globalized media experience, like the fall of the Berlin War and the Gulf War. All three are what Wark would call global media events because "there is some linkage between the sites at which they appear to happen and the sites at which we remote-sense them" (Wark 1994, vii).

Starting with December '89, the several weeks of nonstop live televisual coverage in Romania (the kind of coverage associated with "crisis" in the normal eruption of media flow) were perceived as a return to normal reality and a normal pace. Television, until that point never considered anything but propaganda, became, as Deleuze would say, the measure of the real. There was an overwhelmingly naïve quality at least to my initial reaction to the *seeing machine*.

I thought you watched television to see what was really happening, yet I learned that through television what was happening became real. You want what television promises in its ideal state: to show you everything, at once. This promise to render visible, the core of the realist premise of televisual discourse, is what Romanians never hoped to obtain from television before '89, but it suddenly became very real as Romania entered the "real world" of global television. The promise was soon demystified as an illusion, because we shared the feeling of having been duped.

Romanian television did other things, too. It interpellated excessively, it almost remote-controlled viewers. The contradictory appeals of the television to "stay with it" and simultaneously to "go out there" (to defend the television station or to prevent Securitate members from escaping from the army head-quarters in Cluj) shifted the boundaries between "out there" and "on the screen." In January and February of 1990, this shift became visible and prob-lematized. Those who had *only* watched TV were accused by those who had done more than watch it of having only watched it, while the mandate of real revolutionaries was claimed by, and quickly bestowed on, the ones seen on television by the ones who were, of course, watching. The fiction of a national community in revolution and a commodified identity of the revolutionary coalesced around television. Television became an enabling and distorting national fiction-producing machine. Watching itself became a form of agency, and television became the eyes of this new spectator citizen.

While lived experience distinguished some persons from others, teles-thetic experience offered the mandate of revolutionary not only to those seen on screen but also to those watching. The line between watching and acting was thin, since seeing and being seen on television by "the world" was the crucial driving revolutionary impulse (the hope that world opinion could not ignore Ceauşescu's reprisals). That line grew harder to maintain, although it was frequently rehearsed. Romanian television, in a move symptomatic of tele-vision in general but particularly excessive and revealing, managed to con-stitute a commodified revolutionary identity ("we" at one point were all revolu-tionaries), and along the way it managed to diffuse all responsibility for real shootings, real violence, real terror. From then on, as we watched reruns of the revolution, which of course means reruns of Studio 4 celebrating "our" memo-ries, we might all feel ourselves to be revolutionaries or we might all feel duped. Of course, we are both at the same time.

Reactions to the Romanian revolution in the West deserve at least a brief mention here. In December 1989 and January 1990, U.S. print media, from the *New York Times* to the *Washington Post*, commented enthusiastically on the role of Romanian television in the creation of a virtual community of viewers, in the distribution of uncensored information, and in providing legiti-macy to the Romanian revolution. Furthermore, U.S. journalists compared the images of the "spontaneous" and "unpolished" images from the tele-vised Romanian revolution, which were used to "defy despotism and celebrate a people's impulse for freedom," to the constrictive and "polished perfor-mances" of the televised coverage of U.S. involvement in Panama (Goodman 1989, 18). However, a critical discourse on television and the Romanian revolution quickly emerged thereafter and it is, with few exceptions, articulated from within the realist frame that television itself reproduces: disillusionment with Romanian television, criticism of the way it manipulated its viewers, or criticism of the way Romanians manipulated the West.[9] This critical discourse makes Romanian television the bad guy. What is not taken into account is the specific implication of the gaze of the West or the intimate contamination of gazes (despite the apparent estrangement of East from West), the promises of global television, and the slanted flow of the television vector which delivers East to West and shows the East how it is seen by the West.

While the television vector tends to implicate us all at our receiving terminals, the promises and illusions it fosters are those of complete access to, nonimplication in, and democratic distributions of sites (and/or flow between sites). The fascination with the West, my reading suggests, was and is charged not so much with the illusion that spectral/televisual images of the West *are* the West as with the illusion that being seen by the West and seeing what the West sees means equal positioning in a global televisual community. The televisual drive to see what the West sees, to be seen by the West, and to see itself the way the West sees "us" drove the Romanian revolution. This drive was thus partly an illusion fostered by global television in the sense that being made visible and accessing Romania as it appears on Western television means equal positioning within the economy of virtual geography, based on the promise of democratic distribution of sites. It was also an intuition of what the future held: images from the West, such as those of Romanian orphans and orphanages, producing Romanian identity.

Virtual Geographies: From "Deep Freeze" to "Defrost"

In the condition of post–Cold War television globality, there are different genres within which "America" and "Eastern Europe" are produced and encountered and significant differences between the everyday televisual experiences and positioning toward global television of Romanian and American TV viewers. For a Romanian viewer, "America" appears as an everyday virtual encounter that brings her, as Wark would say, an "everyday perverse intimacy" with a territory/trope that is not her own.[10] The encounter with American programs on television—daytime soaps such as *The Young and The Restless* and evening shows such as *Baywatch*—provides an everyday reassurance that at least on television things are as they should be and as they weren't before '89. It allows one to "play at being American," to watch what "Americans" watch, to see what "they" see. In other words, this encounter gives a Romanian viewer the illusion that seeing what the West sees means equal positioning within a virtual televisual community.

"Eastern Europe" appears on television as an agglomeration of sites assembled in a territory. In late fall and winter of 1989, the sequence of sites was initially constituted as a territory where the "whirlwind of democracy was blowing," and the distinguishable sites (corresponding to different countries opening up to democracy) appeared at times to be interchangeable. In February 1990, the by-now-infamous Romanian television requested a correction from BBC and CNN because images of a burning building in Sofia, Bulgaria, were captioned as from Bucharest, Romania. This slippage points to the structure of the economy of signs of "Eastern Europe": because Romania had a violent revolution, was a site of violence on television, the building must be burning in Bucharest. Subsequently, "Eastern Europe" has been constituted along the coordinates of "the disappearance of communism" and its return. Through television "Eastern Europe" is thawing, is no longer an opaque monolith. There are distinguishable places here, lines that map zones of crisis within the territory: now we have bastions of communism and, in comparison, remarkably democratic zones; we have poverty zones and prosperity zones. But even as the thaw continues, "Eastern Europe" has preserved its blurred opacity. No longer invisible, it is still incomprehensible.

For an American viewer, Romania and "Eastern Europe" appear mainly within the genre of crisis and catastrophe specific to news coverage. Encountering these sites, one does not plug into being Eastern European. Rather, as sites that are supposedly revealed to the eye of an American viewer in their rough nakedness (facts, facts, facts!), they recall his position as distant observer of this territory. Western fascination with "Eastern Europe" follows the promise of global television to access, to views of sites that *were once inaccessible*, and it is infused with the illusion that the West is not implicated in the spectacle of crisis that is "Eastern Europe." According to the illusion, if one actually goes to Romania/Eastern Europe, it will look like this, though just being there means being actually implicated. Perhaps it is much too obvious to note that American travelers, unlike Romanians, go to Romania and East Central Europe to witness the spectacle more closely or to bring back something with them: "real" chunks of communist memorabilia, a picture or memory of participating somehow or intervening in "that mess of a country" and *doing something about it.*

It is maximum visibility, not positive content, that constitutes "Eastern Europe" as a spectacle of crisis on American television. "Eastern Europe" has been defined in terms of previous inaccessibility as the land behind the "Iron Curtain," now accessible to the West through victorious post–Cold War American technology. The trope of "Eastern Europe" is constructed on this shift between invisibility and visibility in relation to global television. Its built-in post–Cold War euphoria feeds on Cold War ideology. Those who access "Eastern Europe" are positioned as winners of the Cold War, as those entitled to the secrets of the losers and as nonimplicated judges or evaluators of the capacity for change of "Eastern Europeans."

To some degree, "Eastern Europe" does appear as a zone where people aspire to be like "us," to aspire to "our" democratic values. But in the murkiness of other events, at points where the post–Cold War narrative of progress from East to West collapses in an ongoing struggle,[11] what is important is "they" are so "unlike 'us'" that "they" are "like each other."[12] On screen "we" as Americans access "their" nationalism (not our patriotism), the cause of their wars. We see "their" orphans with AIDS (*our* AIDS victims are not innocent children), and we hear about "their" ethnic cleansing. The excesses that make "them" different are delivered to "us."

Television thrusts geographic sites into each other, erases lines between constructed identities and/or geographies such as East and West; it makes lines between "watching" and "lived experience" hard to draw; it dislocates actions from their sites. Yet it constantly prompts a countermovement, drawing lines between West and East, between a "Western viewer" and faraway "zones" such as "Eastern Europe" or "Romania."

Nobody's Children: Traveling to Televisual Romania

I suggest we travel back to "Romania" by unfolding two traveling stories. The first story, a television movie, is about a zone constructed in the present tense of an ongoing struggle. The story is self-referential, as television discourse tends to be; it is a story about telesthesia, Romanian orphans, and American viewers. While the television movie is constructed around the trope of the orphans and the impact of this trope on an American viewer, in the second story, a travel memoir, the televisual trope is also disseminated on the landscape; it contaminates the gaze that tries to trace and identify history on the faces and bodies of Romanians. On both sites, television does more than simply hum in the background. Both stories of encounters with "Eastern Europe" emphasize the role of televisual representations of "Eastern Europe" in prompting the travelers to seek it, yet both claim, paradoxically, an encounter with "Romania" and "Eastern Europe" outside of televisual memory and televisual experience. Both encounters take shape as encounters between a Western viewer/traveler and an incomprehensible spectacle of crisis.

Nobody's Children (1994), co-written by an American-Romanian team, concerns an American couple who go to Romania to adopt in 1990. The first scenes of *Nobody's Children* are staged revolutionary scenes that were filmed on site in Bucharest, Romania. From here we move to a car in the driveway of an American neighborhood in Detroit, Michigan. Inside the house, a pregnant Carol (played by Ann-Margret) and her husband open the door for their friends. They walk together into the living room, laughing. From this comfortable home space, we move back to the space of street protest, where protesters gather in large numbers, tanks drive by, and finally soldiers start shooting at the protesters. Back in the American living room, Carol is decorating a Christmas tree, and she starts cramping; in the background we hear shots and news of Ceauşescu's arrest and execution. From Carol's pained face we move to the television screen and, more specifically, to images of deformed Romanian orphans.

After the commercial break, Carol comes out of a hospital room, embracing her husband, and then we see her at home, in bed, crying quietly, watching more images of orphans. At this point, Carol embodies that "American" feminine subject position constructed as/by a certain way of watching Romania that I signal in my discussion of the Olympic team sketch. Her husband wants to turn the television off, convinced it is upsetting her, but in the words of any fascinated television viewer, Carol says "leave it on." At first she is unable to do anything but watch, but seeing the Romanian orphans makes her *do something*. She decides to leave behind the comfort of her home in order to go to Romania to adopt an orphan.

The response to the images of Romanian orphans by Peace Corps volunteers, medical personnel, and people going to adopt resembles to some degree the response to television during the Romanian revolution. Both interventions were enactments starting from television's illusory promise of unmediated reality, but enactments with real effects. Narratives about why one answers the call of television are the retroactive coherence that we give "ourselves." *Nobody's Children* offers us a version of how "Romania" and television touch the lives of American viewers. This movie, based on the real story of an American couple who followed the televisual vector to the image's "source," represents the source according to televisual reality and produces an "American identity" in relation to this reality. Carol responds to the immediacy and urgency that television offers and to the narrative of identity it offers American viewers, of being people who care about what is going on, who *do something* about it.

And so Carol and her husband go to the ominous land of Romania, where they suffer through minor ordeals such as lack of hot water and major fears such as the terror of revolution and the corrupt system, and then they find and manage to adopt one of two children, the second one turning out to be an "AIDS baby." In the process, "Romania" and "America," televisual image and viewer are blurred together, contaminated, but then the lines between "Romanian" and "American" are quickly redrawn. On one side, the incomprehensible; on the other, a story to "relate" to.

The producers make no attempt to anchor viewers or Carol in real time. Is her trip in 1990/1991/1992? "Romania" remains in this mode of crisis and catastrophe, in the time frame of the news genre, throughout the movie. Carol eventually leaves Romania, barely, bringing a baby, the hard kernel of this incomprehensible site.

As it speaks of televised representations of Romania and "Eastern Europe," we might fashion our own story around *Nobody's Children*. From this perspective, we see the self-referential recycling of tropes and genres specific to the televisual; Carol, in other words, travels to televisual Romania. As a palpable trace of the murky past (the decaying body of communism) and present (its return), the trope of the orphans is what we bring from television, the crystallized reality. The Romanian orphans are the heart of the "heart of darkness" of Romania; in the economy of Eastern European tropes, Romania is now completely accessible yet still has an incomprehensible core. This is a symptom of the regime of crisis in which "Eastern Europe" functions on television that, in turn, is imbricated with a crisis in narrative about what is going on in "Eastern Europe." The crisis in narrative speaks of the bankrupt and still-prevalent Cold War symbolic within which "Eastern Europe" is produced and encountered.

"Eastern Europe" in Return: Murky and Incomprehensible Sites

Eva Hoffman's ambitious project *Exit into History* (1993) can only very loosely be called a travel memoir. Its complexity deserves more attention than the analysis I provide here. For the purpose of this essay, however, *Exit into History* allows us to focus more closely on the rhetorical power of the fiction of Eastern Europe. Furthermore, the articulation of the returnee as an Eastern European American subject allows us to focus on the particular relationship between "Eastern European" and "American" identities that the fiction of "Eastern Europe" reproduces. In this hybrid discourse that brings together cultural history, childhood memory, telesthetic memory, and travel memoir within the frame of a personal narrative of an American/"Eastern European" intellectual's return to the land of her childhood, the fiction of Eastern Europe overdetermines personal narrative.

In her introduction to *Exit into History*, the narrator moves from a retrospective presentation of her impulse to return to a brief history of the fiction and the region of "Eastern Europe." There are, Hoffman tells us, two reasons or two impulses that account for her wanting to see "Eastern Europe." The first she calls a "personal impulse," the impulse to see the "lost territory of her childhood" before "it disappeared" (1993, x). The second she calls a "fascination," the same kind of fascination that had "suddenly made the eyes of the world turn on Eastern Europe," a condition that she herself was not immune to (ibid.). Hoffman qualifies her fascination as a desire to see the "history" that "was happening there," a desire to "catch it in the act" (ibid.). Hoffman does say, in passing, that this is not her first journey back to Poland. A journey of return to Poland two years before was the prehistory of this journey. Indeed, this is a return to "Eastern Europe," not to Poland, though she speaks of her "long lost home" of Poland as being *by extension* Eastern Europe (ibid.). The territorialized attachment to Poland, the nostalgic immigrant attachment to the lost nation/childhood, is rewritten here as an attachment to the "territory of Eastern Europe." And thus, *by extension*, "Eastern Europe" becomes the lost territory of childhood, "the land that had stayed arrested in my imagination as a land of childhood, sensuality, lyricism, vividness, and human warmth" (ibid.). The televisual fiction of Eastern Europe doubles and troubles immigrant memory as the televisual encounter redefines the way in which she thinks of and speaks of her "long lost home."

Hoffman proceeds to make her reader aware of the fictional nature of

"Eastern Europe," yet she also wants to retain the notion of "Eastern Europe" as a territory of shared history. She differentiates between "my Eastern Europe" and the "real Eastern Europe." Hoffman makes her reader aware that "her Eastern Europe" is "an idealized landscape in the mind" (ibid.). She acknowledges that "her Eastern Europe" is inflected with immigrant nostalgia, which, as she observes, is responsible for having arrested Eastern Europe in her mind, but insists that there is a "real Eastern Europe" that "stayed arrested in actuality as well" (ibid., ix). According to Hoffman, communism both "inflicted on a large region of the world" what she calls "the ruling narrative that divided whole societies into bipolar oppositions" and imposed the material conditions that transformed that narrative into the reality of Eastern Europe (ibid., x). In Hoffman's terms, the fiction of "an othered Eastern Europe" was actually transformed into actuality, the "real Eastern Europe," by the communist regime. Aside from "my Eastern Europe" and the "real/ Communist Eastern Europe," we can untangle, provisionally, a third and other Eastern Europe, one "that has never quite ceased being 'the other Europe'" (ibid., xi) in the imagination of the West, from the writings of Shakespeare to common Cold War misconceptions of Eastern Europe as "a lifeless, monochrome realm" (ibid., xii). Hoffman means to undo this Cold War fiction through her own memories and through recovery of "the real Eastern Europe" as lived experience.

In *Exit into History*, the fiction of "Eastern Europe" appears to be necessary because it is, according to Hoffman, based on some measure of historical reality. She also must accept this fiction in order to enter the discursive formation on "Eastern Europe," in order to strategically rewrite or recover it from a site of nonidentity and projection to a site that can occasion self-reflection (ibid., 409). And finally, as her Poland of memory is doubled by the "Eastern Europe" of history happening, her attachment to the Poland of memory is doubled and troubled by her attachment to the televisual Eastern Europe of history happening. Thus, although she recognizes its complex constructedness, the fiction of "Eastern Europe" is preserved. Concerned with the fictional nature of "my Eastern Europe," Hoffman gets caught in the larger fiction of "Eastern Europe."

Exit into History consists of six chapters corresponding to each country the returnee visits: there are two chapters about her return to Poland (Poland I and Poland II) and one chapter each about Czechoslovakia, Hungary, Romania, and Bulgaria. While the text is staged as a narrative of return to "Eastern Europe," Hoffman had a great degree of familiarity only with Poland—her country of birth—and had previously visited the Czech Republic. As she moves away from Poland, the traveler moves along/with the media vector and encounters countries and places she had never visited before, in an attempt to find "Eastern Europe." As she moves farther and farther away from familiar ground, in spite of her critical awareness, the accounts of Hoffman the traveler perpetuate the tendency of othering Eastern Europe in two primary ways. On the one hand, the traveler finds and revels in "Eastern Europe" as the "absence of Capitalism" and the beauty of the landscape and people. On the other hand, in Romania, where she is primarily looking for "Eastern Europe" as history happening, she finds instead signs of a "murky mentality" that blocks change (i.e., progress) toward Western values and capitalism, signifying an idea totally different from Europe. In the encounter with "Romania" she finds that idea other than Europe, that incomprehensible spectacle of crisis that Eastern Europe appears to be across discursive lines.

Romanian sites, whether the dark sites of Transylvania or those of Bucharest, are murky and initially incomprehensible. According to Hoffman the narrator, Romania is the "Bermuda Triangle" of the author's fantasy as a traveler, the place that "concentrates all one's anxieties about unnamable dangers and the darkness of the unknown" (ibid., 262). In Transylvania, the traveler finds darkness on the faces of people, and in the unfamiliar and stark reality of Transylvania she finds the "Balkans." Cluj is "a lovely town and unmistakably European in a way that surprises me—recognizable, beautiful Europe, in this far region of the world!" Its architecture has the "comforting" beauty of Europe, but "the atmosphere is somehow . . . well, Balkan" (ibid., 270). The "Balkan" nomen appears here as a symptom of something other than Europe, a symptom of "Eastern Europe."

Following her arrival in Bucharest, she "braves walks" through the city and finds herself overcome by "esthetic torment, of the kind that's nearly indistinguishable from moral torment" (ibid., 289). In Bucharest she sees how "signs of recent violence become depressingly visible" on the facade of buildings "pockmarked with bullets" (ibid., 285). She comments on the poverty in the food displays and the lines of people waiting for fresh bread. The "woebegone items" in the store add to the "sense of absurdity, of an antiworld" (ibid., 289). She finds the "anonymous crowd as disturbing as those eerie buildings" (ibid.). People's lack of energy and of resistance to their situation amaze her:

> Despite the heat, I feel a cold touch of something like devolution, deathliness; why is this acceptable, this slide into chaos? Why isn't everyone shouting in protest? Instead, women walk into those ghastly interiors; in the street, groups of open-shirted men hang out. There's little movement and almost no noise, as if there were no energy to expend even on talk. (ibid., 285)

We can read here, first, frustration in an encounter with a Bucharest that is so unlike her televisual encounter with "history happening." In what the narrator encounters now, "there's little movement and no noise" and no shouts of protest. Second, we can see how the traveler detaches herself from and critically scrutinizes this "antiworld" and the complacency of the Romanians. When faced with "murky" Romanian sites, the traveler withdraws in horror and frustration and draws on both a Balkanist and a Cold War discourse to translate them for her readers.

In her study of historical representations of the Balkans, Maria Todorova traces a symptomatology of Balkanist discourse. The clusters of aimless men with their shirts open recall what Todorova calls a recurring description of the standard Balkan male as "uncivilized, primitive, crude, cruel, and without exception, disheveled" (1997, 14). Observing the anonymous crowd in terms of its aesthetics, the traveler in *Exit into History* withdraws in horror and remarks that "Bucharest seems barely to cling to the edge of the continent, threatening to fall off into some other space, some other idea entirely" (Hoffman 1993, 290). Bucharest's threatening to fall into an "other idea entirely," an idea other than Europe, recalls the "reflected light" of the Orient, as Todorova would say. According to Todorova, "what practically all descriptions of the Balkans offered as a central characteristic was their transitionary status" (1997, 15). The Balkans "have always evoked the image of a bridge or a crossroads" between East and West (ibid.). Hoffman remarks that in Bucharest "some bridge has not been crossed."

While Hoffman's text thus reproduces a symptomatology of Balkanist discourse, it also essentially and excessively recalls televisual representations of "Eastern Europe," the blurred opacity of the spectacle of crisis. Her traveler reads Romania through the narrative of progression from East to West and finds it lacking. Nowhere does Hoffman acknowledge the possibility that the murkiness is an effect of her own gaze, of a mediated (and telemediated) encounter, or of a superimposed narrative that is itself in crisis.

Beyond recalling more generally the blurred opacity of televisual representations of "Eastern Europe," the text also explicitly records the power of the trope of Romanian orphans and presents us, once again, with an encounter with the orphans. The traveler says that it is "out of some sense of duty" that she decides to visit "one of the orphanages that have become so unhappily associated with Romania and its latter-day horrors" (Hoffman 1993, 327–328). She, like many others, had seen "distressing photographs of places where babies with AIDS—all contracted with blood transfusions—are kept" (ibid.). The sense of duty takes her to a site that she has previous familiarity with and that she feels she has to confront. The sight of the children frightens her. However, she is not frightened of them "but for them." She gets tired very quickly and, by the time she sits down in the matron's office, "a sense of sickness descends upon me" (ibid.). Before she leaves, she decides to distribute the cookies she has brought to the children because she distrusts the matron's reassurance that they will be distributed. On the way out, the children surround her and her companion: "One of them puts his arm through mine, and walks with me toward the gate with the look of purest sadness and supplication I'd ever seen in human eyes" (ibid., 329). This departing look makes her feel "instead of a sense of duty fulfilled, a strange guilt for having seen what I did, the guilt of an uninvolved witness at a tragedy" (ibid., 330).

The sadness in the eyes of the orphans was what the Olympics coverage called to our attention in the sketch about the Romanian team: Romania appeared as those sad eyes and faces, in relation to which the coverage articulated a certain way of watching Romania. The viewer was invited to identify with a certain subject position, that of a feminine subject saddened by what she sees. Hoffman's traveler identifies with this subject position, yet the narrator/traveler also records something else. She feels guilt, the guilt of witnessing a tragedy, the guilt of having sought out the familiar encounter with misery.

In *Exit into History*, the narrative of return to a childhood place, of looking with a mature eye for changes in the childhood landscape, shifts into looking for post-1989 changes—traces of democracy, capitalism, and signs of relapse—in landscapes and on bodies, with the eye of a Westerner looking at her Other. In the process, "Eastern Europe" becomes the childhood of the West—its own unspoiled past and the wounded or "retarded" child who cannot progress into Western maturity. "Eastern European identity" becomes that background against which the more mature "American identity" takes shape. In other words, Hoffman's narrative of personal experience reproduces the peculiar rhetorical positioning that the fiction of "Eastern Europe" stages between West and East and Western and Eastern subjects/identity. The encounter with "Eastern Europe" produces "Hoffman" as an American traveler/narrator.

Hoffman's memoir rehearses a familiar argument about the problematic but necessary fiction of "Eastern Europe." The argument shifts from the role of Western representations of Eastern Europe in producing the fiction of a territory/identity defined in terms of its otherness to the reality of Eastern Europeans' "otherness" (arrested development, psychological blocks, etc.) after communist regimes. Thus, "Eastern Europe" appears to be whatever it is without involvement from the West, though the West is there to witness the spectacle.

While the communist regimes incontestably had drastic effects that are traceable on the landscapes of East and Central Europe, it is also true that the Cold War imaginary assigned this territory a consistent opacity with just as much effect on its (in)visibility. Present constructions of Eastern Europe also reinforce its "blurred-ness." On the one hand, "Eastern Europe" is opaque and immobile, and on the other hand, it is thawing or "defrosting": these are the coordinates within which "Eastern European" sites are *produced* for us.

Instead of a Conclusion: News from Dracula

I note an unacknowledged crisis in narrative about what is happening in "Eastern Europe" that comes with the continuous rerun of the story of progression from East to West (and how "Eastern Europe" fits or does not fit within this narrative frame). While a crisis in narrative might work to destabilize the function of the signifier "Eastern Europe" as a pillar for Western identity, we can see that this has not been the case so far. The fiction of a shared community of "Eastern Europe," defined as beyond the realm of Western normality, is in practice disabling. "Eastern European" identity is produced in an unequal discursive configuration, functioning in what we might call a pedocratic regime. "Eastern Europeans" are always children, always under evaluation by a more mature Western gaze: Are they worthy or unworthy of adoption into Europe, into "the West"?[13]

It seems that since 1989 the fiction of "Eastern Europe" has become aggressively active in the political landscape of the countries it refers to. A number of politicians have promoted their countries in international politics, or their parties and values in national politics, as "real" European ones while pointing at others (countries or political parties) that cannot meet European (Western) standards of democracy, tolerance, and the work ethic because "they" are either stuck in an old frame of mind (where "Orient" meets "communism") or simply too irrational, too lazy, too "other." From West to East, old-fashioned and contemporary Orientalism, Balkanism, and Cold War ideology meet, feeding on each other to produce "Eastern European identity." It is an "identity" that, according to this logic, must be surpassed, grown out of, overcome, or denied.[14] Somebody else has it. The truth is indeed always that somebody else has it, since it is produced as a site of estrangement, here on television and "there" as well.

If this fiction, however, is the condition of our visibility—a visibility that is threatened by the bipolar dynamics between the fiction of "Eastern Europe" and the fiction of its disappearance—can it become a space for resignifying practices? An "Eastern European" reader, artist, or student has to accept the kind of restrictions and prohibitions that come from being an other whose "identity" is talked about, superfluous yet missing, exotic yet not exotic enough. Engaging in a cross-cultural dialogue and entering into the discursive formation of "Eastern Europe" is never easy for someone identified as "Eastern European," because one must talk about oneself as other via "Eastern Europe," a trope that quilts experience and discourse. In other words, as *Beyond Belief* clearly reveals, one must accept the fiction in order to enter a dialogue, even on unequal terms.

Beyond Belief produces the illusion of a transparent and equal relationship between viewer and artistic production, between artistic production and the object it presumably "refers" to, and between "Western" viewer and "Eastern European" artist. In other words, the viewer has the illusion that she is accessing and learning about "Eastern Europe" through its vehicle, the Eastern European artist. She is invited to trace in each nationally identified artwork the larger hologram of "Eastern Europe." What is erased is precisely what went into producing this exhibit. In order to design an exhibit of "Eastern European" art, Hoptman turned to the Soros Foundation with a network that gathers artists from East and Central Europe who are willing to cater to a Western sensibility. Moreover, a significant number of the works were done specifically for this exhibit. The *story* of the exhibit's production speaks more generally of how "Eastern European" tropes are produced in the media and circulate from West to East and back; of how the fiction of definable "Eastern European" features takes shape and is reproduced as a power-full production engaging both "Westerners" and "Eastern Europeans" in an unequal distribution of rhetorical privilege.

"News from Dracula" by the Romanian group subReal was one installation featured in the exhibit *Beyond Belief.* I turn to it because it offers a commentary on its own production and implication in this cross-cultural dialogue. To enter this dialogue, subReal goes through the fantasy realm of Western productions of Romania and "Eastern Europe."

"News from Dracula" consists of a gymnastics horse (a vault) that stands off center and is partly dressed in animal skin and wool, metal stands and wooden stakes surrounding the vault, a VCR, and a VHS video loop. As such, it agglomerates what we could call sites of "Romania" in American media and popular culture: the stakes of Dracula, the gymnastics horse of Nadia Comaneci, and the video loop, perhaps representing Romania's eruption onto global television. The collage of juxtaposed historical tropes (Dracula the medieval vampire; Nadia the famous gymnast who escaped Romania) is formally transposed in a juxtaposition of technology and artifact: video, metal, wood, animal skin. The video camera levels the agglomeration of sites in a hybrid collapse of history.

This is a landscape of Romania that, to some degree, we see in travel texts. Specifically, it is almost an anatomy of the traveler's fantasy in Hoffman's *Exit into History*, the encounter with Transylvania. Let us recall that Transylvania, the heart of that "Bermuda triangle" of Romania, activates the traveler's worst fears. Associations with the story of Dracula—and with what Hoffman calls "the real model" for this personage, Vlad "Dracul"—are doubled by closer images of violence, the bloodshed in the Transylvanian city of Timişoara. In "News From Dracula," the trope of Dracula (wooden stakes) is a parodied site of violence waiting to be filmed, circulating in the loop.

"News from Dracula" continues a longtime project of subReal. It exposes the encounter of Romanian Orientalism and Western Orientalism in productions of Romanian sites and celebrates this "zone of contamination" between "Europe" and "Orient," West and East, myth and history. In "News from Dracula," however, the emphasis of the performance shifts to the spectral encounter between East and West via television. In this installation, Romania appears as an agglomeration of sites loosely assembled around images of violence, a televisual effect—in other words, as it appeared on television in 1989. But unlike the mainstream of critical discourse on the Romanian revolution that assigns Romanian television the role of staging the revolution, subReal suggests Western media's implication in producing Romania as a site of spectacle. "News from Dracula" stages the meeting of "Romania" as a constructed, jumbled collage of sites on American film and televisual sites and "Romania" as a site produced for the West in Romania (the televised revolution). The installation produces itself, in the same register as subReal's previous "Dracula" explorations, as a site of cultural miscommunication and reappropriation. The artists' performance lies in staging a "Romania effect" and in revealing that Romanian/Eastern European identity is simply an effect.

I suggest in this very sketchy presentation of their project that subReal presents us with one very compelling way, given the prohibitions set in motion by the fiction of "Eastern Europe," of responding to the interpellation of "Eastern European" identity. Rather than denying it and claiming that someone else has "it," a claim with drastic consequences, subReal performs an overidentification with this position. Through this subReal enters the discursive formation of "Eastern Europe" and exposes the imbricated and constructed nature and limitations of "Romanian," "Eastern European," and "Western" identities.

One caveat: "News From Dracula" reflects back on the construction of Romanian sites in a complicitous and parodic way, exposing and reinforcing them. However, couched as it is within an exhibit of "Eastern European" art, offered as a way for American viewers to encounter and experience "Eastern Europe," subReal's performance might be lost on the art public, might offer only return, confirmation, and reproduction of a Western viewer's fantasy space.

One Last Site: A Healthy Reminder

While I am now a permanent resident of the United States, I vividly remember the lines in front of the U.S. embassy in Bucharest. Standing in line at all hours, struggling to stay awake, leaning on the rail only to be told that they could not do so, people were/are not comparing notes on places to visit in the United States or exchanging travel tips. Documents proving that they own homes and businesses, that they have children and well-paying jobs they will want to return to: these are requisites for the trip to the United States. Instead of travel guides, there are guidelines on the walls of Western European and American embassies. The U.S. embassy in Romania was for me, and still is for many, a good reminder that one *does* possess an Eastern European identity. For some of us, Western embassies are sites at which we encounter our identity through prohibition.

From this perspective, the fiction of "Eastern European" identity can be reappropriated to speak of real and discursive prohibitions, such as the limits that entering a discourse on "Eastern Europe" entail for an Eastern European, the restrictions on possibility of movement, the violence toward Eastern European immigrants in Western Europe—these are real material conditions (among others) that produce an Eastern European identity.

NOTES

1. I have lived in the United States (in the Midwest) since 1991, when I came here for graduate school. I have been working on the ideas in this chapter on and off for years, since the submission of an early draft of it for this anthology. Actually, the early

draft of this essay started me on the book manuscript that I am currently writing; thus, some sections of this article are already developed into chapters of my manuscript.

2. I draw primarily on Edward Said's charting of the rhetoric of Orientalism, Larry Wolff's history and analysis of the idea of "Eastern Europe," and Maria Todorova's discussion of Balkanist rhetoric. Following Said, who is interested in the "internal consistency of Orientalism and its ideas about the Orient . . . despite or beyond any correspondence, or lack thereof, with a 'real' Orient," I am here interested in the consistency of "Eastern Europe," not its correspondence to a real geographic territory (Said 1978, 5). In very general terms, I understand Eastern Europe as a peculiar production of Orientalist rhetoric; it is spoken about as an area that cannot represent itself, it appears as a spectacle of crisis and difference reinforcing the normative idea of "Europe," "Western values," and "capitalism." The invaluable contribution of Larry Wolff, who traces the history of the idea/concept/nomen of "Eastern Europe," as well as those of Maria Todorova and Slavoj Žižek, who both emphasize the persistence of a Balkanist discourse in the articulation/encounter of post-communist sites, also inform and guide my project. According to Žižek, the fantasy that organizes the perception of former Yugoslavia is that of the Balkan as the Other of the West. Within her ground-breaking historical account of Balkanist discourse, a discourse traced as distinct from what Said has called Orientalism (see specifically 1978, 10–20), Todorova demonstrates its persistence in present-day articulations of post-communist sites. The imbrication between the Balkanist, Orientalist, and Cold War inflections of Eastern Europe are in dire need of careful consideration—which exceeds the limits of this essay. What I want to emphasize, though, is the persistence of the Cold War fiction of "Eastern Europe," which also has Balkanist and global televisual/Orientalist inflections.

3. The phrase circulates in written media, loosely. It became more noticeable after the 1995 elections. For example, see Andrew Nagorski, "The Return of the Reds," in *Newsweek*.

4. I have found this phrase to be recurrent in written media in the early and mid-1990s. For an early example, see Charles Lane, "The Undead," in *The New Republic*.

5. Bucharest is presented in very unflattering terms in the American media in general. For this particular reference, see Russel Watson's article in *Newsweek*, in an interview with tennis star Ilie Nastase, who ran for mayor of Bucharest in June 1996.

6. I offer an extensive analysis of the 1996 Olympics coverage as a global/national televisual event and an analysis of the relationship between American girls and "others" in "Nationalizing the Olympics Around and Away from 'Vulnerable' Bodies of Women," *Journal of Sport and Social Issues* 24 (2000): 118–148.

7. Although Judith Butler is not interested in issues of national identity or identification, I recover here her reading of identification to understand the role of representations of "others" in national identification. In this process, "others" appear as "specters of abjection produced by the symbolic as its threatening outside" (Butler 1993, 105). Representations of others (other nations) are produced, in my understanding, as a condition of national identification. They reinforce our reality and at the same time represent the danger of what lies outside. As this process plays out in this coverage and, more generally, in representations of "Eastern Europe," the "Western"/"American" citizen subject is always in danger of becoming a foreigner and the fantasy of "our nation" is constructed against but vulnerable to "others."

8. For example, see Watson's reference to Nastase, who left the country, versus Romanians who "cowered under the regime."

9. The few noticeable exceptions I have encountered are Jean Baudrillard's reading of "The Timisoara Massacre" in *The Illusion of the End* and the works of the Romanian artists subReal. Baudrillard contends that the Romanian revolution reveals about television in general, and about news in particular, its "secret purpose (destination)," which is "to deceive us about the real, but also to undeceive us about the real" (1994, 61).

10. Wark speaks of the "perverse intimacy" he, as an Australian, has with the imaginary of America, a feeling of "growing up in a simulated America" (1994, 14). He draws attention to the fact that the critical task of vectoral analysis needs to be "approached differently on the edge of the American empire from the way it is at its heart" (ibid.). I am attempting here an account of the spectral encounter, or a vectoral analysis of sorts, from both positions; this account/analysis is, of course, made possible by my shifting position of access.

11. Let us consider, for example, a crucial aspect in the media coverage of the mass graves in Bosnia. I was struck at how voice-overs informed viewers/readers of the discovery of mass graves containing Muslim bodies while we saw images (from written captions on the image) of mass graves presumably containing Serbian bodies, and vice versa. Media coverage of the graves did not function to reveal who was responsible but rather to reveal that "they"—Serbs, Muslims, and Croats—were all the same.

12. McKenzie Wark employs John Hartley's notion of Theydom in order to conceptualize the spatial organization of Telesthesia along lines of nonidentity throughout his text (see, for instance, Wark 1994, 10–11). Hartley uses the concept of "Theydom" throughout the two works cited below. However, for a discussion of the logics of accessed identifications (involving representations of others and ex-nomination), see 1992, 24–38.

13. In our contemporary political landscape, this pedocratic regime and the accompanying question have become distinctly clear. Consider, for instance, reactions to the February 2003 statement by Vilnius Group countries in support of the United States, UK, and Spain concerning the use of force against Iraq—a position which itself would merit a lengthy paper. These "outsiders" were accused of being "childish," "reckless," and "lacking manners," and they were reprimanded for their rash behavior in political statements by President Jacques Chirac (see Extraordinary European Council 2003). Political cartoons such as the editorial cartoon "Leçons" in *Le Monde* present the Vilnius countries as schoolchildren, thus echoing Chirac's remarks.

14. The political landscape that I sketch here very roughly should be contextualized via Žižek's notion of a crisis in legitimization. He refers to the opposition characterizing the "new world order" along the "new frontier" between "those who succeeded in remaining 'within' (the 'developed,' those to whom the rules of human rights, social security, and so forth, apply), and the others, the excluded (apropos of whom the main concern of the 'developed' is to contain their explosive potential . . .)" ("Caught in Another's Dream in Bosnia," 235). He highlights the crisis of the postsocialist states as precisely one of legitimization: "who will be admitted 'inside,' integrated into the developed capitalist order, and who will remain excluded from it?" (ibid.). In my view, we can also understand this crisis in legitimization as a response to the "necessary fiction" of Eastern Europe and of Eastern European identity. I argue that Eastern

Europe is always located on the site of an "Other." This form of disavowal of "Eastern European" identity reproduces with drastic consequences the Orientalist and Cold War inflections of the fiction of "Eastern European" identity.

WORKS CITED

Baudrillard, Jean. *The Illusion of the End.* Stanford, Calif.: Stanford University Press, 1994.

Butler, Judith. *Bodies That Matter: On the Discursive Limits of Sex.* New York: Routledge, 1993.

Extraordinary European Council, Press Conference given by Jacques Chirac. Brussels, Belgium, February 17, 2003. Web site of the Embassy of France. Available online at   http://www.info-france-usa.org/news/statmnts/2003/chirac_eurocouncil.asp (accessed February 17, 2004).

Goodman, Walter. "Upheaval in the East: TV Critic's Notebook; Television Has Become a Weapon in Panama and Romania." *New York Times,* December 26, 1989, A18.

Hartley, John. *The Politics of Pictures: The Creation of the Public in the Age of Popular Media.* London: Routledge, 1992.

———. *Tele-Ology: Studies in Television.* London: Routledge, 1992.

Hoffman, Eva. *Exit into History: A Journey through the New Eastern Europe.* New York: Viking, 1993.

Hoptman, Laura J. "Seeing Is Believing." In *Beyond Belief: Contemporary Art from East Central Europe,* 1–15. Chicago Museum of Contemporary Art, 1995.

Lane, Charles. "The Undead." *The New Republic,* December 11, 1995, 10ff.

Nagorski, Andrew. "The Return of the Reds." *Newsweek,* December 4, 1995, 47ff.

Nobody's Children. Dir. David Wheatley. Writ. Petru Popescu and Iris Friedman. USA Pictures, 1994.

Perlez, Jane. "Hillary Clinton Visits Romanian Children." *New York Times,* July 2, 1996, 45ff.

Said, Edward. *Orientalism.* New York: Vintage Press, 1978.

subReal (Calin Dan, Iosif Kiraly). "News From Dracula." Collection of the artists, Bucharest (1994). In *Beyond Belief: Contemporary Art from East Central Europe.* Chicago Museum of Contemporary Art, 1995.

Todorova, Maria. *Imagining the Balkans.* New York: Oxford University Press, 1997.

Wark, McKenzie. *Virtual Geography: Living with Global Media Events.* Bloomington: Indiana University Press, 1994.

Watson, Russel. "Vote for Me, Stupid." *Newsweek,* May 27, 1996, 45.

Wolff, Larry. *Inventing Eastern Europe: The Map of Civilization on the Mind of the Enlightenment.* Stanford, Calif.: Stanford University Press, 1994.

Žižek, Slavoj. "Caught in Another's Dream in Bosnia." In *Why Bosnia? Writings on the Balkan War,* ed. Rabia Ali and Lawrence Lifschutz, 233–241. Stony Creek, Conn.: The Pamphleteer's Press, 1993.

———. *The Metastases of Enjoyment: Six Essays on Women and Causality.* London: Verso, 1994.

———. *Tarrying with the Negative: Kant, Hegel, and the Critique of Ideology.* Durham, N.C.: Duke University Press, 1993.

two

The Nation In Between; or, Why Intellectuals Do Things with Words

Elena Gapova

[U]nless national consciousness at its moment of success was somehow changed into social consciousness, the future would not hold liberation but an extension of imperialism.

Edward Said[1]

Posing the Question

Much as in other former socialist countries, contemporary Belarusian intellectual discourse is focused on the idea of a return to Europe. The idea is mostly based on the belief that the medieval Grand Duchy of Lithuania was a Belarusian state, with old Belarusian as its language of state communication, legal documents, and the first printed books, and the idea of the return to Europe is presented as a nostalgic myth in the Belarusian memory of identity. It resurfaces at times in peculiar forms, like the demand by one group of intellectuals that the "national text" be changed from Cyrillic to the Latin alphabet (*Belaruskaya lacinka*), which was used for brief periods throughout Belarusian history and can hardly be presented as "the script" taken from the nation by the brutal colonizer. The rationale for this act (which is deeply felt by those who feel it) is a vision of belonging with Europe that was allegedly interrupted but not fully destroyed by the Russian incorporation and Soviet experience, since for several hundred years the country had not been present on the European map as an independent state. Since 1991, though, it has

Elena Gapova

been there, following the disintegration of the Soviet Union through a seemingly triumphant realization of the idea that every one of the fifteen major
constituent Soviet nations now deserves a state of its own.

This, though, did not happen through the victory of the Belarusian national ideology, for the Belarusian people did not particularly ask for independence, seemed at a loss about how to utilize it when it was granted, and, having
regained some consciousness after their initial bewilderment, elected Alexander Lukashenka in 1994 as their president. His platform was to return things
to what they had previously been "economy wise" in general and to unify with
the fraternal people of Russia in a common state in particular.

From the very beginning, this "new" nation of Belarus did not strive to be
master of its destiny; both independence and statehood were rejected by too
many Belarusian citizens. Repeated efforts were made to reach closer and
closer union with Russia, and the process seems to have been in the final stages
since April 2, 1997, when the treaty on reunion was signed. It triggered protest
on the part of urban intellectuals, which was severely repressed with arrests
and beatings by police but was met with sincere approval by older people, by
the urban poor, by those residing in the countryside and in the East of the
country, and by more women than men.

Reunification began to develop as a cultural process, starting with a solution to the language dilemma through a referendum in favor of giving Belarusian equal status with Russian (although part of the urban intelligentsia
firmly insisted that it should be the only state language), replacing "independent" national symbols with slightly modified Soviet ones, and decrees pro-
hibiting the use of turn-of-the-twentieth-century Belarusian orthography and
legitimizing the Soviet version as the only possibility. Eventually the process of
reunification became overtly political. Several opposition newspapers were
closed, government media blocked the expression of any alternative opinion,
the legitimate Parliament was dissolved by force, and the new National Assembly was established, one-third of whose members are nominated (!) by the
president. The constitution was changed to place the executive branch over all
others; intolerance of protest has reached a degree where students are expelled
from universities for participating in legal demonstrations and are sentenced to
imprisonment for antipresidential graffiti (at least one 18-year-old served eigh-
teen months in prison for exactly that); nongovernmental organizations are ha-
rassed and outlawed; and several opposition leaders have disappeared for good.

Thus, reunification politics included a nostalgic idealization of socialism,
government control in all spheres of life (economic, social, and symbolic), and
severe curtailment of civil and political rights. The people in general supported reunification, reelecting Mr. Lukashenka in 2001. He tries to preserve
the socialist type of economy and keep the legacy of free health care, university
education, paid maternity leaves, and all kinds of social subsidies (in this
system of centrally controlled resource allocation, he holds overarching executive power) intact and working in the emerging market economy. One can still

call a state doctor, who will pay a free home visit, prescribe medication, and approve paid sick leave for as long as it takes one to get better. The problem is, the medication, which is Swiss or French, may cost half a teacher's monthly salary, and if one is working for a new private company, one's employer may (and most certainly will) not be interested in paying someone on sick leave or in having an employee who gets sick at all. It may prefer to hire someone healthier in order to continue the pursuit of profit with more success. What is more, it may prefer hiring those who will never need a maternity leave.

The Belarusian opposition (called nationalist by the government media and democratic in the West) reacted to the curtailment of liberties by preaching universal values of democracy and a market economy, but first of all insisting on national independence as the precondition for these. The idea was that as soon as the nation recollected its European past and switched to the Belarusian language (and, even better, to the Latin alphabet) in all spheres public and private, justice and economic prosperity would reign among those poor people. Too bad the people would not listen and continue to prefer another form of social justice.

The Belarusian controversy has been theorized by many journalists and political scientists as one over "lost nationhood": the Belarusians allegedly have problems identifying themselves as a nation and lack a sense of shared origin, experience, and culture because their lands were for centuries a contested transitional space between the democratic and European West and totalitarian Asian East, with Soviet experience completing the process to make people forget their true national belonging. The *New York Times* summed up the nation's calamities with the line, "Belarus is a land cursed by geography and history."[2] David Marples entitled one of his books *Belarus: A Denationalized Nation*[3]—originally the title ended with a question mark, which was lost during the publishing process.

Many proponents of their own global citizenship seem to think that people in other parts of the world are entitled to a single clear-cut national (or, rather, ethnic) feeling as their sole and main identity: that "the Irish are only Irish, Indians Indians, Africans Africans."[4] They rule out the possibility of primary self-definition with multiple or nonnational identities. I have argued elsewhere that in the post-Soviet world, discourse on national issues has tended to include such choices as market economy (and liberal democracy) versus socialism (and political coercion) as different ways of resource allocation.[5] This discourse serves to manifest a class discontent, since it is not so much about national belonging as about class interests. The major social process in the post-Soviet world has been class (re)formation (through income inequality, i.e., through the workings of the market) and national issues in their various incarnations— be it demands for autonomy or independence, controversy over language or disputed territories, or some other argument—are mostly manifestations of a class issue. The USSR disintegrated in the first place not because it was "the prison of nations" but because a "new class" was emerging for whom the socialist system of resource allocation became too tight:[6] they strove for the freedom that the market provides. National projects serve to justify the new social order ("class society") by providing emerging elites with a "noble national goal." Today's situation in Belarus is "class struggle" in its pure form: one group, with one set of economic and cultural assets, is interested in changing the status quo, while another wants to preserve it.

Intellectuals are the main articulators of the national cause: post-Soviet national projects are to a great degree about urban intellectuals (and the language they speak; i.e., the symbolic means they use) versus the rural and urban workers who are less educated and have fewer opportunities in the emerging brave new world (and its brave new speak) and who have in the last decade become the rural and urban poor. From the very beginning, "the language issue" (Belarusian versus Russian) has been at the very core of pro-independence discourse, the locus of controversy; intellectuals champion it for the sake of "the people," while the folk very firmly reject it.

Starting from the proposition that "the language" is part of a particular market system—in the sense that Pierre Bourdieu ascribed to the notion—I am interested in how the group (class or "corporate") interests of post-Soviet intellectuals are related to their activities and revealed in the discourse they produce. My questions are simple: Why do intellectuals need the national language or, rather, what can they do with it in both the national and international arenas, if those for whose sake they promote it evidently do not need it? What intellectual purposes are served by the language people are supposed "to recollect"? (Most do not speak it anymore.) I will address these questions analyzing how language discourse revolves around two issues: political and human rights, on the one hand, and cultural projects (starting new journals or translating Western intellectual texts into the Belarusian language), on the other.

What Is the Language of Freedom?

As everyone knows, the language issue first emerged in European history as vernacular against Latin or, later, against the language of the Empire (whichever that was): it was about using one's mother tongue publicly, relating in it to God; it was about literacy, education, access to culture, and, eventually, about modernity and statehood. The turn-of-the-century Belarusian literati (most of whom were educated in Petersburg or Warsaw, for after several uprisings the tsarist government had prohibited universities in the region and closed those which existed) saw their lands as "for several centuries an arena of political, national, religious and cultural struggle"[7] between Russia and Poland. For them, the national cultural idea was simultaneously a goal and a means for social mobilization; working for recognition of the language; eradicating backwardness, illiteracy, and poverty; and joining, as an independent nation, the European project of modernity.

How does language discourse relate to the "people" now, when everyone in the former socialist world is literate, and most are also urban and educated, though they do not speak as intellectuals claim they should speak?

In the mid-1990s my neighbor, a doctor, told me his story in a brief conversation about whether there had been a special Soviet policy which aimed at driving the Belarusian language out of use. "When I first came to Minsk to take my exams at the Medical Institute as a 17-year old village boy," the doctor said, "I could not speak anything but Belarusian (or, rather, countryside Belarusian). I was schooled in it, and no one on the examination committee found fault with me for the way I spoke. Quite the opposite, they smiled (encouragingly) as I answered my examination questions. I was admitted and began to study, and it was only later that I began, slowly, to switch to Russian . . . so no one made me."

Now this doctor, who speaks Russian both at home and in his public life, claims that his Belarusian is poor because he has not used it for many years and never did use it professionally. He is fluent in French, which he spoke while he worked for the Red Cross in Africa and Indochina. The doctor is sure that there was no external force that made him drop his native (village) tongue; it happened "naturally."

Marples describes the seventy Soviet years in Belarus as "repression and urbanization," arguing that the communists both built and destroyed the country,[8] annihilating during Stalin's rule the national intelligentsia nurtured on the turn-of-the-century revival ideals, launching modernization and development (which was especially rapid in the postwar period), and eventually turning these lands into one of the most industrialized regions of the USSR. The doctor's story demonstrates how language use was related to upward social mobility in the Soviet context. Coercion was definitely there, despite what the speaker believes, in a "non-violent," because institutionalized, form: the daily organization of power left very little "other way," and students could so easily switch to a "more developed" language when the languages belong to the same linguistic family. The switch went along with a strong affirmative action policy changing the pattern of social stratification and bringing "village boys" (and probably to an even greater extent girls) into higher education and the professions.

To ask whether modernization could have happened differently (as contemporary Belarusian literati insist it could have), whether all medical (and chemical, electronic, engineering, etc.) books could have been translated into the national language, whether education was about the "colonizer" recruiting locals to run "colonial administration," and so forth—in short, to be able to conceive all these ideas would require the common fundamental presupposition that colonization is actually what took place. But what exactly did it involve and how can one prove it if village boys got into medical schools and were able to advance in their profession? If the imaginary oppressors eat the same food, do the same work, send their children to the same schools, reside in the same apartment buildings, intermarry and, what's more, can in no perceptible way be distinguished from the oppressed because both belong to the same race; if it is only the way one speaks that reveals—reveals what? That this person is Belarusian and that is Russian? No; that this one lives in a city while that one resides in the countryside or is a first-generation urbanite, for by the second generation there is no clear distinction between . . . between whom, again? Ruler and ruled? No: the distinction is about who was born where, of course.

If, in fact, the oppression was not about economic opportunities but about "us" becoming "others," then it is not oppression but *repression,* and it relates to the question of whether the subaltern can speak. For how does one recognize it if one has already become the "other"? How can this "other" remember that mostly unconscious prestage of life in a different language? And if one, in fact, never was in that "other language" but was already born into the new one? In what language is repression described? How does one argue against it? And why should one want to return where one has never been? To recognize oppression/repression, one must already know about it, or at least have people who remember or know something different, however subtle, and can somehow convey this to others.

What later, during perestroika, took on the shape of independence claims, started as a quest for a non-Soviet identity through a nostalgic idealization of the self. A Belarusian rethinking—or building anew—her intellectual being (and, at the same time, trying to get rid of the cliché that the nation had no history before or outside the Soviet context) had nothing ready at hand: neither the idea of great culture (as Russia) nor a church that could speak the national language, nor could an uncontested language itself do so, nor recognized ancient statehood, nor any universally known national genius. But there was national mythology whispering great things into the Belarusian ear. The nation is a European gatekeeper against Russia: the printing of books began earlier here; these lands had a renaissance, a reformation, and a baroque period. The Belarusian language is the most ancient of all Slavic languages and preserves the most ancient words; the bogs of Belarusian Palessie (in the southwest) are the ancient place of origin of the Slavs. Belarusians have retained the ancient Slavic anthropological type, for the Tatar-Mongol hordes were stopped in this country after being exhausted in conquering Russia and did not "spoil" the blood. To support this last intriguing assertion, some recollect that Russian writer Ivan Bunin allegedly said that it is only west of Vitebsk (i.e., in Belarus) that the women do not have wide Mongolian cheekbones; they have narrow Slavic faces instead.

As a child, I heard this intelligentsia "popular culture" from my parents' friends: writers, art critics, journalists, and so forth. The careers or even the lives of some of them were ruined by the KGB for the ideas they had been uttering, for this mythology disrupted the single and monumental Soviet version of history and in so doing it was dangerous. It is probably at this time that the concerns that *mova hine* (the Belarusian language is dying) were also articulated for the first time; they have been growing among some intellectual groups ever since. The strongest concern was voiced by members of the Belarusian Writers' Union, whose books, published with state support in tens of thousands of copies, often remained on store shelves for years and then were pulped for recycling, as the head of the state publishing corporation (Dzyarzhkamdruk) admitted in a newspaper interview.[9] Thinking of anecdotal evidence, I remember one houseguest, a poet, telling my mother that just that day he had walked along the street with a famous writer whose work is included in all the Belarusian anthologies—and no one recognized or greeted him.

Perestroika made it legitimate to articulate those claims publicly, placing history and language in the center of patriotic discourse and relating them to the political vocabulary of national oppression and human rights. It was alleged that the people did not know their true history, were living with a false consciousness and taking it for their own, had forgotten their language. This last is most vividly represented by the emergence of *trasyanka*, the linguistic variant used by those who relocated into cities but retained some of their rural speech. *Trasyanka* (the equivalent of Ukrainian *surzhik*),[10] the linguistic manifestation of a certain social position, is viewed by intellectuals as "the Soviet monster that began to jump out of Belarusian bodies destroyed and ravaged by Soviet experiments."[11] The intellectuals represent some imaginary Belarusian as the norm against which all language practices are measured and judged. The "body of jurists" (as Bourdieu calls them), constituted by grammarians, linguists, and literati in general turned politicians (the head of the Popular Front is a linguist who works on orthography reform), judged *trasyanka* to be a deviation resulting from the political violence of the colonizer, a violation of the human right to live one's life in one's native language. Such an issue can only be dealt with politically.

The desired integration into a different linguistic community had to be articulated through recognized political language and the vocabulary of national oppression, or of violation of rights, served the articulatory purpose. The people just needed to be persuaded that they were oppressed and urged to awaken from their false consciousness. As there was no "proof" of oppression (cf. again the doctor's story), "ordinary" people and intellectuals really were speaking different languages, but in the sense of oppression versus repression.

What interest do intellectuals have in persuading the people that they are oppressed and need to recollect their true identity? Because this concerns the place intellectuals as a group would occupy; being the ones who tell the people they are oppressed and awakening them for protest, they gain symbolic capital. The language (or which language is used where, how it is classified, etc.), or discursive "occupation" of national public space, relates to the status of a group in a system and signifies other nonlinguistic economic and political interests: it justifies the demand to bring a different group of people into office, changing the political order. When newspapers first (during perestroika) introduced a special headline, "Prestige of the Native Tongue," to discuss language matters, one very popular answer to the question "Why is it necessary to make Belarusian the state language?" was "To give it back some prestige."[12] No one ever asked why the language needed prestige, for it went without saying that this was what the" people" must want (they don't yet, but they inevitably will, once they understand that this is how it should be), because they are a "titular nation."

Some city folk switched to Belarusian at work and at home, a political act which demanded considerable effort and self-discipline (some lasted several months, others several yeas, still others may have become Belarusian-speaking for life), in the honest belief that this was about democracy (an anti-Soviet act). Democracy is, however, at least partially about who will represent and implement power. A young nationalist activist explains:

> These people, the friends of the organization [the nationalist youth organization] should in the future become members of parliament, rectors of universities, CEOs, headmasters.[13]

At first, Belarusian was overwhelmingly the language of antigovernment demonstrations, for, as Katherine Verdery points out, nationalities are the only units with organizational history when a centralized system starts to fall apart.[14] With time, though, the anti-Soviet and anti-Lukashenka struggle ceased to be associated with the language. In the special issue of an opposition newspaper devoted to the language situation, several prominent intellectuals noted:

> A noticeable recent tendency in Minsk is that the actions of the opposition are taking place in the Russian language.

> Something no one could have imagined in 1995 is the fact that six years later a democratic struggle would be taking place in Russian.

> Maybe we are so unsuccessful because our democracy and the people speak different languages.[15]

In a certain sense this was supposed to happen, for language is not really the issue at stake in this controversy, nor is nationhood even, but rather the societal method of resource allocation—socialism versus capitalism (nationhood is present only insofar as it accompanies the issue of class).

Intellectuals, who, in honest but not conscious deliberation, were anxious to secure a certain (economic, cultural, and symbolic) profit from the restructuring of the linguistic market (which accompanies the social restructuring), keep adhering to the discourse of human rights as the only publicly recognized representation of their struggle:

> The Russian language is an aggressive tool of Russian chauvinist fascism. The Russian language is the evil tongue of captivity. Belarusians, switch over to your mother tongue. By doing this, you will get rid of the negative effect of the Russian language on our human rights, freedom of speech, and democracy. In this way we shall bring closer the reign of freedom in Belarus.[16]

If there is a connection here between the language issue and human rights, it is an essentialist one which equates Russianness with evil, and the perceptible anxiety, the emotional discomfort, and the sense of deprivation of the speaker provide the missing rationale. Repressed by master signifiers, the intellectual is at a loss about how to act and what to say and produces an almost hysterical discourse that expresses his anxiety about where to belong through what is available in the culture. There seems to be no place left for him, but he still is looking for one.

The Lure of Central Europe

"Europe was a transnational idea based on a civic ideal of the association of free cities," writes Svetlana Boym in *The Future of Nostalgia* (referring to Milan Kundera's definition of "European" as "nostalgic for Europe"). She believes that "alternative thinking urban dwellers in these cities could find more in common among themselves than with their own countries,"[17] and provides the beginning for a list of European cities: Sarajevo-Ljubljana-Budapest-Belgrade-Zagreb-Plovdiv-Timisoara-Bucharest-Prague-Kraków-L'vov/Lviv-Vilnius-Tallinn-Leningrad/St. Petersburg-Gdansk/Danzig.

The list, though unfinished and open to new members (from any part of the world, as long as they feel nostalgic for Europe), has some meaningful omissions. L'vov/Lviv, which had the reputation for being Western throughout the Soviet era with its cafés and across-the-border supply of blue jeans, is there, of course, and Lithuanian Vilnius is too, though without its Polish/Belarusian name Wilna. Kyiv/Kiev is not there, and Minsk is missing. Moscow is closer to Europe than these last two, which in the Soviet Russian cultural imagination were considered peripheral even as republican capitals, for if Ukraine and Belarus were ever allowed to have a pre-Soviet past, it was a peasant, illiterate, stateless one. Even Kievan Rus' could hardly be an argument to the contrary, since in the recognized version of history it was the cradle of the Russian, not Ukrainian, state. As for the Polotsk principality of the same era in Belarusian lands or, later, the medieval Grand Duchy of Lithuania—who ever mentioned these at all? With the demotion of other histories, including those lands into the Russian Empire appeared to be a great civilizing act.

Ukraine and Belarus, which enter the European gaze as "borderlands" as soon as some variant of the *Mitteleuropa* project appears on the horizon, were at the same time "the edge" of the Eastern Slavic lands in official Soviet (and pre-Soviet) historiography.[18] Rus' was the heart of those lands, of course, and our school history textbooks (in fourth or fifth grade) explained the "emergence" of the Belarusian and Ukrainian languages in the following way. At first, all Slavic tribes (*polyane* who lived in steppes, *drevlyane* who inhabited forests, and other nymphs and dryads) were speaking the same language, but eventually the people at the edges (*krai*) of that territory started to pronounce some words and sounds differently ("h" instead of "g," for example), and thus

73

the Belarusian and Ukrainian languages emerged. This implied first of all that that they "emerged" later as derivative dialects; second, that they were formed out of Russian (like a woman from a man's rib) which "was there" from the very beginning instead of emerging as dominant (linguistically and politically) during nation-building; and, third, that they are in some way "different," a deviation from the "correct language," which, of course, is Russian. Invited to think of themselves in this way, Belarusians and Ukrainians were relevant for the Pan-Slavic Russocentric historical mythology. Their presence demonstrated the gradual "lessening" of Russianness when moving from the center (i.e., true Russianness) to the edge and the Other. Poland, though still Slavic, was really "other" in its (Catholic) faith and culture, hence the permanent suspicion of everything Polish: Gogol's Cossack hero Taras Bul'ba fights against it; people there "hiss like snakes" in Gorky's "The Old Woman Izergil," and no "fair Polish lady" (*prekrasnaya polyachka*) in Russian history can ever be trusted. Popular myth supported the belief that Polish women are seductive and dangerous, probably with the same "rationale" as the myth of the "fair Jewess" in European culture.

The post-communist redefinition of geographical space means a major power shift; the former "center" and "periphery" both have to work out different cultural imaginary while rethinking their social subjectivity. Even after Ukraine and Belarus became sovereign states, post-Soviet Russophile historiography, as Andrew Wilson points out, "has so far failed to address seriously the fact of Ukrainian and Belarusian independence, and has remained content to recycle the myths of tsarist and Soviet eras."[19] The meaningful absence of "socialist countries" and "national republics" takes the form of perceptible anxiety. Nationalist politicians are openly anxious, while some intellectuals are uneasy in their own subtle ways, their discontent also concerning domination, albeit in a different domain—that of the symbolic field where meanings are produced. The famous writer Viktor Erofeev, who once took part in the subversive almanac *Metropole* and was expelled from the Soviet Writers' Union, begins a travel essay published in *Ogonyok*, formerly the most antitotalitarian and democratic of all the great perestroika journals, from Orientalist presumptions:

> There were times when Warsaw was ours. Well, maybe not completely the way the Crimea or Gagry were [famous resorts; the second is in the Caucasus—EG], though it used to belong to us in that way too, but that was long ago, during the tsars. But still, as far back as I can remember, it was almost ours, but not completely, and this had some special meaning to it. Overtly tame and submissive, Warsaw was still trying to run away from us or to hide, and we were trying to catch her by the hand, and she behaved strangely, trying to get loose and not trying to at the same time, and . . . laughing, as if a girl. In short, she was a living thing.
>
> Now Warsaw has run so far away from us that Poles do not even think of themselves as Eastern Europe anymore. Now they are Central Europe, and as for Eastern Europe—these are now Belarusians and Ukrainians. . . .

> [I]t is too quiet there now, as if in some European "Slippery Rock," and everything has become extremely provincial. Warsaw hasn't turned into Paris and didn't outdo Berlin, and is like a dull Viennese suburb, where they drink beer and curse unemployment.[20]

Ukrainians and Belarusians, who are now part of Europe (though an Eastern one), reverberate through the short essay mocking a conference which was about—of all things!—"nostalgia for communism" (most probably meaning reflections of the communist past) in the former communist bloc, revealing the author's own pan-Slavic nostalgia. He describes the meeting as

> a lively conference of writers and journalists from countries formerly ours, from Albania to Estonia, including Hungary, Romania and Czech Republic, including those very Ukrainians and Belarusians who have received a European status.

Intellectual anxiety over who belongs among the European nations results from the contest over cultural authority within the new European order: who can be a player in the global intellectual market, who controls participation at an international conference, and, in general, who owns the right to an internationally recognized cultural voice and the glory that goes with it. Before, Russian (its classical literature, Bolshoi ballet, Tchaikovsky's music, the Russian avant-garde, The Hermitage—the list could be a really long one) was the canon in this part of the world, and to be accepted into world culture and be considered for a Nobel Prize, one had to be coded as "Russian." Marc Chagall, a Belarusian-born Jew, is Russian in most world museums.

National writers—those from "national republics" writing in their "national languages," though regularly translated into Russian for all-Union readers (and often by first-class Russian poets) as a part of the Soviet affirmative action policy of internationalism—were still perceived as secondary, though some were quite popular: their topics were too local, their interests too narrow, their concerns too ethnic to express the modern world. The persistent attitude that on all intellectual counts they were "younger brothers" just learning to read and write, despite the fact that many of them belonged to cultures whose great books date back to the times when Slavs were just mastering their first alphabet, springs from the same reasons as the question Linda Nochlin raised about art some thirty years ago, "Why Have There Been No Great Women Artists?"[21]

The answer, formulated since then by the feminist critique of art, is that there have been so few of them because the canon of "great art" is neither objective nor the only one possible. It does not represent the "real" art history—"the way it was"—but the way it was supposed to be according to certain presumptions. There are so few of them because women were seen not as creators but as muses, created by the male gaze and existing for it. Because women were not taught to read or to paint. Because they never had "a room of their own," both metaphorically (as intellectual space) and physically (as a study with no babies crying or stew boiling over). Because the topics inspired by their life experience were considered unimportant or even indecent by authoritative judges. Because to paint as a woman one had to change the canon, that is, to restructure the symbolic field.

These reasons, when taken together, also explain why there have been no "great national writers" (writers not coming from the small group of widely studied world languages) and are metaphors for the notion of censorship, "the structure of the field itself which governs expression by governing both access to expression and the form of expression, and not some legal proceeding which has been specifically adapted. . . . This structural censorship is exercised through the medium of the sanctions of the field, functioning as a market on which the prices of different kinds of expression are formed; it is imposed on all producers of symbolic goods, including the authorized spokesperson . . . and it condemns the occupants of dominated positions either to silence or to shocking outspokenness."[22] Or, I would add, to using what tools are available when it becomes possible to redefine the space.

Symbolic realms are permeated with social relations, and during the postwar period only two Belarusian writers made it to an all-Soviet readership: the late Vasil' Bykau, internationally recognized for his tragic World War II novels (he wrote in Belarusian, and his first books were severely criticized by the Party ideologists for their "defeatist" mood), and Svetlana Aleksievich, whose narratives written in Russian are based on oral history; for example, of the Afghan war or the Chernobyl disaster.[23] The fact that their books, which have been translated into dozens of (European and Asian) languages, are currently not on the readings lists of Slavic departments of Western academia, where Russian writers of their caliber would necessarily have been included, is explained by "censorship" in the form of the structure of the field. The Slavic studies curriculum, which is structured by discipline and by country, is and has been Russia-centered even if it has taught Soviet history and culture, and including Aleksievich would demand rethinking what is considered Russian beyond mere geography.

The post-Soviet restructuring of political space potentially allows redefinition of the global and European intellectual market (of which Western academia is one part) and reconsideration of the roles of intellectual players, but unlike Belarusian independence, which was miraculously granted through the disintegration of the USSR, this kind of contest demands some effort. It needs a special assertive mechanism, and of all the resources available, the "national language" versus Russian is the most powerful.

The Central European relationship with (or to) the Russian language has a long history. In the nineteenth century, after the Polish/Belarusian/Lithuanian uprising of 1863 had been crushed, Polish writer Eliza Orzeszkowa stressed the importance of writing in the national language. That, she believed, would testify that "the people" were not broken, while the very same texts—in translation—would be important vehicles in converting the oppressor: "That which I write in Polish, dressed in the clothing of a different language, reaches the very edges of the state and inspires interest, sympathy, even admiration. If, as I think, we are engaged in a long and complicated historical process, then attentive and even persistent listening to the voice of the oppressed could make an important document."[24]

Imposing a language implies the promotion of certain texts and ideologies, and after World War II almost everyone in the former socialist bloc had to learn Russian. Many knew it, some rejected it, and a few welcomed it (for cultural or career reasons). In the former USSR everyone knew it, of course, and for many outside the Russian Federation it was (and is) a native language. It is "through Russian" that one could get access to world culture, for who knew English then? And who could get those books, even if one did?

In the 1990s, the relationship between Russian and other languages of the region started to change, for it is through the performative rejection of Russian in certain public arenas (even at the cost of convenience) that new cultural agency was negotiated. Participants in various democracy seminars organized at the time through Western efforts to promote civil society mention that English was often the language of after-class communication at such gatherings among former Soviet compatriots. For many of them, Russian was (and is) the language of the private world of their home and families, of their work and educational exchanges. But the seminars were public, not private, and international, not national, spaces of negotiations about the terms on which to enter discourse: when a conference participant spoke English to a Russian from Russia (i.e., as one "foreigner" to another) or a Lithuanian and an Armenian used it in front of a Russian colleague, it was a public statement and a political act. As a Moscow friend of mine described her experience at the conference,

> We [Russian participants] had to take it, had to live through it. It lasted for two days, and then they all realized that we were like them, in the same camp, and they stopped it and then everyone was speaking Russian. But we had to live through those first two days. They needed them, and I can understand why.

The stage of combative and demonstrative rejection of Russian has ended among Central European members of NATO and the European Union, who have made their political statements and hardly need to assert themselves in other ways. Central European intellectual interest in Russia is now of a different nature: those recognized as intellectual voices in Europe expect to be accepted in that world language as well, while those for whom Erofeev speaks—empire-nostalgic intellectuals—would wish to see these countries as dominated by Russian (and not Western) culture:

> Central Europe, though, did not curse Russians, and that was surprising. All the writers wanted to have their books published in Moscow. They would come up to me and ask how that could be arranged. Many of them are now

published in Italy, France, Holland, and Russia wouldn't publish them. Why? I was looking at them in silence. . . .

I noticed that everyone is more eager now to speak Russian, except possibly new Eastern Europe. The new Eastern Europe was speaking Polish and English with a strong Russian accent. . . . Before, Poles would speak Russian only after a heavy drink. Now even sober Warsowians, meeting you, would try to think of some Russian words, which they so stubbornly rejected during the old regime.

In the "new Eastern Europe," which is still an outsider in Europe, the situation continues to be a power play; intellectuals need to assert their meaningful and separate presence in cultural space dominated by Russia, where Russian publishers are the ones with the resources to translate and publish Derrida (to whom they overwhelmingly prefer Stephen King, to be honest) and Russian TV can afford to broadcast the Academy Awards.

If a Russian-speaking Belarusian intellectual is forever marginal in the "Russian" cultural world (a village cousin who can never speak correctly and, even if he or she does, whose topics are too local, concerns too ethnic, etc.), for this world was shaped through the grand imperial tradition, then one way (for there can be others) of contesting the grand narrative is by reinscribing oneself as "totally different," or foreign. Language makes a difference as a "class" marker, but it can only do so if politically loaded, in the same way that it is not biological difference between men and women per se that is the reason for inequality but rather the meaning that difference acquires through a larger social interaction. Linguistic difference is imagined as a raison d'être for cultural nationhood and for joining Central Europe as "an uncertain zone of small nations between Russia and Germany" (according to Milan Kundera);[25] that is, a space which is (currently) not organized through a binary opposition to the former metropolis but is (potentially) a multiplicity of intellectual urban centers, as Svetlana Boym sees them. The names of Kundera himself; of Havel, Czesław Miłosz, Adam Michnik, and Slavoj Žižek; of Polish sociology as an intellectual tradition and Polish posters as an art form; of Czech pantomime theatre, Wajda's films, Chagall's paintings and his famous nostalgia for the Belarusian-Jewish Vitebsk (of which we learned from a poem by Russian poet Andrei Voznesenskii), the humor and bitterness of the lost Ashkenazi culture, and the Bulgarian "seminar" brilliantly presented by Miglena Nikolchina in her recent essay[26] create the aura of a powerful Central European intellectualism, to which the "new Eastern Europe" is so eager to belong, to which it has contributed, and into which it believed it is accepted without being looked down upon as a village fool. It is also important that through this connection one can even enter the "Slavic studies curriculum," making what Edward Said calls "a voyage in": entering, through a conscious effort, the discourse of Europe and the West, mixing with it, transforming it, and making it acknowledge them. Being an intellectual, after all, is about producing texts, preferably for "the whole world."

My further intention is to analyze how textual cultural agency involves "postcolonial" cultural politics. The term is not related to the question of whether the USSR was a colonial empire, but it emerges because of an important parallel: post-communist intellectuals encounter the same structural situations (in relation to Russia as a world culture, to each other, and to the world at large) as postcolonial intellectuals; they are asking the same questions and pondering the same problems of definition of the common self and the common place. This is so because the power centers which used to define their lives were situated outside of them in a similar way.

The Agents and the Cause

The specialized languages that schools of specialists produce and reproduce . . . are, as with all discourses, the product of a *compromise* between an *expressive interest* and a *censorship*.

Pierre Bourdieu[27]

National liberation struggles involve "reclaiming, renaming, reinhabiting the land."[28] In this essay, though, I will not consider (re)invention of the allegedly authentic folk tradition, history, and culture by historians and ethnographers. This work, dating back to a much earlier period, was started by an older generation of scholars (I mean those from the post–World War II period), many of them born in the countryside or in Western Belarus (where modernization started later). Many were (and are) "natural" Belarusian speakers and quite often are first-generation members of the intelligentsia.

I will focus on an intellectual attempt to produce an alternative signification by elaborating a Western-oriented philosophical and literary project by younger literati, most of whom are urban born, belong to the second- (or third-) generation intelligentsia and consciously switched to Belarusian in the early 1990s; some of them were formally educated in the natural sciences and floated to the humanities through participation in nativist cultural initiatives during perestroika.

Anne Applebaum, in her travel book *Between East and West*, mentions a young man, a philosopher, poet, and student of English whom she met in Minsk around 1991. Immersed in the study of postmodernism and Beatnik texts, he explained his credo:

> We young Belarusians can be like gods—we can create the world by inventing new words for things. Where else in the world can I do the first translations of Derrida, or write the definitive work on Hegel? Here I can help create a literary tradition, and influence the thinking of the many generations of people who will follow me.[29]

One of his friends, Applebaum mentions, had translated *Ulysses* into Belarusian, just to see whether it could be done; another was working on Eliot's *The*

Waste Land, and everyone was learning Belarusian, which had become "all the vogue."

The youthful pathos of 1991 was engendered by patriotic enthusiasm mixed with cosmopolitan ambitions: by the (then imaginary) project of (re)creating a nation-state as an epitome of a new brave world, by the opportunity to cross national borders freely (well, not exactly, as we know now but didn't know then), by a sense of joining avant-garde developments in the international humanities, by becoming ambitious participants in a new European order. By the general perestroika elation when "everything is possible" and by intellectual (a.k.a. economic) opportunities. . . .

In those days, culture was almost as big as politics in the inspirational process of new agency that the national project seemed to offer. International foundations were opening their offices in Minsk to start exchange programs, through which the words "grant" and "scholarship" were becoming part of the academic vocabulary: one could get money to travel to a European conference, to work in the Library of Congress, and even to publish one's own work. Reinventing themselves through anticolonial nationalism as a new breed, "public intellectuals" (who "did not exist" in the USSR, in spite of the abundance of intellectual conversations over kitchen tables) launched several journals (two of which, *ARCHE* and *Frahmenty*, declared postcolonial studies the intellectual paradigm that enabled a new analysis of local culture), created "Belaruski Kalegium" to offer courses on topics in the humanities and embarked on various cultural projects, all with foreign support.

Language is the ultimate means of production for intellectuals, and part of their civilizing linguistic effort revolved around orthography, which also became a political dividing line. The now-canonical variant emerged out of the 1933 Russification reform and is called *narkomovka* (from "*narkom*," the communist head of a department); it is the script of government-supported newspapers and all that they stand for. The *Taraszkewitsa*, which was worked out at the turn of the century and was very popular around 1991, still feels outdated; moreover, its use, prohibited by a special decree when the *trasyanka*-speaking government suddenly became concerned with the orthography in opposition newspapers, is a political statement. An even stronger statement is Belarusian *lacinka*: the tradition of using the Latin alphabet dates back, in its most significant appearance, to the 1863 uprising and its anti-tsarist and anti-Russian pamphlets. *Lacinka* is especially popular in *Nasza niva*, the newspaper which in 1991 revived the name of the first-ever Belarusian newspaper, which was published in Wilna (Vilnius) and had been the mouthpiece of the turn-of-the-twentieth-century revival.

Belarusophone intellectual life seems to be blooming, an idea one might get from the announcement in the journal *Frahmenty* that brilliantly plays on myths of national origin and historical continuity and the names of canonical figures and contemporary actors of national revival:

As it is technically impossible to provide an absolute pluralism, the editorial board of Frahmenty *announces that temporarily texts written in Palessian, Prussian, Jatvigian, Great Litvan and Small Litvan languages, texts written in Arabic and Hebrew script, as well as translations made in the "radical Bulgakauka" style will not be accepted. Texts in the Kryvian (Krivichian) language should be sent to "Kryuje" for expertise. As for the orthography, we accept "Kolasauka" and the first five variants of "Taraszkewitsa": classical, Vintsukouka modified, Shupauka, Naszaniuka, emigrantese, as well as individual mutations of the above-mentioned bodies.*[30]

The witty text veils the fact that intellectuals play with five variants of orthography in a world where Belarusian as a standardized language is spoken only by them and by the small diaspora in the United States: elderly inhabitants of the countryside use some form of the vernacular (which is not a tongue usable for translating Derrida), urban workers use *trasyanka*, and intellectual life is mostly Russophone.

The government effort to widen the academic usage of Belarusian in 1991–1995 met with resistance and hostility and was later dropped at the beginning of the reunification process. Thus, the publishers of *ARCHE*, launching the journal with the idea of providing in Belarusian what is unavailable to the intellectual readership otherwise, stated their goals to be "the utmost saturation of the Belarusian intellectual market with world cultural treasures; contributing to creating healthy conditions for intellectual agency in the Belarusian capital city; working out new mechanisms and ways to pursue projects in the sphere of contemporary technologies in the humanities" and, what is more, "publishing 'An Anthology of 20th Century Philosophical Thought' in the Belarusian language," plus several other minor things.[31]

Immediately, publishing one's work in *ARCHE* between "daring" translations of Said and Erica Jong became a sign of belonging to an elite (because Westernized) group, because it implies quality work. It implies "hot" postcolonial topics, use of words such as "creolization" in relation to the Belarusian situation, and . . . that is all. One of the journal's issues was entitled *Medicine*, and I began reading "Mental Disorders in Independent Belarus," looking forward to a Foucaultian perspective on the post-Soviet "clinic" . . . only to discover a medical textbook description (written by a doctor, whose name, alas, is not Fanon) of schizophrenia and neurosis: "If you haven't had a schizophrenic in your family, your chance of having the disease is 1%." Another issue is devoted to the topic of women. It opens with the radical text "Woman and Sex: What, Where and What For" that is long and detailed and begins with the phrase: "Women's sexual organs are usually classified as internal and external. They are separated from each other by a hymen or its remnants after the woman has become sexually active."[32] Because women are seen as bodies, "research" on them consists of description and classification of the object—female sexual anatomy and its uses. Special issues on the topics of Jews, pathologies, postmodernism, and pornography have also been published, and I expect the editors to come up with ideas for issues on Negroes or the poor.

The journals are a project aimed at the Western (via Central Europe) cultural market, where their value is much greater than at home: here they circulate among a small and close group (mostly consisting of those who write for them), while translations of Western texts for a larger audience are supplied by the more powerful and, hence, prestigious Russian-reading market. The profit drawn from this investment is an alternative elite status, that is, recognition as "some of our own" by Central European colleagues and notice from Western scholars whose field of interest in some way includes Belarus and who would mention that "interesting work is being done by those new journals" but, I suspect, may have not read the articles. Through this recognition and the economic support that goes with it, the new intellectuals are able to negate symbolically the hierarchy of local academia, where the capital they possess is rarely recognized, because this is a way for local academia as a "Soviet" institution to protect itself from "disruption" by Western knowledge.

As they develop cultural products, intellectuals take into account market conditions—where those products will circulate—and this is one of the reasons why Belarusophone intellectual life has a distinctly performative character. Their intellectual life does not result from a process in which new words emerge in, as Kristeva describes them, "communities of men and women [who] have ripened them in a concern for singularity in the memory of their language and in the discussions that forge their concepts. I do not see these communities, I do not see these singularities, I do not see this memory of language, I do not see these discussions."[33]

I agree with Alexandra Goujon that this situation with language results from politics,[34] but I would argue that everything results from something and happens in particular contexts. Nothing happens for no reason (though we may not know the reason); we have what is, not what we would rather have if human history were different. Trying to reverse a trend by applying different politics demands an understanding of why, for whom, and for what cause or, as Lenin used to say, in whose interests: *qui prodest?*

Historically, national struggles, starting at the margins, were aimed (at least overtly) at improving the situation for the marginalized; at the turn of the previous century, national oppression and class inequality were often seen as one. In 1905, Yanka Kupala, the founder of contemporary Belarusian literary tradition, wrote "And, Say, Who Goes There?"—a poem recognized as a symbol of the rising people:

> And, say, who goes there? And, say, who goes there?
> In such a mighty throng assembled, O declare?
> Byelorussians!
> And what do those lean shoulders bear as load,
> Those hands stained dark with blood, those feet bast-sandal shod?
> All their grievance!

And to what place do they this grievance bear,
And whither do they take it to declare?
   To the whole world!
And who schooled them thus, many million strong,
Bear their grievance forth, roused them from slumbers long?
   Want and suffering!
And what is it, then, for which so long they pined,
Scorned throughout the years, they, the deaf, the blind?
   To be called human![35]

Almost 100 years later, in 2003, another bard, a poet and a musician, published an essay in *Nasha niva*. His inspiration was also in his people:

Our Folks

Here they are—with harsh faces, reddish with frost, sun or wind. They go East and West to inhabit their marketplaces. They stand there, in these markets, offering their traditional goods: vodka and cigarettes. These are "our folks"—your compatriots, meeting with whom, when abroad, you fear and try to avoid. This is only one category of "our folks," the most primitive and brutal.

Once you were standing in the customs line at the Belarusian-Polish border. What was your luggage? A guitar. Several CDs. Some clothes. A simple Belarusian babushka, who was standing in the line next to you, asked you to take a package across the border. She said, there was just a bottle of vodka there, could you help the old babushka, please. You agreed, and in a moment a customs officer was unfolding the package. Two bottles of cheap brandy, some similar stuff "for sale." Because of that babushka, you could have been sent back across the border, and since then you have not assisted anyone of "our folks" with their smuggling problems, in spite of their lamenting and requests.

You understand only too well why our Western neighbors do not like "our folks." Who could ever like them: their vodka may cause health problems and their cigarettes have a nasty smell. They are cynical, have lost visual sexual features, do not take care of their looks. They curse and speak loudly. . . . They are "second rate" people: that's how the locals take them. By the way, it seems to me that when "our folks" return home (to Slonim, Lida or Baranavichy), they turn—in some miraculous way—into the local elite. Affluent, owning estates, cars and property that they got through decades of hard market work. . . .

But listen, these are your compatriots! They should be closer to you than local Poles, who look at this "marketing horde" from the East with fear and disgust. So why do you feel belonging with the Poles, and not with our folks, why are you ashamed?

Once you were staying for three days in a hotel in Byalystok, where the "bonus" was several swimming pools and saunas, a kind of an aquapark. Staying there is quite expensive, so only "our folks" of the highest category stay there. These do not differ too much from the locals in their clothing and behavior, and their main difference is in the language. They do not make an effort to learn at least a few Polish words. They speak Russian always and everywhere, for they believe that their money would guarantee that everyone understands their Russian language.

You are sitting in the bar room of a hotel and having a small beer (0.3 l). You are looking around. Across from you there are two middle-aged Polish musicians. In the street in front of the hotel there is a continuing concert, for today everywhere in Poland there are concerts and performances, a musical marathon with the money going for handicapped infants. The musicians will perform in an hour, and as it is cold outside (it's winter time) they let themselves have 100 g of tequila. They are sitting there, speaking in low voices, probably, joking. A young man comes up to them (most probably the son of an affluent father staying here with his family) and asks in pure Russian:

"Excuse me, do you by any chance have a cigarette?"

The musicians ask him what he wants, for they do not understand Russian. But the young man does not speak any other language.

You do not know the end of it. You rise and go to your room. Most probably in some way they made sense of each other's languages, and the young man got his cigarette. But why are you so ashamed? And why do you feel internal belonging with the Polish musicians and not with your compatriot, who must have been trying, while his father was not there, to have a beer and a cigarette? Why didn't you help the boy to communicate with the Poles, but went to your room to watch some Polish movie for a whole hour instead? Why? There's no answer. . . .[36]

Today, as Homi Bhabha writes, contextualizing contemporary subversive cultural and intellectual politics, "(in Britain) experimental art and film [is] emerging from the left"[37] and is associated with experience of migration and nomadism, with urban poor, with people of color—that is, with those at the margins; it is *for the subaltern* (who is now beyond "national") that postcolonial thinkers are trying to speak.

The post-Soviet critical intellectual, proudly declaring "a guitar and several CDs" as his property, is full of disgust for the babushkas trying to make money any way they can to survive and despises "lower class" vulgarians living, because other jobs are nonexistent, through across-the-border trade (they are called *chelnoki*, a Russian word meaning "shuttles"); he also dislikes the inelegant new rich but does not mind those who dress and behave like middle-class foreigners. These people become even better if they can speak like foreigners. The snob, sandwiched between the haves and have-nots, has a clear-cut class consciousness, identifying with the Western (or Westernized) conformist class and hoping to be taken for one of them. Texts full of contempt for urban trash and countryside cattle (*bydla*), who forgot "the national language and culture" to become vulgar *homo Sovieticus*, are a feature of Belarusian intellectual publications. Babushkas, that is, the elderly, who are diagnosed as crazy because they vote for Lukashenka (who regularly "updates" their pensions) are a particular target. Really, jet intellectuals (as Richard Rorty describes the category) are closer to each other than to the populace of their own countries.

Concluding Remarks

I started this essay with the presumption that the main process in my part of the world is class formation and that intellectuals are usually the most ardent supporters of a new social order: always representing "others"—that is, acting on behalf of a new rising class—they become central subjects of political discourse[38] and articulators of the new (national, economic, and all other) ideas. Serving the class interests of others (the new rising class), intellectuals justify their action by constructing it as service to the "people's cause."

Though intellectuals are not the ones who get the most from the new societal arrangement economically—quite often they do not understand this—they still have an interest here. The interest is not of an overtly economic nature, and more often than not intellectuals believe that they have no other "interest" in the regime change except the pursuit of justice. But "justice" has never been an abstract thing: it may mean different things and is always bound to certain interests. The purpose of my essay was to establish the fundamental link between "national language" activism and the "class" or "corporate" interests of intellectuals. These interests, which are not economic in the narrow sense (but are definitely related to the economic opportunities), are rather about a general restructuring of political and intellectual spaces. More specifically, they concern opportunities to bring a different group of people into power nationally, to enter the global intellectual market, and to become international players in this field.

NOTES

1. Edward Said, *Culture and Imperialism* (London: Chatto and Windus, 1993), 323.

2. *New York Times* editorial, "The Tyrant of Belarus," August 31, 1996, 20.

3. David Marples, *Belarus: Denationalized Nation* (Amsterdam: Harwood Academic, 1999).

4. Edward Said, "Yeats and Decolonization," in *The Edward Said Reader* (New York: Vintage Books, 2000), 303.

5. See Elena Gapova, "On Nation, Gender and Class Formation in Belarus . . . and Elsewhere in the Post-Soviet World," *Nationalities Papers* 30, no. 4 (2002): 639–662.

6. Contemporary class is not about one's place in production (as in Marxism) but about the distribution of life chances through the workings of the market (a Weberian perspective). Stratification takes place as "the life chances accessible to different groups of the population are distributed unevenly as a collective outcome of the activity of individual economic agents who differ with regard to power in the market," writes Timo Piirainen in *Toward a New Social Order in Russia: Transforming Structures and Everyday Life* (Hanover, N.H.: Dartmouth University Press, 1997), 29.

7. Ivan Lubachko, *Belorussia under Soviet Rule* (Lexington: University Press of Kentucky, 1972), 31.

8. David Marples, *Belarus: From Soviet Rule to Nuclear Catastrophe* (New York: St. Martin's Press, 1996), 79–114.

9. Mikhail Dzyalets, "Vyarnyts' autarytet belaruskai knihi," *Zvyazda*, September 9, 1988, 3.

10. Trasyanka is what Alexander Lukashenka, a man from the countryside, spoke when he was elected president in 1994 and people immediately recognized him as "one of our own." The government media began calling him "the people's president." (After seven years of presidency his speech changed to a degree, and recently he started making speeches in Belarusian.)

11. Uladislau Horbatski, "Bul'ba-taukanichka," *Nasha niva*, June 19, 2000, 2.

12. Ivan Laskou, "Prestyzh rodnai movy," *Zvyazda*, September 15, 1989, 2.

13. Natallya Makovik, "MF pavinen farmovac' elitu," *Nasha niva*, June 26, 2000, 6.

14. Katherine Verdery, *What Was Socialism, and What Comes Next?* (Princeton, N.J.: Princeton University Press, 1996), 85.

15. Siarhei Paulouski, Bartosik Zmitser, Tumar Barys, "Mova jak ahvgara palityli," *Nasha niva*, May 21, 2001, 3–4.

16. "Z nashaniuskaga partfelyu," *Nasha niva*, May 15, 2003, 2.

17. Svetlana Boym, *The Future of Nostalgia* (New York: Basic Books, 2001), 221.

18. "Ukraina" literally means "borderland" (from *krai*, "edge")—this meaning of the word is stressed by the former customary use of "the," to which Ukrainians have been objecting, with some success, since independence. Compare the Croatian province Krajina, which appeared in world media in 1995 as the Croatian army drove out ethnic Serbs living there and which received its name as a military borderland of the Austro-Hungarian empire. [Eds.]

19. Andrew Wilson, "National History and National Identity in Ukraine and Belarus," in *Nation-Building in the Post-Soviet Borderlands* (Cambridge and New York: Cambridge University Press, 1998), 23.

20. Viktor Erofeev, "Nostal'gia po Warszawe," *Ogonyok* 4750 (2002): 22.

21. Linda Nochlin, "Why Have There Been No Great Women Artists?" in *Art and Sexual Politics: Women's Liberation, Women Artists, and Art History*, ed. Thomas B. Hess and Elizabeth C. Baker (New York: Macmillan, 1973), 1–39.

22. Pierre Bourdieu, *Language and Symbolic Power* (Cambridge, Mass.: Harvard University Press, 1991), 138.

23. The most famous books by Svetlana Alexievich are *Voices from Chernobyl: Chronicle of the Future* (London: Aurum Press, 1999) and *Zinky Boys: Soviet Voices from the Afghanistan War* (New York: W.W. Norton & Co., 1992).

24. "Avtobiografiia Elizy Ozheshko v trekh pis'makh," *Russkoe bogatstvo*, no. 11 (1910): 247.

25. Milan Kundera, "The Tragedy of Central Europe," *New York Review of Books*, April 26, 1984.

26. Miglena Nikolchina, "The Seminar: Mode d'emploi. Impure Space in the Light of Late Totalitarianism," *Differences* 13, no. 1 (2002).

27. Bourdieu, *Language and Symbolic Power*, 137.

28. Said, "Yeats and Decolonization," 299.

29. Anne Applebaum, *Between East and West: Across the Borderlands of Europe* (New York: Pantheon Books, 1994), 168.

30. *Frahmenty* no. 9 (2000). I am grateful to Curt Woolhiser and Uladzimir Katkouski for help with translation of this piece and the comments below.

The name Jatvingian is used in reference to the Baltic tribe that once inhabited the Western portions of the Belarusian and Lithuanian speech territory. This term could also be used in reference to the "Jetvyz'ska valoda" (based on the West Palesian dialects) that was promoted by a separatism movement in the early '90s as a separate language.

The term *"vialikalitouskaja mova"* was probably coined by Jan Stankievich by analogy to the Russian *"velikorusskij jazyk."* The English version Stankievich himself employed is "Greatlitvan." As for *"malalitouskaja mova,"* "Little/Lesser Litvan," this term was probably used by Stankievich in reference to the Baltic Lithuanian language (what some contemporary Belarusian nationalists refer to as *"lietuviskaja mova"* [Lietuvian] or *"zhmudskaja mova"* [Zhmudian/Zhemaitian]).

The term *"kryuskaja mova"* can be rendered in English as "Kryvian" or "the Kryvian language," though English-language scholarly works on East Slavic archaeology, history, and linguistics tend to use the adjectival form "Krivichian" in reference to this particular tribe. "Kryuje" may be the name of the journal for Belarusian neopagans.

On orthography variants: Kolasauka is a modification of the 1933 *"narkomauka"* orthography proposed by the Orthographic Commission led by Jakub Kolas and Kandrat Krapiva in 1957. Bulgakauka is a reference to Valerka Bulgakau, editor-in-chief of the journal *ARCHE*, who is quite revolutionary in introducing new words (or long-forgotten words) into our language. "Vincukouka" is a reference to Vincuk Viaczorka (a linguist and a politician) who is currently working on "updating" the Taraszkievica system to fit modern needs. "Szupauka" is a reference to Siarhiej Szupa, the director of Baltic Waves radio and a linguist. The term "Naszaniuka" is a reference to contemporary "Nasza Niva" (not to their ancestor from the beginning of the century).

31. The anthology project can be viewed online at http://arche.home.by/fond.htm (accessed February 17, 2004).

32. *ARCHE*, special issue *Kabety*, no. 3–4 (1999): 64.

33. Julia Kristeva, "Bulgaria, My Suffering," in *Crisis of the European Subject* (New York: Other Press, 2000), 175.

34. Alexandra Goujon, "Language, Nationalism, and Populism in Belarus," *Nationalities Papers* 27, no. 4 (1999): 661–677.

35. *Like Water, Like Fire: An Anthology of Byelorussian Poetry from 1828 to the Present Day*, trans. Vera Rich (London: George Allen & Unwin, 1971).

36. Lyavon Vol'ski, "Nashyja," *Nasha niva*, available online at http://www.nn.by/index.pl?theme=nn/2003/05&article=19 (accessed February 17, 2004).

37. Homi Bhabha, "The Postcolonial and the Postmodern," in *The Location of Culture* (London and New York: Routledge, 1994), 177.

38. Stanley Aronowitz, "On Intellectuals," in *Intellectuals. Aesthetics. Politics. Academics*, ed. Bruce Robbins (Minneapolis: University of Minnesota Press, 1990), 10.

three

Prenzlauer Berg Connections

*The Trajectory of East German Samizdat Culture
from Socialism to Capitalism*

Lisa Whitmore

East German writers and artists found themselves in a unique situation after
the fall of the Wall. Unlike states that suddenly gained their national independence, East Germany buckled under the cultural and economic domination
of West Germany. After the German monetary union, artists and writers had to
begin searching for resources in an acutely competitive climate. Political bias
and misunderstanding compounded the usual market demands in a national
culture industry dominated by the bigger, richer West. Yet many East German
writers and artists continue to bring forth new works. For writers and artists who
had created their own semipublic sphere in the German Democratic Republic, the tradition of a local audience enabled them to continue producing
even in the absence of mainstream national success. The struggle for cultural
identity within unified Germany is a significant chapter in the understanding
of post-totalitarian culture that illustrates the costs of the new system and
exposes as simplistic the popular notion that the lifting of the Iron Curtain
brought forth automatic enlightenment to brainwashed victims of Stalinism.

The experiences of the marginalized authors and artists of East Germany's
well-documented "unofficial culture" best illustrate the serendipitous intellectual advantages gained at the edges of the old system and what was at stake in
the new. The subculture, sometimes known as the Prenzlauer Berg Scene, was

a loose network of artists and poets who congregated in the neglected Wilhelmine working-class neighborhoods of East German cities during the 1980s. With the subterranean production of artbooks and periodicals, occasionally referred to using the Russian word samizdat, meaning "self-published," it gained attention as an oppositional avant-garde movement. Participants found ways to navigate labor and political requirements and to benefit from subsidization of basic necessities, thereby allowing them enough resources to concentrate on their art.

The work incorporated an eclectic array of styles such as Dada, Moscow futurism, Kafkaesque surrealism, and poststructuralist literary theory. Despite the artists' exploration of the avant-garde, their work diverged from traditional leftist art in their rejection of utopianism. For them, motifs of "changing the world" were inextricably tied to the official Marxist-Leninist ideology of the GDR state and its corruption. The state categorized this emphasis on style and the rejection of utopianism as subversive. Thus, in an ironic twist, the group's anti-activism was viewed as oppositional, both by the secret police and by Western *feuilleton*, proving that the politicizing dynamics of the highly ideological state were inescapable. For these experimental writers and artists, who explored the critique of ideology long before unification, the most significant change was not the freedom from propaganda and ideology that might have been portrayed by the American news. Rather, it was the open door to make their work public and the resulting financial responsibility.

After German unification, the politicizing context was replaced by the semiotic vacuum of the global economy, in which opposition was quickly commodified into the fashion of radical chic. In the first decade after unification, public figures from the former GDR continued to be judged by the old for-or-against dichotomy, though any verdict now resulted in a loss of market value. Writers who had published in the GDR were marginalized for their past conformity, while writers who had been banned in the GDR came to be viewed as tokens of past opposition rather than as relevant artists in the new society. In an anthology that explores the samizdat veterans' role in unified Germany, Frauke Meyer-Gosau, a West German publisher, outlines the publishers' pre-1989 interest in the samizdat writers, describing the writers as a "youthful manifestation of a literary outsider movement" (2001, 21). Underlying her analysis is the belief that the samizdat texts lacked appeal independent of their gesture of autonomy. She points out that West German publishers lost interest in the writers when it was disclosed in 1992 that two active figures in the self-publishing network had been informers for the Ministry of State Security (Stasi), since this disclosure undermined the quality of artistic sovereignty that the publishers had aimed to market. However, despite Meyer-Gosau's pronouncements, many of the artists and writers continued to be prolific a decade after the opening of the market. As much as they claimed in the 1980s that their work had nothing to do with opposition, now they might claim that it had nothing to do with the market.

Since the self-publishing writers and artists had already begun to question the socialist political system in the 1980s, the fall of the Wall allowed them to speak their minds more than it changed their views. In fact, it is surprising how little the new experiences influenced them. This attitude differs greatly from the attempts that emerged after the end of the Nazi regime to describe possible relationships to the totalitarian past. Two rhetorical tropes emerged in the 1940s and 1950s with which the attitudes of the 1990s can be contrasted. The West produced the idea of *Stunde null* (tabula rasa, or zero hour). In the GDR, the idea of a cultural "blank slate" was not an acceptable model, because social theorists deemed fascism too pervasive to wipe away (Emmerich 1989, 439). Instead, socialist culture was to be the new tool with which to fight the constant threat of fascism. A third concept, *Vergangenheitsbewältigung* (dealing with the past), arose later in the 1960s on both sides of the Wall when a new generation of Germans began to face their recent history.

The self-publishing poets of the 1980s deal consciously with these rhetorical reactions to historical rupture, simultaneously calling the concepts into question and reformulating them in their work. Following their predecessors, they reject the naïveté and historical amnesia of tabula rasa rhetoric, but they also reject their parents' goal of seeking atonement in a new way of life. Unlike the Nazi past, the GDR past does not fuel a drive for reconciliation.

Among former samizdat writers, Kurt Drawert has led the way in exploring the issue of ideological change since unification. His first anthology, *Privateigentum (Private Property)*, grew out of self-published texts. It was first published in the GDR by Aufbau in 1987 and was republished by the large West German publisher Suhrkamp in 1989. Although the end of the GDR was still three years away when Drawert completed the poem "Zweite Inventur" ("Second Inventory"), it alludes to the West German poet Günther Eich, who poetically explored the possibilities of tabula rasa following the end of the Nazi era. Eich is representative of the literary style called *Kahlschlagliteratur*, which translates literally into "clear-cut literature." Following the ideological confusion and complexity of the Third Reich, Eich and others sought peace of mind in poetic simplicity. Eich's poem "Inventur" ("Inventory") is composed of a list of basic belongings: "this is my towel / this is my thread" (1947, 17). It is a meditation on the essential in the hope that clarity might arise from literary quietness. Drawert's variation on "Inventur" is composed of a much longer list, and the items—used subway tickets, crumpled paper, and dirty laundry—represent clutter (1989, 27f.). Helmut Höge theorizes in the Berlin newspaper *Tageszeitung* that the samizdat writers immersed themselves in artistic chaos as an antidote against boredom in the overregulated GDR (2001, 23). Drawert's list portrays welcome disorder and rejects the *Kahlschlag* project of seeking purity in simple language. In a later text, Drawert presents a more explicit critique of the idea that a society can drop its ideological baggage with a change of government. In his narrative *Spiegelland: ein deutscher Monolog (Mirrorland: A German Monologue)*, he writes, "of course the concepts don't yet die with the nation that brought them forth" (1992, 12). He insists on the pervasiveness of ideology despite changes of government and economic landscape.

Thus, the third rhetorical concept that arose in the wake of the Third Reich, the concept of coming to terms with the past, is replaced by the expanded project of coming to terms with a variety of pasts and a questionable future. In several texts, the poets even conflate past and present by exploring the turnover of political power as one in a series of continuous reversals. Not only do they write about remnants of GDR mentality and experience that continue to be influential; they depict traces of the Nazi past emerging unexpectedly as the return of the repressed. In *Spiegelland*, the father is sent as a young boy to destroy the grandfather's Nazi documents by dropping them into a river (ibid., 146). The floating documents do not sink but instead line the riverbank. In a novel by Kerstin Hensel, letters written by fictional biology professor Malvenrath during the war surface randomly between specimens in the university's biological sciences collections (1991, 8). In Thomas Rosenlöcher's *Die Wiederentdeckung des Gehens beim Wandern* (*The Rediscovery of Walking While Hiking*), the narrator observes, "The new era had suddenly become the old. While the old era, which had been overcome long ago, was suddenly the new, creating new start-up problems" (ibid., 16). The writers' depiction of the tenacity of ideology breaks down the notion of clean historical epochs.

Rosenlöcher's narrative takes place within the setting of unification and exhibits skepticism toward both past and present. The narrator recollects, "A few months prior at the same kiosk I would have purchased the central organ of so-called socialism without the slightest hesitation and paged through the daily report of continuous successes" (1991, 10). The narrator goes on to wonder, "How could I [have done that] back then?" (ibid., 11) He contemplates the recent past for a moment but turns to current events, going on to consider the new "weightier" newspapers for sale at the kiosk the morning after the monetary union. The linguistic connection between weight, *Gewicht*, and importance, *Wichtigkeit*, creates an equation he then calls into question. Rosenlöcher's narrator postulates further that being informed does not lead to real social participation but only to the illusion that one can participate (ibid., 12). Drawert shares Rosenlöcher's skepticism of public expression in the new system. He writes, "but the *book*, the right to an opinion, the completion of the unsolicited text: how ridiculous, how pretentious" (1992, 150). Despite their doubts about the viability of public expression, Rosenlöcher and Drawert continued to publish throughout the 1990s.

Whereas Westerners think of the "free" market economy as the absence of ideology, it takes on the contours of an ideology through the eyes of the critical Eastern German narrator. Rosenlöcher weaves economic problems into the semiotics of East, West, and German nationalism. The bearded narrator, who personifies Karl Marx to the other characters, is confronted by a Western pharmacist whom he, in turn, envisions as the German national poet Goethe. Marx comments acerbically, "I should have known that Goethe drove a Mercedes" (1991, 61). The narrator celebrates the monetary union by making an excursion to the Harz Mountains. The Harz symbolize the footsteps of Goethe and Goethe's role as a poetic role model, but the region, lying on the former border between GDR and BRD, comes to represent a national unity that privileges the rich. Rosenlöcher rewrites the scene from Goethe's *Faust* of the Harz witch festival called *Walpurgisnacht*. In Rosenlöcher's text, *Walpurgisnacht* is the German World Cup victory of July 7, 1990, six days after the monetary union. The witches are the patriotic soccer rowdies. In the finale of Rosenlöcher's narrative, the ridicule of reds and pharmacists, past and present, gives way to anxiety about the pending national unification and its potential to ignite German nationalism.

The socialist literary program referred to the past in light of an improved future. Rosenlöcher is not convinced of the moral superiority of the present, and Drawert cannot complete the literary work of resolving the past because he suspects himself to be trapped in the language of his father and grandfather (ibid., 26). Both *Wiederentdeckung* and *Spiegelland* show anxieties about nationalism that are not present in early literary texts of either the GDR or the FRG.

Despite the communicative skepticism shown by Drawert and Rosenlöcher, publishing skyrocketed after Honecker resigned. The literature showed no break in the style or philosophy that had emerged in the previous decade, partly because a wave of unpublished manuscripts from the 1980s came out along with new material. Industrial "republishing" blurs the distinction between new and old work. The industrially republished versions of samizdat texts seldom provide original dates or version information.

Kerstin Hensel's 1991 novel *Auditorium panopticum* is an example of a postunification text that looks critically at the GDR without referencing the German unification and therefore leaving the context of its conception open. The title of the novel alludes to Hermann Kant's canonical socialist-realist novel *Die Aula* (*The Auditorium*), but Hensel explodes the socialist-realist model of authoritatively "mirroring" the successes of socialist reality from a single superior perspective, as prescribed by Lukács. Despite its fractured style, the novel depicts an atmosphere of oppression resulting from inept institutions. Hensel breaks up the narrative into the multiple perspectives of several exaggerated dysfunctional characters, such as the best student, the dropout, and a nude Valkyrie, who continuously encounter one another in a confined world. The story centers on a university in which not even the research interests go beyond the university basement, where biology professor Malvenrath discovers an albino cave amphibian. A montage of informers' reports for the secret police constitutes some of the chapters. Thus, in addition to its play on the title of Kant's novel, *Auditorium Panopticum* alludes to Foucault's analysis of surveillance, "panopticism" (Foucault 1979, 195), as a modern penal technique. No social niche is spared from the novel's ridicule. Hensel implicates the self-publishing writers as collaborators with the Ministry of State Security. "The People's Office of Projection and Subversion: Department of Current Events" organizes a fictional literary conference in the novel. The novel thus presents the self-publishing writers in an act of staged opposition. The question of whether the supposedly autonomous Prenzlauer Berg Scene writers were covertly involved with the Ministry of State Security first became an issue in 1991. Thus, historical knowledge available in 1991 is used to shape the story, but Hensel "deals with the past" without reference to the present, especially avoiding any teleological framework of future progress.

The story's obsession with surveillance and containment is surprising during a period of falling boundaries. Though the critique was in some ways dated, there was a demand for publication, finally, of critical views of the GDR that had until then circulated only "unofficially."

The new freedom to publish transformed the self-publishing writers into published authors. At the same time, the conversion to a system based on hard currency and capital growth brought the expectation that Germans from the "new states" would seek gainful employment, profoundly changing the context of writing and dividing professional from leisure-time writers. Political oppression was exchanged for the growth imperative.

A Prenzlauer Berg neighborhood periodical first published in 1994 under the title *Sklaven* (*Slaves*) has been taking issue with the labor expectations of the new system. In the 1920s, Franz Jung, a famous figure from the European Bohemia, first proposed a periodical called *Sklaven*, but it never came to fruition. The *Sklaven* of the 1990s reprinted and analyzed Jung's essays and letters as a way to address the problem of alienation of labor, which was suddenly taking on new meaning. Jung, who portrayed himself in his fictionalized autobiography *Der Weg nach Unten* (*The Way to the Bottom*) as a scam artist in capitalist Weimar Germany, maintained an interest throughout his life in the distribution of wealth, labor, and leisure. Walter Fähnders, writing on Jung for *Sklaven*, compares the thirteenth-century fantasy of luxury for all, Schlaraffenland (in the land of Cockaigne), with the sixteenth-century fantasy of full employment for all, *Utopia*. For the editors of *Sklaven*, Jung represents a critique of capitalism that avoids the dogmatism of GDR Marxism-Leninism.

Sklaven founders also organized weekly events, featuring, for example, a group called the Glücklichen Arbeitslosen (The Happily Unemployed). Poised somewhere between activists and satirists, the Glücklichen Arbeitslosen argue in their manifesto that it is not the condition of being unemployed that is regrettable but the condition of being "unfunded." Like Jung, they attempt to deconstruct the work ethic and the distribution of leisure. They use humor to raise awareness of contradictions in the system. For example, they carry to the next logical level the concept that full employment is corporate waste: "Logically one should thank the unemployed [person] that he is supporting the system more than anybody else [by making it more efficient]. Instead he doesn't get a single fart of the profit that he is helping to create" (1996, n.p.).

The Sklavenmarkt reached a poignant end in the year 2000, when the new management of the venue where events took place, the Prater, began requiring that all beverages be purchased on site (Gröschner 2001, 14). Annette Gröschner, a former editor of *Sklaven*, describes the 1990s as a transition period in which the rising cost of living changed the Eastern German urban neighborhoods, such as Prenzlauer Berg, by making work and meeting spaces unaffordable (ibid., 16). However, Gröschner also writes, "[The Prenzlauer Berg Scene] dies gladly and with fervor every few years" (ibid., 13). The phoenix-like quality of this subculture makes it unpredictable, and it is especially interesting with respect to the ways it overcomes the financial challenges of unification. After the Prater was closed to Sklaven events, one participant, Bert Papenfuß, opened his own bar, Kaffee Burger, where events could continue.

In order to procure the new hard currency, many of the artists and writers continued to freelance, supported by government funding and prizes as well as sales. But in the Prenzlauer Berg Scene, *freischaffend*, translated literally as "freely productive," never referred simply to the occupation of "freelance writer." It always had an entrepreneurial facet.

The first of several author-run publishing houses undertaken in Eastern Germany after the fall of the wall was BasisDruck, which quickly released a bestseller about the Ministry of State Security, *Ich liebe euch doch alle! Befehle und Lageberichte des Ministeriums für Staatssicherheit (But I Love You All! Orders and Reports of the Ministry of State Security)*. Printed in 1990, this book was the first analysis of the East German secret police to be published by and for East Germans. BasisDruck continued to publish books on sensational and popular East German topics such as life near the Berlin Wall (Scholze and Blask 1992) and the history of the East Berlin soccer club (Luther and Willmann 2000).

In the 1980s, artists in the GDR developed resource networks to deal with restrictions on information, such as the unreliable telephone infrastructure. The ability to exchange professional information helped artists and writers translate the self-publishing projects into incorporated businesses. Whereas writers and artists once passed information to each other about potential West German publishers, they might now inform each other about grants or galleries or how to incorporate a business. For example, the founders of BasisDruck coached Gerhard Wolf as he initiated the literary publishing house Janus Press before it was purchased by the bigger Western publisher Luchterhand. And wherever one finds one Prenzlauer Berg artist exhibiting, one can usually discover additional names from the 1980s artbooks.

The women artists' collective Dresdner Sezession 89 was still in business a decade after it was founded. Organized in part by Angela Hampel, an artist whose androgynous female figures stare piercingly from at least thirteen different self-published booklets, the members of Sezession operate a shared gallery, Galerie Drei (Gallery Three) in Dresden. They have produced diverse collective exhibitions since becoming the first organization of women artists in Dresden history. Sharing costs lightens the burden of financing gallery space. The artists' collective spans a range of age and experience, but the talent and innovations of each artist attracts attention to the entire collective. Furthermore, in a climate of political "agnosticism," the agenda of female cooperation lends the project an identity that other galleries lack. The Sezession was founded on the premise that female artists have been on the margins of Dresden's art tradition. There is no further reflection on theories of gender at the business level: "We focus ourselves on our existence as artistically productive women in a dominantly patriarchal society" (Dresdner Sezession 89 1991). However, despite these strategies, the exhibitions are mostly reviewed by local newspapers eager to promote Dresden as an art city.

A freelancer and an entrepreneur both require market courage. But as Rosenlöcher implies, more than freedom of speech is necessary for participation in public discourse. A sense of literary authority and the ability to navigate the culture industry are also necessary for an entry into public culture. A sense of authority built up in one social political context may not be impervious to the rigors of another. Indeed, some of the writers, such as Lothar Fiedler or Hendrik Melle, faded from the publishing world after emigrating West in the mid-1980s, in contrast to those who remained.

In many ways the attempt to "own the means of production" is a continuation of the autonomous spirit of samizdat. Those writers and artists who know both systems and who experienced a climate with less-sophisticated forces of marketing and advertising have the potential to provide an invaluable perspective. The radiance of these entrepreneurial cultural projects lies especially in their attempt to salvage from political and economic pressures space for intellectual and creative work, without which there can be no self-knowledge. The persistence of this active culture, even as local culture, is far more important for the richness of human experience than the writers' and artists' failure or success within the capitalism of unified Germany and the world market.

WORKS CITED

Danek, Sabine. "Art Cologne. Kunst ist Geld." *Spiegel Online*, November 5, 2000. Available online at http://www.spiegel.de/kultur/gesellschaft/0,1518,101440,00. html (accessed February 17, 2004).

Drawert, Kurt. *Privateigentum*. Frankfurt am Main: Suhrkamp, 1989.

———. *Spiegelland. Ein deutscher Monolog*. Frankfurt am Main: Suhrkamp, 1992.

Dresdner Sezession 89. *Dresdner Sezession 89*. Dresden: Druckhaus Dresden, 1991.

Lisa Whitmore

Eich, Günter. "Inventur." In *Deine Söhne, Europa. Gedichte deutscher Kriegsgefangener*, ed. Hans Werner Richter, 17. München: Nymphenburger Verlagshandlung, 1947.

Emmerich, Wolfgang. "Kein 'Nullpunkt': Das Programm der antifaschistisch-demokratischen Erneuerung (1945–49)." In *Deutsche Literaturgeschichte Von den Anfängen bis zur Gegenwart*, 3rd ed. Stuttgart: Metzler, 1989.

Fähnders, Walter. " '. . . daß Produktion Glück ist': Das Schlaraffenland ist eine plebejische Phantasie." Part 1. *Sklaven. Migranten, Melefikanten, Kombattanten* 20–21 (1996): 23–27.

Foucault, Michel. *Discipline and Punish: The Birth of The Prison*. Translated by Alan Sheridan. New York: Vintage, 1979.

Glücklichen Arbeitslosen aus Berlin. "Manifest der Glücklichen Arbeitslosen aus Berlin." Berlin: self-published, 1996.

Gröschner, Annett. "Szenenwechsel." In *Zersammelt. Die inoffizielle Literaturszene der DDR nach 1990. Eine Bestandsaufnahme*, ed. Roland Berbig, Birgit Dahlke, Michael Kämper-van den Boogaart, and Uwe Schoor, 12–19. Literaturforum im Brechthaus Recherchen 6. Berlin: Theater der Zeit, 2001.

Hensel, Kerstin. *Auditorium panopticum*. Leipzig: Mitteldeutscher Verlag, 1991.

Höge, Helmut. "Ausdehnung durch Reduktion." *Tageszeitung*, 1 April 2001, local edition, 23.

Jung, Franz. *Der Weg nach Unten*. Frankfurt am Main: Luchterhand, 1961.

Kant, Hermann. *Die Aula*. Berlin: Rütten & Loening, 1965.

Luther, Jörn, and Frank Willmann. *Und niemals vergessen—Eisern Union. Die Geschichte des Berliner Fußballclubs (And Never Forget—Mighty Union: The History of the Berlin Soccer Club)*. Berlin: BasisDruck, 2000.

Meyer-Gosau, Frauke. "Zu Markte getragen: Texte vom Prenzlauer Berg in der BRD." In *Zersammelt. Die inoffizielle Literaturszene der DDR nach 1990. Eine Bestandsaufnahme*, ed. Roland Berbig, Birgit Dahlke, Michael Kämper-van den Boogaart, and Uwe Schoor, 20–36. Literaturforum im Brechthaus Recherchen 6. Berlin: Theater der Zeit, 2001.

Michael, Klaus, and Thomas Wohlfahrt, eds. *Vogel oder Käfig sein. Kunst und Literatur aus unabhängigen Zeitschriften in der DDR 1979–1989*. Berlin: Galrev, 1992.

Michel, Elke. "Porree zu Geld. Wie schaffen es Künstler, von ihrer Kunst zu leben? Zwei Beispiele." *Die Zeit*, February 8, 2001, 51–52.

Mitter, Armin, and Stefan Wolle eds. *Ich liebe Euch doch alle*. Berlin: BasisDruck, 1990.

Rosenlöcher, Thomas. *Die Wiederentdeckung des Gehens beim Wandern. Harzreise*. Frankfurt am Main: Suhrkamp, 1991.

Schedlinski, Rainer, and Andreas Koziol, eds. *Abriß der Ariadnefabrik*. Berlin: Galrev, 1990.

Scholze, Thomas, and Falk Blask. *Halt. Grenzgebiet. Leben im Schatten der Mauer (Halt. Border. Life in the Shadow of the Wall)*. Berlin: BasisDruck, 1992.

four

Reading Transparent "Constructions of History"; or, Three Passages through (In)Visible Warsaw

Magdalena J. Zaborowska

The constructions of history are comparable to military orders that discipline the true life and confine it to barracks. On the other hand: the street insurgence of the anecdote. The anecdote brings things near to us spatially, lets them enter our life. It represents the strict antithesis to the sort of history which demands "empathy," which makes everything abstract. . . . Thus, the image of a historical course of time is totally transformed as soon as one brings to bear on it a standard adequate and comprehensible to human life.

—Walter Benjamin[1]

At the end of 1938, I wandered through [the] Warsaw night in fast-forward motion . . . [for] in the unconscious of a passerby it already swelled up with fires, screams, blood. . . . [T]he ever-changing, dynamic Warsaw of President Starzynski was becoming a mirage. . . .

[After the war] Warsaw emerges already petrified into a moonscape brightly lit up with memory—cool, because seen from another planet [London]. . . . Only after having known a different layout, different warmth, a different sense of homes elsewhere, could I appreciate and register the details of past life.

—Maria Kuncewicz[2]

Many years after Polish émigrée writer Maria Kuncewicz described walking through her beloved Warsaw on the brink of World War II, Elizabeth Wilson used similar imagery to map the modern city: "[O]ne never retraces the same pathway twice, for the city is [in] a constant process of change, and thus becomes dreamlike and magical, yet also terrifying in the way a dream can be. Life and its certainties slither away from underfoot. This continual flux and change is one of the most disquieting aspects of the modern city."[3] As European capitals go, Warsaw is an especially disquieting one. Its scarred layout and confusing structures have been determined by the kinds of nightmarish history that Benjamin describes as determined by "military orders," but they are also incomprehensible without the anecdotal evidence he deems essential, preserved by generations of dwellers, visitors, and artists. The three brief passages through Warsaw sketched out in this essay take the "flux and change" of the Polish capital for granted, for its turbulent history and oddly mixed architecture make it an example of modernity in its own right, one that puts to test modernity's Western definitions.

In the first passage, Warsaw emerges as a space of martyrdom, the invisible Jewish city wiped out by the Holocaust, whose haunting presence and resilient survivors have inspired efforts to recreate living memorials of departed people, spaces, and forms. The second brings back the post–World War II Warsaw, which became a testing ground for various processes of socialist and communist urban, economic, political, and ideological change, some of which were blamed for causing "the second demise of the city."[4] The last passage ends on the millennial threshold and glimpses Warsaw's ongoing colonization by office towers haphazardly erected by "globalized" corporations and the city's "building back," or responding with architectural assertions of its liminal, hybridic, post-communist identity.

My focus on these three moments in Warsaw's twentieth-century history arises from a desire to illustrate the ways in which its intricate urban fabric is woven of spaces narrating the interpenetration of extremes: past and present, death and survival, demolition and reconstruction, suppression and innovation, communism and capitalism, East and West.[5] Warsaw's overwhelming destruction during World War II and its subsequent ambivalent "(re)building" under the communist government largely erased the historic continuity of its cityscapes and architecture which had once earned it the nickname "the Paris of the North."[6] The socialist-realist capital built atop the rubble celebrated visibility and excess—of scale, decorativeness, and open space—and was seen by some writers as a "strange center of Europe and cosmos, a transparent desert outside of time."[7]

This odd mix of transparency of vision and desert landscape provides a useful metaphor that helps us see the Polish capital today as a fascinating hybrid: of World War II memorials, painstakingly reconstructed past splendor, and communist grayness and grotesque monumentality, as well as the new office parks, fast food restaurants, chain hotels, and omnipresent billboards that mark or mar the post-1989 period. Warsaw becomes a fascinating textbook of East European and world history as city narrative. Walter Benjamin envisioned nineteenth-century Paris as a prism though which to view Western historic and ideological processes in *The Arcades Project*. Warsaw's development in the last century certainly reflects and refracts Poland's changing fate and historic contribution as a country in the "former Soviet bloc," poised between East and West and burdened with legacies of "otherness" that make it both similar and unique among post-communist capitals. Its complex story also challenges the hegemony of the "modern European city," whose narrative has largely excluded urban complexes outside of the West and whose readers paid little attention to specific "standard[s] adequate and comprehensible to human life" in the Other/East Central Europe.[8]

The Largest (Invisible) Jewish City in Europe

Many visitors would agree with Marta Zielińska, whose popular book pronounces Warsaw a "strange city."[9] The Polish capital's nearly 80 percent destruction during World War II and subsequent near-miraculous reconstruction under the Soviet-imposed communist government make it not only "strange" but also sad and difficult to approach in comparison with other European cities. Today, growing as fast as Berlin, Warsaw seems different every day, and one can get lost very easily in the maze of new streets, high-rises, ditches, and towering webs of cranes. Deprived of anything lasting or immortal in its architectural fabric, Warsaw is filled with a longing for eternity; it is a city that has embraced otherness, impermanence, and liminality as its normal condition (Zielińska 1995, 28–30).

Warsaw's temporal, geographic, and cultural situation is indeed strange—it exists suspended between past and present, East and West, and is "neither ancient, nor especially civilized," as Zielińska points out. Unlike that of Rome, Warsaw's "'immortality' has a negative character"; it nurses at its core a certain lack and absence (ibid., 39). This is so because the Polish "unvanquished capital" is built on top of a vast cemetery—"the symbols of death are always present in [the] streets and do not arouse anybody's surprise," Zielińska stresses. "[There are] hundreds of plaques commemorating occupation-time executions. They are a kind of everyday 'memento mori.'" And how does one manage while living among ghosts? "If we wanted always to remember over what kinds of deposits of horror we walked every day, no one could sleep peacefully here. . . . Death in Warsaw . . . has been domesticated. . . . Life feeds on death and death on life. The boundaries between them are fluid" (ibid., 180–182).

Zielińska's statement that Warsaw has "domesticated" death, on the one hand, and has no claim to eternity, on the other, has an especially poignant and ambivalent ring to it when one considers that it was "resurrected" on the rubble of a Jewish city. The most tragic absence and deadly lack at the heart of the Polish capital was caused by the extermination of its Jewish population during the Holocaust. Between 1918 and 1939, Warsaw had the second-largest number of Jewish inhabitants in the world (after New York) and the largest in Europe. Its 380,000 Jews lived in several large neighborhoods and constituted

Magdalena J. Zaborowska

almost 30 percent of its citizens. These citizens and the parts of the city where they lived became the immediate target of Hitler's meticulously planned genocide. At the period of greatest congestion, the ghetto, which was cut off from the rest of the city in the fall of 1940, contained 450,000 people from Warsaw and the surrounding region. The vast majority of them fell victim to deadly diseases, starved to death, or were murdered, executed, and massively exterminated in concentration camps, especially Treblinka, if they did not die by fire or commit suicide during the Warsaw Ghetto Uprising in 1943.

Forced emigration of the majority of survivors in the wake of postwar pogroms,[10] deliberate silencing of the memory of the Holocaust and of the Jewish contributions to the country by the Polish government, and anti-Semitic political purges in 1968 deepened the already tragic invisibility of Polish Jews in the postwar capital. Today, Jewish Warsaw is a phantom, a haunting, invisible metropolis. It embraces a ghost network of erased streets, alien structures, and empty spaces in place of the once-vibrant districts that became a sea of rubble three to four stories high in the wake of the SS "Grossaktion" in the ghetto. As long as the Holocaust is remembered, this city will remain one of its most tragic and perhaps most ambivalent monuments, precisely because of the nearly complete erasure of its Jewishness. In the presence of war monuments and memorials, of which Warsaw has many, this poignant invisibility of the spaces and structures marking vibrant everyday Jewish life—streets, synagogues, squares—speaks the loudest. In the context of post-communist resurgences of nationalism, anti-Semitism, and white supremacist movements in Poland and all over the "New Europe," it inspires reflection about the ways architecture and urbanism are inextricably woven into, become active agents in, and bear witness to the historic and political processes that shape whole nations and continents.

Echoing Theodor Adorno and Günter Grass, Niels Gutschow and Barbara Klain ask whether urbanism is "possible after the experience of Auschwitz."[11] What that city and Warsaw underwent during the Nazi occupation— the simultaneity of "extermination and [architectural] utopia"—seems incomprehensible and astonishing to postwar generations. According to Gutschow, German architects never had so much freedom and power as during the war years of 1942–1944: "A circle of [them], friends of one another since the time of their studies in the early 1920s, invite each other to express opinions, causing thus a self-perpetuating process, one that was perceived as reality." In similar circumstances, Oskar Dengel ordered a project for the "new German city, Warsaw" from his colleagues in Würzburg. As Gutschow stresses: "Dengel did not have to have a client behind him, he didn't need an 'order from above.' On the contrary: this initiative was to propel his career. . . . Dengel's worldview was assessed thus [by Hitler's party]: 'positive, with no reservations, hates blacks'" (1995, 10).

In terms of spatial management, systematic genocide, like city planning, or like the transatlantic slave trade, requires careful design and efficiency.

Form must follow function, as the builders of the concentration camps (or slave ships) and those in charge of the so-called liquidation of the Warsaw ghetto knew only too well. Perhaps it is not sufficiently remembered that the Nazi war and death machine was in part constructed according to modernist ideals of progress and visions for a new city[12] and that Adolf Hitler thought architecture the supreme expression of Nazi ideology. Impressed with Le Corbusier's urban visions, such as "Plan Voisin," for example, many Nazi architects wished for a city like a tabula rasa, one that could be laid out and built from scratch according to their totalitarian visions. Placed in the "undeveloped" and "culturally inferior" East,[13] Warsaw offered Nazi engineers and architects a unique chance to remake it as a "new German city"[14] after the planned "removal" of the Jewish population and enslavement of the Poles. In particular, the Warsaw Jewish ghetto became, as Elizabeth Wilson writes, "the 'real' Nazi city . . . orderliness run mad in pursuit of extermination" (1991, 99).

Marek Edelman, one of the few surviving Ghetto Uprising leaders, describes the transformation of architecture at the Umschlagplatz—the point of deportation from which thousands were packed into cattle cars and taken to Treblinka during the "liquidation" of the ghetto: "It is a long way to the 'Umschlag.' . . . The tall walls surrounding it and closely guarded by gendarmes are broken at only one narrow place. Through this entrance the groups of helpless, powerless people are brought in. . . . The human torrent grows, deepens, floods the square, floods three large three-storey buildings, former schools. . . . People fill every inch of free space, crowd the buildings, bivouac in empty rooms, hallways, on the stairs."[15] While awaiting trial in postwar Warsaw, Briggadführer Jürgen Stroop, the SS officer in charge of the "Grossaktion"—the "architect" of the ghetto's final extermination—remembered his hard work: "[We had to] prepare the area of the former ghetto to answer the call of the present and the future . . . preparing the construction of a model residential district . . . which was to be created according to the architectonic and urban vision of German engineers."[16]

The German model "residential district" never came to be. By the end of 1944, the city was a sea of ruins, a metropolitan tabula rasa indeed, after the defeat of the Warsaw Uprising and the systematic destruction carried out by Nazi troops who were fleeing the Red Army offensive not even two years after the funeral pyre of the ghetto stopped burning. Images of Warsaw from that time persist in blurred photographs and documentary footage and have been movingly recreated in Roman Polanski's acclaimed 2002 film *The Pianist*, which recounts the story of one man's survival in wartime Warsaw. The hero, Władysław Szpilman, a composer and pianist, was accidentally saved from deportation from the Umschlagplatz, from where his whole family was taken to their deaths. Hidden by friends in a series of abandoned and sealed-off apartments, day after day he witnessed the death and annihilation of his people and city. *The Pianist* is full of excruciatingly detailed claustrophobic interiors, where Szpilman is vegetating unbeknown to his neighbors, and long perspectives of burned-out city blocks, where he wanders alone searching for food and shelter. Szpilman's autobiographical account, which inspired the screenplay by Ronald Harwood, relays the end of Warsaw by binding its Holocaust survivor and the butchered city in an intimate embrace. The new Crusoe, as he refers to himself, survives to tell the story:

> I was alone. Not just in a house or a neighborhood, but alone in the whole city, which until recently contained over a million and a half people and was one of the richer and more beautiful cities of Europe. Today it has been turned into ruins, filled with burnt out and demolished buildings, under which lay buried the whole nation's cultural treasures that had been collected for centuries, and the bodies of thousands of murdered people, who were decaying in the warmth of the last days of this autumn.[17]

After the war, areas where Jewish neighborhoods once thrived were erased and built over with drab socialist-realist apartment buildings. Jan Lebenstein comments ambivalently that postwar Warsaw "lacks a heart." He stresses that the demise of the city progressed in three stages: the bombardments of 1939, the "liquidation" of the ghetto in 1943, and the slow agony following the 1944 uprising, when the Red Army stationed on the Praga bank of the Vistula River passively watched Warsaw bleeding to death. "Warsaw's demolition was completed after the war," Lebenstein emphasizes. "It was conducted by the authorities and the so-called architects, who thought that progress meant the elimination of all that was old."[18] The tragic disappearance of architecture, city fabric, and citizens often brought a wreckage of human sympathy and solidarity as well, as the new authorities rushed to create a new, homogeneous culture. On the 60th anniversary of the Ghetto Uprising, Halina Bortnowska remembers what it felt like on the other side of the wall:

> Spring, sunshine, April clouds, dark, imposing. And swirling black snow is falling—flakes of soot. "It's from the Ghetto," says my mother wiping off this black snow from the window seal, from her face, eyes. "It's nothing, it's in the Ghetto." "In the Ghetto"—means not here, not by our place, this fire will not reach us, will not consume our street or my backyard (this would happen, but later and will be remembered with a separate anniversary). . . . And still, today, I am ashamed of that distance. I see in it the evil shadow of the wall reaching right into the soul. It was as if the authors of the Warsaw Holocaust succeeded in the effort of segregating them, the Jews, from the reach of human sympathy, as well as in excluding us from reaching where it could be felt.[19]

In Warsaw, life breeds death and death breeds life in ambivalent and unpredictable ways. The district of Muranów—or the area of the former ghetto—was filled with so much rubble that it was impossible to clear it after the war. Nathan Rappaport's 1948 monument to the Warsaw Ghetto Uprising now stands surrounded by uniform socialist-realist apartment buildings that are home to hundreds of families. Designed by Bohdan Lahert, these three- and

Nathan Rappaport's 1948 monument of the Warsaw Ghetto Uprising. 2000.
Photograph by Magdalena J. Zaborowska. Used by permission.

four-story structures were literally made from the ghetto debris, which provided "recycled" material for the concrete building blocks and the escarpment
on which the whole residential complex was erected (Szmit-Zawierucha 2000,
84–86). Unlike those in the ghetto, many Jewish structures outside of it could
have been preserved and reconstructed. In a deeply ironic bout of yet another
"utopian" city planning, this time under communism, such unique remnants
of Jewish Warsaw as Kronenberg Palace or the tenement house on Bagno
Street and Plac Grzybowski were demolished to make space for ugly structures
and streets sanctioned by the government and official ideology.

As Jan Sujecki reminds us, rebuilding often went hand in hand with clear
attempts at profanation. In 1956, there was a proposal to build a new thoroughfare that would cut in half the Jewish cemetery at Okopowa Street and
result in the destruction of 5,400 *matzva* and tombs (Sujecki 1998, 196). The
cemetery was spared, but the historic house in Bagno and the street itself
disappeared forever. A similar fate met a residential area at the lower edge of
the ghetto, which was rebuilt after the war and then demolished to provide
space for the gigantic structure of Joseph Stalin's Palace of Culture and Science in 1953–1955. That erection, "Poland's only skyscraper" during the
Cold War, meant the resettlement—or brutal uprooting—of people housed in
3,500 rooms.

At the turn of the millennium, as structures built according to the whims
of Party officials have begun to crumble, Jewish Warsaw persists through narrative and architectural shards of the past. A fragment of the external ghetto wall

Wojciech Klamerus and Hanna Szmalenberg's 1998 Umschlag Memorial. 2000.
Photographs by Magdalena J. Zaborowska. Used by permission.

still remains at Zlota Street #60 and is a regular stop for international tourists. A brick shed that once housed a school run by the "famed Rabbi Alter from Góra Kalwaria—the only trace of the ultra-orthodox Hassidic movement" was recently saved by Eleonora Bergman, an architect from Warsaw's Jewish Historical Institute.[20] The 1998 memorial at the Umschlagplatz,[21] situated on the upper edge of the ghetto and Stawki Street, from which hundreds of thousands were taken to death, replicates the actual narrow "entrance of no return" remembered in Edelman's narrative, "The Ghetto Fights." However, as Nora FitzGerald suggests, the "despairing trek from monument to plaque" fails to give one a sense of the past richness of Jewish Warsaw as a vibrant living city.[22]

A recent project of the Jewish Renaissance Foundation[23] aims to remedy this by rebuilding and redeveloping Nos. 7 and 9 at Próżna Street—two houses near Plac Grzybowski that were miraculously spared by the war and socialist urban developers. The $10 million project involves a complete and painstaking restoration of every element of the buildings, which used to house elegant residences and neighborhood shops. The project arises from what Menachem Rosensaft of the Jewish Renaissance Foundation calls "the beginning of a new era of people trying to build a community again . . . [one that will] also have its intellectual, cultural, and religious roots in what once was" (quoted in FitzGerald 1991). The buildings will house a kosher restaurant and bakery, a hardware store, a Jewish bookstore, a café, and a Judaica shop. There will also be an apartment recreated as a tribute to late-nineteenth-century Jewish life in Warsaw.

Próżna Street lies near Warsaw's Yiddish-language theater, whose dull gray modernist building also houses a German bank. The Lauder Community Center for Jewish Education and Youth Club are located in nearby Twarda Street as well, next door to the early-twentieth-century Little Knives (Nożyk) Synagogue. These signs of the returning visibility of Polish Jewish culture are aided by the Lauder Foundation Genealogy Project at the Jewish Historical Institute of Poland, which has helped many survivors and their descendants trace family roots or find long-lost relatives. As the publishers of *Midrasz*, a Jewish monthly launched in Poland in 1997, introduce their audience, it is clear that there is a whole new generation of "Poles of Jewish origin who have relatively recently become aware of their Jewishness, and are exploring it, or contemplating that possibility." These people, whose number *Midrasz* assesses "at some 25 thousand" and "whose needs [it] wants to satisfy, with the goal of bringing them closer to the Jewish world,"[24] may have the greatest impact on assuring the survival of Jewish culture and spaces in Poland.[25]

Those living in and visiting Warsaw will soon be able to frequent the restored neighborhood at Próżna Street and witness the construction of the Museum of the History of Polish Jews to stand opposite the memorial to the Warsaw Ghetto Uprising. The building, designed by Frank Gehry, with exhibition space by Event Communications of London, may become an architectural representation of new Jewish Warsaw. Its main purpose is to invite visitors

Little Knives (Nożyk)
Synagogue at Twarda Street.
2000. Photograph by
Magdalena J. Zaborowska.
Used by permission.

to take part in "a [multimedia] visual narrative of the millennial Jewish civilization that flourished in the lands of Poland, the civilization known as Eastern Ashkenaz." As a flier available at the site also states, the museum's goal is to recreate a vibrant and lively culture so that the visitors "will not view artifacts in display cases, but will be transported into a virtual world of marketplaces, and study houses, theaters and rallies."

The project is an international venue spearheaded by Jeshajahu Weinberg, who created the Museum of Diaspora in Tel Aviv and collaborated on the Holocaust Museum in Washington, D.C. The architecture, interiors, and displays, designed by an international team led by Jerzy Halbersztadt, will lend themselves to narrative and interactive participation. The invisible Jewish city and lost national culture will thus be recreated in multimedia displays and high-tech life-size dioramas, such as the one depicting a section of famous Nalewki Street in Warsaw. Visitors will be able to walk through the street while mingling with images of its inhabitants preserved on the recovered 1918 film footage; listening to the then-customary mixture of Yiddish, Polish, and Hebrew spoken there; and smelling traditional foods being cooked in the surrounding apartments.[26] The actual building of the Museum of the History of

Polish Jews is still years from being built, but the project has already gathered an enormous archive of over 40,000 catalogued, digitized, and replicated artifacts, and enthusiasts and fund-raisers are working in several countries across the Atlantic.

Can a Gehry building spell an end to Jewish Warsaw's invisibility? *World Architecture* thinks it would provide the "icing on the cake" in its rapidly developing economy, and might give the Polish capital "something to satisfy the international public's craving for fashionable novelty and distinctive form-making, even though it may lack the size and budget of Bilbao's Guggenheim."[27] The Lauder Foundation Web site records the controversy over whether the money might be better spent on aiding the living rather than preserving the artifacts and information about the past.[28] No matter what the controversy, publicity, and budget issues are, once erected, Warsaw's Jewish Museum will certainly help to restore rich multicultural spaces as much in Poland's capital city as in the minds and hearts of its dwellers and visitors, whose identities are being continually formed, contested, and reshaped by the challenges of our past.

Socialist Realist Chic, or the Second Coming of Pop Culture

For the first time in its history, Polish architecture—whose greatest values were formed on the basis of the struggle of the masses and the creativity of the people—has ceased to be the possession usurped by a narrow stratum of aristocracy or bourgeoisie and [has] become the property of all the people.

—Edmund Goldzamt[29]

A recent issue of *Newsweek* recalls a joke about a Frenchman and a Russian traveling in opposite directions on the Paris-Moscow train. When both trains stop at the same time in Warsaw, the Frenchman looks around surprised and asks, "Is this Moscow?" And the Russian asks, "Is this Paris?"[30] Apart from illustrating how much our perceptions of urban spaces are informed—if not conditioned—by where we live and come from, the joke comments on the historic paradoxes and bipolar representations of the Polish capital. In the myopic eye of the Westerner, Warsaw's ugly, "gargantuan," or "revolting" socialist-realist architecture marks the city as irrevocably stamped by Soviet domination and thus makes it barely distinguishable from Moscow.[31] Conversely, to a non-cosmopolitan stereotyped Russian deprived of cultural freedom, Poland's largest city, with its reconstructed charming old architecture, looms as great and glamorous as the "West" in its difference from home and exotic attractiveness.

Between the imperative to embrace the new, socialist, and modern and the desire to preserve the old, Warsaw of 1945–1989 was shaped by curious paradoxes of city planning and (re)construction. In the last decade, amid the growing fashion and nostalgia for what in Polish is known as PRL (Polish People's Republic) culture, on the one hand, and increasingly reactionary views on Polishness, on the other, a discussion of the ideological and political underpinnings of the city's architectural remaking has finally begun to take place. Apart from confusion about the ways in which Warsaw should develop these days, this reassessment of its postwar design has revealed a profound hunger for spatial participation not only among architects and cultural critics but also among average citizens. For despite the repressive and garish aesthetic of the period that shaped the majority, Warsovians have been able to interact with their city and make its architecture theirs in their own strange and often-paradoxical ways.

Writing in 1979, irreverent journalist Stefan Kisielewski inveighed against "the kingdom of concrete-covered, devoid of style, anti-artistic, and destructive ugliness" of most of rural Poland.[32] Unlike the countryside, Warsaw was to be Poland's representational space, a loud advertisement for the new system and the new man who came in the wake of Big Brother's *homo sovieticus*. In a painfully ironic twist of fate, postwar urban planners and architects were offered in ravaged Warsaw a city that was virtually a tabula rasa, on which avant-garde theories of a "functional" socialist capital could be freely tested. Among the overexposed structures and urban spaces that resulted from that process are the headquarters of the Polish United Workers Party at Jerozolimskie Avenue, Plac Konstytucji and the MDM residential district (Marszałkowska Dzielnica Mieszkaniowa), the East-West Artery (Trasa W-Z), and the "gift" from Stalin—the Palace of Culture and Science (Pałac Kultury i Nauki) that rests in the heart of the largest square in Europe.

With the advent of 1989, these structures that were once the socialist capital's architectural pride and joy could finally be criticized. Many architectural historians angrily condemned the postwar period, agreeing with Sujecki's and Lebenstein's claims that it had spelled "the other demise of the city." In a badly needed reassessment of the capital's post-1945 urban planning, Jerzy S. Majewski and Tomasz Markiewicz speak about the "mass-scale ideological postwar demolitions" sanctioned by the Bureau for Reconstruction of the Capital (Biuro Odbudowy Stolicy, BOS) (1998, 155). The main group of architects employed by BOS was educated under the influence of modernist ideas, especially those of Le Corbusier, whose ville radieuse they thought an especially attractive inspiration for planning the new Warsaw.[33] Their vision coincided with the propaganda designs of the Party, which embraced architecture as a metaphor and vehicle for the country's new ideology. Amid creation of the new political system—or the "dictatorship of the proletariat"—the (re)building of Warsaw became a pet project of party officials, who often meddled in actual designs and labeled whatever they disliked "bourgeois" or "Western modernist."

While some were erecting a new downtown for the proletariat, brigades of Stakhanovite work-norm-breaking laborers were also sent to begin the reconstruction of some of Warsaw's old sections—an ideological move meant to win support for the Party among tradition-loving and largely anti-Soviet Poles. The best-known and most-familiar of these structures and areas are the Old Town and the Royal Castle, parts of the Royal Tract, and the boutique- and souvenir shop–lined streets of Krakowskie Przedmieście and Nowy Świat. In 1950, Grażyna Woysznis-Terlikowska's *Warsaw of Yesterday-Today-Tomorrow* offered a curious example of how the rhetoric of the old and the new, of tradition and modernization, the homeland that was gone for ever and the one still in the making, intertwined in the official newspeak:

> And when on July 22, 1949, amid a sudden silence which fell upon the emotional masses, the President of the Polish People's Republic, Bolesław Bierut, cut the white-and-red ribbon, thus giving to Warsaw the East-West Artery, thousands of eyes turned toward the wreckage of the Royal Castle to the rubble of the Old Town. Because everyone knew then that the battle of Warsaw had been won. That the opening of the East-West Artery meant the opening of new, magnificent perspectives. That the Castle would soon rise again. That the Old Town would rise up. Because we knew that after the creation of the East-West Artery, there was nothing impossible for our city.[34]

In this dramatic rendition of a carefully staged communist ritual, the debris of the old Warsaw is anthropomorphized and resurrected in the futurist utopian gaze of the masses. In a moment of collectively envisioning the transparent city of the future, the crowd communes in conversion to the new ideology. The reconstruction task that faces them is "incredibly difficult," yet it "inspires passion" and is "filled with revolutionary romanticism." All through the passage, the East-West Artery serves as the proof and tangible guarantee, the axis supporting the reality and materiality of the ideological message. Its scale and geographic orientation—like the revolution, the dawn of freedom, it comes from the East—anchor the "spiritual" and "romantic" elements of the vision, in which the city's "bourgeois" past is rendered harmless. After this compressed collective epiphany/initiation, workers and spectators recognize one another in the rubble of the Old Town, united by their passionate labor (Woysznis-Terlikowska 1950, 46).

It is important to realize that the masses of consumers and producers of socialist-realist spaces portrayed in such propagandistic visions were more than brainwashed puppets in the hands of the regime, indifferent to changes in their environment. David Crawley writes that in the West, the Poles were often seen as "no more than dramatis personae: occasionally acting as heroic re-sisters and sometimes as victims" within the "monolithic officially sanctioned sphere" of socialist culture. Such a view downplays the possibility of agency; that is, the fact "that the culture which was made available through centralised provision might be used by its consumers in ways unimagined by those who produced it . . . [or that] the Poles may have been selective in the pleasure that they took in the forms of culture available to them."[35]

A faded photograph of my grandfather and aunts taken in front of the newly opened Palace of Culture about 1954–1955 in no way registered their support for Soviet hegemony in the region. It was simply a snapshot from a sunny-day excursion to the capital city that boasted the country's only sky-scraper. Who cared that the Palace was Stalin's idea and "gift"? It was quite a spectacle to behold, and everybody wanted to own some part of it. A Warsaw architect who practiced underground during the war, Zygmunt Skibniewski, remembers 1945 thus: "Right after the war—the reconstruction years. I must admit that this was the most intense and beautiful period of my life. There was lots of work and I was in love" (Gutschow and Klain 1995, 12). I, too, can't help recalling how fun the May Day parades could be once the boredom of speeches, obedient clapping, and synchronized cheering was over. Children had a day off from school and were given all kinds of colorful props to wave and play with during the parade, and they could keep them after it ended; people watching gained a new dimension as we trod the streets that were closed to traffic that one day in the year. Dad took us out for ice cream and soda when the march was over (our fiercely antiregime mother usually stayed home); it felt like playing hooky, but with the First Secretary's blessing. This anecdotal evidence of the complexity and usability of the past confirms Benjamin's argument that such bits and pieces of local history "bring . . . things near to us spatially, let . . . them enter our life."

Looking at the changes that have taken place in Warsaw during the past decade, Szmit-Zawierucha criticizes Warsaw's "un-European" relationship to its past. On the one hand, the Old Town, no matter that it was resurrected by the communists and stripped of some of its historic, religious, and bourgeois details in the process, has become an integral part of the city. On the other, post-1989 Warsaw does not seem to value the lessons of its recent past. As if trying to outdo the communists, who enacted their conquest of the city with architecture and language, the new rulers change street names left and right as if they bear no connection to national history and collective memory (2000, 134). The nostalgia of some citizens and politicians for the invisible, irrevocably lost "Paris of the North" often disguises reactionary and nationalistic sentiments. First ravaged by Nazis, then by Soviets, and now made even more invisible by free-marketers of so-called globalization, Warsaw is a changing set of historic transparencies to each of its dwellers. Conflicting views on what it should be are not as surprising as the most recent interest in the material culture of the communist era.

Two exhibits devoted to this topic opened in Warsaw during the summer of 2000. Both of the organizers of the exhibits, Zachęta Gallery and the National Museum, experienced an unusually high turnout of visitors hungry for what could perhaps be translated as soc-realist retro, PRL chic, or a campy comeback of communist culture. Suddenly a hair dryer, a poster with a red Party slogan, or a beat-up Syrenka—a popular family means of transportation, a two-cylinder car known for its foul-smelling exhaust and popularly nicknamed "a dirty sock"—regained cultural value. These objects or fetishes of the past that had been safely sealed and nearly forgotten were not the only attraction. In

Visiting the Palace for
pleasure. Ca. 1954.
Zaborowska family archives.
Used by permission.

the National Museum, people were lining up to sample meals in a realistically replicated "dairy bar" (*bar mleczny*)—the chain eatery of choice for students and the poor in the old days of shortages and rations.[36] There was even a dead-serious proposal to open a "museum of communism" in the Palace of Culture, which suggests a longing for more permanent access to spaces and objects from the Soviet-bloc past. On the other hand, in the post-1989 spirit, the idea might also have signaled a more enterprising and prosaic attempt to capitalize on the fashion for *Ostalgia* Polish style, especially given the growing tourist interest in hunting the remnants of "exotic" red-hued history in East European countries.

For the time being, the exhibits of soc-art and soc-space will have to do for the Warsovians, because the museum of communism project has been put on hold.[37] But this budding interest in its most recent past, some hope, may also mean that Poland is not embracing the transitional cultural forms that accompany its new fast-paced economy and the political makeover brought about by the "West-to-East Tract" as easily as enthusiasts of NATO and the EU might like to think. Warsaw's rapidly changing skyline signals yet another process of rendering transparent or invisible a period of history whose difficult but valuable lessons should reach far outside the city limits. As the country and its capital are poised to be assumed into the European Union in 2004, this need to embrace and learn from the past manifests itself in some of its newest architecture.

"Hinc Omnia": Open Stacks and Free Access, or City as Library

A homogenous and utterly simultaneous space would be strictly imperceptible. It would lack the conflictual component . . . of the contrast between symmetry and asymmetry. . . . [T]he architectural and urbanistic space of modernity tends precisely towards this homogenous state of affairs, towards a place of confusion and fusion between geometrical and visual which inspires a kind of physical discomfort. Everything is alike. Localization—and lateralization— are no more. Signifier and signified, marks and markers, are added after the fact—as decorations, so to speak. This reinforces . . . the feeling of desertedness, and adds to the malaise.

—Henri Lefebvre[38]

Over a decade after the fall of communism in East Central Europe, Warsaw still retains some of its neither-West-nor-East, a-little-Moscow-and-a-little-Paris liminal character. As Elizabeth Grosz states, the city "has become . . . the point of reference, the centerpiece of a notion of economic/Socialist/political/cultural exchange"[39] Perhaps more than any other capital in post-1989 Europe, Warsaw is a textbook on the politics of urban planning, the social and ethical responsibilities of architecture, and ways to rebuild communities and spaces in newly independent nations. In the wake of the often-ruthless and predatory encroachment of foreign businesses—what some Poles refer to as a rapacious capitalist "colonization" of their country weakened by decades of communist economic devastation—this city seems overrun, if not besieged, by haphazardly placed specimens of "Western" architecture. New office towers and parks, banks, apartments, motels, and shopping malls seem to have been lifted from Greenville/Spartanburg, South Carolina, or Bakersville, California, and dropped in the Polish capital to disrupt the city's already-chaotic fabric further and to compete in ugliness with the worst of the socialist-realist relics. Asked why this is happening, the Warsovians shake their heads and shrug, much the way they used to twenty years ago, except that now they can say out loud that it's the corrupt politicians and local government who pander to the highest bidder with no concern for the city's needs. It's a free country, after all, and no one censors anyone anymore (except perhaps for the truly Foucauldian self-censoring practiced by much of the media and business in the face of the resurgent cultural and political hegemony of the Catholic church). The new enterprising reborn Catholics in the capital, like my high school friend Artur, combine the new and the traditional—he carries a credit card–like rectangle of plastic with the image of Poland's Black Madonna, the Częstochowa Virgin Mary, on one side and miniature rosary beads on the other. "It's a great space saver," he says.

How is it possible to retain, revise, and (re)construct a city identity in such a climate? What stories can buildings tell at a time when corporate sponsorship provides an inevitable narrative matrix for—or erases any possibility of—the majority of projects? Amid the post-1989 construction chaos, with a coherent and publicly accepted plan for the city's long-term growth still in the making, the recently opened Warsaw University Library (BUW) is an example of a team effort that has made the paradoxes of the past and present work on behalf of public architecture. It was designed by a team which won a national competition: Marek Budzyński, Anna Chmura, Zbigniew Badowski, Jacek Rzyski, Urszula Lewy, and Wojciech Kłos. The building's eclectic and self-conscious design reinterprets modernist and postmodernist traditions while playfully nodding at monumental symbols familiar from recent decades and engaging cutting-edge approaches to public space and material.

Post-1989 newly capitalist Warsaw is a fertile ground for testing and contesting Henri Lefebvre's ideas about the social production of space. As an example of "talking" architecture,[40] Warsaw University Library joins other successful Polish projects of the last decade that have attempted to "build back" against the blandness of Western commercialism, to inscribe through architectural forms a search for cultural identity that is rooted in both tradition and experimentation. "Talking architecture," or a desire for links between oral expression and spatial form, between language and material texture, is nothing new. But, as I hope I have shown, Warsaw stories are not easily accommodated, and the pleasures of a good read, like those of a city tour, can be hard won here. They entail long hours of study and confrontation with facts, spaces, people, ideas, structures, passages, monuments, and meanings that challenge, sadden, and disturb as often as they move and delight us.

The new library is a book—its gently arched frontal elevation is composed of open "pages" seven meters high that carry inscriptions in Sanskrit, Hebrew, Arabic, Greek, Old Church Slavonic, and Old Polish. There is also a page of mathematical formulae and a musical score. Like the city's, this building's story, its genesis, is a hybrid of paradoxes; it builds on the painful past and opens into spaces of the present. Quite like a post-communist fairy tale, the story begins with a generous decision by the first post-communist prime minister, Tadeusz Mazowiecki, who gave Warsaw University the profits from leasing the former headquarters of the Central Committee of the Polish United Workers Party at Aleje Jerozolimskie. $80 million later, from this venue and other funds, the dreams of over 50,000 students, librarians, and faculty that had once been deemed "impossible" were realized. The state-of-the-art facility has an estimated capacity of 6 million volumes, and it boasts the most accessible system of open stacks in the country. "Hinc Omnia"—"From here, everything"—is the project's motto, inscribed on the bronzed pages of a volume that hangs suspended in transparent glass over the internal library entrance.

The authors of the project emphasize its ecological design, which includes vegetation climbing over and covering the concrete, copper, steel, and glass elevation, while the transparent roof carries a garden that connects the

Warsaw University Library, façade. 2000. Photograph by Magdalena J. Zaborowska.
Used by permission.

structure to the land around it. This pastoral setting for leisurely strolls and
relaxed reading during good weather exists because of and in an interesting
symbiosis with commerce that is hidden from view. To make money for future
expansions of the university, the so-called croissant wing of the building, the
one that bears the "holy pages" of human knowledge, also houses a bank, an
advertising agency, and commercial spaces. Thus, the pages of wisdom—like a
"fig leaf of culture" (Bartosiewicz 1999, 17)—cover the economic mechanism
that makes the "production of knowledge" possible in the light-flooded, open-
to-all-with-a-valid-card halls of the library. Once they have turned the anticipated profit, these commercial spaces will in the future become library offices
and storage facilities. Like them, the former Party headquarters is still making
money for the University "on the side"—a condition necessary for sustenance
in the free-market economy after decades of uneasy state sponsorship.

With the money and the students, the whole city comes to the library.
Inside the cobblestone entry hall, which may remind one of Paris's *passages
couverts* and add yet another postsocialist twist to Benjamin's musings on the
topic, there are cafés, a bookstore, exhibition halls, and spaces to sit. From that
public passage and space of commerce and consumerism, one enters the
temple of the library, which greets one with four unmistakably pseudo-socialist-
realist figures of famous male philosophers mounted on concrete pedestals.
The only element of the interior they seem to match is the out-of-place-looking
chair where His Holiness the Pope once sat. All together, these slightly outland-

Warsaw University Library,
interior passage. 2000.
Photograph by Magdalena J.
Zaborowska. Used by
permission.

ish elements provide a bit of unexpected, almost comic relief in the library's
otherwise uplifting and impressive central space. It is important, however, that
the sacred and the profound mix freely right below the library, where a family
recreation center holds a climbing wall, billiard tables, an eatery, and a bowl-
ing alley, enabling one to spend hours and lots of money in idle pursuits.

The profitable family entertainments in the basement are not the only
Western imports and signs of pop-cultural and technological globalization.
The call-number system upstairs, on the level devoted to intellectual labor, has
been imported from the U.S. Library of Congress, while the general contrac-
tor, PORR Projekt und Hochbau AG from Austria, represents a sound investment by the European Union. To ensure the support of both the goddess
Fortuna and official religious powers, the pope was invited to consecrate the
finished building. Now a plaque devoted to that event, along with his chair,
marks the presence of the country's new official belief system inside the structure. (When I was visiting, there was a ladder propped up against the wall right
by the plaque; for a moment I mistakenly took it for an art installation because
it looked so appealing. A real art installation would not have surprised me
more than the fact that it was not.)

Warsaw University Library, interior, view from the first floor. 2000. Photograph by
Magdalena J. Zaborowska. Used by permission.

A postmodern temple above the marketplace of commercial pleasures,
the library is still marked by past destruction. Because Warsaw lost almost all of
its rich, painstakingly maintained book, archive, and precious print collections
during World War II, the library performs an important function as a reposi-
tory of surviving national heritage and a space where new knowledge is produced. A fan of book bonfires, Hitler unleashed his hordes with special vicious-
ness against Warsaw's collections. The Krasińskich Library was destroyed with
methodical precision: "the Germans . . . carrying flame throwers went from
floor to floor, for as long as it took to send up in smoke two hundred fifty
thousand old prints . . . a collection of maps, manuscripts, incunabula" (Szmit-
Zawierucha 2000, 83).

As much as Warsaw wants to distance itself not only from the horrors of the
war but also from the repressive period of communist rule, it cannot escape the
fact that it has been irrevocably scarred and formed by both. Ghosts of people,
books, and architecture—a whole Jewish city and national past preserved on
paper burned alive—will haunt it forever but also quicken the beating of its
(in)visible heart. This part of Warsaw's story makes the Warsaw University
Library a memorial to what has been lost. But it also makes it embody hope
and freedom, a space of living memory for the generations who have finally
been granted "open access" to the production of human and humane knowledge, forms, and structures. In the punch line in a Polish joke about a conven-

tion of East European architects who argue over which is the most beautiful city in the region, the Polish architect says to the Czech from Prague that it is definitely Warsaw, "because it was worth fighting for."[41]

NOTES

An earlier version of this essay, entitled "Three Passages through (In)Visible Warsaw," was published in *Harvard Design Magazine* 13 (Winter/Spring 2001): 52–59. I would like to thank Coleman A. Jordan and Leszek Cicirko for their assistance with obtaining the visual material for this project.

1. Walter Benjamin, *The Arcades Project,* trans. Howard Eiland and Kevin McLaughlin (Cambridge, Mass., and London: The Belknap Press of Harvard University Press, 1999), 545.

2. Maria Kuncewiczowa, *Dyliżans warszawski* (*Warsaw Stagecoach*) (Warszawa: Instytut Wydawniczy Pax, 1997), 6–7. All translations from Polish are mine, unless otherwise noted.

3. Elizabeth Wilson, *The Sphinx and the City: Urban Life, the Control of Disorder, and Women* (Berkeley: University of California Press, 1991), 3.

4. See Janusz Sujecki, "Druga śmierć miasta. Przyczyny i konsekwencje," in *Historyczne centrum Warszawy: Urbanistyka, architektura, problemy konserwatorskie,* ed. Bożena Wierzbicka (Warszawa: Biblioteka Towarzystwa Opieki nad Zabytkami, 1998), 191.

5. The trope of weaving was inspired by Jennifer Bloomer's work on the "slippage of the boundary between visual and verbal criteria." I refer to it as signaling a connection rather than developing a deeper theoretical argument, which lies beyond the scope of the present project. See Jennifer Bloomer, *Architecture and the Texts: The (S)crypts of Joyce and Piranesi* (New Haven, Conn., and London: Yale University Press, 1993), 7–11.

6. See Danuta Szmit-Zawierucha, *Opowieści o Warszawie* (Warszawa: Wydawnictwo DiG, 2000), 24–25.

7. See Marta Zielińska, who discusses Tadeusz Konwicki, Miron Białoszewski, and Leopold Tyrmand in *Warszawa—dziwne miasto* (Warszawa: Instytut Badań Literackich, 1995), 59.

8. It is not my intention to discuss the complex semantics of the terms used to refer to the whole region, as they have been dealt with in the introduction to this volume. Rather, my essay provides a glimpse—somewhat "Polish" and "Warsovian"—of the multiplicity, hybridity, and even inaccuracy of the vocabularies developed to define and make appear as separate the two elusive cultural spheres of the post–World War II "East" and "West."

9. Zielińska's title translates as *Warsaw: A Strange City.*

10. Space constraints do not permit me to engage this topic in greater depth. Recent scholarship and discussions in the Polish media on wartime and postwar Polish-Jewish relations provide a larger historic and geographic background for my subject.

11. Niels Gutschow and Barbara Klain, *Zagłada i utopia. Urbanistyka Warszawy w latach 1939–1945. Vernichtung und Utopie. Stadtplanung Warschau 1939–1945* (Frankfurt/Main and Warsaw: Deutscher Werkbund e.V., Muzeum Historyczne m.st. Warszawy, 1995), 10–11.

12. Elizabeth Wilson discusses ambivalent responses to modernism in Nazi Germany and Le Corbusier's willingness to "flirt both with socialism and with fascism if they would support him." *The Sphinx in the City*, 95–99.

13. Larry Wolff discusses the historic roots of invented Eastern European "backwardness" in *Inventing Eastern Europe: The Map of Civilization on the Mind of the Enlightenment* (Stanford, Calif.: Stanford University Press, 1994).

14. See Gutschow and Klain, *Zagłada i utopia*, 15–16, 22–24.

15. Marek Edelman, "The Ghetto Fights," in *The Warsaw Ghetto: Das Warschauer Ghetto*, designed and produced by Bożena and Marek Potyralscy (Warsaw: Drukarnia Naukowo-Techniczna, n.d.), 32.

16. Quoted in Gutschow and Klain, *Zagłada i utopia*, 62–63.

17. Władysław Szpilman, *Pianista* (Kraków: Wydawnictwo Znak, 2002), 157.

18. Jan Lebenstein, "Czy Warszawa jest miastem z ludzką twarzą?" *Architektura/Murator* 4, no. 55 (April 1999): 81.

19. Quoted at http://www.jewish.org.pl/polskie/materialy/powstanie/powstanie.html (accessed February 17, 2004).

20. See Christopher Bobinski, "Warsaw Is Acknowledging Its Jewish Past," *The Financial Times* (London), September 27, 1997, 22.

21. Design by Wojciech Klamerus and Hanna Szmalenberg.

22. Nora FitzGerald, "In Warsaw, a Jewish Street Reborn," *The Washington Post*, July 13, 1999, C1, C8.

23. Funded by Ronald Lauder.

24. Publicity materials obtained at the Jewish Visitors Information Center at Twarda 6 in Warsaw.

25. For the 60th anniversary of the Ghetto Uprising, Wirydarz, a "group for collective action and study against anti-Semitism and xenophobia" prepared a project that included an installation and a photo reportage, "spaces behind the wall": see http://wirydarz.w.interia.pl/projekt_swiadomy/archiwum/04/index.html (accessed February 20, 2004).

26. For more information, see Joanna Podgórska, "Powrócić tu" ("To Return Here"), *Polityka*, 20, no. 2350 (May 18, 2002): 70–72.

27. Peter Wislocki, "Warsaw's Identity Crisis," *World Architecture* 86 (May 2000): 35.

28. See http://www.jewish.org.pl/polskie/materialy/index.html (accessed February 17, 2004).

29. Edmund Goldzamt, *Architektura zespołów śródmiejskich i problemy dziedzictwa* (Warszawa: Państwowe Wydawnictwo Naukowe, 1956), 403.

30. Andrew Nagorski, "The Polish-Russian Gap," *Newsweek*, July 17, 2000, 4.

31. Wolff stresses that the Western invention of Warsaw's and Poland's "Easternness" actually originated during the Enlightenment. See *Inventing Eastern Europe*, especially 235–283.

32. Stefan Kisielewski, *Wołanie na puszczy. Pisma wybrane* (Warszawa: Iskry, 1997), 256.

33. See Jerzy S. Majewski and Tomasz Markiewicz, *Warszawa nie odbudowana* (Warszawa: Wydawnictwo-DiG, 1998), 10–11.

34. Grażyna Woysznis-Terlikowska, *Wczoraj-dziś-jutro Warszawy* (Warszawa: Książka i Wiedza, 1950), 46.

35. David Crawley, "People's Warsaw, Popular Warsaw," *Journal of Design History* 10, no. 2 (1997): 206.

36. See Zdzisław Pietrasik, "Odkurzony Peerel," *Polityka* 30 (22 lipca 2000): 3–9.

37. On the controversy surrounding this project, see Ewa Rozwadowska, "Socland, sosland—Czy powstanie muzeum komunizmu w Warszawie?" *Architektura/ Murator* 1, no. 64 (styczeń 2000): 51–55. A Museum of Socialist Realism already exists, in the Zamoyski Palace in Kozłowka.

38. Henri Lefebvre, *The Production of Space*, trans. Donald Nicholson-Smith (Oxford and Cambridge: Blackwell Publishers, 1994), 200.

39. Elizabeth Grosz, "Bodies-Cities," in *Sexuality and Space*, ed. Beatriz Colomina (New York: Princeton Architectural Press, 1992), 242–243.

40. Dariusz Bartosiewicz, "Nadwiślański cud biblioteczny," *Magazyn Budowalny* 7 (1999): 16–21.

41. Quoted in Ian Fisher, "Too Picturesque for Its Own Good?" *New York Times Magazine,* June 15, 2003, 20. (While I interpret the joke differently for my purposes here, I agree somewhat with Fisher's conclusion about Prague, too.)

five
Can Prague Learn from L.A.?

Frank Gehry's Netherlands
National Building in Prague

David Houston

As the countries of East and Central Europe emerge from under the weight of Soviet occupation, they each face a variety of urban challenges, from rebuilding Bosnia-Herzegovina to protecting historic districts from the corrosive influence of unbridled new development. The issue of weighing historic preservation against new development has been at the center of the debate over the Netherlands National Building, designed by American architect Frank Gehry, in Prague's historic core. Working with a program and site previously proposed by Yugoslav-born architect Vladimir Milunić, Gehry designed a building that immediately became a potent symbol of post-Soviet Prague's refusal (and inability) to remain suspended in a museum-like stasis. The ensuing debate over the Netherlands project has extended far beyond preservationist concerns and has rekindled discussions on national architectural identity and self-determination that were last argued in 1937, prior to the Nazi invasion.

In June of 1993, President Václav Havel addressed the Pritzker Prize award ceremony in the great hall of Hradčany Castle and invited the architects of the West to build in Prague. The unceremonious delivery of this invitation sent waves of surprise through the audience. The many representatives of the Czech architectural establishment registered obvious concern about the idea's implications, while the potential invitees were obviously delighted. The first

Western architect to benefit from the invitation, Frank Gehry, was present in that audience. The construction of his Netherlands National Building thus clearly demonstrates that Prague's architectural character is not fixed and that its future integrity is not secure either, no matter what zoning and historical ordinances might protect it. The mark of an American postmodern architect has added a new layer of contemporary architectural activity, reawakening the city's urban development and rekindling smoldering debates over Czech architectural and national identity.

The initial controversy over Gehry's proposed mixed-use building—for office, commercial, and entertainment space—involved site and context. Located just across from the National Theater on the Vltava River, the prominent corner site was only one of three such sites available for new construction in Prague's highly regulated historic district. The lot had remained vacant since its accidental bombing by an American plane during the Second World War. Located at the end of a row of undistinguished predominantly nineteenth-century buildings, Gehry's project is visible from as far away as the Charles Bridge and the Castle, thus assuming an important presence amid a complex fabric of more than five centuries of urban development.

From the outset, both the dynamic character and the overwhelming scale of the building raised concerns within the Czech architectural community. Projecting twin towers over the sidewalk, in a dancelike counterpoint to the bulging mass of the main structure, the building required significant variances in zoning ordinances that called for buildings to be set back to the edge of the sidewalk. Since the Gehry building is located near the apartment of President Václav Havel—who inspired the original Milunić proposal—the expediency with which zoning variances[1] were granted for such a controversial and aesthetically dominant project raised lasting concerns over the city's ability to regulate the character of its architectural future. These concerns appear especially well founded in the face of the potent alliance among power politics, foreign investment capital, and a celebrated American architect.

Dubbed "Fred and Ginger" by the architect himself, Gehry's building employs the metaphor of the dancers in the overwhelming stance of self-display inherent in its dynamic character. Depending on one's point of view, the building embodies either the elegance and playful interaction of dance or the awkwardness of an unwelcome guest dancing at an inappropriate place or time. Arguably, one can see an affinity between elements of the building and the baroque and art nouveau layers in the city. The Medusa-like sculpture crowning the Netherlands Building echoes the rounded medieval tower just upriver, and it bears a passing similarity to domes atop Wilson Station, Municipal Station, and the white art nouveau house at the corner of Jungunan Square. However, contextuality is not one of Gehry's values or overwhelming concerns.[2] With a technically sophisticated and aesthetically daring design, the building exhibits a tension between the architect's playful sculptural style and the responsibility to respect the historical context of the neighborhood.

But this strategy ultimately works to the detriment of both. In choosing neither to ignore the urban fabric of the neighborhood nor to attempt to come to terms with it fully, Gehry's gesture toward contextuality skews the design so that it smacks of architectural caricature. Thus, his vocabulary clearly draws from the architectural layers of the city but nevertheless remains uncomfortably alien to the spirit and character of Prague. The resulting building is to Prague's architecture what Kafkalogy is to Kafka.

But perhaps like Kafka studies, the assimilation of outside influences in architecture is not a new phenomenon in Prague.[3] The Netherlands National Building may be understood as the most recent in a lineage of distinguished buildings that announce the addition of another layer to the historical fabric of the city. The renaissance, baroque, art nouveau, and modernist functionalist styles all overturned the existing architectural order through the introduction of a new aesthetic. The most glaring difference between these historical examples and Gehry's design is linked to the unique character of Czech history. All of the city's stylistic layers, from the gothic to the modern, were the fruit of Bohemia's active participation in European history, signifying values that have been important in the country's historical evolution. Since the end of the Second World War, deprived of its linkage both to Western Europe and to its immediate precommunist past, the region could not itself have developed the advanced capitalist media-based society that has yielded the cultural fruit of postmodernity. As Ioana Sandi has suggested, the Czech Republic emerged from Soviet domination facing the "crisis of a yet incomplete modernity."[4] One response to this problem that emerges within the young Republic is a nostalgia for functionalist architecture and the design of the 1930s. Miroslav Masek understands recent architectural trends in the Republic as "our convalescence from a difficult past," arguing that "the characteristic features of our recent architecture are sobriety, materiality and austerity, which harmonize with and which in a certain way are kindred with our national mentality."[5] Benjamin Fraguer is not alone in linking the reevaluation of functionalism with the renewal of democracy: "Czech architecture is re-evaluating the values of early modern architecture, its view of life and morality. For many architects today they symbolize democracy."[6]

However, Masek himself clearly outlines the present dilemma of the Czech architectural community. Architect of the controversial Maj Department Store, Masek is one of the most important Czech architects to emerge from the Soviet occupation. His notion of an architectural "convalescence" from the trauma of Soviet dominance is a significant one, and his prescription for a renewed Czech architecture recognizes the importance of the past and the near-impossibility of simply restarting the Czech functionalist architecture last seen prior to the Nazi invasion in 1938. "There are some 70 to 80 years between the prewar avant-garde and nationalist movements," he writes, "and it's not possible just to leap over those years, forget history, and say 'We stopped in 37 and we'll start up again in the 1990's.' "[7]

Gehry's "Fred and Ginger."
Photograph by Ing. Arch.
Dobroslav Szpuk, Prague.
Used by permission.

In this context, as the most visible and widely publicized contemporary building in Prague, the Netherlands National Building will continue to represent an important moment in the ongoing debate over Prague's architectural future. For many, the transposition of the signature style of an important American architect into the pristine center of Prague connotes Western cultural imperialism. However, for many Czechs, the building also symbolizes renewed cultural and economic links to the West. Where an American critic may see yet another prestigious sculptural building that functions primarily as monument to itself and its maker, many Czechs see a new symbol of creativity and freedom regained.

The directions architectural solutions suggest in Prague, and indeed in all of Central and East Europe, have the potential to serve as important test cases, examining the inherent contradictions and fragility of the Western model of postmodern architecture.[8] That model legitimizes itself mostly in terms of the status provided by luxury commodities designed by a handful of star architects. In rethinking the place of building and urban thinking in the newly emerging social and economic orders, European architecture must examine not only the aesthetic qualities of a project but also the underlying cultural, political, and historical assumptions involved in realizing a specific building. The refusal of the Czech architectural community to embrace Frank Gehry's Netherlands National Building uncritically suggests the possibility of a more local architectural movement developing alongside Western postmodern models. In Western Europe and America, important architecture is often considered to be little more than an extension of public relations, and it is primarily experienced through reproductions in publications. The challenge of building within a Central European urban context is to restore architecture's lost dimension and practical function and to reconnect the profession to cultural values that should go beyond commerce.

The problems and merits of Gehry's Netherlands National Building are best understood within the context of the Czech Republic's recent contact with the postmodern West. In choosing to traverse zoning codes and construct yet another remarkable building that functions largely to embody its own and its maker's prestige, Gehry's Netherlands National Building exudes the arrogance that has followed Western architecture's inability to legitimize itself except in the terms of a metacommodity. In *The Spirit of Prague*, Ivan Klíma makes the following observation about the architecture of Prague:

> One of the most striking features of Prague is its lack of ostentation. Franz Kafka (like many other intellectuals) used to complain that everything in Prague was small and cramped. . . . Prague is one of the few big cities where you will not find a single tall building or a triumphal arch in the centre, and where many of the palaces, though magnificent inside, put on an inconspicuous and plain face, almost like a military barracks, and seem to be trying to look smaller than they really are. . . .

> What might have been felt as pettiness and provinciality at the beginning of the century, we perceive today as a human dimension, miraculously preserved.

> A sense of proportion permeated the life of people as well. Czech life does not go in for a great deal of ostentation.[9]

Another Prague native, Milan Kundera, develops a notion of the dancer that seems not unrelated to Gehry's "dancing" building in his novel *Slowness*. For Kundera, the dancer is compelled "to take over the stage so as to beam forth his self. . . . Taking over the stage requires keeping other people off it."[10] "Fred and Ginger" commands center stage and announces the presence of a new set of architectural values in post–Cold War Prague. These values are innovation, individuality, and commodification, all of which pose a distinct challenge to the integrity of the city's distinguished architectural history and deepen the identity crisis that is perhaps necessary for the completion of a remarkable Czech "convalescence" from its troubled past. As we examine the ways in which an individual building can affect a larger urban context, the Netherlands National Building offers an excellent opportunity for Prague to learn an invaluable and irreversible lesson from the architecture more often associated with L.A.

NOTES

1. On the issue of local zoning issues, I am indebted to lectures and conversations with Vladimir Slapeta, dean of the School of Architecture, Czech Technical University.

2. A precedent for Gehry's acontextual approach to building within an historically sensitive European urban context is the unsuccessful proposal for unifying a city block around Berlin's Alte Museum. Here the intervention completely and purposefully overwhelms the character of the nineteenth-century buildings.

3. I develop this topic elsewhere in a dialogue with the Czech-American architect Jasan Burin.

4. Ioana Sandi, "Ethics for and Architecture of Another Europe," *Architectural Design* 60, no. 1 (January/February 1996): 28.

5. Miroslav Masek, "Six Years after the Velvet Revolution," *Architectural Design* 60, no. 1 (January/February 1996): 37.

6. Benjamin Fraguer, "Different Yet Again," *Architectural Design* 66 (February 1996): 40–41.

7. Cited in Ivana Edwards, "Constructing a New Czech Republic," *Metropolis* 15 (May 1996), 108n9.

8. In my conversations with Jasan Burin, he pointed out the important fact that the Czech point of reference for eclectic postmodern buildings are the Stalinist pastiches of the 1950s, which influenced the Czech architect Pavel Bares.

9. Ivan Klíma, "The Spirit of Prague," in *The Spirit of Prague and Other Essays* (New York: Granta, 1994), 42–43.

10. Milan Kundera, *Slowness: A Novel* (New York: HarperCollins Publishers, 1996), 19.

Heteroglossia and Linguistic Neocolonialism

English Teaching in Post-1989 Poland

Bill Johnston

For the length and breadth of the former communist bloc, from the Czech Republic to Kazakhstan and from Estonia to Armenia, a largely unreported yet vitally important battle has been lost and won over the last dozen years: the struggle over what is to be the dominant foreign language for the new East. The loser in this battle is Russian; the victor, without a shadow of a doubt, is English. All across the old Soviet empire and its satellites, the English language is ousting Russian from its place as the primary foreign language. Massive reforms in the public sector aimed at introducing English in public schools are accompanied by the opening of countless private language schools. Agencies such as the British Council and the United States Information Agency (USIA) have expanded their operations in virtually every country in the region and are promoting the use of English whenever and wherever possible. English has come to be regarded as a sine qua non for those with serious ambitions in business. And anyone who owns a computer or visits the movies is confronted with English at every step.

This essay examines the rise of English in Poland, where possibly of all the post-communist[1] countries it has taken root most firmly, and it proposes a way in which the spread of English can be theorized. Finally, it shows how traces of this process can be found in the ways teachers of English in Poland discursively construct their lives and their professional work.

The Spread of English in the New Poland

Under communism, Russian was the dominant foreign language in Poland, as in other countries of the East.[2] Every schoolchild was exposed to up to eight years of compulsory Russian classes in primary and secondary school. Other foreign languages such as English and German were increasingly in evidence after the 1960s, but Russian continued to dominate. Fisiak (1994) estimates that in 1989 (when the linguistic grip of Russian had already weakened considerably compared to previous decades), there were 8,000 Russian teachers in the Polish educational system, compared to only 1,700 teachers of English, the second most common language.

This situation changed rapidly after 1989. To begin with, immediately after the fall of the communist regime, educationalists and the new ministers in the Ministry of National Education began work on a radical reform of foreign-language teaching in Poland. The overall goal, in line with Council of Europe guidelines, was to have in place by the year 2000 a system in which every primary school student would have instruction in one foreign language and every secondary school student would be taught in two foreign languages (Ministry of National Education 1991). These languages were to be predominantly Western ones; English first, followed by German and French, then Russian (Komorowska n.d.).

To meet the huge need for language teachers, seventy language-teacher-training colleges were set up across the country, both in major cities and in smaller towns. The ambitious goal of these colleges was to produce 20,000 new teachers of English and proportionate numbers of teachers of other languages by the end of the decade (Ministry of National Education, Department of Teacher Training 1992; Komorowska 1991).

Yet still the demand for English teaching in the public schools far outstrips the supply. As a result, at the elementary level in particular there are considerable numbers of underqualified teachers who have been pressed into service. One interesting development is that rather than designing a Polish national examination for English teachers, the Ministry of National Education initially decreed that a pass in the University of Cambridge First Certificate in English examination qualifies a teacher to teach in the elementary schools, while a pass in the Certificate of Proficiency in English entitles one to work in a public high school.[3]

Alongside the public sector, private language teaching has exploded onto the Polish scene. Private tuition in English was popular long before 1989. From the mid-1980s on, private schools began to appear; this process accelerated after 1989, and at the time the research for this essay was conducted, in the fall of 1994, there was no sign that the great demand for classes was dropping.

Along with the rise of private language schools, publishers of English-language textbooks have found Poland an extremely lucrative market. Many of the major companies (e.g., Longman, Cambridge University Press, Oxford University Press, Heinemann) have representatives in Warsaw and other major cities. One highly placed representative of a leading British publishing company described post-1989 Poland to me as a "gold mine." Given the market economy on which post-1989 Poland has prided itself, it hardly needs to be pointed out that the spread of English in public and private sectors is fueled by a so-far-unremitting demand for these goods and services. The nature of this demand is itself fertile material for a separate study.

Finally, the spread of English is also—perhaps primarily—to be found in the macrostructures of business, politics, and commerce. The election of Aleksander Kwaśniewski as president in November 1995 represented among other things the choice of a head of state with some command of English over one without that language skill. Poland's "return to Europe" coincides with the growing dominance of English in Europe across a wide range of domains, from scientific research through technology to entertainment (Berns 1992).

The political dominance of English is mirrored by its importance in the business world. The celebrated "joint ventures" so popular after 1989 almost always required expertise in a West European language; increasingly often, this language is English. English also appeared through the establishment of Polish representations of Western companies in Poland. In 1990, the British Council set up a special center to promote the teaching of English for business purposes, a program which went hand in hand with the British government's Know-How Fund, which sought to encourage links between the Polish and British business worlds.

One area in which the English language is visibly dominant is that of entertainment. English has traditionally been the accepted language of popular music (the Polish punk bands formed in the 1980s, for instance, often had pseudo-English names such as Lady Pank); now that cassettes, CDs, and MTV are readily accessible, this linguistic hegemony has come into its own. It is accompanied by the domination of television and film by Western languages, especially English, and especially American English. A newspaper I have from January 1996 lists the films playing in Kraków cinemas: of thirty different movies showing, twenty-one (70 percent) were American productions, eight were from various West European countries (including one from Britain), and only one was Polish. Similarly, a considerable percentage of television films and serials on Polish television channels are foreign, predominantly American, British, German, or French. To this must be added the English-language television channels available on satellite TV, which a growing number of Polish homes now have: CNN International, Sky News, MTV, and so on.

As already mentioned, the rise of English in Poland has been actively promoted by the British Council and, to a lesser extent, American agencies such as the USIA. British Council annual reports for 1990 and subsequent years (British Council 1990–1994) specifically target the former communist countries for language teaching along with other activities.[4] The British Council has aggressively pursued the establishment of British studies centers at Polish universities. Finally, several charitable agencies have been active in recruiting volunteer teachers with varying levels of experience and training to work in the Polish education system. For example, the British organization VSO (Voluntary Service Overseas), which traditionally dispatched volunteers to Third World countries, has established a separate subagency to handle the placement of volunteer teachers in schools and colleges in the former communist countries. The American-based Peace Corps has also been active in providing similar placement for U.S. volunteers.

Finally, the influence of English is inscribed in the Polish language itself. While all languages borrow from other languages, this process has shifted into warp drive over the last few years as far as English borrowings in Polish are concerned. Mańczak-Wohlfeld, in her study of English loanwords in Polish, finds that "most English loanwords entered Polish after World War II and particularly after the change in the political system in Poland" (1994, 155), even though her data collection ended in May 1993. While many of the borrowings belong to the domains mentioned above, such as business, politics, and language education, others do not.

A cursory glance through a few recent Polish newspapers and magazines, for example, reveals, virtually at random, examples such as the following: *dealer* and the adjective *dealerski, ranking, menedżer* (manager), *faks, koncern, leasing,* and *gej* (gay). Many words and phrases are translated directly or in some other way "Polonized": one sees terms such as *liposukcja* and *twardy dysk*, a travel agent offers *optymalna aranżacja tras*, and an advertisement for fax machines talks of *inteligentne powtarzanie numerów*. Once again, this phenomenon cries out for a separate detailed analysis.

In some domains, the two languages mix freely. In talking and writing about computers, one may come across terms such as *przemysł software'owy* or *notebooki i serwery*; one such *serwer* is advertised as having *przeinstalowany MS-DOS 6.2, opcjonalnie Novell NetWare, SCO Unix, Windows NT*. The same code-mixing (Myers-Scotton 1993) occurs in advertising. A recent magazine advertisement for hair replacement, entitled "H.M.: 'Handsome Men' to włosy dla ciebie," includes the following list:

>   -Polecamy metody:
>   -hair pieces,
>   -implant Micro-Derme,
>   -free & action,
>   -intensyfikatory. (*Wprost* 1996)

129

Finally, though I have little more than anecdotal evidence and thus the idea is highly speculative, I am increasingly struck with the impression that the pragmatics of Polish may be changing and that this may partly be influenced by English pragmatic conventions that are commonly encountered in Polish translations of television programs, movies, and popular literature. For instance, the conventions of use of the informal pronoun *ty* versus the formal *pan/pani* seem to me to be shifting in favor of greater informality, while diminutives of given names are being increasingly used in traditionally formal settings such as television interviews or published material. The author of the much-discussed novel *Panna nikt* (Tryzna 1995), for example, gives his name as Tomek (not Tomasz) Tryzna; as far as I am aware, this was the first use of a diminutive in an author's name on the cover of a book published in Poland. In a different domain, a judge I know reports that she is increasingly addressed by plaintiffs in court as *"wysoki sądzie,"* the term used as a translation of "your honor" in American courtroom dramas on television, rather than the conventional Polish form of address (*"Proszę sądu"*). I offer these observations as food for thought in considering the spread of English in Poland.

Theorizing English in Poland

The role of the English language in establishing, maintaining, reinforcing, and perpetuating the economic, cultural, and political dominance of English-speaking countries across the world has been clearly documented and analyzed (Phillipson 1992; Pennycook 1994). Scholarship has shown that the promotion of English serves the interests of specific groups of native speakers and that language teaching, far from being a neutral and beneficial activity, is profoundly ideological in nature (Benesch 1993) and is inescapably tied to social, cultural, and political values associated with the English language.

However, the literature cited above has focused almost entirely on the countries of what is known as the Third World, primarily Africa and Asia. Phillipson looks in detail at the African situation and the promotion of English (and resistance to it) in countries such as Kenya, Ghana, or Namibia. Pennycook analyzes the position of English in Malaysia and Singapore. While both authors are concerned with the global spread of English, the postcolonial setting of their research naturally influences their accounts and leads them to talk of this spread in terms of neocolonialism and what Phillipson calls "linguistic imperialism." Phillipson portrays the promotion of English as serving to maintain inequalities of power and resources between "core" or "center" countries (primarily the United States and Britain) and the countries of the "periphery." Interwoven in this is the cultural imperialism exercised by means of English in many Third World settings, which has met resistance in the writings of authors such as Ali Mazrui (1975), Edward Said (1993), Homi Bhabha (1994), and novelist Ngũgĩ wa Thiong'o (1986a). Ngũgĩ, for instance, has publicly renounced English and has vowed to write only in Gikuyu.

Yet the situation in Poland and other post-communist countries is different in important ways and may require a somewhat different theoretical approach. Poland is neither a core English-speaking country (like the United States, Britain, Australia, or Canada) nor a periphery country of the type represented by former colonies such as Nigeria, Malaysia, or India. The Polish language is not a major world language (like English, Spanish, or Russian), but with 40 million speakers, it is also not a threatened minority language such as Irish, Hawaiian, or Lakota. More important, while the teaching and use of Russian in Poland *was* imposed by force in a quasi-colonial situation, under both communism and Russian imperial rule, the same cannot be said of English. The spread of English is a voluntary phenomenon, visible in the popular demand for teaching and materials in both the public and private sectors.

How can the rise of English in Poland be theorized? One might object that it is patronizing to talk of linguistic imperialism or cultural neocolonialism in the Polish context. After all, Polish language and culture have a history almost as long as that of English and have survived what appear to be worse ordeals than the present one: the banning of books, the imposition of Russian or German in schools in the nineteenth century, the stultifying *nowomowa* or "newspeak" of the communist media (Głowiński 1990), even the "perils" of multilingualism.[5]

I wish to propose here one way of theorizing the success of English in post-1989 Poland. This will involve two sets of theoretical constructs: Bakhtin's (1981) opposition of authoritative versus internally persuasive discourse and Foucault's (1977) panopticism.

Bakhtin sees language as heteroglossic: composed of multiple discourses that often compete with each other and are in constant dialogue even within the language of a single speaker. His notion of discourses is similar to that of Gee (1991): discourses are "verbal-ideological belief systems" (Bakhtin 1981, 311; see also Johnston 1996). Bakhtin, however, makes a crucial distinction between authoritative discourse and internally persuasive discourse. The former is "conjoined with authority" (1981, 343) of some kind, whether religious, political, or moral. It is "the word of the fathers" (ibid., 342). Internally persuasive discourse, on the other hand, is "affirmed though assimilation, tightly interwoven with 'one's own word'" (ibid., 345); it "organizes masses of our words from within" (ibid., 345).

Finally, Bakhtin portrays this assimilation or "appropriation" (ibid., 294) of the discourses of others as a constant struggle:

> Language is not a neutral medium that passes freely and easily into the private property of the speaker's intentions; it is populated—overpopulated—with the intentions of others. Expropriating it, forcing it to submit to one's own intentions and accents, is a difficult and complicated process. (ibid., 294)

In the Polish context, the battle for dominance between Russian and English can be seen as a heteroglossic competition for discursive (and hence ideological) dominance in Poland: a struggle between two authoritative discourses to be accepted and to become assimilated as internally persuasive discourse.

Yet the discursive contexts in which these two languages have operated in Poland are very different indeed. Before it was a foreign language and a "neutral" school subject, Russian was the language of communism, of oppression, of forced learning. Linguistic resistance to communist ideology through language (Wierzbicka 1990; Buchowski et al. 1994) attempted to counter the "ideological Russification" of Polish: the introduction into the language of ideological terms that had first been coined, or put into action, in Russian. Even before communism, Polish nationalism had at least since the eighteenth century been virulently anti-Russian, equating the Russian language with tsarism and the privations of partition.[6]

The English language, on the other hand, has since the end of the Second World War been an ally of those who resisted the ideology of communism and its discursive realization. It was the language of the BBC World Service and the Voice of America, sources of information that countered the disinformation of the regime. It was the language of Margaret Thatcher and Ronald Reagan, both of whom were widely admired in Poland for "standing up to communism." Furthermore, it was the language of forbidden fruits: pop music, film and video, pornography, advertising, business, computers, and travel. In a word, it was the language of the accumulation of wealth, of consumerism and materialism, perhaps the most persuasive counterdiscourses to those of communism.

Thus, when the time came, there was in fact little need for those interested in promoting the English language in Poland to perform much overt propaganda. To a large extent, through the experience of communism, the Poles had already internalized the ideologies associated with English and thus also the need for the language itself. While of course some minimal publicity is conducted by the British Council and by various private and public institutions offering English classes, this is mostly a question of internal competition among the institutions themselves. The Poles do not need to be persuaded to learn English; they only need to be persuaded to go to one school rather than another. The emergence of the schools, courses, and programs themselves was a spontaneous reaction to values internalized as part of the resistance to the discourses and ideology of communism.

In this way, English, with the discursive ideologies it carries, can be seen as a "*simultaneously* authoritative and internally persuasive" discourse (Bakhtin 1981, 342), a situation Bakhtin recognizes as possible though rare. This discursive combination goes a long way toward explaining the lack of discursive or other resistance to the spread of English in post-1989 Poland.

This voluntary internalization of the worth of English, and hence of its ideologies, its values, and the power relations it represents, also recalls Foucault's panopticism, in which power relations are also internalized. The Poles, like the inmates in Bentham's model prison, are "caught up in a power situation of which they are themselves the bearers" (Foucault 1977, 201). It is interesting that Foucault's central theme in *Discipline and Punish* is the shift from the exercise of power through externally imposed violence to the creation of "docile bodies" (ibid., 136) through the "subtle coercion" (ibid., 209) provided by an internalized surveillance:

> [T]he productive increase of power can be assured only if, on the one hand, it can be exercised continuously in the very foundations of society, in the subtlest possible way, and if, on the other hand, it functions outside these sudden, violent, discontinuous forms that are bound up with the exercise of sovereignty. (ibid., 208)

This shift can be seen plainly in the failure of the Russian-based discourse of communism to take hold in postwar Poland, compared with the instant acceptance of English-based discourses of consumerism after 1989. The discourse and practice of communism was precisely one that was imposed, in the last instance, through violence and physical coercion. Little or no additional propaganda, on the other hand, was needed to set in motion the massive engine of expanded English teaching (and the suppression of Russian) in Poland after the fall of communism, for the values inherent in English had already been internalized by the Poles themselves, and had "spread throughout the social body" (ibid., 207). Put otherwise, having internalized the new discourses, the Poles had begun to take part in their own surveillance.

In order to comprehend fully the significance of this idea, it is vital to recognize that, as pointed out above, the spread of English is in fact by no means a neutral or benign process. First, there is a relatively overt political agenda behind the promotion of English language teaching and learning by the British and American governments, and this agenda is not restricted to so-called Third World countries (Phillipson 1992). The English language is seen as a vital component in the pursuit of cultural, political, and economic influence in Poland and other post-communist countries. For the British Council, for example, an organization whose stated aim is the promotion of British interests worldwide, "the most crucial role . . . in Eastern and Central Europe remains the development of English language teaching" (British Council 1990, 17).

Second, both Bakhtin (1981) and Gee (1991) have stressed that any discourse is inextricably associated with specific ideologies and political-moral values (Pennycook 1994; Hodge and Kress 1992). To take the example of language teaching itself, the use of British coursebooks entails particular ideologies of appropriate methods and techniques in language education, which may in fact be unsuitable in a non-British context for any number of reasons (Holliday 1994). The use of British language exams as qualifications for Polish teachers of English also leaves questions of standards (and therefore of values) in the hands of native English speakers who live outside of Poland and have little or no personal experience or understanding of Polish social and educational realities.

Third, in connection with the preceding, in the Third World, the armed intervention of the colonial powers has, in most cases, given way to a subtler yet no-less-effective economic control. Phillipson quotes President Nyerere of Tanzania as saying: "Instead of gunboats, economic power is used one-sidedly to push through the will of the powerful" (Phillipson 1992, 51). Ngũgĩ describes the "age of neocolonialism" in the 1970s as one that "saw the clear ascendancy of US-dominated transnational financial and industrial monopolies in most of Asia, Africa and Latin America. This ascendancy was to be symbolized by the dominance of the IMF and the World Bank" (1986b, 12).

Just at the point when we are about to console ourselves that the Polish situation is different from that of Third World countries, Ngũgĩ mentions the World Bank and the International Monetary Fund—the very two organizations who have a stranglehold over the Polish economy. This fact alone suggests that terms such as cultural neocolonialism and linguistic imperialism may not be so out of place in the Polish context.

Finally, while the future of the Polish language may not be in danger, the spread of English is quite literally threatening the existence of a large and ever-growing number of languages. Krauss (1992) estimates that up to 90 percent of the world's approximately 6,000 languages may be extinct by the end of the twenty-first century; a major factor in this process is the globalization of a small number of majority languages, English foremost among them. Krauss further points to the fact that the predatory action of English no longer relies principally on crude forms of violence such as genocide and enforced assimilation but operates through economic and cultural pressure, including what he calls the "cultural nerve gas" of the electronic mass media, television in particular. In the Polish context, these phenomena are prominent. Whether or not they will lead to the displacement (Phillipson 1992, 27) of Polish in selected domains is a matter for speculation.[7] At the very least, it seems that a failure to address the spread of English amounts to complicity in its effects elsewhere in the world. On this subject, it would be instructive to compare Polish governmental policy with regard to English and its policies toward minority languages within Poland, a matter which is beyond the scope of this essay.

Yet in the face of the internalized panoptic gaze and the convergence of authoritative and internally persuasive discourses, the preceding issues of economic, cultural, and political hegemony are rarely mentioned. Rather, this internalization produces a state of affairs where such things seem natural, unavoidable, and even desirable.

Teachers Talk about Their Working Lives

Data for this section is taken from my study of teachers' professional life stories (Johnston 1995, 1997). For this study, I conducted extended interviews in fall 1994 with seventeen teachers of English in a major provincial city. In the present essay I focus on the twelve Polish informants; I have written elsewhere about the five expatriate teachers (Johnston 1999). This section will present selected data and findings from the original study.

To begin with, I wish to examine the presence of the new discourses analyzed above in the speech of the informants in my study. In this analysis, I will be assuming not just that discourse creates, mediates, and negotiates social reality (Gee 1991) but also that, as Bourdieu has pointed out from a sociological perspective, language is not a neutral and transparent device for encoding meanings but is "an instrument of action and power" (1991, 37). Thus, my observations about teachers' constructions of self and profession are not situated in a vacuum but are firmly linked to the sociological realities of post-1989 Poland.

In many cases, at first glance it seemed as if the new ideologies had taken firm root. Rafał was a graduate of the English department in N.[8] and worked in a public high school. When asked his opinion of developments since 1989 in Poland, he came out with statements such as the following:

> I think the changes were necessary, unavoidable, because the whole period of communist and postcommunist economy was living on credit. It just seems to me that that economy had no justification; often it was illogical, the central planning, and all those five- and six-year plans and other things. And the central administration of everything. Only, really only a free market is the one solution that, in my opinion, is justified in a modern state, and I believe the changes were necessary. (tr.)[9]

The discourse Rafał draws on sounds almost propagandistic in its support for the "changes," an impression confirmed by what he says next:

> True, it's a complex situation, and a lot of people are complaining about what's going on at the moment, because everything changed so abruptly and a lot of people lost more than they gained in the transition. But it seems to me that it's a necessary stage. Things can't be perfect right away, and, as is often predicted, the period of change will last a good few years yet. Unfortunately, we simply have to stick it out and try to do as much as possible to catch up to the rest of the world, which has left us a bit behind. (tr.)

From examples like these, found in many of the transcripts, it is clear that the new discourses of capitalism and the free-market economy have found their way into the teachers' speech. To what extent, though, have these discourses become internalized, or appropriated, by the teachers?

At this point, we must remember that these interviews are primarily discursive self-presentations rather than necessarily reflections of teachers' inner values. There is a strong element of what Bakhtin calls addressivity, the "quality of being directed to someone" (1986, 95) that characterizes any given contextualized utterance.[10] In this case, the addressee is me, a Western researcher and a stranger; it seems at least possible that this particular discursive presentation is influenced by this fact. In other words, it is not possible to conclude that these are Rafał's "own" values. It may be that in the context of the new Poland, Rafał is "performing the new Pole"—presenting what he perceives as the current authoritative discourse.

This analysis is complicated further by the position of the new discourses in Polish social and political life. As outlined above, the optimistic discourses of the benevolent effect of market capitalism are today the authoritative discourses of the new Poland; yet only a few years ago they were themselves counterdiscourses to the quasi-Marxist ideologies of the communist regime. In that period, such discourses represented resistance to the oppressor and were valued as such (Wierzbicka 1990). Today, the discourses of communism would provide a counterdiscourse to the dominant discourses; yet they are thoroughly discredited (for good reason) and cannot provide the counterbalance necessary for an effective dialogical relationship—they lack any authority and to a large extent were never internalized. Discursively speaking, they barely exist.

Thus, the dominant ideologies of the day, which are realized through their discourses, go relatively unchallenged in post-1989 Poland. There is no effective oppositional discourse. Even politicians of the former left have adopted the new discourses: no serious contender in Polish politics argues for a return to communist values and ideologies. This absence of an effective counterdiscourse with any chance of being internalized by individuals goes some way toward explaining the propagandistic sound of Rafał's account. In the post-1989 sociopolitical context, it has been extremely difficult to come up with persuasive alternative accounts.

Yet at least the potential for counterdiscourses exists. In a number of cases, when I proposed counterdiscourses drawn from my own political orientation and my reading of the Polish situation, the teachers, without automatically agreeing with me, accepted these counterdiscourses as valid discursive oppositions that could enter into dialogue with the discourses of the new "party line." This was the case with Marek, a recent graduate of the teacher-training college who taught in a private high school. Marek's discursive representation of the post-1989 situation was similar to Rafał's. Marek extended his account to a defense of private schooling, drawing on the same kinds of arguments as those used in speaking of market capitalism: "While today these schools have, you know, various financial problems and sometimes they have to accept people out of, just out of financial considerations, in a few years things will be different. It's pure economics, pure market demands. Adapting to needs" (tr.). Yet when I countered this account with the objection that private education can be seen as an elitist system based on financial wealth rather than on ability, Marek recognized this objection as valid. To begin with, he argued that there is no alternative and that one must come to terms with this state of affairs:

> Interviewer: But isn't that just creating a kind of class system?
>
> Marek: Well, I do wonder; maybe, maybe. But really, I don't think it can be avoided. . . . You know, this school happens to be for people with money, I admit. And that's why I think the social system, the education system should offer the opportunity for exceptional individuals to be supported, that it should provide a firm foundation, but if you're exceptional, you have the opportunity to excel, and to excel in such a way that you get, you know, state grants and so on. And if you're rich, by all means you should be able to afford to send your child to a private school. Why not? That's how things are, and I don't think you can, I don't think there's any getting away from it. (tr.)

Yet later in the discussion, he seemed to have internalized the counterdiscourse much more:

> And from that point of view, this is a country where money plays a major role; where elites are formed often largely financially. And that appalls me; that it's not supporting people who are talented, but people who have money, that's the most appalling thing for me. (tr.)

It can be seen, then, that even where an authoritative discourse appears to have been internalized, the possibility of heteroglossic dialogue is always present.

One area which reveals the complexities of the competing discourses facing English teachers is the professional discourse of language teaching (Johnston 1997). Here, the opposition is not a simplistic ideological one between the "bad" old system and the "good" new one but also between an educational tradition (whether good or bad) which predates the communist period and which is familiar and in a sense homegrown and another which is partly attractive and partly inimical to the first. In education generally, and in language teaching in particular, Western teaching philosophies have tended toward more humanistic, student-centered ideologies which emphasize features such as choice of subjects and materials, student control of learning processes, learner independence, alternative forms of evaluation, collaboration between students, and the integration of "real-life" materials and activities into classroom learning. While the realization of such ideologies has often fallen far short of these ideals, the principles remain.

In language teaching, especially the teaching of English as a second or foreign language, this tendency has resulted in a number of more-or-less clearly articulated teaching methodologies, prominent among which is Communicative Language Teaching, an approach developed in Britain and the United States in the 1970s and 1980s. With modifications, it remains the dominant influence on textbook design and classroom teaching methods today (Little-

wood 1981; Brumfit and Johnson 1979). Communicative teaching is characterized inter alia by features such as extensive use of pair work and group work
in the classroom, an emphasis on fluency and oral use of language with a
concomitant deemphasis on grammatical accuracy, an emphasis on colloquial
forms of language as much as formal uses, and a concern with communicative
competence (Hymes 1966) in addition to grammatical competence.

Language teaching in Poland, on the other hand, has traditionally emphasized other values. Grammatical and phonological accuracy is prized above
fluency. The distinction between procedural and declarative knowledge is
largely obliterated, so that knowing the language is equated with the ability,
for example, to articulate grammatical rules. Evaluation is by discrete-item
exams, and success in these is crucial in making progress through the educational system.

As described above, the Western-based sources which draw on communicative methodology—coursebook publishers, private schools, agencies such
as the British Council and the Cambridge examiners—have made considerable inroads into language teaching in Poland in the years since 1989. Given
that Western-published materials and methods are so common, it seems inevitable that conflict between the Polish and Western ideologies of teaching
will emerge in the teachers' accounts of their work. Krystyna, the director of
the teacher-training college in N., says of these methods: "It's wrong, it goes
against common sense to believe that there will be miraculous results when
students start to talk with each other. Of course it produces a relaxed atmosphere, it's pleasant; but I wouldn't entirely agree that everything should be
taught communicatively, for instance grammar" (tr.).

A close analysis of this quotation reveals the dialogic nature of Krystyna's
position. On the one hand, the use of the word "miraculous" (*cudowne*) shows
that she is ironizing the value Communicative Language Teaching places on
pair work, while her own choice of the less dramatic "pleasant" (*przyjemne*)
damns with faint praise. On the other hand, the cautious tone of her statement
that "I wouldn't entirely agree that everything should be taught communicatively" brings up another aspect of the question of addressivity. Here we may
ask: Why is Krystyna even saying this? Why is her tone so cautious? It seems
plausible, at least, to suggest that the reason is the dominance of the opposing
position: in present-day Polish EFL teaching, at least in a context such as the
college where Western expertise and materials are widely used, the default
ideology—that is, the authoritative discourse—holds precisely that the communicative approach *is* the best way to teach. A panoptic sense of discursive self-
surveillance causes Krystyna to defer to the ideology of Communicative Language Teaching even as an internally persuasive discourse leads her to oppose
its values.

The effects of the discursive conditions of the new Poland can perhaps
above all be traced in the way the teachers in this study discursively con-

structed their lives. This was the principal focus of my dissertation (Johnston 1995). My findings included the following:

First, in very nondiscursive terms, all of the teachers in the study led extremely busy lives. Many of them held down three or more jobs, teaching in both public and private sectors, giving private lessons, or working outside of teaching, for example selling real estate or life insurance. Indeed, in my research it was difficult if not impossible to establish basic facts such as principal place of work, length of teaching experience, and so on, notions which are unproblematic in Western-based research on teachers' lives (e.g., Fessler and Christensen 1992).

These "multiple careers" were motivated almost exclusively by the need to make enough money to survive and prosper in the new Poland. As was seen above, many of the teachers accepted the dominance of economic factors as "natural." It is clear too that teachers had internalized the inevitability of their position as foot soldiers in the army of the English language. There was no mention of the fact that as they were busy promoting the interests of the most powerful language on the planet, little or none of that power trickled down to them. Rather, in panoptic fashion, they were accomplices in the preservation of existing power relations.

Second, these economic exigencies were leading many of the teachers to consider leaving teaching. Some, like Rafał, already had a foot out of the door; others, like Wojtek, regarded it as a real possibility. Not one of the teachers I spoke to was able to say for sure that she or he would remain in teaching over the long term.[11] This lack of commitment is of course entirely understandable at an individual level. Yet it is also very damaging for Polish education. If we agree that an effective educational system hinges above all on a highly qualified and competent teaching body, then instability in that teaching body will lead to instability across the system. This is precisely what is found in a wide range of English teaching contexts in Poland: constant changes of teachers make it impossible for school students to achieve continuity and thus to progress in their learning.

This lack of long-term commitment reflects a more general absence of a discourse of profession in the teachers (Freidson 1994), which also has a negative impact on the practice of education in Poland. While the teachers interviewed all seemed competent and reasonably conscientious, they had no common understanding of professionalism. For Danka, being a professional meant above all doing one's job successfully, as measured for instance by exam results. For Ewa, her co-worker, the key quality of a professional was a "one hundred percent dedication" to one's job and devotion to one occupation only. For Ania, a professional was someone with long-term commitment to a job: a new teacher by definition cannot yet be called a professional. For Adam, it meant earning a respectable salary.

At best, the absence of a sense of profession produced the kind of impermanence referred to above. In the worst case, there was an outright refusal to embrace professional standards of practice. Joanna, a young graduate of the teacher-training college, explained that she was not always as well prepared for classes as she might be:

> But I'm not going to do more because first of all I don't have time, and secondly it's not paid enough to work more, I think; and then I'm not going to do something, as I said, I'm not an altruist, and it's a cheat-off, actually, what we're doing, with the, well, the Ministry of Education, and what's going on in this country, I mean the work you have and the money you get for it, I think it's a huge misunderstanding and I'm not going to put up with it.

This quote, part confession and part accusation, demonstrates once again how the authoritative discourses of the new Poland are predominantly economic in nature. In the context of teaching in England, MacLure has written that "the old iconographies of teacherhood, with their virtues of vocation, care, dedication and self-investment, are being eroded under the pressures and interventions of the late twentieth century" (1993, 319). It is clear that these virtues are also out of place in the discursive world of the new Poland.

The final finding I wish to mention here relates directly to telling of the life story. Linde (1993) points out that in discursively representing disjunctures in the life story (of precisely the kind found in this study), speakers have recourse to discursive means to establish coherence and continuity in their accounts. For many of the Polish teachers, this was achieved by assuming the identity of expert speaker of English rather than teacher of English. For instance, Marek states the following:

> It's certain that any job I do will be connected with English, because it's something I like, and I just feel comfortable in it; and whether for example I'll devote more time to doing translations, or whether I'll try to set up for instance some kind of business school, or whether I'll be a partner in negotiations, more in the way of working with some firm, some representation [of a foreign company], or whatever, we shall see. (tr.)

From the position of the individual teacher, such a strategy is advantageous in the volatile and money-focused situation of the new Poland. Yet in other ways the assumption of this identity is dangerous. First, as in the case of professionalism and commitment above, it creates more instability for the Polish educational system. Second, it equates teaching ability with language ability. This is the same value that led the Ministry of National Education to recognize success in the Cambridge exams—which are purely language qualifications—as entitling one to teach. It is this value that makes it difficult to create a professional discourse of expertise in teaching, since teaching expertise is seen as no more than language expertise. It is also this value that places the native speaker of English in a naturally superior position to any nonnative speaker; the superiority of the native speaker, in turn, as Phillipson (1992) has documented, has long been an axiomatic principle of organizations such as the

British Council, inter alia, because it can easily be linked to the superiority of British (or American) know-how and materials.

Thus, the effects of the spread of English in Poland can be traced into the speech of the teachers who carry it out; these individuals form the loci at which competing discourses meet and the points at which authoritative and panoptic discursive forces operate.

The spread of English in post-communist Poland can be seen as linguistic neocolonialism of a specific kind. It is not a military colonialism, yet it is profoundly rooted in the exercise of political power and economic influence. The spread of English represents the continuing hegemony of core countries over those of the periphery. In Poland, and countries like it, this assumes slightly different forms than in "Third World" countries, yet uncomfortable parallels remain. It cannot be overemphasized that the peculiar status of English in Poland, as both an authoritative *and* an internally persuasive discourse, makes its spread particularly unchallenged and particularly threatening.

Throughout this essay, I have indicated certain aspects of the situation that deserve further investigation. In seeking to understand the post-1989 changes, especially those that concern the learning and teaching of English, there is a pressing need to know more about the exact nature of popular demand for English and the attitudes and beliefs underlying it; to monitor closely the spread of English in advertising, business, technology (especially computing), and elsewhere and to continue to be aware of the ideologies it brings with it; and to set the use of English and official policies regarding its promotion within the broader context of policies and attitudes regarding other indigenous and foreign languages in Poland.

These are still early days, and change continues at a rapid pace. From the present study, however, certain tentative conclusions can be drawn. First, English language use and learning seem already to have gained a firm place in the linguistic realities of post-1989 Poland. Second, while some of the discourses and ideologies associated with it (notably those concerning education) are resisted by many teachers, others (for example, political and social ideologies) seem to lack an effective counterdiscourse. Third, unless working conditions improve considerably, it is unlikely that the occupation will be able to attract and retain in the long term a corps of trained and effective teachers.

While it is of course useful for Poles to have increased access to the resources and opportunities that knowledge of English can provide, it is also vital to remain aware of the cultural, social, political, and economic ideologies that the English language bears and of the interests its promotion represents. This is all the more important because of the apparently voluntary and unquestioned nature of its acceptance by the vast majority of Poles. The spread of English has taken very different paths than the promotion of Russian under the communist regime, and it has been infinitely more successful. For this very reason, its success should be closely and critically analyzed and monitored.

Bill Johnston

NOTES

1. I use this term to mean "post-1989," aware that neither term is value-neutral and that by the use of such expressions I am creating the very subject of my discourse. My only excuse is that such is the nature of the present volume.

2. In applied linguistics, it is common to draw a distinction between a *second* language and a *foreign* language. A second language is one spoken by nonnative speakers in a country where that language is officially sanctioned or widely spoken: for example, speakers of Spanish or Polish using English in the United States. A foreign language refers to a language spoken by nonnative speakers in situations outside of countries where the language is indigenous: for example, the use of Russian in the United States or English in Poland. In practice this distinction is sometimes hard to maintain, but it will be employed here for the sake of convention.

3. The University of Cambridge Local Examinations Syndicate produces a suite of exams in English for nonnative speakers which are offered in a large number of countries around the world, including Poland. Enrollment in these exams, which are held twice a year in several major Polish cities, has increased severalfold since 1989; they have been made an integral part of the programs of many of the teacher-training colleges, and private schools prepare students to take them. The First Certificate in English (FCE) is an upper-intermediate qualification, while the Certificate of Proficiency in English (CPE, or "Proficiency") requires advanced knowledge of the language. Neither examination has anything to do with teaching.

4. In fact, from the British point of view, Poland represents the Western end of a linguistic and cultural *Drang nach Osten* aiming to bring British "expertise" and cultural exchanges and the English language to points farther east than the Council's range of influence hitherto: in the years since 1989, the Council has set up or considerably expanded operations both in the former satellite countries (Hungary, Bulgaria, Romania, etc.) and in the newly independent states within the former Soviet Union (e.g., Ukraine, Estonia, Georgia, Kazakhstan, and Kyrgyzstan).

5. Norman Davies, among others, has discussed the extent to which Poland's cultural heritage is multilingual (1984, 316–323). A magnificent example of this can be found in Jan Lam's 1873 novel *Wielki świat Capowic* (Lam 1938), which draws much of its humor from the Babel-like mixture of Polish, German, Ukrainian, Czech, Yiddish, French, Latin, and other languages used in a small Galician town. Multilingualism, in turn, is seen by many (for instance the political right in the present-day United States) as a threat to linguistic purism and the dominant role of the majority language (Donahue 1995).

6. In Polish literature, for example, anti-Russian sentiment can be traced throughout the period of the partitions, from Mickiewicz's *Dziady* (*Forefathers' Eve*, 1832) to Żeromski's *Przedwiośnie* (*The Coming Spring*, 1925).

7. An example of displacement can be seen in the fact that in Germany, board meetings in the BMW company are now conducted in English.

8. To maintain confidentiality, the city in question has not been identified. For the same reason, the names used here are pseudonyms chosen by the teachers themselves.

9. This indicates that the original interview was conducted in Polish and that this extract has been translated into English.

10. Bakhtin's notion of addressivity is akin to the sociolinguistic concept of *recipient design* (Sacks and Schegloff 1979).

11. This finding is supported by early survey research on teacher-training college graduates, which indicated that only between 35 percent (Tann 1994) and 60 percent (Drury 1994) of graduates enter public-sector teaching even in their first year after graduation, though this trend was reversed to some degree by subsequent reentry into teaching.

REFERENCES

Bakhtin, M. M. *The Dialogic Imagination.* Trans. C. Emerson and M. Holquist. Austin: University of Texas Press, 1981.
———. *Speech Genres and Other Late Essays.* Trans. Vern W. McGhee. Austin: University of Texas Press, 1986.
Benesch, S. "ESL, Ideology, and the Politics of Pragmatism." *TESOL Quarterly* 27 (1993): 705–717.
Berns, M. "The Role of English in Europe: EIL or EFL?" Paper presented at the Conference on World Englishes Today, Urbana, Ill., April 1992.
Bhabha, H. *The Location of Culture.* London: Routledge, 1994.
Bourdieu, P. *Language and Symbolic Power.* Trans. G. Raymond and M. Adamson. Cambridge, Mass.: Harvard University Press, 1991.
British Council. *Annual Report.* London: British Council, 1990–1994.
Brumfit, C. J., and K. Johnson. *The Communicative Approach to Language Teaching.* Oxford: Oxford University Press, 1979.
Buchowski, M., D. B. Kronenfeld, W. Peterman, and L. Thomas. "Language, *Nineteen Eighty-Four,* and 1989." *Language in Society* 23 (1994): 555–578.
Davies, N. *Heart of Europe: A Short History of Poland.* Oxford: Oxford University Press, 1984.
Donahue, T. S. "American Language Policy and Compensatory Opinion." In *Power and Inequality in Language Education,* ed. J. W. Tollefson, 112–141. Cambridge: Cambridge University Press, 1995.
Drury, J. "Pre-Service English Teacher Training in Poland: The Need, the Demand and the Supply." In *Directions towards 2000: Guidelines for the Teaching of English in Poland,* ed. C. Gough and A. Jankowska, 39–45. Poznań: Instytut Filologii Angielskiej, UAM, 1994.
Fessler, R., and J. C. Christensen. *The Teacher Career Cycle.* Boston: Allyn & Bacon, 1992.
Fisiak, J. "Training English Language Teachers in Poland: Recent Reform and Its Future Prospects." In *Directions towards 2000: Guidelines for the Teaching of English in Poland,* ed. C. Gough and A. Jankowska, 7–15. Poznań: Instytut Filologii Angielskiej, UAM, 1994.
Foucault, M. *Discipline and Punish.* Trans. A. M. Sheridan Smith. New York: Pantheon, 1977.
Freidson, E. *Professionalism Reborn: Theory, Prophecy, and Policy.* Chicago: University of Chicago Press, 1994.
Gee, J. P. *Social Linguistics and Literacies: Ideology in Discourses.* London: Falmer, 1991.

Głowiński, M. *Nowomowa po polsku*. Warsaw: PEN, 1990.

Hodge, R., and G. Kress. *Language as Ideology*. 2nd ed. London: Routledge, 1993.

Holliday, A. *Appropriate Methodology and Social Context*. Cambridge: Cambridge University Press, 1994.

Hymes, D. "On Communicative Competence." Paper presented at the Research Planning Conference on Language Development in Disadvantaged Children, New York, New York, June 1966.

Johnston, B. "Do EFL Teachers in Poland Have Careers?" Ph.D. diss., University of Hawai'i at Mānoa, 1995.

———. "Do EFL Teachers Have Careers?" *TESOL Quarterly* 31 (1997): 681–712.

———. "The Expatriate Teacher as Postmodern Paladin." *Research in the Teaching of English* 34 (1999): 255–280.

———. "Towards a Bakhtinian Discourse Analysis." Paper presented at the Annual Meeting of the American Association for Applied Linguistics, Chicago, Ill., March 1996.

Komorowska, H. "Language Education Policy: A Proposal." Unpublished manuscript, n.d.

———. "Second Language Teaching in Poland Prior to the Reform of 1990." *Georgetown University Round Table on Languages and Linguistics 1991*, 501–508. Washington, D.C.: Georgetown University Press, 1991.

Krauss, M. "The World's Languages in Crisis." *Language* 68 (1992): 4–10.

Lam, J. *Wielki świat Capowic*. In vol. 1 of *Pisma Jana Lama*. 1873; reprint, Kraków: Trzasko, Evert and Michalski, 1938.

Linde, C. *Life Stories: The Creation of Coherence*. New York: Oxford University Press, 1993.

Littlewood, W. *Communicative Language Teaching: An Introduction*. Cambridge: Cambridge University Press, 1981.

MacLure, M. "Arguing for Your Self: Identity as an Organising Principle in Teachers' Jobs and Lives." *British Educational Research Journal* 19 (1993): 311–322.

Mańczak-Wohlfeld, E. *Angielskie elementy leksykalne w języku polskim*. Kraków: Universitas, 1994.

Mazrui, A. *The Political Sociology of the English Language*. The Hague: Mouton, 1975.

Ministry of National Education. "Directions of Changes in Education in 1990s." Unpublished manuscript. Warsaw: Ministry of National Education, 1991.

Ministry of National Education, Department of Teacher Training. *Teacher Training: Present Situation and Prospects for Changes*. Warsaw: Ministry of National Education, 1992.

Myers-Scotton, C. *Duelling Languages: Grammatical Structure in Codeswitching*. Oxford: Oxford University Press, 1993.

Ngũgĩ wa Thiong'o. *Decolonising the Mind: The Politics of Language in African Literature*. Portsmouth, N.H.: Heinemann, 1986a.

———. *Writing against Neocolonialism*. Wembley: VITA, 1986b.

Pennycook, A. *The Cultural Politics of English as an International Language*. London: Longman, 1994.

Phillipson, R. *Linguistic Imperialism*. Oxford: Oxford University Press, 1992.

Sacks, H., and E. A. Schegloff. "Two Preferences in the Organization of Reference to Persons in Conversation and Their Interaction." In *Everyday Language: Studies in Ethnomethodology*, ed. G. Psathas, 15–21. New York: Irvington, 1979.

Said, E. *Culture and Imperialism*. New York: Knopf, 1993.

Tann, S. "Initial Results from the Tracer Study." Unpublished manuscript. Lublin: Katolicki Uniwersytet Lubelski, 1994.

Tryzna, T. *Panna nikt*. Warsaw: B&C, 1995.

Wierzbicka, A. "Antitotalitarian Language in Poland: Some Mechanisms of Linguistic Self-Defense." *Language in Society* 19 (1990): 1–59.

Wprost. "AHM: 'Handsome Men' to włosy dla ciebie." Advertisement, June 2, 1996, 108.

seven
Projections of Desire

Robert D. Kaplan's Balkan Ghosts *and the Crisis of Self-Definition*

Anca Rosu

Robert D. Kaplan's *Balkan Ghosts: A Journey through History* is a successful travel book. The classification doubles its success, since the genre has lost momentum in the last century and a half. Good travel books are rare, according to Kaplan, because of the decline of travel itself: "In a world rapidly becoming homogenized through the proliferation of luxury hotels, mass tourism, and satellite communications, fewer and fewer unsimulated adventures remain" (1994, ix). Examining writers who express a similar concern, Michael Kowalewski identifies the same culprit: "A fear of diminishing cultural alternatives . . . seems partly attributable to contemporary forms of mass travel" (1992, 3). Tzvetan Todorov, however, blames the deterioration of travel writing on the disappearance of colonial conditions: "In order to ensure the tension necessary to the travel narrative, the specific position of the colonizer is required: curious about the other, and secure in his own superiority" (1987, 69). Kaplan's success in writing about his travels in the Balkans is the result of his ability to create such a tension.

The "specific position of the colonizer" that Kaplan adopts is perhaps the most important aspect of the book, because it reveals an acute crisis of self-definition in postcolonial America. For while anticolonialist ideology has done a great deal to discredit any blatant disdain for the former colonies (which are usually identified as races rather than cultures), it has never quite eradicated the need to define the self through negative images of others. Kaplan's journey into the unfamiliar Balkans is an ideal occasion to regain the position of colonial superiority without resuscitating racism or violating any present-day pieties. Kaplan's position is all the more interesting because he has written, and continues to write, about many countries in Africa and the Middle East.[1] His success as an expert in the cultures of the countries he visits testifies to a way of seeing shared by many Americans.

Like older colonial writings, Kaplan's book confronts us with epistemological questions that ultimately lead to a politics of self-definition. The relationship between the data of the senses and the representation of that knowledge in this modern travelogue proves that in the process of acquiring knowledge, the empirical evidence plays a lesser part than the alternative representations of the world the author was exposed to. Kaplan's worldview is threatened not when his senses are violated by strange landscapes and unsavory smells but rather when his subjects present him with an alternative value system whose coherence shakes his own convictions and unhinges his self-assuredness. Since in this case the object of inquiry is in fact another subject, acquiring knowledge takes the form of a struggle between one self and another. It is, as such, a threat to identity, and the self spends as much energy rejecting as it does embracing new knowledge.

Two forces are at work in Kaplan's writing: one that pushes him toward an authentic experience, toward exploration and discovery that, when it reaches its extreme, threatens the self with annihilation and another that restrains exploration, urges self-validation, and, at its extreme, proclaims the self superior to others in true colonial fashion.

The purpose of this modern knight in quest of "unsimulated adventure" is to acquire knowledge, which he makes clear from the outset with sentences such as: "If the intruder from the West is not willing to feel with his whole being, he cannot hope to understand" (Kaplan 1994, xv). "To feel with his whole being," the traveler must give up not only his comfort but also something of himself. Understanding thus must take the form of surrender, and the writer's own self may be on the line. But, in spite of Kaplan's desire to give himself up for knowledge, an essentially defensive mechanism animates his cognitive enterprise.

The task Kaplan sets for himself is one common to colonial explorers turned writers. He has to find a way to process the reality of a region that is not only unfamiliar but also hard to measure by Western standards. Kaplan is also a journalist with experience in writing about foreign lands, and he has developed specific methods for getting to the "truth." He looks for guidance to the past with a heightened awareness of his mission: "These lands require a love for the obscure. For months I ransacked rare-book shops and dealers. I knew that the books that best explained the violence of Romania's December 1989 revolution had been out of print for decades, in some cases for half a century or more" (ibid., xxi). Yet this dedication to obscurity is only an apparent surrender, for the sources of knowledge (the rare books) do more than explain the Romanian revolution; they give Kaplan a higher ground from which to contemplate it.[2]

Instead of testing the limits of his capacity to understand others, the writings of the past place the journalist in a position of already-established superiority. One function of the historical sources is, of course, to inform the reader about past events that determine events in the present, such as the reference to the writings of Rebecca West: "Dame Rebecca had already capsulized the situation in Serbia, in the rest of former Yugoslavia, and in the other Balkan states for the 1990s. Now that Communism has fallen and the Soviets have been expelled, *there is a lot of emotion loose about the Balkans which has lost its legitimate employment*" (ibid., 32). A formulation such as "*a lot of emotion loose about the Balkans which has lost its legitimate employment*" is not neutral; it is an interpretation that includes the position of both observer and observed. Kaplan borrows more than the beautiful turn of phrase of a talented travel writer; he also borrows her "civilized" stance against the emotion-ridden "savages."

Kaplan does not stop at using the past writings as an aid to decipher present mysteries. He willingly seeks in the past a confirmation for his present impressions by repeatedly juxtaposing what he has read with what he sees to support his contention that "Communism had been the Great Preserver" (ibid., xxvii) and that what it has preserved is an essentially medieval mentality. If "Dame Rebecca described [Prishtina] as a 'dull and dusty little village,' inhabited by 'men in Western clothes more fantastic than any peasant costume could be, because they and their tailors had never seen a suit till they were grown men'" (ibid., 40–41), then, according to Kaplan's logic, it follows that "[t]oday, . . . Prishtina . . . is the same 'dusty little village' filled with men who still look as though they had never seen a Western suit until yesterday" (ibid., 41). The reiteration of the description down to the slightest detail reinforces the near-immutability of Prishtina's reality. In similar fashion, Romania, Macedonia, or Bulgaria look, and presumably are, exactly like the countries of exotic primitivism described by John Reed, Walter Starkie, Olivia Manning, or other intrepid travelers of the past.

The balance between the knowledge acquired through direct perception and the knowledge already sanctified by the writers of the past tips in favor of the latter. Previously constructed knowledge, whether it is a fact-based account or pure fiction, takes the lead and guides the writer's perception to the point of perverting it. In Romania, Kaplan is impressed by the smell of the trains: "The train carriage reeked of concrete dust, urine, old cheese, sausage, tobacco, plum brandy, sour body odor, and long-unwashed clothes" (ibid., 100–101), but neither the immediacy of the experience nor the detailed list of ingredients that generate the smell seem to have any authenticity before they are endorsed by one of Olivia Manning's characters: "In Manning's story, the smell made

Prince Yakimov think of 'stale beer' " (ibid., 101). Kaplan is convinced that he smells the same odor that a fictional character described, and the conclusiveness of the sentence shows his readiness to accept the superiority of the fictional description.

This willingness to submit to the fictions created by past writers paves the road for Kaplan to take a fantasymonger such as Bram Stoker at his word. "This region, unrolling from the back windows of Count Dracula's mythical castle, was still, nearly 100 years after Stoker published *Dracula*, 'one of the wildest and least known portions of Europe,'" he exclaims (ibid., 135). It is known, and Kaplan himself admits, that Bram Stoker never visited Romania and that he based his descriptions on other people's accounts and his fertile imagination. But the image is too powerful for the American traveler to seek evidence to the contrary; its power resides in its familiarity, its nondisturbing readiness to fit whatever knowledge he had of the region. It is not by chance that Bram Stoker's *Dracula* is the source Kaplan quotes most often, for this fiction competes successfully with other, more fact-oriented sources because of the popularity of the myth it created. And Kaplan is not the first to confuse myth and reality. Analyses of both travel and anthropological writings demonstrate that in the process of acquiring knowledge of other people and places, already-mythologized images often compete with the data of the senses.[3]

Since Thomas Kuhn theorized about *The Structure of Scientific Revolutions,* we have all become aware that in order to understand new data we must fit them in an already-existing cognitive matrix (1970, 184). Yet Kaplan's use of historical and fictional sources to guide his contact with reality goes beyond the usual trade-offs between old and new knowledge, because he lets the past almost entirely shape what he perceives. Knowledge of the Balkan countries thus grows from image to image, from description to description—a process in which reality dissolves as soon as it has stopped shocking the traveler. This is not a simple effort to gain knowledge; it is rather a willed subordination of the empirical evidence to the fictions of history and literature that protect the writer from confusion and buttress his superior position as *subject* rather than *object* of knowledge. This position gives him the right to define the very limits of civilization. The region around Dracula's castle is "wildest" because it is "least known," both to Kaplan and to Stoker's narrator.

The willingness to submit to past impressions and interpretations is only partly determined by the demands of the process of acquiring knowledge. Another factor to be taken into consideration is the difficulty of representing the unknown and the unfamiliar. Representing and communicating one's perceptions are inextricable from cognitive activity, which is not complete until one finds a form in, or gives a form to, the raw data. Kaplan's task as an explorer/writer is to transform his own chaotic perceptions into an intelligible account for his reader. In other words, his mission is not only to understand but also to make himself understood. In this regard, he finds past writers useful as mediators between himself as traveler/writer and his readers.

Most of the time, the guides of the past that dominate Kaplan's book surpass their function as mediators, just as they exceed their importance as sources of information. His reliance on their fictions turns his writing into modern-day fable-making. In this age of deconstruction, Kaplan continues to construct the Balkans, even as the Balkans stand in his way. His own metaphors seem to be natural extensions of past myths about the region. Myth-making contradicts the usual goals of journalism, which is supposed to stick to the facts. That is perhaps why Kaplan, as a good professional, uses metaphors sparingly. However, there are times when the data of the senses fit so poorly into the culture's already-existing images and are so alien to what his readers would be able to digest that metaphor becomes his only defense against total obscurity.

Kaplan's metaphors move unprocessed chaotic reality into the domain of comfortable stereotype. The editor of a newly founded Romanian newspaper who disconcerts Kaplan with his view of the future is encapsulated into a metaphoric description: "His hair, short and unwashed, and his expression, so posed and so severe, made him look like a 1917 Russian revolutionary. His green eyes were like those of a prisoner in a mine shaft, intensely focusing on a small circle of sunlight above, not knowing quite how to reach it" (1994, 123). The editor does not resemble anything that Kaplan or his readers have seen before, but the images of a "Russian revolutionary" and of "a prisoner in a mine shaft" (whose sources may be photographs, newsreels, or movies) successfully perform the task of making his uncomfortable reality fit for American consumption.

Rare as they are in a book concerned with exploring the unknown, these metaphors play to the reader's most basic, and by now obsolete, prejudices. One metaphoric vehicle that dominates the descriptive passages is "Africa." The cluster of connotations the word carries makes it a convenient vehicle for Kaplan's colonialist perspective on the countries he visits. "Africa" plays in his book just about the same part that Moorish civilization played in the accounts of Mexico written by the conquistadors. As Tzvetan Todorov observes, "When the conquistadors saw the Indian temples, they spontaneously called them 'mosques.' . . . When the Spaniards discovered a somewhat larger city, they immediately called it 'Cairo.' . . . The illustrations of the time also attest to this projection of the familiar (even if it is somewhat strange) onto the unknown" (1995, 61–62). The projection of a familiar strangeness over an even stranger reality serves to produce the desired impression upon the reader.

The basis of the analogy between just about any part of the Balkans and Africa is, in most instances, the discomfort of the traveler. Stranded in a Bucharest hotel, Kaplan congratulates himself for his foresight: "As in Africa, I knew enough to bring a flashlight and my own toilet paper" (1994, 83). Like many modern travelers from the West, Kaplan is nearly obsessed with the lack of paper products in the remote regions he reaches: the natives lack Kleenex and wipe their noses with their fingers like the natives of Africa and Asia. What connects Africans, Asians, and Romanians is not what they have but what they lack; not what makes them distinct from each other but what makes them the same in the eyes of the traveler.

Aside from Kaplan's sense of discomfort and shock, the reader receives little material with which to imagine what he perceives. But if the analogies are not sufficient to form a clear image of the author's experience, they do have the power to produce the desired effect on the reader, in the sense that they evoke long-established and familiar "truths." In *Balkan Ghosts*, the references to Africa and other former colonies of the Western world awaken the reader's sense of superiority over the primitive, just as the conquistadors' references to "mosques" aroused the Spaniards' hostility for the religion of their enemies.

Kaplan does not always succeed in taming the unfamiliar with an appropriate stylistic device. The impulse to explore and surrender to new knowledge endangers clarity. When they do not rely on solid stereotypes, Kaplan's metaphors send mixed messages that may become disorienting to his readers. One recurring metaphoric vehicle, for instance, is prostitution. At first, it seems that it is suggested by the landscape of former Yugoslavia: "The earth here had the harsh, exhausted face of a prostitute, cursing bitterly between coughs" (ibid., xxvii). Later, in Romania, Kaplan paints a portrait of the nation by analogy with the royal mistress: "Lupescu's story is the story of Romania. . . . Romania, too, was always alone, always surrounded by enemies who wanted pieces of her" (ibid., 89). Both images contain a suggestion of helplessness in the face of abuse (which are seemingly derived from romantic representations of prostitutes, such as Dumas's Camille) doubled by the more current view (supported by Kaplan's own distaste for the prostitutes at a Bucharest hotel) that such victims deserve their fate. The relationship between travel writer and reader, in this case, is at best ambiguous, for the writer communicates uncertainty rather than a definitely superior stance.

Sometimes Kaplan becomes nearly incoherent in his effort to communicate the strangeness of what he sees. The connotations of his metaphoric vehicles are at odds with their denotations and render their tenors obscure. Kemal Ataturk, the founder of modern Turkey, is described as "an Aryan Dracula." The analogies underlying this description cannot be sustained under analysis. They imply that Ataturk is Aryan and Dracula is not. Maybe Ataturk appears Aryan because of the Western clothes he wears or because he is seen as some kind of fascist. The suggestion of fascism contained in the word "Aryan" is indeed more powerful than its literal meaning, but Hitler would never have referred to a Turk as an Aryan. On the other hand, Dracula, Bram Stoker notwithstanding, would have no trouble qualifying as one of the "master race," since Romania was an ally of Germany in World War II. Kaplan appears to be at a loss about where his own superiority resides in those "savage lands," inhabited by suave vampires and fierce-looking reformers.

The mixed messages of Kaplan's metaphors indicate his own confusion. However, that confusion is not produced simply by contact with reality but by an underlying confrontation between the worldview the writer represents and the worldview of the people he describes. This confusion leads to a near-surrender of the self, but a less-than-voluntary one. It is a paradox that in Kaplan's narrative, confusion begins in moments of clarity, moments when the traveler seems to feel at ease among the natives.

The easiest opportunity to identify with the natives is the coincidence of prejudices between the culture Kaplan comes from and the one he has made an object of study. He seems subliminally delighted to find anti-Semitism alive in Romania, after he almost deplored its disappearance in Austria. Kaplan, who is Jewish himself, has little reason to sympathize with anti-Semites, but the presence of the prejudice gives him an illusion of familiarity that sustains him through the strangeness of the culture. Kaplan also seems to feel comfortable when he finds other forms of racism, which create a connection between what he already knows and what he perceives: "The Gypsies I saw on the boat seemed to fit the worst stereotypes of Gypsies: drunk, dangerous, with restless hands bent on theft" (ibid., 109). One may wonder where Kaplan learned about these Gypsy stereotypes, if not through local prejudice. His usual sources—past travel writers—seem to offer a more romanticized image of Gypsies as born musicians, inseparable from their fiddles.

Locals help Kaplan make inroads into their culture by presenting him with images of themselves that have been fabricated for foreign use. They produce something similar to what Mary Louise Pratt has called an auto-ethnography, "in which colonized subjects undertake to represent themselves in ways that engage with the colonizer's own terms. If ethnographic texts are a means by which Europeans represent to themselves their (usually subjugated) others, autoethnographic texts are those the others construct in response to or in dialogue with those metropolitan representations" (ibid., 7). Simply put, autoethnography is a representation of the colonized done by themselves in the language of and for the benefit of the colonizers. Kaplan is greeted with representations in which the natives stereotype themselves to meet his stereo-types at every turn. When he arrives in Bulgaria, he is accosted by a local journalist, who, by way of introduction, tries to get the Western stereotype of Communists out of the way: "Do you think that just because I am a Commu-nist I am going to brainwash you?" (ibid., 197). The receptionist at the Athenée Palace Hotel in Bucharest confirms Kaplan's disdain for local depravity by offering him prostitutes, women or men. Aware that the American journalist will find their country backward, a couple of Romanians in Sfîntu Gheorghe greet him with "Welcome to Africa" (ibid., 113). A Romanian journalist dis-parages his own culture, saying: "All the influences upon us are Oriental, bad" (ibid., 125). The standards of the West are thoroughly applied in these self-characterizations, and what shocks us is perhaps only their crudity.

These awkward self-portrayals do, nonetheless, bring the natives and the explorer to common ground and facilitate what amounts to an attempt on Kaplan's part to translate the worldview of the natives. But translation in the sense of transposing a text from one language into another is not exactly what happens here. It is rather, as Thomas Kuhn proposes, a risky appropriation:

> To translate a theory or worldview into one's own language is not to make it one's own. For that one must go native, discover that one is thinking and working in, not simply translating out of, a language that was previously foreign. That transition is not, however, one that an individual may make or refrain from making by deliberation and choice, however good his reason for wishing to do so. Instead, at some point in the process of learning to translate, he finds that the transition has occurred, that he has slipped into the new language without a decision having been made. (1970, 204)

When a worldview is the object of knowledge, a transformation of the self is thus implied. We rely on a worldview in order to be who we are. Kuhn sees the process as a transition without awareness, a risk that one takes in the attempt to translate another worldview. It is the risk one takes in order to know it—in Kuhn's words, "make it one's own." A transition of this kind takes place in Kaplan's writing, albeit only at certain moments. His desire to know his subjects sometimes takes him beyond ordinary translation and gets him close to "going native."

Those are the moments when Kaplan seems ready to give in to local charm. He retrospectively gives credence to a fortuneteller who predicted his marriage in a Bulgarian restaurant: "(As it happened[,] fifteen months afterward, I met my future wife)" (1994, 199). In Romania, he almost capitulates to lax morality and perceives his surrender as a natural phenomenon: "First you were shocked. Then, after a few weeks in Romania, you gave in to the environment. A perverse side of your nature allowed you to fall in love with the country and people. You even thought that, perhaps, the Romanians possessed a peculiar wisdom about life and survival that the rest of the world lacked. And thus you would begin to understand. . . ." (1994, 81). Understanding is, of course, the journalist's objective here, as it is everywhere else in the book, and Kaplan allows himself to surrender to local views on life because it helps him advance his knowledge.

For a traveler, who has to maintain a critical distance from the natives in order to keep his or her superior position, the inroads he or she makes in the cultures he or she studies easily become treacherous. The lure of what anthropologist Clifford Geertz has called "local knowledge" can be even more powerful when it is presented in a coherent form.[4] Kaplan is astounded by the way locals conceptualize their politics, especially by their accuracy in predicting the outcome of events. Predictions give his informants an aura of wisdom that he positively covets: "I realized that Djilas was always right. He was able to predict the future. His technique was a simple one for an East European, but a difficult one for an American: he seemed to ignore the daily newspapers and think purely historically" (ibid., 74). His Romanian and Bulgarian informants share the talent of this Montenegrin politician. They perfectly understand what is happening and predict the future with absolute correctness. The coherence of their vision determines Kaplan's surrender to it: "[P]erhaps the nuns in Bucovina were right: a savior could only emerge from a place where this much evil had been committed" (ibid., 159). This surrender is all the more significant since it takes place in pure mythology. An almost-mystical attitude is not exactly what Kaplan brought with him from the States.

Kaplan is well aware of the local tendency to fit everything into a mythical vision: "In the Balkans, history is not viewed as tracing a chronological progression as it is in the West. Instead, history jumps around and moves in circles; and where history is perceived in such a way, myths take root" (ibid., 58). In this passage, which is placed very early in the book, Kaplan appears in full control of himself and totally detached from the worldview he describes. But later in the book, when he yields to the temptation of making sense of the world the way the natives do, Kaplan becomes, like Conrad's Marlow, fascinated with an abyss into which he is nonetheless reluctant to fall. The danger here is that the traveler may "go native" and drag his reader into the bottomless pit of his own uncertainty.

One wonders what would have happened if Kaplan had let moments like these dominate the book, if he had not recoiled in horror. Would his readers have accepted the terrifying vision of a traveler gone native? Kaplan does not seem to think so, since he works hard to regain his self-assuredness. Local knowledge not only threatens his ability to communicate, it also threatens him directly. The threat becomes all the more evident when Kaplan has to admit his fear and actually describe what he abhors. Crowded by Albanian Muslims on a bus to Prishtina, Kaplan exclaims, "Suddenly I didn't feel quite safe" (ibid., 41). The religious fervor of Romanians triggers the same reaction: "Only in Shiite holy places in the Middle East had I experienced such a charged and suffocating religious climate, rippling with explosive energy. It frightened me" (ibid., 122–123). The reality of the Balkans threatens to destroy not just Kaplan's image of the world but the very core of his identity based on that image as well. At such moments, Kaplan the traveler no longer strives to internalize his discoveries but works to construct inner truths germane to his identity—a defense against the outer assault.

In a recent essay on travel writing, Rockwell Gray observes that "our projections of desire define for us the map and the meaning of discovery" (Kowalewski 1992, 35). The desire that defines the meaning of Kaplan's discoveries does not, however, lead to a simple inability to see beyond the self: it signals a crisis in self-definition. This crisis is not in any way personal, for the writer is engaged with his readers in intimate ways. He responds to their sensibilities, and he succeeds, as the sales figures for his book indicate, in touching them in meaningful ways.

Kaplan is aware that in order to remain himself and write his story he must, as Marlow did, stop before becoming Kurtz, before "going native." His account would have no value if he did so. It would mean nothing if it lost its intelligibility for his readers. It is probably because of this awareness that at the most disquieting moments in his account, when the Western moral value system is strongly threatened, Kaplan chooses to abstract himself from his writing.

Such moments occur when the negative or positive values American culture attaches to certain notions are reversed by local history and politics. The way America views political allegiances makes it hard, even impossible, for Americans to understand why the local anticommunist heroes were fascists in Yugoslavia, why Jews supported communism in Romania, why Hitler is considered a benefactor by the Saxons of Transylvania. When relating such opinions, Kaplan simply lets his informants speak: "We had our own national pride. . . . [T]here was a mass psychology among us that encouraged many of the young men to enlist in the Waffen SS. . . . The Hitler years were quite pleasant" (1994, 173). No comment follows, because the candor of the informant baffles the journalist.

If forced to narrate events that are significant to people he cannot classify, Kaplan borrows the minimalist neutral style cultivated by followers of Hemingway: "Soviet soldiers, their bayonets drawn, entered Mrs. Pastior's home, taking her father and her fifteen-year-old brother away on a forced labor conscription. Her brother escaped. Her father died in 1946, while working in the mines of the Donets basin" (ibid., 173–174). There is nothing here to indicate what Kaplan feels about Mrs. Pastior's story. The burden of the moral dilemma—who is good and who is bad in a situation where communists imprison fascists in a labor camp—is transferred to the reader.

Beyond this self-imposed neutrality, which is meant to protect a wavering self, Kaplan makes more obvious rhetorical gestures that establish and maintain the superiority of the traveler and cast him in the position of the colonizer. They pervade the book from start to finish and function as a protective shield against the self's annihilation. One of Kaplan's ongoing rhetorical gestures is to set boundaries. Some are strictly geographical—lines on the changing map of the region—but most of them are intellectual, even spiritual, buffers between himself and the subjects he describes. The line between the West and the Balkans lies in Zagreb, but it is more than a border; it is a time warp: "I arrived in Zagreb by train from Klagenfurt. The last decade of the century was upon me. My ears were tuned to smoldering, phantom voices that I knew were about to explode once again" (ibid., 5). Zagreb engulfs the past and the future but seems to evade the present. To Kaplan, the time warp is not an accidental feature of Zagreb but a characteristic of the region: "This was a time-capsule world: a dim stage upon which people raged, spilled blood, experienced visions and ecstasies" (ibid., xxi). In true colonial fashion, Kaplan places the Balkans in the past of civilization, dominated by violence, savagery, and mysticism.

Violence is what Kaplan wants his reader to perceive as the dominant characteristic of the region. The prologue reconstructs scenes of medieval gore and World War II atrocities that are hardly distinguishable from one another. " 'You don't know what it is to kill with a hammer, with nails, clubs, do you?' "

exclaims one of his Serbian informants (ibid., xvii). "They made the victims, all Jews, strip naked in the freezing dark and get down on all fours on the conveyor ramp. Whining in terror, the Jews were driven through all the automated stages of slaughter" (ibid., xviii). Although he has no opportunity to witness any violence, Kaplan relishes such accounts of bloodshed that, he suggests, are unique to the Balkans. "What does the earth look like in the places where people commit atrocities?" (ibid.), wonders Kaplan, with a righteous indignation doubled by the satisfaction of having found the one place on earth that concentrates all evil and can prove his own moral superiority by contrast. For what Kaplan has found in the Balkans is not only the "unsimulated adventure" he tells us he is seeking but the opportunity to become, in Todorov's words, "secure in his own superiority" as well.

Another Western stereotype that Kaplan reinforces is that Balkan "savages" are sexually depraved. His proof of "the triumph of violence and sexual instinct over the rule of law" (ibid., 6) still lingers in modern day Bucharest, where he is assailed by prostitutes. Overt sexuality marks the appearance of Bulgarians: "Traikov had an extremely virile and lecherous grin" (ibid., 211). In Serbia, even a nun "had a strong, lusty appearance, with high cheekbones and fiery, maternal eyes" (ibid., 33–34). Delving into Romanian history, Kaplan unearths juicy gossip about corrupt monarchs such as Carol II, who "had gone native in the worst possible way" (ibid., 85). The king's Anglo-German extraction does not matter, since his sexual appetite, which takes on mythical proportions in the accounts of local historians, whom Kaplan does not doubt, is explained by his affinity with the natives. In old colonial fashion, sexuality is not only condemned from the perspective of Puritan principles but is also perceived as a "native" primitive trait, a mark of moral underdevelopment.

Kaplan shares the attitude of older colonial writers in intricate detail. The lack of technology, or simply of Western products, leads him to conclude that the violence, sexuality, and mysticism of the natives are their direct results: "The Albanian men crowding next to me on the back seat of the bus south from Zagreb had eyes glazed over by trachoma. They wore threadbare pants held up by safety pins in places where zippers should have been. . . . There was a fight over a seat. Two men began shouting at each other: this I was used to. They began shoving each other and would have come to blows if others had not intervened" (ibid., 41). People wearing threadbare pants with no zippers can only be violent. In *The Conquest of America*, Todorov shows how, to Columbus, the nudity of the Indians suggested intellectual and spiritual poverty. Five hundred years after Columbus, Kaplan still takes the clothes of the natives for indices of their character. On the rare occasions when he meets people dressed in Western clothes, he finds them more enlightened and congenial: "Mungiu had a friendly face. He smiled easily, had black wavy hair of ordinary length, and wore a Western-made dungaree jacket. Unlike the others in the office of *Opinia Studenţească*, Mungiu could have been taken for a university student in America" (1994, 124). We are not surprised to learn Mungiu is most receptive to advanced democratic ideas. He is as ready for democracy as the Indians admired by Bartolomé de las Casas were for Christianity. Democracy and "the American way" in Kaplan's writing play the part that Christianity played in the time of America's or Africa's colonization.

Given the magnitude of the threat to his identity, Kaplan's gesture of reverting to an old-fashioned colonial stance must be seen not as a shortcoming but as a defense against the alien worldview that both seduces and threatens him. His desire to understand "with his whole being" is genuine, but it cannot carry him past the limit where his own self is in danger. Knowledge, for which the self was to be sacrificed, is sacrificed to the self.

Kaplan's attitude is in no way personal; it signals a crisis of American self-definition where a colonial attitude remains central, even in the absence of colonialism. Although anticolonialist ideology has banished racism and ethnocentrism, it may not have erased the need to find nations that one can, in all moral rectitude, despise and put down. Such a need is essential to an identity that depends on the negative images of others to construct an image of the self. And it is in this context that knowledge of the other threatens the self with annihilation. The vilification of others is nothing but the defense mechanism of a self that knows no other center than the one outside. The question for those who seek to know the other, then, is not how to acquire that knowledge, or how to integrate the data of the senses with the mindset that processes them, but rather how to find a way to think about the self independently of the images of others, how to define the self in a positive way.

NOTES

1. His books include *Marking Our Past: West Virginia's Historical Highway Markers* (2002), *Soldiers of God: With Islamic Warriors in Afghanistan and Pakistan* (2001), *Warrior Politics: Why Leadership Requires a Pagan Ethos* (2001), *Eastward to Tartary: Travels in the Balkans, the Middle East, and the Caucasus* (2000), *An Empire Wilderness. Travels into America's Future* (1998), *The Ends of the Earth: From Togo to Turkmenistan, from Iran to Cambodia, a Journey to the Frontier of Anarchy* (1995), *The Arabists: The Romance of an American Elite* (1993), *Balkan Ghosts: A Journey through History* (1993), *Soldiers of God: With the Mujahidin in Afghanistan* (1990), and *Surrender or Starve: The Wars behind the Famine* (1988).

2. The reviews were mixed on Kaplan's use of past writings about the Balkans. Joseph F. Constance found it appropriate: "Kaplan takes the reader on a marvelous tour through the [Balkan] peninsula, using as his own guides the writings of John Reed, C. L. Sulzberger, and Rebecca West. In each nation he encounters characters who are both fascinating and frightening and accompanies each adventure with a concise and powerful historical sketch that makes for a superior narrative" (1993, 179). István Deak, on he other hand, thought this led to simplifications: "Mr. Kaplan is often judicious in his assessments, but almost as often he is unable to distinguish among diverse forms of political oppression. It makes no sense, for instance, to repeat Rebecca West's preju-

diced attacks on Austria-Hungary in her famous *Black Lamb and Grey Falcon*. Hapsburg misrule does not deserve the same label as, say, the tyranny of Nicolae Ceauşescu in Romania" (1993, 3).

3. See Clifford Geertz's critique of Malinowski in *Local Knowledge*, 55–70.

4. Geertz uses the term to argue that knowledge is always local; that is, culturally determined. As such, the "knowledge" of each culture presents a different worldview.

WORKS CITED

Constance, Joseph W. Review of Robert D. Kaplan, *Balkan Ghosts: A Journey through History*. *Library Journal* 118 (1993): 179.

Deak, István. "A World Gone Raving Mad." Review of Robert D. Kaplan, *Balkan Ghosts: A Journey through History*. *New York Times Book Review* March 28, 1993, 3.

Geertz, Clifford. *Local Knowledge: Further Essays in Interpretive Anthropology*. New York: Basic Books, 1983.

Gray, Rockwell. "Travel." In *Temperamental Journeys: Essays on the Modern Literature of Travel*, ed. Michael Kowalewski, 33–52. Athens and London: University of Georgia Press, 1992.

Kaplan, Robert D. *Balkan Ghosts: A Journey through History*. New York: Vintage Books, 1994.

Kowalewski, Michael. "Introduction: The Modern Literature of Travel." In *Temperamental Journeys: The Modern Literature of Travel*, ed. Michael Kowalewski, 1–18. Athens and London: University of Georgia Press, 1992.

Kuhn, Thomas S. *The Structure of Scientific Revolutions*. Chicago: University of Chicago Press, 1970.

Pratt, Mary Louise. *Imperial Eyes: Travel Writing and Transculturation*. New York: Routledge, 1992.

Todorov, Tzvetan. *The Conquest of America: The Question of the Other*. Trans. Richard Howard. New York: Harper Torchbooks, 1987.

———. *The Morals of History*. Trans. Alyson Waters. Minneapolis: University of Minnesota Press, 1995.

Part Two

(Re-)Adaptations

In school, we all knew that Paweł's father was a prominent Party official. He had things none of the rest of us had—real blue jeans, trips abroad, special lessons, any book or toy he wanted. (At that time, feeling jealous, no doubt, I often thought that the healthy flush on his cheeks resembled the shape of the Soviet Union.) Even aside from the fact that no teacher would risk crossing him, all these things gave him a big head start. Of course, he was also very smart, healthy, and easygoing. He was part of the aristocracy of our time. Once we saw him with these things, we thought of desiring them ourselves: clearly travel and luxuries were good if they were the treats the elite saved for themselves and their children.

So I showed up at my fifteenth high school reunion—you know, the successful but unpretentious American-educated university professor, nicely dressed in the informal American style, happy to visit old friends now that travel back and forth from West to East is easy. And who should drive up but Paweł, in a Mercedes, very elegant. His new capitalist-style business was doing well; soon he had to leave, apologetically, to make it to an important meeting. Before taking his leave, he managed to mention that he comes through the States quite often, usually to see friends or to do some business on his way to the Caribbean.

Some things don't change: once you get a head start, you can easily stay ahead. The former communist nomenklatura now flourishes as a new commercial elite. The old aristocracy lost the revolution, but this aristocracy has held tightly and yet flexibly to its privileges, passing them down to the next generation in spite of political change. (I am no longer sure, though, that I can link Paweł's coloring to any specific country.) (MZ)

Woman at an open-air market in Nowy Targ, Poland. 1997.
Photograph by Willard Pate. Used by permission.

The struggle for identity in the new Eastern Europe is not only the familiar competition between classes and individuals but also a question of understanding old, traditional, or ongoing cultural values and practices in new ways. If the first part of this volume concentrated on reading what is present in order to understand it more deeply and usefully, this second part focuses in on continuing commercial and artistic elements, in particular on the ways these transforming continuities are read and misread, appropriated, adapted, and variously understood. Our title, "(Re-)Adaptations," reflects as well the chameleon-like quality of the best of postsocialist cultural production and scholarship—that is, the ability to take in the new and even blend in with the puzzling and unexpected while one's shape and backbone remain the "same." The seven chapters included here reveal both misunderstood and outmoded elements in the interpretive moves between and within East and West and an energetic resilience among high-culture and popular artistic producers in Eastern Europe—as well as some surprising second chances at life for cultural products that no one in the East had much respect for back in "the good old days" of mature socialism.

Halina Filipowicz's essay, "Shifting a Cultural Paradigm: Between the Mystique and the Marketing of Polish Theatre," addresses the performativity of critical discourse. Especially when faced with a prestigious tradition such as Polish theater, critics may be stubborn in refusing to give up the mythic dichotomies and heroic or patronizing readings of Eastern Europe—where, after all, until recently art still counted for a lot more than it does in Peoria. Polish theater gained fame after the Second World War with productions that were both politically significant and artistically innovative; its mystique was as assiduously cultivated by Western scholars and admirers as by its local practitioners. The loss of its oppositional position today may lead to nostalgia or regret in some quarters, but as Filipowicz, a Polish scholar teaching in the United States, shows, the conception of that theater's past is centrally important in its continuing development. She demands fidelity to historical fact in evaluating the institution and honesty about what artists and directors might undertake in the present, including tendentious choices or interpretation of repertoire. Rainer Gries presents the prehistory of a well-known East German soft drink, Club Cola, whose reintroduction after unification served as the occasion for some canny employment of Cold War film footage and propaganda clichés in "'Hurrah, I'm Still Alive!' East German Products Demonstrating East German Identities." His study brings out both the gentle humor of current advertisements, which is suited to the peddling of refreshments, and the deeper significance of their product's appeal to consumers with a common history of experience and interpretation.

Slovak-American painter and art professor Paul Krainak offers an in-depth reading of several recent works in "Cryptographic Art of Bratislava: Configurations of Absence in Post-Communist Installation Art." Krainak offers keys to interpretation of artworks from Slovakia in which densely packed and subtle cultural codes are not only an Aesopic response to censorship but also part of a well-developed artistic strategy with a long tradition, one that requires a different approach and awareness from the Western viewer. Ethnomusicologist and performer Carol Silverman traces a different encounter between Eastern European tradition and Western audience: the rise to international fame and peculiar representation in the West of Bulgarian female folk choirs, especially the Mystère des Voix Bulgares. Her chapter, " 'Move Over Madonna': Gender, Representation, and the 'Mystery' of Bulgarian Voices," tells as much about economic relationships between and within East and West as about the distortions in cultural values and practices that cut across political and monetary systems. She illustrates how Western admiration for ethnically or racially marked practitioners of "world" music need not preclude exploitation of their music and creative gifts—in ways not so different from the Bulgarian vocalists' previous exploitation as socialist producers of music.

Mark Andryczyk, himself a musician, singer, and composer who travels frequently to Ukraine and collaborates with musicians there, offers a brief outline of the art scene in the cultural center of western Ukraine, the city of Lviv, in "Four Bearings of West for the Lviv Bohema." Working from a history that combines Austro-Hungarian tradition with Soviet experience, a particular closeness to Polish culture, and a sometimes-vexed relationship with Ukrainian diaspora communities elsewhere, most artists do not regret the shift from Soviet-style organization, where the demand for compromise fueled a lively private and underground culture. Andryczyk suggests that for young artists the experience of a socialist command economy in the arts was not bad preparation for negotiating the Western art market: this community seems to be making the transition with both humor and style. Věra Sokolová offers a more sociological examination of the (mis-)uses of humor and traditions of representation in her essay, " 'Don't Get Pricked!' Representation and the Politics of Sexuality in the Czech Republic." Among many other connections, she elegantly demonstrates the ways sexism and heterosexism feed off one another in a developing public discourse.

The last word in our collection is an idiosyncratic and performative essay by "Benni Goodman, PhD." He offers an imaginative and improvisatory version of the post-communist intellectual landscape in and about Bulgaria today, moving between past and present, fiction and analysis, U.S. academe and a café in the main square of Sofia. Such slippages pervade our experience of space as "an imaginary foundation" (Geyer-Ryan 1996, 120): in the new economies of visual and narrative exchange, the past does not necessarily yield to the present. Like artifacts, buildings, and cities, human beings too are transformed into symbols of new orders and new relationships.

eight

Shifting a Cultural Paradigm

Between the Mystique and the
Marketing of Polish Theatre

Halina Filipowicz

I

It will not be controversial, I suspect, to suggest that post-communist Polish culture has sprung a not-so-subtle surprise on even its most astute interpreters. In the early 1990s, when I began research for this essay during one of my (all-too-) many furloughs from work on Polish cultural mythology, leading Polish intellectuals were enthusiastic about the prospects of culture in new democratic Poland. Scholars such as Maria Janion were convinced that the end of communism in 1989 marked the beginning of a new era of Polish culture. No longer trapped within a demoralizing system of ideological constraints and censorship restrictions, the cultural scene would thrive on open-minded encounters with ideas and images. My own view was less optimistic. Where others saw a transition to participatory democracy and free enterprise, I saw shrines of patriotic martyrdom, litanies of accusations, and museums of taboos, so I went back to my project on Polish cultural mythology.

A decade later, Janion conceded that the euphoric predictions of the early 1990s were "utopian illusions" (Janion 2001). According to Janion, the Polish cultural scene is fraught with complacency, obscurantism, and defensiveness, which make a free and open exchange of ideas difficult. "Something really terrible is going on in Poland," she concluded (ibid.). At that point I knew I had to return to this essay, at least in part as a way of working through the issues (and taboos) encountered in researching it.

The post-1989 changes have been sufficiently intense (and we are sufficiently in thrall to hyped-up rhetoric) to compel some among us to call them revolutionary: the collapse of communism in Eastern Europe has been tagged "the quiet revolution," "the Velvet Revolution," even "a market revolution." It is evident, though, that not every change affects every institution and cultural practice in precisely the same way. I want to focus on the dynamics of encounter and conflict, of resistance and exchange between the "East" and the "West" as they have played out in Polish theatre since 1989.[1]

The questions I want to take up in this essay are these: What effect does the post-communist transformation have on Polish theatre as a cultural practice as well as an institution? What new topics, issues, and problems does a shift to a different paradigm—to democratic values such as pluralism and to a competitive capitalist culture—bring into Polish theatre? How does theatre respond to the changes that are affecting Polish society? Does it still tack up a blazing, bracing series of warning signs on the perimeter of mainstream culture, as it did, famously, in the 1970s and 1980s?[2] How can a discussion of post-1989 theatre, through the use of comparative and other dialogic techniques, enable something like a mutual interrogation between the "East" and the "West" to throw fresh light on the cultural contests of our own day and perhaps on those of the past too?

I have enclosed the terms "East" and "West" in skeptical quotation marks to suggest that the line separating the "East" from the "West" is less a fact of nature than it is a trait of imaginative geography. The point I am making here is a rudimentary one: the concepts "East" and "West" are discursive constructs whose boundaries are under perpetual negotiation, but the constructs continue to exercise disciplinary power in the formation of new knowledge. One reason for this is that scholarship continues to be framed by traditional linguistic, ethnic, and national boundaries. For example, one can specialize in Polish cultural studies and know little about Jewish culture, and vice versa, in both cases ignoring the dynamic relationship of interaction and exchange between Poles and Jews over the past eight centuries.

I will speak here as an expatriate Polish critic who examines Polish theatre and drama from within a cultural space that is heterogeneous and polyvocal. Within this space, however, the non-Russian cultures of Eastern Europe do not have the same institutional and intellectual status as Russian culture. As Richard Schechner has pointed out, for example, most young Americans who are interested in theatre do not know much about the Polish artist and theorist Jerzy Grotowski, even though he is "one of the four great directors of Western twentieth-century theatre" (Stanislavsky, Meyerhold, and Brecht round out the list) (Schechner 2001, xxv). To put these points another way, working on cultures which had been rarely considered in the American academy before may sometimes feel like swimming against the tide.

Halina Filipowicz

I will also speak as a feminist critic who writes about a society that, for all its rhetoric about a transition to democracy, holds on to patriarchal principles: "[M]en are consistently overrated, while women are underrated" (Valian 1999, 2).[3] It is socially acceptable for a highly respected Polish critic to announce in his rebuttal to a book review by a woman colleague that his opponent is "a decidedly attractive blonde" (Jarzębski 2001, 15). It is not surprising that Polish feminist critics tend to tread gently and support ideas about gender that harm women—ideas such as the hypothesis that women are naturally affectionate and nurturing. It is not unusual for Polish feminist critics to promote "safe" women writers while ignoring those who, like Manuela Gretkowska, refuse to write and behave like "correctly" gendered women.[4] What passes for feminist criticism, then, is often some version of apolitical "images-of-women" methodology, while gender analysis remains largely a blind spot.

I will speak, moreover, as a worker in the vineyard called Polish studies in North America. In 2000, the publication of Jan Tomasz Gross's *Neighbors: The Destruction of the Jewish Community in Jedwabne, Poland*, which documents the massacre of the Jewish residents of the town of Jedwabne by their Polish neighbors in 1941, sent shock waves that continue to reverberate across the Polish-American community. Many Polish-Americans have reacted with indignation, believing that Gross's portrait of Polish society adds up to character assassination. As a result, the Polish-American community has increasingly come to expect the field of Polish studies in North America to promote a uniformly positive image of Polish culture instead of concentrating on open-minded scholarly inquiry. It is not uncommon for scholars in this field to hear from Polish-American students and their parents: "You ought to be inspiring us. You ought to help us build up our pride and spread the word about our great Polish culture." This line of reasoning rescripts Polish studies into a site of struggle for control over the terms of Polish-American identity. To accept this argument, however, is to turn Polish studies into a clearinghouse for portable Polishness, a rather limiting proposition.

Inevitably, then, my queries for myself resonate with a question posed by Gilles Deleuze and Félix Guattari: "How to become a nomad and an immigrant and a gypsy in relation to one's own language?" (Deleuze and Guattari 1986, 19). Caught between my Polish "deep-rootedness" and my American "naturalization," I rephrase the question. How to become a nomad and an immigrant and a gypsy in relation to my home culture as well as my adopted culture? This notion of in-betweenness opens the theoretical space my essay explores.

II

Reports on post-1989 Polish theatre usually begin with dire pronouncements about financial constraints that put pressure on repertory companies. "The more desperate organize strikes," notes a prominent theatre critic, "as if they didn't want to comprehend that under capitalism not every educated person has to have a job, especially in the arts" (Baniewicz 1996, 462; trans. modified). It is evident that theatre was not prepared for a sea change in the economics of Polish culture. I will come back to this issue later. First, I propose to contextualize the dilemmas of Polish theatre within a broader framework.

Many Western observers find it difficult to reconcile the transformation of post-communist Poland with Polish society's fierce and enduring attachment to traditional nonliberal scripts. Indeed, what could be more natural for Western observers, having contested communist autocracy in the name of democratic freedom, than to presume that the undoing of communism would sweep away all obstacles to democracy? The notion that democratic political institutions require the support of a democratic political culture is pervasive in political theory; many scholars treat democratic virtues and liberal values as synonymous.[5] Yet post-communist Poland has embraced predominantly nonliberal values, as evidenced by the imposition of religious instruction in public schools and by restrictions on divorce and women's reproductive rights.[6] What has emerged from the quiet revolution in Poland, then, is a very traditional culture rooted in religious fundamentalism, patriarchal mythology, and exclusivist ethnonationalism. Seen in this context, the reluctance of many Poles to challenge the "hidden" taboo of particular forms of inequality (such as gender discrimination) as well as "unspoken" (yet still active) nationalist narratives becomes less puzzling.

Some of the fundamental democratic values such as pluralism and gender equality create a terrible dilemma in post-communist Poland. When communism collapsed, the need for clear-cut identities of "us" and "them" became especially urgent, and a demand for scapegoats was (and still is) at its highest to feed the totalizing desire for order, stability, and control. Poles still nourish a collective memory of having suffered unjustly, of having been betrayed by the West, of having been victimized by history. Without the myth of victimization, who are we? I am not saying that victimization is a myth but that it has served as a myth for Poles who claim it as part of their national identity.

The self-representation of Poles as history's victims is, paradoxically, conflated with a self-definition that claims agency for Poles, vigorously denying any suspicion of Polish passivity. This self-definition narcissistically overflows with reputedly stock Polish attributes: honor, love of freedom, and courage in adversity. With expert use of the traditional discourse of military heroism, Poles have constructed for themselves a position that relies on the terms of the male heroics of action: they attribute their ethical authority to the courage of willing self-sacrifice for God, nation, and "your freedom and ours" (to use a Polish rallying cry). Thus, Polish cultural mythology wants us to believe that Poles have passionate military heroism stitched into their genetic code. In short, the Polish nation is that extraordinary community which joins the roles of hero and victim into one. Anything that challenges the self-image of Polish exceptionalism is viewed as an affront to Polish pride and therefore meets with indignation and denial.

But there is more at issue. Underlying my argument is a disquieting recognition that the relationship between cultures is uneven. For much of modern history, Poland has not been an interlocutor of the West but its silent Other. As a result, Polish culture is seen in the West as one of the weaker cultures, and Western perceptions of Poles tend to fall into Orientalizing stereotypes. This fosters cultural insecurities in Polish society, making open-minded debates all the more difficult. Poles are indeed victims of unflattering stereotypes. I would argue, however, that they are also players in their own right as they forge and manipulate their identities and others' beliefs about these identities. We need to know more about how Poles invent self-invention: How do they construct their own sense of who they are and how do their perceptions of the Other inform these identity formations?

An obvious place to begin examining these questions is live theatre. It seems almost a banality to say that live theatre is the most communal of all the arts: it depends on public performance and collective viewing. It seems almost another banality—yet one that we, as participants in "a rampantly visualist culture" (Ong 1967, 10) or, more precisely, in the twentieth century's surrender to the monocular imagery of the photograph, cinema, and television, can lose sight of—to point out that live theatre is differently visual. In the epistemological sense, of course, theatre subscribes to a kind of visual absolutism: it tends to represent reality as though a thing can be known only if it is seen and seen clearly, at times even as if seeing was constitutive of truth. Theatre's visualism, however, always carries a subversive propensity because, unlike the camera, it offers unmediated and decentered vantage points and thus challenges all unitary ambitions.

III

Poland's transformation poses a particular challenge for those critics in the West who have followed the Polish theatre scene. To report on Polish theatre when it articulated social discontent and suffered political repressions was gallant, noble, ethically necessary. By writing about the blacklisted Eighth Day Theatre or clandestine performances of the Home Theatre, critics felt that they were making a contribution to the Polish struggle for democracy. They were no longer just critics but spokespersons for the oppressed in the international forum; their writings were no longer just essays but acts of solidarity and support. The emergence of a new democratic Poland has made this kind of ethical engagement redundant. How does one write about a Polish theatre that has lost its political mystique?

There are other challenges as well. The work of Jerzy Grotowski and Tadeusz Kantor, Eighth Day and Gardzienice has shaped Western perceptions of Polish theatre. As a result, it is tempting to move within a magic circle of the familiar—to trace the influence of Grotowski and Kantor, to pay homage to Eighth Day, to make one more pilgrimage to Gardzienice. I would argue, however, that while Polish theatre will undoubtedly continue to draw on the achievements of Grotowski and Kantor, Eighth Day and Gardzienice, the newcomers will determine, as always, the course that theatre will take. These newcomers, some of them noisy and some reclusive, work on the fringes of mainstream culture, providing an oppositional voice and alternative forms to the self-esteeming cul-de-sac in which post-1989 Polish theatre has found itself.

Yet the focus of Western theatre critics tends to be elsewhere. Some of them see ambitious projects by star directors such as Jerzy Grzegorzewski, Jerzy Jarocki, Krystian Lupa, and Andrzej Wajda jostling with Western-style commercial productions and they are quick to applaud what seems to be a new vitality of Polish theatre. Others lament Polish theatre's flight from the political commitment that was its honorable hallmark in the past. These opposing views—the enthusiasm for new productions by leading directors and the disappointment with the post-1989 theatre scene—are not contradictory. Both rest on the assumption that a political revolution generates a revolution in the arts. Some Western observers of Polish theatre are apt to conclude that this process is already under way; others voice their disappointment that it is so slow in coming.

But the issue is even more complex, more paradoxical. On the one hand, Western commentators on Polish theatre welcome the processes that have dismantled an oppressive political system. On the other hand, they look back with nostalgia to the mystique that attracted them to the "exotic" theatre behind the Iron Curtain in the first place. For example, director and critic Paul Allain was drawn to Polish experimental theatre in the late 1980s while "searching for inspiration in the flagging British theatre" (Allain 1995, 93). For several years, he was associated with Gardzienice, a performance group that makes its home in a village of the same name in Poland's neglected eastern border area.[7] Analyzing Gardzienice's *Carmina Burana* (1990), he cannot hold back his sense of disappointment and even betrayal: "[A]s both a Westerner and as one of those who [are] too young to have directly witnessed the heyday of Polish theatre, I must confess some nostalgia for what I have read so much about but have never actually known" (Allain 1995, 113).

How has *Carmina Burana* failed to meet Allain's expectations? His frame of reference is defined by Gardzienice's earlier production, *Avvakum* (1983), which conflates the story of the eponymous leader of a religious movement in seventeenth-century Russia and the exilic imagery of Adam Mickiewicz's Romantic drama *Forefathers' Eve* (*Dziady*, 1832). Gardzienice developed *Avvakum* during a period of martial law imposed by the communist authorities in 1981 to suppress the democratic opposition. One could argue that the forbidden issue of Russian neocolonial hegemony in the so-called Soviet bloc was central to the production and that therefore Avvakum's story was as much an inspiration as it was a smokescreen to evade censorship. Yet it could also be argued that the production refused the familiar polarization of "us" versus

169

"them" and instead explored what Edward Said would call, in *Culture and Imperialism*, "intertwined histories": the experiences of ruler and ruled that could not be easily disentangled, even though a hard and fast line separated one from the other in matters of rule and authority (Said 1994, 3).

In contrast to *Avvakum*, *Carmina Burana* is unequivocally Western, beginning with the Latin title, which can be translated as *The Songs of Beuern*. The production draws on a cycle of medieval Latin songs known as *Codex Buranus* and on the legends of Tristan, Isolde, Merlin, and Vivian. One could argue that by staging a production set during the anarchic and hedonistic period of the early thirteenth century, Gardzienice has found an idiom to capture the disequilibrium, the indeterminacy, the "anything goes" sensibility of the post-1989 age. Not so, claims Allain. He writes: "For me, the performance is apolitical, and has few specific contemporary implications. . . . In this timeless, abstract piece, Gardzienice has moved from the specific and political to the universal and broadly mythological, from the more objective to the personal" (Allain 1995, 113). From Allain's perspective, the "Western" *Carmina Burana* loses to the "Eastern" *Avvakum*.

To put the shift from *Avvakum* to *Carmina Burana* in broader terms, Gardzienice has deterritorialized its creative work.[8] To Allain, this is a bad thing, since deterritorialization destabilizes conventions of identity. Predictably, he cautions that Gardzienice's "firmly established identity" is in jeopardy (ibid., 113). He concedes that Polish audiences watching *Carmina Burana* "perhaps feel closer to Western culture" (ibid.). He admits that many viewers in Poland "are tired of the now clichéd images of oppression and exile, theatricalized religious symbolism and, to put it crudely, the sight of black boots stomping in the darkness" (ibid.). He hedges his argument with such caveats throughout, but it is obvious that he is troubled by Gardzienice's transgression of cultural boundaries between the "East" and the "West." The result can only be a denaturalized product such as *Carmina Burana*.[9]

While Gardzienice is clearly entering a condition of borderless culture, Allain asserts a renewed insistence on cultural difference. As a judicious and well-informed critic, he is sensitive to the problems of his undertaking. He is aware that his position as a Western theatre practitioner has shaped his image of Polish theatre. He bravely confronts his Western perspective vis-à-vis the aspirations of Polish artists and audiences. He neither camouflages his expectations nor censures his disappointment. In his incisive study of Gardzienice, he documents a change from an "Eastern" to a "Western" theatre—a change that forces a realignment of "us" and "them." But his self-reflexivity does not extend beyond a certain point. He never examines questions such as these: Why has he come to view Polish theatre as a monolithic body of political commitment? Why does he insist on measuring *Carmina Burana* in terms of its relevance to political developments in Poland? Why does he fail to mention that the company often performed *Avvakum* and *Carmina Burana* back to back in a single evening? Why does he want to keep Gardzienice in its place by denying

"Eastern" theatre artists the right to draw on diverse materials? In short, Allain never interrogates his own mythologization of the hierarchies of experience, which has led him to locate an alternative to "the flagging British theatre" in Gardzienice's interactive performances on the borders of professional and amateur theatre.

These silences subvert Allain's seemingly fair-minded critique. Thus, when he expresses his concern about Gardzienice's identity and lectures about the dangers of cultural transgression, he unwittingly assumes the paternalistic voice of the Westerner offering advice to underdeveloped nations with an air of cultural superiority. He remains enmortgaged to a mythic "Polishness" locked in the torture chamber of the familiar binaries: rural rather than urban, communal rather than individual, engagé rather than merely aesthetic.

IV

A realignment of "us" and "them" has been thrust on the Polish theatre community as well. Those who were previously enthralled by the "West" as an embodiment of creative freedom now confront a free-market economy. As Elżbieta Baniewicz has aptly observed:

> Free market policies were welcomed with open arms, but without full awareness of how destructive they are for culture, and for theatre in particular—especially in a poor country without a strong middle class prepared to assist culture voluntarily. . . . Today, theatre luminaries speak loudly of theatre's downfall . . . and the necessity of maintaining state support for culture—something they were willing to abolish completely just a few years ago in exchange for the free market's invisible hand. (Baniewicz 1996, 461)

The system of subsidized repertory companies was established in the late 1940s as part of the communist government's cultural agenda, which conflated education and indoctrination. State subsidies ensured full year-round employment to theatre companies, including technical crews and administrative staff. It was possible to create stable ensembles, to have long rehearsal periods, to explore problems of acting and stagecraft without the commercial pressures of the box office. Artistic innovation could be nurtured not just in a handful of studio or experimental theatres but in mainstream theatres as well, as part of their day-to-day work. After 1989, only about a dozen theatres, which were deemed particularly prestigious, retain state support. Others have been turned over to local governments. The problem is that while some local governments see theatre as a valuable cultural asset to a particular city or region, others have different priorities.

The economic impoverishment of Polish theatre is real, and I do not suggest that we ignore the material realities in which theatre operates. But the focus on decreasing resources and financial constraints has obscured some hard questions. Does Poland need some sixty repertory companies that stage approximately 300 new productions each year? Is there enough interest in live theatre to generate public support for these companies? Have theatre schools examined scrupulously the size and operations of their training programs? These questions are tactfully evaded in debates on Polish theatre.

It is a truism that theatre requires only a steady supply of money and talent in order to flourish. But is it really a truism? The need for live and hence "warm" theatre is ever more problematic in the era of packaged, distant, "cool" culture. Polish theatre is now confronting what the state subsidies have helped mask: live theatre is something that many people can do without. Of course, one could argue that declining attendance has to do with higher ticket prices.[10] However, the relentless exodus of theatre audiences began in the mid-1950s when free and inexpensive tickets were widely available. Until 1980, labor unions bought blocks of tickets and distributed them among union members. Those tickets often remained unused, and actors performed before rows of mostly empty chairs. But box offices posted "Sold Out" signs, and annual statistics looked impressive. The system of so-called sponsored audiences is now over, and there is nothing to mask the disagreeable fact that between 1988 and 1994, theatre attendance fell by 50 percent.

The so-called sponsored audiences were a false or captive market, but from the theatres' point of view they were the market. Together with state subsidies, they kept theatres afloat. Today, however, the tables are turned. In a cruel twist of evolutionary fate, theatres have lost their major market. They have had to face the hard facts of a new economic reality. This change in perspective has forced theatres to become more commercially minded, more competitive, and more aggressive.

Before 1989, theatres did not worry too much about the audience as audience. Now theatres woo audiences with a predictable mix of musicals, melodramas, comedies, and farces, many of them imported from the West. These survivalist measures, however, are precisely what many critics see as a threat to the integrity of Polish theatre. To put it in more general terms, they fear that Western-style commercialization is leading to a careless jettisoning of the Polish cultural tradition. Though their concern has validity, it has become a tactic for demeaning anything that does not fit a particular construction of Polish culture. Baniewicz's article is a case in point.

Writing for an American audience, Baniewicz highlights the point that theatre has been a pivotal institution in Polish culture since the Enlightenment and a major source of Polish pride and self-image. She presents Polish theatre as a historically constituted stronghold of high art, patriotic morality, and civic conscience. This model of theatre grew out of the exigencies of national survival when Poland was under foreign control (1772–1918). Today, argues Baniewicz, the concept of theatre as a conflation of high art, ethical commitment, and public good still defines "the tradition that has shaped the unique character of Polish theatre and the special expectations of Polish theatregoers" (Baniewicz 1996, 466; see also Braun 1996, 4–6). In making this argument, she claims that theatre in the West is "a place for noncommittal reflection and entertainment," while theatre in Poland aspires to be "art with a capital 'A'; . . . a place where people stand before their Fate, God, History, and Society" (Baniewicz 1996, 465–466).

However, Baniewicz's sweeping argument about the unique tradition of Polish theatre rests on incomplete evidence. Polish theatre was alive and well not only in well-upholstered houses in metropolitan centers but also in ramshackle spaces where provincial actors eked out a meager living and in dusty classrooms where students acted in plays. Moreover, while it is true that theatre in Poland under foreign occupation was a major public forum for transmitting cultural mythology with its seductive emotional rhetoric of patriotism, this mythology was articulated primarily through the genre of popular drama designed to attract large audiences. For most playgoers, then, their patriotic desire was constructed and consumed by works such as Władysław Ludwik Anczyc's *Kościuszko at Racławice* (*Kościuszko pod Racławicami*, 1880), which regularly played to sold-out houses. *Kościuszko at Racławice* skillfully joins patriotic pageantry with melodramatic sentimentalism, a combination that appealed in a truly democratic way to thousands of spectators regardless of their social status and educational background. Today *Kościuszko at Racławice* may appear naive, but in its own time it admirably performed "responsibilities over and above purely artistic ones" (to borrow Kazimierz Braun's phrase from a different context [Braun 1996, 6]).

I am not saying that Polish theatre artists should abandon their aspirations to high art and revive *Kościuszko at Racławice*. Rather, I argue that the history of Polish theatre and drama is much richer, much more diverse than many Polish critics are willing to admit.[11] I also contend that we must move beyond grand synthesizing modes that are based on the monuments of Polish drama and theatre and uncover the enormously interesting and constantly shifting networks of relations between different voices and traditions within what might otherwise seem to be a monolithic cultural enterprise. There is simply no end to that sort of work. At present, however, the popular tradition of Polish drama and theatre is rarely mentioned in debates in Poland, and it is always suppressed in publications intended for non-Polish audiences. Thus, foreign readers are informed that Polish theatre owes its "unique character" to the masterpieces of Romantic and modernist writers such as Adam Mickiewicz and Stanisław Wyspiański, who are among the most audacious playwrights to put pen to paper.

Baniewicz is willing to concede that these masterpieces are not well qualified to speak to the concerns of post-1989 audiences. From her perspective, though, post-1989 theatre has lapsed from high art and intellectual rigor—to the detriment of the institution, audiences, and art itself. Thus, she returns to her earlier claim about "the unique character of Polish theatre" and concludes the article with a sigh of relief: "Fortunately the negative trends are slowly reversing. After unsuccessful attempts at commercialization and bringing the repertory up-to-date, theatres are going back to the well-tested canon, back to their own best tradition" (Baniewicz 1996, 477–478).

The rhetorical strain perceptible in Baniewicz's article from beginning to end suggests that the resistance to "bringing the repertory up-to-date" is not a purely artistic issue. It would not be too much to say that the insistence on "the unique character of Polish theatre"—the insistence which Baniewicz shares with many critics—is an attempt to revive the Polish mystique by upholding the superiority of spirit over matter in the larger theatre of the "East" versus the "West." Post-1989 Poland may be a newcomer to the modern commonwealth of Western democracies, but it does not come empty-handed. Against what many see as a frightening onslaught of postmodern nihilism in which "any-thing goes," Polish theatre, suggests Baniewicz, can still claim privileged access to "art with a capital 'A,' " which the West has lost.

V

Confronted with dwindling resources and the erosion of the repertory system, many theatre artists and critics speak bitterly about fickle and ungrateful audiences who have succumbed to the seduction of Western-style popular culture. One could argue, however, that theatres might attract audiences by becoming more conscious of potential spectators out there. That is, theatres might attract audiences by thinking of their primary market not as a faceless mass but as individuals who, as we all know, are varied, unpredictable, and demanding.

How to make theatre that matters? For advocates of participatory democracy, for example, Poland makes an excellent test case because it challenges the common assumption that liberal and democratic attitudes are inextricably linked. Is there a metaphor that might capture this challenge? Let me offer this one: the abortion debate. Yet no Polish theatre is interested in grappling with the implications, metaphorical or otherwise, of this debate.[12]

Among the topics that are edited out of post-1989 Polish theatre is the Catholic church, which continues to be the most powerful institution in Poland. Among the topics inadequately represented on stage is the vexed subject of certain blind spots in Poles' construction of their collective history, especially the taboos that distort and falsify the public memory of Poles' behavior during the Second World War. For Poles, the most "loaded" subject is the Jews. No serious historian would argue that Poles had direct responsibility for the Holocaust. Complicity, though, is a very different issue. Poles acted ambiguously during the Holocaust—some saving Jews, others helping Hitler murder them, the majority simply standing by. Poles' complicity in the Holo-caust—what Jan Błoński, in his well-known 1987 essay, has called "shared responsibility through failure to act" (Błoński 1990, 234)—was blurred and obfuscated, ignored or denied for over fifty years, or until the publication of Gross's *Neighbors*. Polish theatre, however, is not particularly eager to explore the politics of Polish memory with its national and nationalist imaginings. This is at a time when, sadly, the need for understanding the historical roots and contemporary manifestations of bigotry has never been more urgent.

As a Polish theatre scholar working in the West, I am especially interested in Polish theatre's negotiations of what John Rouse has called "the dubious gift of mainstream Western theatre, particularly Western drama" (Rouse 1996, 404). My starting point is a deceptively simple query: Why were post-1989 Polish audiences annoyed by *Hunting Cockroaches* (*Polowanie na karaluchy*, 1985) and *Antigone in New York* (*Antygona w Nowym Jorku*, 1992), the "American" plays of Polish writer Janusz Głowacki, who has lived in New York since 1982? The answer seems obvious. Both plays reveal disagreeable aspects of contemporary American culture by focusing on the dead-end existence of recent immigrants. Thus, Głowacki denies the construction of the United States as a site of Polish spectatorial desire. It is not surprising, then, that Polish theatregoers resented his subversion of the familiar myth of America as a land of freedom, success, and abundance.

At the same time, however, Polish revivals of two British plays of the 1950s, John Osborne's *Look Back in Anger* and Keith Waterhouse and Willis Hall's *Billy Liar*, have enjoyed successful runs. Both plays offer a trenchant critique of English middle-class mores, yet Polish theatregoers did not mind that. The different responses to Głowacki's critique of his adopted culture and to the British playwrights' critique of their own culture may suggest that Polish audiences used a double standard. One of "our kind" is not permitted to criticize the West. Moreover, an interrogation of the social and political attitudes of the British middle class does not have the same subversive power as a dismantling of the American Dream. At a time when Poland's economic makeover is accompanied by high unemployment and widespread poverty, the American myth has a therapeutic function, hence one should not tamper with it.

My test case for this argument is David Mamet's *Oleanna* (1992), which had three successful productions in Poland, each in a prestigious theatre: the Stary in Kraków (premiere on April 29, 1994), the Ateneum in Warsaw (premiere on May 7, 1994), and the Nowy in Poznań (premiere on May 1, 2002). The play's plotline involves encounters, or collisions, between a female student and a male professor. Carol, who is failing John's course, stops by his office to seek his advice. She catches him at a particularly bad time: he is on his way out to negotiate an offer on a new house. She is inarticulate; he is rushed and impatient. Misunderstandings escalate. Carol eventually files charges against John, accusing him of sexist behavior and attempted rape. He is denied tenure, and the case goes to court.

The Polish productions of *Oleanna* raise a host of questions, some of which I want to explore here. Why did three theatres choose to invest in a production of this particular play? After all, Mamet is not well known in Poland, and the subject matter—sexual harassment in the American academy—might be construed as yet another attack on the cherished American myth. What could Polish theaters gain by staging *Oleanna*?

Before I turn to the Polish productions of *Oleanna*, I want to examine the interpretive possibilities of Mamet's text. The setting—an American university—seems to be crucial. The Polish media have been eager to portray American universities as obscurantist bastions of political correctness, presided over by feminists and other Others. *Oleanna* can be read as a text that validates this cultural construction while eliciting our sympathy for John as a victim of political correctness. John may lack the qualities that make a good teacher, but he is under a lot of stress, hence he is not in control of his emotions. While we get insights into John's life outside the university to justify his behavior, we know very little about Carol. For example, we never find out where the initially timid and confused student has found her new strength or what has brought about this sudden change in her. Thus, she appears merely to confirm the traditional notion that women are "naturally" cunning and deceptive.

It seems evident, then, that *Oleanna* is not a feminist text. As Toril Moi has pointed out, however, "There is not, unfortunately, such a thing as an intrinsically feminist text: given the right historical and social context, all texts can be recuperated by the ruling powers—or appropriated by the feminist opposition" (Moi 1986, 220). Plays in particular are open to contradictory interpretations. For example, it is possible to imagine a feminist production of *Oleanna*—one that would take Carol seriously. After all, the play shows not only Carol's entrapment within narrow gender-specific expectations but also her empowerment and liberation, even though we do not know all the details. And perhaps we do not know all the details precisely because Carol has been socialized to behave like a "correctly" gendered woman—stammering, uncertain, hesitant, alternately sullen and eager to please as she tries desperately to figure out what she is expected to say, do, and be. In the end, the play offers an encounter with the transgressive Carol whose "unfeminine" difference challenges the gender codes of patriarchal mythology.

At the Stary Theatre in Kraków, director Paul Lampert chose not to take the character Carol seriously. As a result, Beata Fudalej, cast as Carol, did her best to discredit and ridicule her, while Jacek Romanowski played, with gentle humor, a clumsy yet sensitive John.

Directing *Oleanna* at Warsaw's Ateneum Theatre, Feliks Falk went a step farther and revised the ending. In the original, John hits Carol and knocks her to the floor. A moment later, he returns to his desk and arranges some papers. There is a long silence that, one could argue, compels us to reflect on the scene we have just witnessed. Perhaps the silence even turns us into actors, challenging us to act in the larger theatre of life. At the very least, it prevents us from applauding John's violence. In the Warsaw production, the final scene became a triumphant assertion of John's power. He spanked Carol with a belt, reducing her to cowering submissiveness. Message received; we can leave the theatre.

At the Nowy Theatre in Poznań, Kazimierz Braun offered yet another take on *Oleanna*. This production was fraught with a pervasive concern: with feminists such as Carol policing college campuses and enforcing political correctness, the Western world is clearly in the grip of implacable forces. Where will all this end? A tempting analogy was hard to resist. Braun set the encounters between Carol and John in an office with a view of the World Trade Center in New York. Anna Piróg played the increasingly assertive Carol as a terrorist in the making. The sound track featured the roar of approaching planes. By a directorial sleight of hand, then, the plotline of *Oleanna* was revealed to have an oblique connection with—perhaps even to foreshadow—the events of September 11th. At the same time, September 11th became an excuse to invite the audience to reflect on feminism as yet another terrorist phenomenon. In other words, Braun as director in shining armor set out to show why we need live theatre in the wired world of the information revolution, which promises to tell us more and more while preferring us to know less and less. In the process, he transformed the terrorist attacks on the World Trade Center into hard antifeminist currency and thus made his own contribution to the war on terrorism.

In the Polish productions of *Oleanna*, Carol's challenge to patriarchal ideology and practice was ridiculed, condemned, and suppressed. It is not surprising that the productions failed to activate the play's feminist potential. Indeed, it makes sense, given a neoconservative backlash against feminism in Poland. It is surprising, though, that at a time when Polish critics treat simplifications of popular culture with contemptuous dismissal, three leading theatres ignored the nuances of Mamet's play, which are suggested by a double epigraph: one from Samuel Butler's *The Way of All Flesh*, the other from an American folk song.[13] Thus, the conflict between John and Carol was reduced to a confrontation between a good guy and a scheming female driven by authoritarian, even terrorist, ambitions. Unlike Głowacki's plays, however, *Oleanna* was a godsend to post-1989 Polish theatre. With its nuances silenced, Mamet's play was put to work as a champion of the American myth. We can learn from "their" mistakes and keep "our" culture free of the feminist malaise.

VI

It goes almost without saying that Polish theatre is at a critical moment in its postwar history. The fabric of practices, ideas, and institutional frameworks that sustained it since the late 1940s has come unraveled, exposing serious gaps in the ways it has functioned. Can the fabric be mended or will it have to be rewoven and if so, on what basis?

Rather provocatively, I have been using here the term "Polish theatre." But is there such a thing as a quintessential Polish theatre? How far has "Polishness" itself changed? And what is "Polishness" anyway? Is it a feeling, an experience, a state of mind, the sense of a particular cultural tradition? To put these points more broadly, is culture a "thing" we have or, rather, a complex repertory we experience, learn, perform, and revise in our daily lives—a repertory of shared sentiments, assumptions, beliefs, symbols, and practices, all of which are continuously (though not necessarily equally rapidly) changing?

Contemporary Polish society is, of course, multicultural, especially with regard to social class. What effect will this have on Polish theatre? It may well be that the reconfiguration of Polish theatre in the twenty-first century will depend to a large extent on giving serious attention to the limitations of what monoculturalists are pleased to consider "our" culture; that is, a concept of Polish culture as a stable, fixed entity whose boundaries do not exceed the dictates of a polonocentric vision of self and community.

NOTES

I would like to thank Sibelan Forrester, Magdalena Zaborowska, and Elena Gapova for giving me this opportunity to explore several touchy subjects. For generous help in my research, I am indebted to Elwira M. Grossman, Ewa Szymańska, and Grzegorz Ziółkowski.

1. Concise accounts of post-1989 Polish theatre can be found in Baniewicz 1996; Gołaczyńska 2000; Stefanova 2000; Tyszka 1996. For more extended discussion, see Baniewicz, *Lata tłuste czy chude?*; Gołaczyńska, *Mozaika współczesności*.

2. For further discussion of this point, see Cioffi 1996.

3. Titkow 2001 offers a helpful historicized overview of contradictory and ambivalent responses to feminism in Poland. For insights into Polish women's negative attitudes toward feminism, see Fuszara 2000, 282.

4. This is particularly evident in *Pisarki polskie od średniowiecza do współczesności* (*Polish Women Writers from the Middle Ages to the Present*) by Grażyna Borkowska, Małgorzata Czermińska, and Ursula Phillips, the first Polish lexicon of this kind. In her review of the lexicon, Renata Lis takes the authors to task for their "quasi-censorship" that has edited out "the 'bad girls' of Polish literature" (Lis 2001, 35). For a shorter version of the lexicon in English, see chapters on Poland in Hawkesworth.

5. For an overview of this argument, see Feldman 2003.

6. In 1993, the predominantly male Parliament repealed the 1956 law that had legalized abortion. As a result, abortion is now allowed only in rare cases.

7. Those borderlands are actual as well as broadly metaphoric: "It is a point between the East and the West, between Russia and Europe. The routes from Gardzienice lead in both directions, marking out two different perspectives. To understand the theatre, one has to accept both, . . . regardless of the direction taken" (Zagańczyk 1991, 6). On Gardzienice's work in "Eastern" and "Western" contexts, see Filipowicz 1983 and 1987.

8. My use of the term *deterritorialization* follows Deleuze and Guattari 1986, 16–27.

9. The "Westernization" of Gardzienice continues with their latest production, *Metamorphoses, or the Golden Ass* (*Metamorfozy albo Złoty osioł*, 1997), adapted from Lucius Apuleius's tale of the same title. For an appreciative review of this production, see, e.g., Babb 2001.

10. For this argument, see Baniewicz 1996, 462.

11. I have discussed this issue in greater detail in Filipowicz 2002.

12. For the argument that the abortion debate in Poland is not only about abortion but also about political power and concepts of democracy, see Titkow 2001; Zielińska 2000.

13. Both epigraphs are missing from the Polish translation of the play (see Mamet 1994).

WORKS CITED

Allain, Paul. "Coming Home: The New Ecology of the Gardzienice Theatre Association of Poland." *The Drama Review* 39, no. 1 (Spring 1995): 93–121.

Babb, Roger. Review of *Metamorphoses, or the Golden Ass*, by Gardzienice. *Theatre Journal* 53, no. 4 (December 2001): 657–659.

Baniewicz, Elżbieta. *Lata tłuste czy chude? Szkice o teatrze 1990–2000*. Warszawa: Errata, 2000.

———. "Theatre's Lean Years in Free Poland." Trans. Joanna Dutkiewicz. *Theatre Journal* 48, no. 4 (December 1996): 461–478.

Błoński, Jan. "The Poor Poles Look at the Ghetto." 1987. In *Four Decades of Polish Essays*, ed. Jan Kott, 222–235. Evanston, Ill.: Northwestern University Press, 1990.

Borkowska, Grażyna, Małgorzata Czermińska, and Ursula Phillips. *Pisarki polskie od średniowiecza do współczesności: Przewodnik*. Gdańsk: słowo/obraz terytoria, 2000.

Braun, Kazimierz. *A History of Polish Theater, 1939–1989: Spheres of Captivity and Freedom*. Westport, Conn.: Greenwood Press, 1996.

Cioffi, Kathleen M. *Alternative Theatre in Poland 1954–1989*. Amsterdam: Harwood Academic Publishers, 1996.

Deleuze, Gilles, and Félix Guattari. *Kafka: Toward a Minor Literature*. Trans. Dana Polan. Minneapolis: University of Minnesota Press, 1986.

Feldman, Jan. *Lubavitchers as Citizens: A Paradox of Liberal Democracy*. Ithaca, N.Y.: Cornell University Press, 2003.

Filipowicz, Halina. "Expedition into Culture: The Gardzienice (Poland)." *The Drama Review* 27, no. 1 (Spring 1983): 54–71.

———. "Gardzienice: A Polish Expedition to Baltimore." *The Drama Review* 31, no. 1 (Spring 1987): 137–163.

———. "Othering the Kościuszko Uprising: Women as Problem in Polish Insurgent Discourse." In *Studies in Language, Literature, and Cultural Mythology in Poland: Investigating "The Other,"* ed. Elwira M. Grossman, 55–83. Lewiston, Maine: Edwin Mellen Press, 2002.

Fuszara, Małgorzata. "New Gender Relations in Poland in the 1990s." In *Reproducing Gender: Politics, Publics, and Everyday Life after Socialism*, ed. Susan Gal and Gail Kligman, 259–285. Princeton, N.J.: Princeton University Press, 2000.

Geyer-Ryan, Helga. "Imaginary Identity: Space, Gender, Nation." In *Vision in Context: Historical and Contemporary Perspectives on Sight*, ed. Teresa Brennan and Martin Say. (New York: Routledge, 1996), 117–126.

Gołaczyńska, Magdalena. "The Alternative Theatre in Poland since 1989." Trans. Marcin Wąsiel. *New Theatre Quarterly* 17, no. 2 (May 2001): 186–194.

———. *Mozaika współczesności: Teatr alternatywny w Polsce po roku 1989*. Wrocław: Wydawnictwo Uniwersytetu Wrocławskiego, 2002.

Gross, Jan Tomasz. *Neighbors: The Destruction of the Jewish Community in Jedwabne, Poland*. Princeton, N.J.: Princeton University Press, 2001.

——. *Sąsiedzi: Historia zagłady żydowskiego miasteczka*. Sejny: Pogranicze, 2000.

Hawkesworth, Celia, ed. *A History of Central European Women's Writing*. Basingstoke and New York: Palgrave, 2001.

Janion, Maria. "Do Europy tak, ale razem z naszymi umarłymi: Rozmowa z prof. Marią Janion o jej nowej książce." *Gazeta Wyborcza*, February 16, 2001. Available online at http://www.gazeta.pl/alfa/artykul.jsp?xx=135854&dzial=010501 (accessed February 16, 2001).

Jarzębski, Jerzy. "Mocny Anioł i Słaba Płeć." *Tygodnik Powszechny*, March 31, 2001, 15.

Lis, Renata. "Koszmar z ulicy syntez: Co to jest 'literatura kobieca'?" *Gazeta Wyborcza*, March 15, 2001, 35.

Mamet, David. *Oleanna*. Trans. Marek Kędzierski. *Dialog*, May 1994, 78–104.

Moi, Toril. "Feminist Literary Criticism." In *Modern Literary Theory: A Comparative Introduction*, ed. Ann Jefferson and David Robery, 204–221. Totowa: Barnes and Noble Books, 1986.

Ong, Walter. *The Presence of the Word: Some Prolegomena for Cultural and Religious History*. New Haven, Conn., and London: Yale University Press, 1967.

Rouse, John. "Comment." *Theatre Journal* 48, no. 4 (December 1996): 404.

Said, Edward W. *Culture and Imperialism*. New York: Random House, 1994.

Schechner, Richard. "Preface." In *The Grotowski Sourcebook*, ed. Lisa Wolford and Richard Schechner, xxv–xxviii. 1997; reprint, London and New York: Routledge, 2001.

Stefanova, Kalina, ed. *Eastern European Theater after the Iron Curtain*. Amsterdam: Harwood Academic Publishers, 2000.

Titkow, Anna. "On the Appreciated Role of Women." Trans. Paweł Cichawa. In *Women on the Polish Labor Market*, ed. Mike Ingham, Hilary Ingham, and Henryk Domański, 21–40. Budapest and New York: Central European University Press, 2001.

Tyszka, Juliusz. "Polish Alternative Theatre during the Period of Transition, 1989–94." Trans. Jolanta Cynkutis and Tom Randolph. *New Theatre Quarterly* 12, no. 1 (February 1996): 71–78.

Valian, Virginia. *Why So Slow? The Advancement of Women*. Cambridge, Mass., and London: MIT Press, 1999.

Zagańczyk, Marek. "Between the East and the West: *Carmina Burana* by Włodzimierz Staniewski at the Gardzienice Theatre Association." *The Theatre in Poland*, May 1991, 6–8.

Zielińska, Eleonora. "Between Ideology, Politics, and Common Sense: The Discourse of Reproductive Rights in Poland." In *Reproducing Gender: Politics, Publics, and Everyday Life After Socialism*, ed. Susan Gal and Gail Kligman, 23–57. Princeton, N.J.: Princeton University Press, 2000.

nine

"Hurrah, I'm Still Alive!"

East German Products Demonstrating
East German Identities

Rainer Gries

"Atlanta? New York?" The answer to these exceedingly cryptic questions is equally laconic—a simple, definite, self-confident: "Berlin!" Constituting the headline of an advertisement, this question-and-answer exchange invoking these three cities heralds a product's return to the stage of the market place and of brand names. It is "Club Cola. Our Cola."

"Our Cola"—who are "we"? What kind of "we" could claim, in early 1992, that "the Cola from Berlin" is one of "ours"? Who hides behind this strong possessive pronoun with its very own peculiar history in the GDR? How could advertising strategists dare to present this manner of word association in public, one which to this day resonates powerfully with the propagandistic slogans of times past? Indeed, in the GDR there was incessant talk of "our best": the people who worked for "our Republic," loved "our socialist home," defended "our fatherland."

As a historian, I wish to use objects traditionally associated with economic history in order to examine issues of culture and identity.[1] By studying the economic, social, and cultural history of East German products both before and after the transition of 1989, one can explore questions of collective identity in East Germany. Such products trace paths that not only consist of a few

181

First appearance of Club Cola after the transition: tastefully native and historically conscious. 1992. Photograph by Spreequell GmBH, Berlin. Used by permission.

peripheral manifestations but also allow us to determine the structures of "identity formation" and "identity transformation." In fact, quite beyond that, products themselves communicate messages that contribute significantly to the creation and articulation of social and cultural identity patterns. These are conveyed and reinforced in the communicative process through the medium of the product. Thus, the product and its connotations by no means reflect purely economic matters; they also reflect social and even political matters.

An examination of the conditions that facilitated a successful relaunching of Club Cola, at least in the regional Berlin-Brandenburg soft-drink market, not only helps us comprehend the history and personality of the product but, far more significantly, enables us to reconstruct the history and fundamental building-blocks of its consumers' identities. This narrow and almost symbiotic relationship becomes especially obvious in the case of Club Cola, given that this product was able to get by without need of character witnesses on its behalf after the transition of 1989. The East German Cola stands and speaks for itself, plays its own protagonist, and provides its own most convincing testimonial.

Admittedly, when it was reintroduced, the Cola arrived with "new product design and improved quality," but the aesthetic modernization actually proved to be quite modest and cautious. The half-liter reusable bottle remains, the brand label still has a red background,[2] and the typography has been only subtly adapted to the new conditions. Club Cola in no way denies its GDR physiognomy or its history before 1989. In terms of its layout, the product remains true to itself. Celebrating its comeback in 1992, it does not project itself as some kind of completely restyled turncoat but as a tasteful historically conscious native (see Fig. 9.1). Without a doubt that is an important reason for its successful renaissance, but it also partly explains why Berlin's media rolled out the red carpet to welcome it back as "the legendary" GDR soft drink and "a fine old acquaintance."[3]

A Short History of the Socialist Cola

Club Cola is a typical "product of the East." Originally it was intended as a "gift" of the German Socialist Unity Party (SED) to the state youth of the GDR. For the twentieth anniversary of the founding of the Socialist German Republic, on October 7, 1969, the heads of the Party were determined that there should also finally be a socialist Cola (Fig. 9.2). Every ten years the GDR wrote another chapter in the mythology of its founding, organizing pompous pageantry. Economic stabilization during the 1960s soon created the basis for Honecker's ambitious 1971 program for "Unity of Economic and Social Policy," but it had also provided the impetus for the earlier decennial celebrations of 1969.

The dramaturgy of the "XXth Birthday of the Republic"[4] took place in the promising context of a materialist and consumerist upswing. Economic dynamism and social progress were finally to become perceptible and accessible to everyone. Under the propagandistic formulation "We are Twenty!" citizens of the GDR were treated to numerous "gifts." A few city centers were renovated and made more friendly to shoppers through the addition of new supermarkets; new products were thrown onto the socialist market. The extensive program of "gifts" featured the epitome of prestige products at that time. "Praesent 20,"[5] for instance, was a new, ready-to-wear line of outer clothing for ladies and men made entirely of plastic. And for the young people of the Republic: Club Cola.

After the trademark was registered in 1968, Cola (East) went into production on schedule for the anniversary year 1969, bottled at a plant built especially for that purpose in Berlin-Weissensee. The brand name brought to mind the so-called clubs—leisure facilities built in the 1950s for the official GDR youth, the Freie Deutsche Jugend (FDJ). "The whole world was drinking cola, but not in the first Socialist state on German soil. And so the authorities felt that it was certainly high time to finally treat 'our people' to a cola," one commentator recalls in retrospect. "What the native laboratories finally mixed up in their kitchens was admittedly not particularly thrilling on first sip. That is, unless three centimeters of fire-water were added to the glass. The Club Cola of the time was less a refreshing drink than a rather thin syrup. Nonetheless it was regularly subject to the same fate as every other product in that country. At some point it would always disappear from the shelves. In summer, production at the soft-drink factory could never keep up with demand. Then the only resort for thirsty East Berliners was to divide the city into planning quadrants and undertake a systematic search." Nonetheless, as the trained citizen of the East continues, "the deepest, unquenchable yearning was for the red cans from the West, empties of which could often be found decorating the living rooms and kitchens of poor GDR soft-drinkers."[6]

First appearance of Club Cola in the GDR: a gift for the Twentieth Birthday. 1969. Photograph by Kultur- und werbegeschichtliches Archiv (KWAF), Freiburg. Used by permission.

Thus, while Cola-East was intended to represent the material and spiritual contributions of GDR youth to the success of socialism at the end of the 1960s, it was in fact rather an unpopular—if highly coveted—and poor imitation of Cola-West. But the new East Cola of the period following German unification was able to drop the image of a mere copy-cola.

The old Club Cola had belonged to the GDR like Goldbroilers (roast chicken) and Mocca-Fix (instant coffee), according to *Berliner Kurier am Abend.* Despite being the butt of jokes, and notwithstanding its insipid taste and sticky sweetness, the capital-city cola flowed down thirsty GDR throats at a rate of 26 million liters every year.[7] After the soft-drink shelves of the two GDR retail monopolies Konsum and HO (Handelsorganisation) were conquered by the two Western brands Coca-Cola and Pepsi, however, the market for Eastern Cola collapsed quickly and radically. While 300,000 hectoliters were still sold in business year 1987–1988, the curve plunged dramatically during the transitional events of business year 1989–1990, bottoming out at a minuscule 10,000 hectoliters.[8] It had been intended as a symbol of the GDR's consumerist modernity and generosity at the end of the 1960s, above all for young people, but with the end of the socialist state on German soil, the end of socialist cola seemed inevitably to have arrived as well.

With many products made in Eastern Germany the farewell was not difficult, wrote a leading West German daily soon after the historical changes. "Anyone who ever tried out the People's Cola, 'Club' or 'Brisant' by brand-name, will shed no tears for that glue. Naturally the Western brown caffeinated lemonades are also not everyone's cup of tea, but anyone who has tried and liked 'Coke' or 'Pepsi' will not stand still for some poor imitation."[9]

Yet at the beginning of 1992, merely half a year after this devastating cola verdict from the West, the East German fizz was back. And the new-old cola from Berlin was able to hold its own respectably in the gleaming spotlights of West Germany's "social market economy." Thirty to thirty-five thousand hectoliters again flowed into the market in 1993, a figure amounting to 10 per-

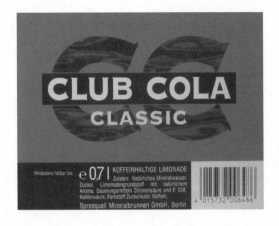

Proven layout in traditional color and formal scheme: modernization. 1995. Photograph by Spreequell GmBH, Berlin. Used by permission.

cent of GDR sales before the 1989 transition. Admittedly, this was only possible because of the tremendous capacity to modernize of Brau- und Brunnen-AG of Dortmund, one of the largest German refreshment companies, which had taken over Mineralbrunnen GmbH of Weissensee as a subsidiary and could provide listings, distribution, and strong marketing. Following a further wave of modernization at the beginning of 1995 (Fig. 9.3), along with stronger references to the color and formal language of GDR times, the cola in fact approached a regional market share of 5 percent. The future of the East German brand name seems bright. "If everything goes as expected, the next Cult Cola will be coming soon from Berlin," the daily *Die Welt* commented on the economic and social chances of the Eastern Cola in 1995.[10] The future prospects of this Eastern brand lie in its uninterrupted connection to the past. In 1996, Club Cola remained a familiar term to 85 of 100 citizens in the five new German states, and only 2 of 100 persons surveyed in eastern Berlin had no idea what this product name signified.[11]

This success is certainly also due to clever and sensitive product marketing. Club Cola came back not only because it did not deny its past but also because it showed that it could learn and be honest. It never tires now in claiming that henceforth it will be "naturally fresh." In the GDR, it was sometimes made from tap water, but now its main ingredient is always mineral water. And it never ceases to emphasize that it is now "less sweet" and has "more taste." Thus, it indirectly admits to the universally known defects of its GDR past and dedicates itself henceforth to improvement and quality. The Berlin cola producers sensed that their cola customers did not desire the image of a Western lifestyle or fashionable lightness, but that they held to their accustomed tastes. To create more taste and cola intensity, the recipe was again adjusted to suit the preferences of the Eastern German cola public in 1995. Admittedly, the nuances of the old GDR taste could not be completely recaptured, as the People's Recipe had toyed with some ingredients that today are prohibited by the German Nutritional Index. The evolution in its taste made Club Cola the big exception among the various East German food products and other goods that were able to reestablish themselves after the transition. Eastern German consumers were seeking their very own unmistakable taste, which had been socialized through the product landscape of the GDR, when they brought about a second product transition following the political transition of 1989.

A Short History of Eastern German Products after the Transition

In the wake of the revolution, faith in the quality of West German brand products, and thus in the creditworthiness of the Western system that they epitomized, at first seemed to be entirely without boundaries. The people of the GDR had seized their freedom to choose. And the citizens of the GDR voted not just for the *Grundgesetz* (basic law)—the political, economic, and social constitution of the Federal Republic of Germany; it is in fact largely overlooked that East German consumers simultaneously, and with great optimism, also chose the product constitution of the West.

In the early days of the transition, traveling salespeople overflowed East German marketplaces, threw products of poor quality off their trucks, and charged a passive, stunned, and helpless population horrific prices. Itinerant cutthroats charged the old GDR price for a kilo of highly coveted bananas in the new Western currency. Through the end of the year 1990 there was a phase of experimentation and curiosity. During the first six months after the introduction of the Western Deutsche Mark, Eastern products were neither offered nor demanded nor even listed—not even fresh produce from Mecklenburg, Thuringia, or Saxony. Merchants who still had Eastern products in stock rushed to sell them off as quickly as possible, at whatever price—an initial "wasteful" market "purification" that was impressed onto the collective memory of East Germans. Advertising in Eastern Germany, including the marketing for Club Cola, would later cleverly and successfully return to these experiences.

This first phase of partially disappointing product experiences had already run its course by 1991, and East Germans returned to those products that could offer the accustomed "taste of home."[12] The first signs of a change in orientation, according to the Institute for Market Research in Leipzig, were detectable toward the end of 1990. Asked by market and opinion researchers whether they consciously favored Eastern products, nearly 50 percent of surveyed heads of household in East Germany answered "yes." A half-year later, in the middle of 1991, the figure was already at 65 percent, and by December 1991 that number had climbed to nearly 75 percent. This trend continued uninterrupted throughout the year 1992. And by 1993, responding to the question of whether they consciously decided in favor of purchasing Eastern German products for their daily needs, 65 percent answered "often," 31 per-

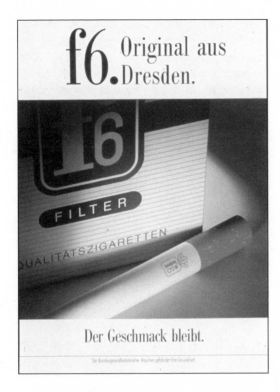

Staging of an eastern German local hero: cigarette brand f6 from Dresden. 1991. Photograph by Kultur- und werbegeschichtliches Archiv (KWAF), Freiburg. Used by permission.

cent said "sometimes," and only 3 percent said this was "seldom" or "never" the case.[13]

It was not an accident that a cigarette moved up to an uncontested position of market leadership in the new states in the first year of German unification by advertising with the programmatic slogan, "The Taste Remains" (Fig. 9.4). Decisive for the success of the traditional GDR brand f6 from Dresden was a marketing concept that called for extremely cautious and sensitive renewal. Just as with the revival of Club Cola, matters of appearance and aesthetic layout were changed only peripherally and, most important, the "unmistakably strong and spicy taste" remained untouched. "East German consumers were happy," according to the product manager of the Eastern cigarette, "that their products were being handled with such care." f6 is simply a "piece of Eastern Germany, a 'local hero.'"[14] Another Dresden cigarette brand subsequently took this kind of self-understanding to its extreme, depicting itself as an assassin with the slogan "Attack on Unified Taste." This approach articulated the discontent of a more-or-less silent majority, not only with the new products of a reunited Germany but also with the new leaders. The genuine and real were now no longer goods from the West but products from "Our Heimat." Their traditional taste— forceful and robust, unfalsified and unperfumed—combined with high moral characteristics such as good quality, decent value for money, honesty, and honor. All of this was recognized and honored when shopping, in a downright revolutionary swing of opinion that would have been unthinkable in the GDR. The West and its products, according to one of the most fundamental lessons of unification from the point of view of former GDR citizens, had promised more than they could ever deliver.

Since 1992 at the latest, the new love Eastern Germans discovered for "their" products should be understood as a conscious act of self-maintenance, in an individual as well as social sense. Asked by Leipzig market researchers for their reasons for purchasing Eastern products, 80 of 100 respondents admitted that the "quality is just as good," 74 percent claimed they wanted to "give local companies a chance," and 81 percent also expressed their hope that in this manner they might contribute to the security of jobs in the eastern German regions.

In the final analysis, the affirmation of local products is tantamount to a referendum with the shopping basket. A product-political plebiscite takes place every day in the supermarkets and department stores of the five new states, and sides are taken in favor of local history and for the future of a region that had seemingly been written off.

Product Identities—Subject Identities

"Atlanta? New York? Berlin!"

Let us return again to the advertisement mentioned at the beginning of this chapter, with its triad of cities as a headline. The superficial objective here, of course, is to recall to consciousness the regional connection of Club Cola, the "Cola from Berlin." To begin with, that strategy has the banal significance of stressing that this is no cola from the former GDR provinces, such as Vita Cola from Schmalkalden in Thuringia, but the cola from Berlin. And what does Berlin stand for? In contrast to the two major U.S. cities also mentioned, Berlin is equipped with a self-confident exclamation point. Is this merely a profession of loyalty to Germany's largest city? At the beginning of 1992, the German-German discussion about the national capital and seat of federal government had been completed for half a year, but carrying out the decision still hung in the balance.[15] Surely the cola of the capital was to some degree casting an unmistakable vote for Berlin as the federal capital and Berlin as a national symbol. But the slogan also unmistakably resonates with a propagandistic essential of the former Workers' and Farmers' State, namely that incessantly repeated formulation: "Berlin, Capital of the GDR." One message of Club Cola might thus be expressed as follows: Who are "we?" "We" are the people who know that Berlin was the capital and remains the capital and that Club Cola was our cola and remains our cola.

"Test the West"[16]

Club Cola does more than positively profess its loyalty to Berlin; it also draws lines and exclaims: "Why roam so far afield with cola? . . . You need no longer drink with strange colas." Far afield is America; the presumably strange comes from Atlanta, headquarters of competitor Coca-Cola, or New York, headquarters of the Pepsi Corporation. The ad not only defiantly declares that "Berlin can keep up worldwide"; it also expresses loyalty to a Berlin that is "our" metropolis and that makes no glittering promises that later prove to have been impossible all along. By the end of 1991, Eastern Germans believed they had on the whole gotten their fill and knew enough not just about Western products but about "the West" as a whole. The West test often had negative results. Whom was Club Cola supposed to address? "Either those who could not particularly stomach the taste of the newly opened 'wide world,' or those on the other side who wanted to try out the taste of a different world," the cola strategists of the East believed.[17] "Atlanta" and "New York" thus stood for the mounting disappointments which followed the transition. These started building up individually and collectively at the latest after the monetary, economic, and social union had been carried out and finally led to skepticism, withdrawal, and even rejection of certain Western behavioral patterns and thus also of Western values and standards. Seen from this perspective, the topographical metaphor "Berlin" provides a good foundation of orientating knowledge, appearing as a fortress of familiar traditions and securities.

Nevertheless the others, the construed out-group, remain quite indefinite. Only the following seems to be of significance here: Who are "we"? "We" are those who have had negative experiences with strange products—"Western people" and "the West"—and who in the future no longer need to depend upon them. "We" are specifically those who are ready to return if necessary to the "old" values.[18] Certainly it must be added here that such perceptions of difference can by no stretch of the imagination be interpreted simplistically as a profession of loyalty to the GDR.

In the future, Club Cola intends to continue to present itself as the cola "from the metropolis Berlin with [an] East Berlin lifestyle." The marketing for Club Cola will thus continue to employ the mental building-block "Berlin," especially the specific Berlin consciousness. The intended target market for the Eastern cola in the coming years includes eastern Germans in their twenties and thirties who feel a tie to the "East Berlin lifestyle." A personification of this "East Berlin lifestyle" might be fantasized as a figure that "has a distinct Eastern German heritage" and whose air and habits reflect the "full range between Marzahn desolateness, international metropolitan feeling, and Prenzelberg scene flair."[19]

"Hurrah, I'm Still Alive!"

Like no other print communication, the ad with this headline, which nearly acquired the status of a slogan, helped summarize the feel of life in Eastern Germany around the winter of 1991/1992 (Fig. 9.5). This pronounced call combines two entirely divergent worlds of emotion and thought that at the time were nonetheless closely interwoven. On the one hand, it contains all the recently renewed doubts about everyday life: the loss of a job once thought so secure, the breakdown in private friendships and social relations, the rash transformation of spatial and temporal day-to-day categories, and, in the final analysis, the mass devaluation of personal biographies.[20]

Previous patterns of identity upon which social life and individual self-consciousness were based, such as "our brigade," could not be carried over into the new age. Given the threatening vacuum of social identities and possibilities for identification, what other "latent" we-constructions[21] were available? "From the experience of individual self-understanding and reproduction of self," according to historian Lutz Niethammer, "we know that the thematization of identity is a phenomenon suggesting something that is missing, or a pathological indicator. Much like the similarly indefinable concept of 'health,' one only speaks of it when it is lacking or disadvantaged—classically in times of changing status and life crises. That apparently also applies to collective ideas of identity. They are constructed as a means of bridging social discrepancies."[22]

Club Cola makes an existential offer. Aware of the history of its clients, the Berlin Cola expresses solidarity. It too had to go through and experience, along with everyone else, the pains suffered by the citizens of the GDR following the

A slogan ("Hurrah! I'm Still Alive!") condenses the feeling of a time: advertisement for Club Cola. 1991/1992. Photograph by Kultur- und werbegeschichtliches Archiv (KWAF), Freiburg. Used by permission.

transition: devaluation and removal, declassification and deindustrialization. In this situation of extreme social upheaval, this product takes on the task of formulating the most elementary possible statement of a collective securing itself. The survival slogan: We're still alive.

The former GDR cola defiantly insists on its right to exist—and thus simultaneously on its right to compete, to do business. Moreover, like hundreds of thousands of former GDR citizens, it has successfully maintained into the present the necessary quantum of hope and optimism, and this despite great hostility.

Who are "we"? We are those who have survived despite everything and those who must be reckoned with in the future. All attempts to bring us down—yes, to take our very lives—have failed. That is now reason enough for restrained triumph and fighting defiance. That is why we are encouraged. Join us, "take joy with us."

"I know one day a miracle will come . . ."

Finally, socially effective and executable "we" communication also requires, as a central component, a valid consensus in relation to the canonization, presentation, and interpretation of a shared past. States and nations organize and finance discourses surrounding this agreement about the past as a science of history. Who "organized," however, who sponsored the "historical" self-understanding of the citizens of the ex-GDR following the transition? At first glance such an effort might seem foolhardy—but here too, Club Cola jumped into a gaping breach.

Working together with graduates of the ex-GDR film school in Potsdam-Babelsberg,[23] the Spreequell marketing team developed a one-minute commercial. Starting in July 1992, it ran for one year as part of the advertising block that normally precedes movies at German theaters. Moviegoers apparently reacted in a "very lively and thoroughly positive" fashion, the filmmakers from Prenzlauer Berg report: "[R]elieved laughter comes over many in the audience like a liberation. . . . Whoever is already able to laugh about the past can view the future more calmly. . . . The joyful, happy-lifestyle image of the big brands would never have even been realizable on the comparatively low [Club Cola] budget. And certainly not realistic." This had forcibly posed the Leninist question of "What is to be done?" "All at once the history of Club Cola appeared thoroughly helpful to us. Over 17 million Germans grew up with it. Let's remind them of that! Using old DEFA documentary film stock, we edited together typical everyday GDR events chronologically, and connected them directly to Club Cola."[24]

The East Berlin admen lead us into a small pictorial mosaic of historical footage, whereby the pictures from the past are rounded off—indeed answered and remarked upon—by the commercial slogans mixed in. This documentation of GDR histories is acoustically accompanied by 1930s singer Zarah

Propaganda heroes of the GDR as advertising vehicles for Club Cola: "Titan" Adolf Hennecke. Club Cola trailer storyboard, 1992. Photograph by Fritsch & Mackat Werbeagentur GmGH, Berlin. Used by permission.

Leander, who reassures us: "I know one day a miracle will come. And then a thousand dreams will come true."

The spot, as humorous as it is sensitive, begins with one of the first "titans of socialism," Adolf Hennecke, shown accomplishing his amazing feat of endurance in October 1948.[25] Admittedly, the legendary mineworker was bringing coal, not cola, out of the ground (Fig. 9.6). He exceeded the prescribed performance standard by 287 percent. Sacrosanct in the GDR, his masterful act now receives succinct dismissal from the brown soft drink: "Fresh!" We are promptly treated to another ancestral hero of the GDR: two-time world bicycling champion (1958 and 1959) Gustav Adolf "Täve" Schur (Fig. 9.7). The friendly rider for peace and later member of the People's Assembly (SED) was the most popular athlete among young and old in the GDR right up to 1989.[26] The refreshment now disrespectfully calls after him that Club Cola has become "Less Sweet!" The following scene shows two nameless "heroes of labor" employed at the Warnow shipyards, an engineer and a worker, who are full of pride and teary-eyed as they follow the launching of a freighter named after the German Communist and resistance fighter Anton Saefkow. Club Cola takes this Baltic episode as the opportunity to point once again to its "Natural Mineral Water!" Following the conquest of the high seas, the Red conquerors of space are also presented. The thrusting force of socialism catapulted cosmonauts Valerij Bykowski and Sigmund Jähn[27]—the first German in orbit—

Victor of History: "Peace Rider" Gustav Adolf "Täve" Schur. Club Cola trailer storyboard, 1992. Photograph by Fritsch & Mackat Werbeagentur GmGH, Berlin. Used by permission.

into weightlessness in 1978. We see them agilely bounding about within their space capsule (Fig. 9.8). "Now Available as Light!" Club Cola cleverly retorts. Rounding off the series of images, the directors recall the annual German Gymnastics and Sports Festival in Leipzig. We see Erich Honecker demonstrating his connection to the masses by performing gymnastic exercises. The scene is abruptly interrupted to show the well-known slogan, "Hurrah! I'm Still Alive!" on the red background of the Cola label, which briefly metamorphoses into a red flag covering the entire screen.[28] Thus, the slogan of the cola and its consumers also becomes the final statement of the last general secretary of the Socialist Unity Party. "And I know that we will meet again," sings Zarah Leander, not only to the audience but also to Honecker himself, at the time still in his brief Moscow exile. The spot then concludes with a last look at members of the top levels of Party and state playing ball in the grandstand of Leipzig Central Stadium.[29]

With this commercial, Club Cola provides an excellent source for the historical culture of the new German states in the year 1992.[30] GDR "history" can for the first time once again be displayed in public "with success." This is made possible not only through the temporal distance from the historical events depicted but also through a consistent and effective ironic reworking of the pictorial documentation.

The pictures are intended as a way to symbolize "GDR history" much

The "Red Columbus": Conqueror of Gravity Cosmonaut Sigmund Jähn. Club Cola trailer storyboard, 1992. Photograph by Fritsch & Mackat Werbeagentur GmGH, Berlin. Used by permission.

more than as a way actually to represent it. They prove to be very carefully edited. The filmmakers are not throwing together random events from GDR history; they are consciously presenting "our best," the "titans" and "heroes" of socialism—which, incidentally, is a purely male society. To be precise, we are leafing not through a history book but through the GDR book of fairy tales. In a matter of seconds we tour a pictorial history of GDR myths intended to produce legitimacy and loyalty.[31] In short, it is the propaganda pictures of the Workers' and Farmers' State that hit home with the audiences of 1992. While we are not seeing documents of everyday life in the GDR, the propaganda film is understood as part of a particular GDR everyday culture, although it is not possible within the framework of this chapter to consider in detail the rich historical and historical-cultural content in such agitational and propaganda visuals.[32] Here, after all, our interest is primarily directed at the question of the emotional and cognitive "we" structures referred to, reflected, and possibly reinforced by such mosaics of the past.

It may at first sound paradoxical, but in 1992 nothing proved better as a source of material for creating a viable consensus on which to base a new East German identity than the propaganda of the GDR, particularly because of its ironic failure. As we have seen, the collective pattern of "East German identity" is normally experienced "negatively" in the perception of otherness and difference, specifically in the everyday confrontation with the West and its protagonists. By contrast, the historical pictures,[33] conveyed by the one-time cola of the GDR, provide "positive" building blocks for a self-understanding as former GDR citizens. They may very well deliver a model that the open adherents, silent "collaborators," and active opponents of the GDR regime could all equally accept for a time.

Who are "we?" We are the ones who were addressed by these propagandistic efforts "for forty years," and we therefore know exactly how these pictures are to be categorized. Wherever we may have stood politically, we are the ones for whom these pictures were created with the specific intentions of expressing politically binding power. Today these propagandistic intentions are forever obsolete. We know they are "history." And we are thus also the ones who can once again laugh about these pictures from the long-gone past.

So much for a brief inventory of elements of a collective identity discourse in the new German states in the year 1992. Obviously, such a depiction by necessity remains incomplete. Nonetheless, Club Cola's communications do allow us to distinguish and portray central elements of the eastern German identity discourse in the second year of unification. The formulation of social and collective identity "textures" can in the final analysis never be carved in stone or seen apart from history; it is always situational and contextual. It is the result of continuous processes of communication and interpretation, taking place under particular societal and political conditions. In the process, many potential identity patterns compete with each other simultaneously and can be called upon or formulated at will. Thus, it is no wonder that an idea of "floating identities" has recently been coined in feminist theory.[34]

"East Nostalgia: Club Cola Again Filling Shelves"[35]

Since 1992, the pejoratives *"Nostalgie"* (nostalgia) and *"Ostalgie"* (literally "Eastalgia") have been used too glibly in public discussion to describe the manner in which citizens in the five new states are handling their pasts. The devaluing label throws highly divergent behavioral modes into the same pot, ranging from the collective vote for Eastern products described above to the votes received by the Party of Democratic Socialism (PDS), successor party to the communist SED, and from mere thematization of GDR history to its mystification. Indeed, mere reference to a personal "biography before 1989" tends to arouse public mistrust immediately. The decision by eastern Germans in favor of the traditional products of their home and the profession of loyalty to these products by their potential consumers can however by no means be devalued as a nostalgic yearning for a socialist past. The smokers of f6 cigarettes and buyers of Club Cola are not backward-looking or eternally stuck in the past, as some people certainly must be; they are seeking, by way of products, to nourish their complicated mixture of identities as citizens living in Saxony and Saxony Anhalt, in Berlin and Brandenburg, in Thuringia and Mecklenburg.[36]

Rainer Gries

> Supraindividual uniformity in perception, interpretation, and evaluation of facts of reality and social uniformity in dealing with these realities are natural end products of cognition and behavioral modes of many individuals. But the interesting question is how it happens that these many individuals arrive at these uniform, socially divisible modes of viewing and behaving, under what conditions these similarities appear, become more widespread, or are reduced.[37]

The history of product connotations and communications may well provide a key to answering these central questions. "A brand has a face just like a person," product theorist Hans Domizlaff taught whole generations of advertising experts in Germany.[38] The history of Club Cola may pointedly demonstrate the validity of this axiom. "Eastern Germans should be told that their Club Cola still exists, and that it hasn't adapted, just gotten better. That corresponds to the mental situation of many eastern Germans who are grieving over their own culture."[39] In the final analysis, at least this is surely the case:

Who are "we"? Our cola is "we." And we are our cola.

Translated from the German by Nicholas Levis

NOTES

This essay represents an expanded version of a lecture delivered to the 21st New Hampshire Symposium 1995 in Conway, which under the general theme of "Who's 'We'?" considered "The Identity Dispute in the New German States Five Years after Unification." See Rainer Gries, "Who's 'We'? Deutsche Identitaetsdiskurse im fünften Jahr der Einheit," *Deutschland Archiv* 28, no. 10 (1995): 1095–1099. It emerged from my theory and history of product communications. See Rainer Gries, *Produkte als Medien. Kulturgeschichte der Produktkommunikation in der Bundesrepublik und der DDR* (Leipzig: Leipziger Universitätsverlag, 2003). For the translation into English I am most grateful to Nicholas Levis, Berlin.

1. This work arose originally as part of the author's comparative research efforts toward a political and societal semiotics of product landscapes in the two German societies, sponsored as a postdoctoral thesis by the Fritz Thyssen Foundation in Cologne. See the project sketches by Gerald Diesener and Rainer Gries, "Nachkriegsgeschichte als Kommunikationsgeschichte. Deutsch-deutsche Projekte zur Produktwerbung und Politikpropaganda," *Deutschland Archiv* 1 (1993): 21–30. For an in-depth theoretical discussion see also Gries, *Produkte als Medien. Kulturgeschichte der Produktkommunikation in der Bundesrepublik und der DDR* (Leipzig: Leipziger Universitätsverlag, 2003).

2. In the GDR, the product design also emphasized red, a color characteristic of cola products in general.

3. "Legendary 'Club Cola' from Weißensee Is on Its Way Back," *Der Tagesspiegel* (Berlin), January 31, 1992, 11; "Spreequell Gets Club Cola Fizzing Again," *Berliner Kurier*, January 31, 1992. [Translator's Note: Original titles are given for academic sources, but newspaper headlines are translated into English.]

4. On the social, political, and propagandistic semantics of the major birthdays of the Republic, see the anthology *Wiedergeburten. Zur Geschichte des runden Jahrstage*

der DDR, ed. Monika Gibas, Rainer Gries, Barbara Jakoby, and Doris Mueller (Leipzig: Leipziger Universitätsverlag, 1999).

5. On the cultural history of this exemplary gift, see Cordula Günther, " 'Praesent 20.' Der Stoff aus dem die Träume sind," *Universitas. Zeitschrift für interdisziplinäre Wissenschaft* 51, no. 2 (1996): 116–126.

6. Wolfgang Kohrt, "A Personal Sip," *Die Zeit Magazin* 31 (July 30, 1993): 22–25. ["Trained citizen of the East" = *"gelernte Ostbürger,"* an idiomatic appellation of years past. Translator's Note].

7. "Club Cola Starts Comeback with New Taste," *Berliner Kurier am Abend*, February 7, 1992.

8. Michael Marquardt and Christine Krasel of Spreequell Mineralbrunnen GmbH, writing to the author of the present essay on November 22, 1993.

9. *Frankfurter Allgemeine Zeitung* (FAZ), May 1991.

10. "New Cult Cola Coming from Berlin: Successful Relaunching of Traditional GDR Brand Achieved with Small Advertising Budget," *Die Welt*, May 16, 1995.

11. Alexander Mackat of the advertising agency Fritzsch & Mackat, Berlin, writing to the author on July 3, 1996.

12. For an extensive treatment of this phenomenon, see Rainer Gries, "Der Geschmack der Heimat. Bausteine zu einer Mentalitätsgeschichte der Ostprodukte nach der Wende," *Deutschland Archiv* 10 (1994): 1041–1058.

13. Berichtsreihe Konsumklima-Forschung, "Institut für Marktforschung Leipzig: Verbrauch und Verbrauchsverhalten in den fünf neuen Bundesländern," unpublished paper.

14. "The Brand Is a Piece of East Germany," *Horizont. Zeitung für Marketing, Werbung und Medien*, no. 44 (November 1, 1991).

15. By the narrowest of margins, the German Bundestag determined on June 19, 1991, that Berlin would be not only the official national capital but also the actual seat of government and Parliament.

16. ["Test the West": the wildly successful marketing slogan for the "West" brand from Reemtsma, the leading West German cigarette maker, for nearly two decades. An appeal consciously directed at East-bloc markets both before and after 1989—Translator's Note]

17. Alexander Mackat in a letter to the International Advertising Film Festival, London, April 23, 1993.

18. See, among others, Thomas Gensicke, *Mentalitätsentwicklung im Osten Deutschlands seit den 70er Jahren. Vorstellung und Erläuterung von Ergebnissen einiger empirischer Untersuchungen in der DDR und in den neuen Bundesländern von 1977 bis 1991.* Speyer: Forschungsinstitut für Öffentliche Verwaltung bei der Hochschule für Verwaltungswissenschaften, 1992.

19. A. Mackat to the author. [Marzahn is a bleak and endless collection of massive apartment blocks in typical GDR style at the outer edge of East Berlin, now best known as a stronghold of the post-communist PDS. "Prenzelberg," diminutive of Prenzlauer Berg, largely succeeded West Berlin's Kreuzberg as the city's main night "scene" and artist's quarter following 1989—Translator's Note. See Lisa Whitmore's article in this anthology—Eds.]

20. The "mass factual or imagined experience of inferiority" is commonly cited as "the main cause of belated 'GDR identity.'" See, for example, Wendelin Szalai, "Wie

'funktionierte' Identitätsbildung in der DDR?" in *Identitätsbildung und Geschichts-bewusstsein nach der Vereinigung Deutschlands*, ed. Uwe Uffelmann (Weinheim: Beltz Fachverlag, 1993), 92.

21. The formulation borrows from Norbert Elias, *Studien über die Deutschen* (Frankfurt/Main: Suhrkamp Verlag, 1989), 457.

22. Lutz Niethammer, "Konjunkturen und Konkurrenzen kollektiver Identität. Ideologie, Infrastruktur und Gedächtnis in der Zeitgeschichte," Commencement Address, Friedrich Schiller University, Jena, 1994, published in *Prokla: Zeitschrift für kritische Sozialwissenschaft*, no. 96 (1994): 397.

23. The two former students founded a full-service marketing agency in 1993 that specialized in communications in the new states and today is still entrusted with the modest Club Cola advertising budget. For their gracious assistance I am very grateful to the two partners in the Fritzsch & Mackat advertising agency of Berlin.

24. A. Mackat, letter to International Advertising Film Festival, London, April 23, 1993. "DEFA" is the acronym for Deutsche Film-Aktiengesellschaft, the state-owned studios of the former GDR.

25. For a biography of Adolf Hennecke, see Jochen Czerny, ed., *Wer war Wer—DDR. Ein biographisches Lexikon* (Berlin: Ch. Links Verlag, 1992), 180. For the history of the heroes of socialism, see *Sozialistische Helden. Eine Kulturgeschichte con Propagandafiguren in Osteuropa und der DDR*, ed. Rainer Gries and Silke Satjukow (Berlin: Ch. Links Verlag, 2002).

26. For a biography and bibliography on "Täve" Schur, see ibid., 416.

27. For a biography and bibliography on the cosmonaut from the Vogtland, see ibid., 206.

28. "Party Red," frowned upon during the transition, was apparently once again acceptable in the year 1992. RFT Stassfurt, a manufacturer of TV receivers, used this color later in the year as the background for its slogan "East German, Therefore Good." See Gries, "Der Geschmack der Heimat," 1055ff.

29. On the role of the grandstand in GDR history, see Monika Gibas and Rainer Gries, " 'Vorschlag für den Ersten Mai: die Führung zieht am Volk vorbei!' Überlegungen zur Geschichte der Tribüne in der DDR," *Deutschland Archiv* 5 (1995): 481–494.

30. "The entirety of forms in which historical knowledge is present in a society can be summarized in the term 'historical culture [*Geschichtskultur*].' Historical culture is a collective description for highly divergent, complementary or overlapping, at any rate directly or indirectly related forms of presentation of the past in a present. It is nothing static, but permanently in transformation, and arises as the result of a variety of conditional factors." Wolfgang Hardtwig, *Geschichtskultur und Wissenschaft* (Munich: dtv, 1990), 8ff.

31. On the history of "legitimacy" and "loyalty" in the GDR, see Sigrid Meuschel, *Legitimation und Parteiherrschaft in der DDR* (Frankfurt: Suhrkamp Verlag, 1992).

32. The primary mission of the DFG Project on History of Propaganda Freiburg & Leipzig is documentation and analysis of propaganda and public relations in German-German comparison. The first results of the work have been published in Monika Gibas and Dirk Schindelbeck, eds., "Die Heimat hat sich schön gemacht . . . ," 1959: *Fallstudien zur deutsch-deutschen Propagandageschichte* (Leipzig: Leipziger Universitätsverlag, 1994); and in Gerald Diesener and Rainer Gries, eds., *Propaganda in*

Deutschland. Politische Massenbeeinflussung im 20. Jahrhundert (Darmstadt: Wissenschaftliche Buchgesellschaft, 1996).

33. On historical pictures see Rainer Gries, Volker Ilgen, and Dirk Schindelbeck, *Gestylte Geschichte. Vom alltäglichen Umgang mit Geschichtsbildern* (Münster: Verlag Westfälisches Dampfboot, 1989).

34. See, for example, Judith Butler, *Das Unbehagen der Geschlechter* (Frankfurt am Main: Suhrkamp Verlag, 1991); and: Rosi Braidotti, *Nomadic Subjects: Embodiment and Sexual Differences in Contemporary Feminist Theory* (New York: Columbia University Press, 1994).

35. "A Personal Sip," *Die Zeit Magazin* 31 (July 1993): 22–25.

36. On the nostalgia debate in Germany, see Margaret Talbot, "Back to the Future: Pining for the Old Days in Germany," *The New Republic*, July 18 and 25, 1994, 11ff; Lothar Fritze, "Identifikation mit dem gelebten Leben—Gibt es DDR-Nostalgie in den neuen Bundesländern?" in *Das wiedervereinigte Deutschland. Zwischenbilanz und Perspektiven*, ed. Ralf Altenhof and Eckard Jesse (Munich: Bayerische Landeszentrale für politische Bildungsarbeit, 1995), 275–292; and Rainer Gries, "Nostalgie—Legende—Zukunft? Geschichtskultur und Produktkultur in Ostdeutschland," *Universitas. Zeitschrift für interdisziplinäre Wissenschaft* 51, no. 2 (1996): 102–115.

37. Amelie Mummendey, "Verhalten zwischen sozialen Gruppen: Die Theorie der sozialen Identität," in *Theorien der Sozialpsychologie*, vol. II: *Gruppen-und Lerntheorien*, ed. Dieter Frey and Martin Irle (Bern/Stuttgart/Toronto: Huber, 1985), 211.

38. Hans Domizlaff, *Die Gewinnung des öffentlichen Vertrauens. Ein Lehrbuch der Markentechnik. Neu zusammengestellte Ausgabe* (1939/1940; reprint, Hamburg: Verlag Marketing Journal, 1992), 141. On the biography of the German "brand-name philosopher" Hans Domizlaff, see Dirk Schindelbeck, "Stilgedanken zur Macht. 'Lerne wirken ohne zu handeln!': Hans Domizlaff, eines Werbeberaters Geschichte," in *"Ins Gehirn der Masse kriechen!" Werbung und Mentalitätsgeschichte*, by Rainer Gries, Volker Ilgen, and Dirk Schindelbeck. (Darmstadt: Wissenschaftliche Buchgesellschaft, 1995).

39. Mackat to the International Advertising Film Festival.

ten
Cryptographic Art of Bratislava

Configurations of Absence in
Post-Communist Installation Art

Paul Krainak

The American public has been weaned on formalist and ahistorical art theory. We are seduced by spectacle, obsessed with the present and with presence. The enduring subject of American art, linking the work of Pollock, Johns, Smithson, and Warhol, is the "act" itself—not so much a rite but a record of individual will in the ledger of a secular universe. Our art world is contoured by academic politics and market strategies. We are not likely to decipher Slavic artists' sensitivity to folk tradition and religious ritual, not accustomed to comprehending the historic suspension of Eastern Europe between Western European influences on one hand and Asian on the other, between Christian and Islamic religions, and between Latin or Germanic and Slavic tongues. There are few phantoms in mainstream American culture. Absences in our art world are simply empty spaces. Conversely, for artists who endured decades of censorship, absence or silence is poignant. One faces a confounding issue of actual or virtual location, physical and psychological displacement, and authentic versus fictional history when Central European art is exhibited in the West.

In late socialist Czechoslovakia, progressive artists, who were unrecognized by the Party, cultivated the secure, contemplative ambiance of private domains out of inherent opposition to the public spectacle of official art. This was facilitated with homegrown ritual-based surrealism, conceptualism, and performance art practices. Many commentators have assumed that these practices were prevalent in part because smuggled Western art magazines prominently featured corresponding styles. Although Slavic artists responded favorably to American culture, they did not slavishly adopt specific trends from the West. That resemblance is hardly valid, in any case, for defining a generation of artists whose work matured in the late days of the socialist regime, when such stylistic categorizations are conceived by Western art-market customs and New York art discourse. Conceptual art and installation art had been developing internationally for decades, and the popular art literature from the West only helped us to frame the work as generally comprehensible for critiques of dominant cultural institutions.

One may assume that this generation from the last years of socialism viewed ideology and aesthetics as experiential rather than rhetorical. The critical contours of much Central European art were more a tactical response to the realities of having to disguise dissenting expression, camouflage it, hide it totally, or else exhibit it abroad, sometimes under an assumed name. These realities demanded specific physical limitations that granted work portability and confidentiality. Since this was coupled with limitations on the availability of quality materials and regional exhibiting venues, artists learned to be extremely resourceful and focused in their research.

While art from Slovakia today is not explicitly about the experience of censorship and the resulting secrecy of exhibiting and criticizing works, there is still covert evidence of the "underground" in works shown abroad by artists who came of age in the last days of that regime. Small, carefully chosen sites in private, domestic environments such as churches, artists' homes, or summer cottages once safeguarded the object and inevitably contoured the language of production. One need only compare the look and feel of installation art in the West, which is dominated by a blurring of public and private spaces and an interest in celebrity and spectacle, to note stark differences in aesthetic attitude and intention. In contrast to the United States, in Europe, the history of art is incomprehensible without explicit linkage to profound historical narratives. Satellite socialist regimes understood that some of the most radical and proscriptive early modernism emanated from Moscow, Berlin, Prague and Vienna,[1] and they did not want the spirit of avant-gardism reborn under their watch. By the 1980s, dissident artists of Central Europe needed to resuscitate those suppressed revolutionary connections between radical form and real events which activated Dada and constructivism, two movements born in Central and Eastern Europe and in Russia. How to rehabilitate such a tradition so synonymous with reform was a constant struggle of the underground that can still be traced in today's art.

Related to former conditions of secrecy and seclusion, a notable series of signs appears in the installation art of today's most notable Slovak artists. At first glance they appear to be signatures of minimalism: they employ spareness of expression and simplicity of means. They might include an absence of color other than black or white, sculpture that recalls rudimentary tools, narration rather than pictorialism. In the United States, they would be read merely as antagonistic to the cultivation of beauty and connoisseurship. But here these devices are more imaginatively arranged, more ritualized. They delineate feelings of absence and omission and are remnants of the fortunes of pre-revolutionary Czechoslovakia. It is significant for Western viewers that they demand that the observer abandon familiar associations with the language of exclusion inherent in our purist and chaste high modernism.

Central European, Russian, and Baltic artists complained bitterly about the decontextualization of their work when it was first shown in America and Western Europe after 1990. Reading Central European signs of absence and concealment and other residues of censorship as akin to formalist negation or mystified as an inscrutable cultural Other misses the target. The tendency of the West to "internationalize" culture into dominant trends continues today by way of a discourse on "international conceptualism." More recently applied to emerging art in Asia and Africa, a common conceptualist orientation is now purportedly shared by all progressive international artists. This flawed notion had its beginnings in the reception of Eastern European art in the 1980s and 1990s. However, instead of seeing an art that mirrors the West or stereotypes a cultural temperament, it would be more instructive to acknowledge regional histories, such as the repercussions of generations of prohibitions on free speech. Today, after more than a decade of experimentation with unconstrained themes and formats, the installations of one group of Slovak artists are still informed by the strategies used to overcome social oppression. These take the form of obscured images, indecipherable texts, blackened objects, and faint shapes. Former survival strategies are sometimes evinced in unsolvable riddles, irrelevant observations, and private rituals amid subtle reconstructions and critiques of local histories. These dislocations are detritus from a past when creative activity and the frustrations of deferred liberties were synonymous.

Catastrophe and Decay

Daniel Fischer, one of the most widely known painters from Bratislava, has built a reputation on the aesthetics of location and disappearance. He utilizes processes of landscape imaging and displacement by siting a canvas in an environment and abstractly reinterpreting what the canvas has masked out. The image he paints contains the same color, light, and compositional structure of the site, so the painting blends seamlessly with the actual background. This artistic and ideological camouflage is accompanied by large-scale photo-documentation of the site when the painting is shown in a white-walled gallery, so viewers understand that it is not common abstraction. Through this

Daniel Fischer's "Memento." 1995. Photograph by Mattress Factory, Pittsburgh, Pa., courtesy of John Charley. Used by permission.

process the observer comes to consider the art as a kind of anthropological evidence. Fischer coyly naturalizes the cultural construct of abstraction, making chameleon-like objects which use the expressionist painting style once banned by the Party to critique standardized gallery viewing and collecting. His exhibitions, combining the painting and the photodocumentation of its original integrated setting, question which image contains the real art. They emphasize the innovative processes that many Slovak artists rely on to articulate that real experiences and events are the source of their art, though they are regularly disguised.

In the 1990s, Fischer also produced installations that involve controlled spaces, with light, text, and sound as his formal apparatus. An installation which is clearly coded with signs of secrecy and concealment is entitled "Memento."[2] The work involves a gear-shaped contraption about four feet in diameter which appears to have been exhumed from some medieval factory. A center wheel rotates incrementally, tautly strung by a band driven by an electric motor. The machine hovers at ankle height in the center of a rectangular white-walled room. On the back wall are a series of framed texts revealing typographic and semantic relationships between dichotomous constructions such as wisdom/stupidity, altruism/egoism, or charity/envy. Between each is a graduated blending of words, which establishes an imaginary structure bonding the contrary meanings. According to Fischer, these are formal models designed to articulate "the fragile balance between good and evil."

Paul Krainak

Fischer, "Memento," a closer look. 1995. Photograph by John Charley, courtesy of the Mattress Factory, Pittsburgh, Pa. Used by permission.

At the end of each cycle of the precisely torqued wheel, the central mechanism splits open into four claw-shaped sections. Instantly the lights in the gallery go out and the claws flail menacingly outward. Flames seem to spit from the armature, and the gallery walls are suddenly backlit by colored texts conveying only abject human conditions. Before the observer (victim) can adjust to this assault, the lights come up again and the slow tortuous cycle is resumed. Fischer is attempting to demonstrate Peter Zeeman's theory of catastrophes. Zeeman, a Dutch physicist, proposed that systems which develop via continuous, gradual change, be they natural, mechanical, or social, are eventually due to produce calamitous events—this despite their apparent prior order and tranquil surface appearance. Fischer's staging of a crisis that erupts like the pressure of tectonic plates on a civic fault line is an apt one. It clearly refers to the relentless oppression of the earlier regime, but it could also remind the viewer of postseparation Slovakia, whose people continue to weather a cycle of ineffectual economic reforms.

Several striking aspects of the installation seem at first glance to be peripheral to the subject and the site. These have to do with formal devices chosen to flavor the impression of the work. Dimmed lighting is a finely tuned feature which also recurs in the work of Fischer's peers. Fischer uses low lighting to de-compose the objects in the room so that as we walk into the space our eyes must adjust from the clarity of the hallway. The sudden plunge into darkness instills anxiety, feelings of entrapment, and ultimately impressions of death. In addition, the obscuring of language through indecipherable

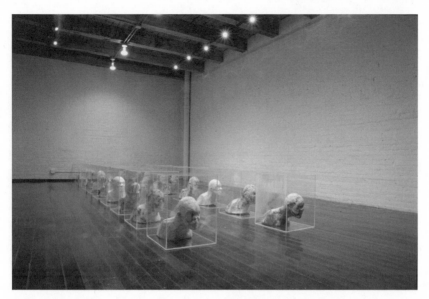

Ladislav Čharny, "Phase of Nigreda." 1995. Photograph by John Charley, courtesy of the Mattress Factory, Pittsburgh, Pa. Used by permission.

Closeup of Čarny's "Phase of Nigreda" showing the bacteria on the busts. 1995. Photograph by John Charley, courtesy of the Mattress Factory, Pittsburgh, Pa. Used by permission.

Paul Krainak

Čarny's "Phase of Nigreda": glowing in the darkness. 1995. Photograph by John Charley, courtesy of the Mattress Factory, Pittsburgh, Pa. Used by permission.

symbols creates a breakdown of logic and provokes anxiety about not knowing. The continual appearance and disappearance of larger wall texts simulates the allusiveness and relativity of human virtues as they are made unintelligible in the machinery of a decaying social system.

Another Bratislavan, Ladislav Čarny, also addresses social dynamics—survival, disease, and institutionalization—in a project called "Phase of Nigreda." In it the artist reflects on the work of eighteenth-century sculptor F. X. Messerschmidt, whose statue he has reconformed and serialized.[3] Twenty cast-paper life-size busts are sealed inside Plexiglas cubes and aligned in two precise rows toward the rear of the gallery. Each is in various stages of grotesque disfigurement, having been infected by the artist with slow-rotting bacteria. As the gallery lights fade, the heads, which have also been treated with phosphorous, begin to glow. Mold on the paper-pulp busts now looks like dark cavities, demarcations of absence rather than merely surface abrasions. The procession of these disembodied souls is radiant, even though they are scarred by putridity and suffocate in an aura of decay. Regimentation, confinement, and deterioration all relate to the repression of the subject and the relocation and reconfiguration of speech. For Čarny, however, the transmutation made possible by the cycle of decay and rebirth is full of hope and opposes the morbidity of submission. He remains somewhat more optimistic than Fischer, presenting a poignant and resourceful hybridization of history, philosophy, and religious veneration.

Vulgar Testimonials

Two more Bratislavans, Desider Toth and Roman Ondák, have created works which subvert symbols of private and public life. Former state policies limiting the scope of free expression are internalized in unique ways in the production of their art. How these repressive policies became recoded is perhaps more evident in the following works, which use books as material and as a catalyst for critique.

Desider Toth's installation "Reservations" is a kind of library to unknowing that illuminates the past and present state of literacy in Slovakia. This installation displays scores of books on ten small wooden shelves, each large enough to support four or five hardbound texts. The shelves are suspended about every three feet, one at eye level, one at chest height and so on, the display being somewhat more like a rare books boutique than a library. However, some books have been mutilated, sawn diagonally in half or three-quarters so that they disappear inexplicably into the shelf. All the covers are painted black except for the spine, and the pages are glued shut.

References to the obscenity of censorship, limitations on information, the bleakness of not knowing, and being in the dark are obvious. The suppression of history, the official erasure of basic pleasures under the auspices of moral authority, resonates in such stark configurations. But Toth tells us more about the experience of oppression if we examine the blackened volumes carefully. Although anonymous when approached point blank, they reveal their titles when viewed obliquely. Only surface fragments of their former selves, they still suggest that there is more information to be decoded if you take an alternative route to their core.

Toth's piece speaks to the peripheral perception of artists that was regularly exercised before the revolution. Because the former Czechoslovakia had the highest percentage of paid informants per capita in all of the satellite countries, the experience of finding fault with and speaking frankly about social conditions was fraught with deception and guilt. To uncover truths, one always had to enter discreetly from the side. Fine details of events may have been obscured by fear or Party policy, but the structure of truth was sometimes discernible underneath the garment of official propaganda. Immediately after the Velvet Revolution, the desire for alternative voices in the East was stemmed by a book market flooded with Western-style pulp novels and soft porn. The odyssey from essentially opaque to totally transparent literature engenders a new set of surrogates for open discourse and diversity that serves as a postscript to Toth's chronicle of deferred narratives.

Finally, "A Taste of Thinking," by conceptualist Roman Ondák, is a gritty reconstruction of a holding cell with bilious-colored wall tiles and a concrete floor. With its paint-chipped desk, gray bookshelf, bare mattress, dingy carpet, and rusted hot plate, it offers all the amenities of a Khrushchev-era bunker on

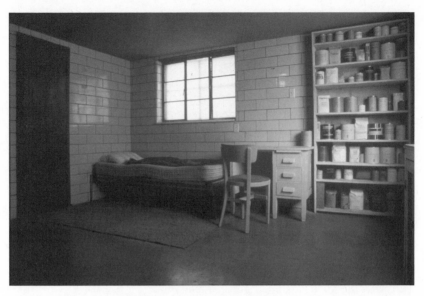

Roman Ondák's "Taste of Thinking." 1995. Photograph by John Charley, courtesy of the Mattress Factory, Pittsburgh, Pa. Used by permission.

the Sino-Soviet frontier. The ceiling-high shelf is crammed with tins and sacks of storable food. At first glance, their muted generic labels suggest military provisions, reinforcing the room's institutional setting. On closer view, the ersatz bean and flour labels turn out to be book titles. They are mostly psychology, sociology, and medical primers with titles as bland as the expected rations. These include *The Modern Home Medical Advisor, Use and Abuse of Psychology, Human Neuroanatomy*, and *The Handbook of Medical Psychology*, along with the more droll *Emergency Psychiatry at the Crossroads* and *Art in Elementary Education*. The majority of the titled labels are gray, faded green, beige, or brick-colored, and the authors' names are missing.

Ondák's cell is a hard-nosed appraisal of Enlightenment logic. It is the karmic residue of history's most totalizing social experiment. The plethora of technical texts and the absence of muses condemn any occupant to consume only the most artless expressions of civic conformity and cultural mediocrity. Like Fischer's and Čarny's constructions, the chamber of regret in "A Taste of Thinking" resonates with absences and conveys the risks of digesting any grand-scale sociological regimen over a balanced ideological diet. Like the other artists listed here, Ondák exploits the medium of installation art to displace the viewer. He offers observers an alternative non-Western context from which to flesh out the inhabitant of this metaphoric space. But Ondák is the lord of this manor, and he wants us to "taste" the condition of being an absent or anonymous subject.

All these artists' installations are full of quiet but telling omissions, intellec-

Supplies for surviving a long
intellectual famine. 1995.
Photograph by John Charley,
courtesy of the Mattress
Factory, Pittsburgh, Pa. Used
by permission.

tual blind alleys, and sideshow sleights of hand which animate their makers'
experience and our imaginations. Those who chose to remain and work in
postrevolutionary Middle European nations still contend with alarming political and economic conditions. The breakup of former Czechoslovakia left
Slovaks with high unemployment rates and a corrupt leadership that lacked
any mandate or interest in supporting the arts. The National Academy for the
Arts in Bratislava, a haven for the artists who founded Slovakia's intellectual
underground, has experienced a decade of severe cutbacks and neglect in arts
education. The ordeal of democratic and capitalistic reform remains sluggish
and painful. A dramatic swing to the right has adversely affected the artistic
discourse which was so optimistic in 1990.[4] Attempts to conform to a more
eclectic Western notion of free expression has been problematic for artists who
were not accustomed to art that is market driven and ahistorical. Some Slovak
artists still contend with civic adversity by addressing larger concerns—
religion, politics, identity, and so forth—as interdependent aesthetic constructs that have a language rooted in real histories and reflect a memory of
preserving artistic expression under forty years of official condemnation.

In 2000, Daniel Fischer produced an exhibition titled *Retrospection* in

Ondák's labels combine naïve idealism, socialist-style self-help, and wry humor. 1995. Photograph by John Charley, courtesy of the Mattress Factory, Pittsburgh, Pa. Used by permission.

Vienna at the Kunst Raum Mitteleuropa. The work is a testament to Slovak Jews who were deported during World War II. The centerpiece of the show is a mural-sized photo composite of a crowd of Jewish detainees. Upon close inspection one finds that the mosaic is made up of pictures of luxurious commodities—watches, jewelry, automobiles, furs, and so forth, all turned upside down. The only way to comprehend the larger images of victims is to view the picture through small lenses suspended in the middle of the galley. Fischer is still using subterfuge to criticize the instruments of political power and cultural determinism. His immediate subject is the Holocaust and the absence of Jewry in Bratislava. The images of luxury reflect the spoils of oppression as well as the specter of capitalism that has haunted the region's political rhetoric for the last fifty years. Fischer's attention to this tragedy is intended to remind us that the dilemmas of Slovakia's current crisis are a legacy of World War II. The artist asks us to imagine which next sacrificial lamb will be slaughtered in the name of political autonomy and power. Thousands of émigrés in the arts and sciences have abandoned their homes in the last ten years for opportunity and wealth, and their departure has left Slovakia culturally poorer. This is a bitter pill for those who have stayed at home and struggled to bring closure to everything they have sacrificed. The prohibitions, suppression, and confinement of one era have been replaced by indifference, isolation, and exile in another. The connotations of loss and issues of culpability are stinging in the camouflage of *Retrospections,* and a veil is lifted from the surface of consumerism that was supposed to placate the average citizen.

The aforementioned installations from Slovakia reflect on life under "the regime," but that is not their subject. The subject of this art, and the subjects of Central European art in general, are extremely diverse. Because artists during the regime were required to be so guarded with language, subtlety and cryptic traditions became ingrained. Even now, art and language are not taken so cavalierly as in the West. And it is bitterly ironic that the artists' sense of community, once strong enough to unseat a corrupt monolith, resilient enough to keep confidence and trust alive in a culture of stifling paranoia, is now, after gaining the requisite personal freedoms, largely dismissed by their citizens and their government. The absence of community, disappearance of consensus, and splintering of cultural destination are now embedded in the code of omissions in contemporary Slovak aesthetics.

NOTES

1. For more information on Middle European avant-garde of the 1920s, see Rostisav Svacha, ed., *Devetsil: Czech Avant-Garde of the 1920's and 30's* (Oxford: Museum of Modern Art, and London: Design Museum, 1990).

2. Several of the works described in this essay were part of the exhibition "Artists of Central and Eastern Europe," curated by Michael Olijnyk at the Mattress Factory, Pittsburgh, Pa., 1995. An earlier examination of the works can be found in a *New Art Examiner* essay by the author entitled "Siting Slavs at the Factory," March 1996.

3. Messerschmidt has special significance to Central European artists, as he was a resident of Bratislava. His expressionist aesthetics are considered to have prefigured the German Expressionist movement of the 1930s. See the exhibition catalog by Jana Gerzova, *Ladislav Čarny: Pictures Objects Installations* (Zilina: Museum of Art, 1995), 19.

4. In spite of this a Bratislavan art journal, *Profil,* under the editorial direction of Jana Gerzova, has managed to survive and champion the work of artists such as Toth, Ondák, Fischer, Čarny, and others.

eleven

"Move Over Madonna"

Gender, Representation, and
The "Mystery" of Bulgarian Voices

Carol Silverman

When New York Times critic Jon Pareles wrote "Move over Madonna, taste-
makers on two continents are embracing a Bulgarian women's choir" (1988,
27), he both reflected and promoted the Bulgarian music craze that swept the
United States and Western Europe in the late 1980s and early 1990s. Whereas
people used to stare at me incredulously when I said I was studying Bulgarian
folk music, in that era Bulgarian CDs were prominently displayed in Tower
Records, critics proclaimed Bulgarian folk music "the most beautiful music on
the planet,"[1] and rock and classical stars waxed eloquent about the group Le
Mystère des Voix Bulgares (The Mystery of the Bulgarian Voices) and collaborated with them in "crossover" productions. Following Steven Feld, who wrote
that "transcultural record productions tell specific stories about accountability,
authorship and agency, about the workings of capitalism, control and compromise" (1994, 258), I discuss the historical background of Bulgarian choral
music, highlighting issues of labor (both socialist and capitalist), representation, and gender in the transcultural dialogue between East and West.[2] Furthermore, I locate my discussion of Bulgarian choirs within the theoretical
frameworks of the emerging literature on the conception, marketing, and
imagery of "world music."

It is no accident that the term "world music" was gaining ground precisely at the time when the Bulgarian choirs first toured the West; the choir's fame in the West was intricately entwined with the emerging marketing success of "world music." According to Timothy Taylor, this term gained currency when it replaced the terms "ethnic," "folk," and "international" and began to be used as a sales category, marked by the debut of *Billboard*'s world music chart in 1990 (1997, 3–5; also see Feld 2000, 146–150). As Steven Feld remarks, "the phrase swept through the public sphere first and foremost signaling a global industry, one focused on marketing danceable ethnicity and exotic alterity on the world pleasure and commodity map" (2000, 151). World music is, indeed, a fruitful arena for examining global flows of commodities and symbols in a charged atmosphere revealing multiple representations of "difference" and conflicts over who has rights to sell what to whom. The Bulgarian case is particularly rich because we may examine all of the above within the contrasting contexts of socialism and postsocialism.

Steven Feld characterizes the scholarship on world music of the last decade as focusing either on anxiety or celebration, loss or gain. On one hand, anxious accounts stress the loss of musical diversity that accompanies increased homogeneity (Alan Lomax's cultural "gray-out") and the "complicity of world music in commodifying ethnicity," noting that there is little possibility of resistance to world capitalistic institutions. On the other hand, celebratory accounts uncover active resistance, laud reappropriations of Western forms, and revere the emergence of local, creative, hybrid genres (ibid., 53). My analysis of Bulgarian choirs is an anxious tale, but it is not one that isolates capitalism as the enemy. A significant danger of the anxious narrative is the tendency to essentialize a prior authenticity (socialist or presocialist), which is then contrasted with a degraded and exploitative capitalist commodity. In my analysis, there is no prior authenticity, rather merely a series of historical moves wherein music is part of ideological and commodity exchanges within both socialism and postsocialism.

The Emergence of Bulgarian Choirs

The form of Bulgarian vocal music which attracted the most attention in the West in the 1980s was the a cappella female chorus, a form "invented"[3] in 1951 by the Bulgarian composer Filip Kutev (1903–1982). Kutev's brilliant idea was to take traditional village songs, which are monophonic in most of Bulgaria or have drone-based harmony in the southwest region of the country, and arrange them into four- or five-part Western harmonies and add dynamics and tempo changes while preserving the throat-placed vocal quality.[4] With the goal of creating a national folk chorus, Kutev traveled around Bulgaria in the early 1950s to recruit the best female village singers and instrumentalists for the newly formed state-sponsored music ensembles.[5] Choruses featured female singers because singing in Bulgaria is predominantly a female tradition; ritual and work songs, for example, are almost exclusively sung by women.

Moreover, women are symbolically associated with tradition and nationalism, a point I develop below. Singer Kremena Stancheva recounts, "The Radio had a competition for folk singers. At that time the Radio had a small group of singers and instrumentalists but they decided to create a large ensemble—a female choir and male instrumentalists. . . . I also received an invitation from Filip Kutev to be in his ensemble, but they constantly traveled inside and outside the country, while the Radio choir just made recordings. The working hours were fixed, so I decided to try. Singers from all regions were accepted into our ensemble."

With the formation of the choruses, singers from all parts of the country sang together for the first time, not their own local music but ensemble compositions based on traditional songs and authored by composers. Stancheva remarks, "Our choir was a school for conductors and composers. Those that could compose and those that couldn't all wrote music for the Radio Choir. We had no choice but to sing these songs." Singers were taught how to alter dynamics and tempos, how to harmonize in complex polyphony, and how to blend in a chorus. They were paid a state salary, but they were not paid for singing a village song to a composer, who then used it as the core of his composition, called an *obrabotka* (an arrangement; literally, a reworking; from the verb *rabotja*, to work). I use the male possessive pronoun deliberately because all composers were male except for Kutev's wife, Maria Kuteva. Once an arrangement was written, the composer's name was attached to it and the singer's name disappeared. The composer received an arrangement fee from the government plus a royalty fee every time the composition was performed or played on the radio. These fees were quite substantial during the socialist period and were terribly resented by singers, who felt exploited.[6] According to Stancheva, "In terms of royalties, folk singers were in the most disadvantaged position. We sing the songs; the composer arranges them, changes them; they get the royalties . . . we get nothing." Note that the linguistic coding of how Bulgarian singers conceive of singing a song for composer is with the verb "to give"—"I gave a song to a composer." This illustrates the lack of control a singer exerted over her song once it was "given" to a composer.

The gender coding of the above arrangement was obvious: females/singers worked for and delivered material to males/composers; the latter received the profit from the former's work. But more than just an unequal labor relationship, this was also an unequal artistic relationship. The songs were commodities delivered into the hands of males who often had radically different ideas of musical taste. Stancheva remarks that when her solo songs were recorded by Radio Sofia, the instrumental accompaniments fashioned by composers destroyed the regional style: "The first time we singers would hear the instrumental accompaniments was at the recording sessions. Some of these accompaniments ruined our songs—often they had no connection with the style of our music. We weren't allowed to comment or object to these accompaniments—we were only singers."

The above practices demonstrate that despite the rhetoric of socialist equality, women in the arts held less decision-making power than men. Furthermore, despite claims to employment equality, females held inferior positions in the labor hierarchy—they were paid less and had fewer benefits. As Daskalova remarks, "Despite the communist regime's self-congratulatory assertions about gender equality and equal employment opportunities, these patterns are well documented for the communist period" (2000, 341). In Bulgaria, the situation within the arts paralleled the larger occupational hierarchy: women were clustered in low-paying professions, including the textile, shoe, and leather industries and in teaching, health care, and accounting. The arts were considered one notch up from these professions, but within the arts, singers were indeed many notches down from composers and arrangers. As we will see below, this hierarchy changed little after the introduction of capitalism.

In the socialist period, ensemble music became a significant ideological marker of the elevation of "folk" (or "peasant") to the realm of "nation": it was hailed as the "national music" of Bulgaria, as opposed to competing regional and ethnic musics and the popular/folk fusions played at weddings.[7] Composers, ethnomusicologists, and Party ideologues boasted that they were raising the level of folk music to that of Western art music.[8] This was part of a state-sponsored initiative to "modernize" peasant culture in diverse realms. Folklore had to be "cleaned up" and reworked to make it "art." During the socialist period, ensemble music received prime media space; ensemble music was almost ubiquitous on the radio and represented Bulgaria at festivals of music held in various socialist countries. Moreover, two high schools and a pedagogical institute at the college level were formed to train young people for ensembles. In spite of government sponsorship, however, ensemble music never was and still is not widely accepted by the Bulgarian public. Perhaps because of its homogenized sound, its predictability, its removal from the "folk," and its association with socialism, ensemble music was rejected by most Bulgarians.[9] Bulgarians were certainly proud that the West admired Bulgarian choral music, but at home nobody listened to it. At home, a very different kind of music swept the country in a craze during the 1970s and 1980s—"wedding music." Combining the loudness and intensity of rock music with breakneck speed, dazzling improvisations, and eclectic quotes reminiscent of jazz, wedding music embodied a Western modernity which was tantalizingly forbidden under regulated socialism (Silverman 1996). Ironically, then, as Bulgarian audiences rejected the socialist music of choirs, the West embraced it as "mysterious, ancient, and seductive."

Even though males as well as females were part of government ensembles, the socialist government promoted the symbolic association of women with traditional music through visual and aural means. For example, Bulgarian women in peasant costume were ubiquitous images for concerts, records, and tourist posters. Women were perceived as closer to local custom and lore, and indeed during the 1950s some villages lost most of their males in outmigration

Carol Silverman

to town industry. As Kligman pointed out for Romania, "Women are now the practical tenders of tradition for their families, their villages and the state" (1988, 257). It is ironic that women were displayed symbolically as tradition-bearers precisely at the time that women were being recruited away from villages into wage labor for music ensembles which did not perform traditional music. The latter were part of a larger trend in all East European socialist countries, whereby women were mobilized away from private village agriculture into industry. The symbol, however, transcended the specific circumstances; the power of the equation women = tradition is intertwined with a related association, that of women with nation.[10] As Martha Lampland points out, "The frequency with which the nation was represented as women in Europe in the eighteenth and nineteenth centuries is well known. . . . Visual representation gave form and physical presence to these symbols" (1994, 288). Furthermore, European nationalism required a particular form of gender relationships, most notably the regulation of female sexuality and reproduction in the service of the state: "The trope of the nation-as-women of course depends for its representational efficacy on a particular woman as chaste, dutiful, daughterly and maternal" (Parker, Russo, Sommer, and Yaeger 1992, 6). As we will see below, the image of the chaste or maternal female peasant needed to be altered significantly to refashion Bulgarian women into pop stars.

Western Promoters Invent the "Mystery"

The female Bulgarian singer was reinvented when Western music producers and marketers entered the representation process. In 1987, Nonesuch/ Elektra Records released an album of the Bulgarian State Radio and Television Female Vocal Choir (henceforth referred to as the Choir) with the title *Le Mystère des Voix Bulgares* (*The Mystery of Bulgarian Voices*), and the public went wild, first in Western Europe and then in the United States.[11] Volume one of *Le Mystère* sold over a quarter of a million copies (Kohanov 1991, 73), and volume two won the 1990 Grammy for Best Traditional Folk Performance.[12] Also in 1987, Hannibal issued the LP *Balkana: The Music of Bulgaria*, which featured vocal arrangements by the Trio Bulgarka (composed of former members of the Choir), plus solos and instrumental performances. This record was also a hit in Western Europe and the United States and was followed by the Trio's *The Forest Is Crying* (*Lament for Indje Voivode*). The Choir first toured the United States in 1988 to sold-out audiences. A bevy of other choruses formed and reformed in Bulgaria after 1989 to capitalize on the success of the Choir and Trio Bulgarka. Subsequent tours of the Choir and other related choirs during the 1990s created what *USA Today* called "Bulgaria Hysteria: What has 52 feet, the voice of an angel and counts Linda Ronstadt and Jerry Garcia as fans? The Bulgarian State Radio and Television Female Vocal Choir" (1988).

Why the sudden popularity of Bulgarian music in the West? There is no doubt that the 1980s craze of world beat and ethnopop had opened listeners to many kinds of folk music (Miller 1988, 72–74). No doubt the dissonant harmonies, additive rhythms,[13] expressive ornamentation, throat-placed vocal style, and superb technical abilities of the singers were all very striking. But whereas African and Caribbean musics have had points of entry into American popular music via jazz and gospel, Bulgarian a cappella singing has little in common with the drum kits and synthesizers of world beat.[14] The marketing strategy of Nonesuch and other companies deliberately exoticized the music as ethereal and ancient, perhaps the opposite pole from ethnic and peasant.[15] By now, this has become a common technique in world music marketing, as witnessed by the marketing of the music of the Gyuto Monks and other Tibetan and Mongolian groups. In their case, although the musical style was largely remote for Western audiences, the appeal was in its "spirituality." Taylor reminds us that the popularity of New Age cultures fits right into the trend of "spiritualization that western listeners impose on this decontextualized and reritualized music" (1997, 25).

In the case of the Bulgarian choirs, marketing tropes capitalized on remoteness, but they were less about the "sacred" and more about the "mystery." In fact, the choir soon began to be referred to as "The Mystery." Composer Ingram Marshall wrote in volume one's liner notes that "it is really the uniqueness of these singing voices, the 'mystery' of their clarity, tempered by seductive loveliness, which ultimately enchants our ears" (1987). Reviewers and journalists expanded the theme of mystery: *Rolling Stone* said the music "offered transporting sensual experiences to audiences" (De Curtis 1988). *Newsday* said it "achieves a spectral sonic beauty . . . is hypnotic. . . . The notes seem to float" (Williams 1988). *The Christian Science Monitor* lauded "shimmering, other-worldly voices" (Duncan 1988), and the Hult Center for the Performing Arts (Eugene, Oregon) wrote:

> Trained in centuries-old, secret vocal tradition, their voices resonate with a dense, ravishing mixture of exotic dissonances and gorgeous romantic timbres. Listeners the world over have been drawn to the mysteriously haunting songs of the all-female 24-voice Bulgarian State Radio and Television Female Vocal Choir. Performing arrangements of ancient East European folk songs and chants, these women sweep through a profusion of eerie, heartbreaking harmonies. Dark sighs. Strong, cutting resonant power. . . . Hear the other-worldly sounds that evoke a heartbreakingly distant past. (1990–1991)

Promoters highlighted three main elements of the music: mystery, women, and antiquity. The East European female voice became a discursive symbol for interwoven fantasies about power, mystery, and mythology. First, various historical ages are invoked by reviewers in an effort to convince us that this music is ancient. I have dated the choral style to the 1950s,[16] but nevertheless, reviewers remark that "they sound . . . like the chorus of some prehistoric golden age delivered to us in a time machine" (Migaldi 1988). The Orpheus story connects Bulgaria to Greek mythology: "What do the Bulgarians sound like? It may be suggesting too much, but according to Greek myth, Orpheus, the great musician, was born in Thrace which is now part of Bulgaria. And it is said that he was able to charm the gods of the underworld with his divine playing of the lyre. The Mysterious Voices of Bulgaria conjure exactly the kind of thrilling, unearthly beauty and purity of sound that this music suggests" (Weiss 1988).[17]

Second, critics slide easily from the ancient era to the middle ages, perhaps because Ingram Marshall, in the liner notes to *Le Mystère* volume one, refers to Bulgarian singing as a "mysterium; in the middle ages, this word was used to denote a guild of craftsmen, a group of people who practiced an art or skill known only to them" (1987). But in Bulgaria, all villagers sing in this manner; there are no secret groups. Few, of course, sing well. The critics, however, fantasize as follows: "Their specialty is an open-throated vocal resonance that is something of a tool of the trade, handed down in guild-like secrecy" (Moon 1988, 4D), and "There is something medieval about the Bulgarians' sound too—as if it emanated from a remote monastery where chosen women were trained in musical secrets from childhood" (Weiss 1988).[18] Finally, not only is time displaced to the past, but place is also displaced to the East. The Eastern influences in the music are noted with "Orientalist" clichés: "There is the oriental component to the Bulgarians' music—full of haunting nasal wails and vocal twists, and mesmerizing dissonances" (Weiss 1988).[19]

In the context of hyperbole and ethereal associations in liner notes, concert notes, and press releases, critics freely embellished the discursive symbols of mystery. Some brave critics criticized the lack of information in print and media (Dyer 1988); others delved into Balkan history to explain this singing style as due to the oppression of the Ottoman empire (Alarik 1988). This line of reasoning, although supported by Bulgarian nationalist anti-Turkish propaganda and espoused by the Choir's conductor and producers, has no scholarly basis. Most critics, however, simply expanded on the given mystery and dealt with the music in terms of sound (melody, harmony, and rhythm), omitting text, context, and performer background. Popular music stars and marketers alike have emphasized that the sound of the music has universal appeal: claims state that it is not tied to one ethnicity and is part of an avant-garde aesthetic. National Public Radio commented that "perhaps this is a musical truth that opens the gates to the timeless realm of all human song."[20] And Danny Kahn, director of promotions for Nonesuch said, "This music is magical. There is a difference between ethnic musics from around the world . . . but some things transcend them. . . . Everyone can listen to this."[21] There is a profound irony here: as Taylor asserts, world music lays claims to "authenticity" by virtue of its "positionality" (that is, being from a faraway place), its "emotionality" (that is, its spirituality or "realness"), and its "primality" (that is, its age) at the same time that a universal appeal is made in terms of sound

(1997, 21–28). The central irony is that world music is both strange and familiar. It also claims to be timeless and new at the same time (ibid., 28).

Perhaps more than any other marketing strategy, the endorsements of rock and popular music stars guaranteed that Bulgarian music would have an audience far wider than ethnic music fans. This phenomenon is noted by Taylor, who calls these Western stars "intermediaries" (ibid., 28). At the first press conference of the choir in November 1988, just prior to their first tour, Graham Nash was the featured speaker.[22] In addition to Nash, Pat Metheny, Paul Simon, Linda Ronstadt, George Harrison, Jackson Browne, Jerry Garcia, and David Byrne have at various times lavished praise on the music, many of whom claim to have been fans well before the 1980s. During the 1988 press conference, Graham Nash chronicled his own interest: "In 1966 Paul Simon called me over and said 'I want you to sit down and listen to this. . . . It was an overwhelming album. . . . For a member of a band somewhat renowned for harmonies, it was truly amazing music. I feel somewhat responsible for having given away over 100 of these albums." Choir concerts through the 1990s continued to draw a huge array of rock and popular music stars, and name-dropping about which famous stars were attending Choir concerts became a favorite sport of journalists.

Women, Work, and Voices

How have gender ideologies molded the female Bulgarian choir phenomenon? My analysis reveals two notions of the female singer, the first as socialist worker and the second as capitalist pop star. These radically different notions, the former a product of planned economies and the latter a product of Western media, clashed boldly during the era of the post-1989 transition. As Gal and Kligman state, "We begin with the observation that the economic and political processes of the 'transition' . . . are not gender neutral, and that one of our primary tasks would be to explore the various ways gender has been a factor in the current transformations" (*Reproducing Gender*, 4). To deconstruct gender appropriations, we must first return to history: in the 1950s, it was entirely reasonable that Filip Kutev recruited only women into the newly formed national choirs, for women were considered the preservers of Bulgarian tradition and women traditionally sang in groups more often than men. However, Kutev faced opposition from many families of excellent female singers because they were appalled at the thought of a young girl leaving a village or small town to live alone in Sofia, the capital city, to work as a professional singer. In the patriarchal family, women were expected to marry in or near their village and to adjust to a husband's career aims. I do not wish to imply that Bulgarian women did not work outside the home. Historians such as Maria Todorova have shown that many Bulgarian women worked outside the home even prior to the twentieth century, and when they worked at home in peasant agriculture they were an essential part of decision-making and resource allocation (1993). Furthermore, as noted above, the recruitment of women into various forms of state labor, such as industry and agricultural collectives, was happening precisely at the time of the formation of the ensembles. Despite these demographic trends of the 1950s, many parents rejected Kutev's offer to move their young (often unmarried) daughters far away to initiate independent careers; surely this offer conjured notions of the breakup of family life.

Two additional factors influenced families: first, ensemble singers traveled a great deal (from the 1950s to the 1970s to socialist countries, but in the 1980s and 1990s all over the world), taking them away from their families and domestic duties. The second factor is that traditional village values associated females singing professionally (i.e., for money) with lack of morality and lack of respect. A woman singing at family and village events for no remuneration was praiseworthy, but female singers who worked in "wedding bands" or in restaurants for tips were labeled "loose."[23] One Thracian singer remarked to me that her parents refused the offer "because it was simply out of their realm of the acceptable; it was shameful." According to singers I have interviewed, just as many families said no as said yes to the idea of their daughters joining the ensembles in the 1950s. As singer Kremena Stancheva narrated, "In general, my parents didn't want singing to be my profession, they didn't consider it prestigious enough." Clandestinely Stancheva became involved in singing; at one point she was asked to travel with the Choir to Germany: "But I didn't have a passport then; I needed my parents' permission to leave the country. So I needed to tell my parents about my secret involvement. It was the first time my father visited me in Sofia. He agreed and then decided that I could sing."

As Bulgaria developed as a socialist nation, the notion of the female professional ensemble singer became more positive, more acceptable, and more ideological. By the 1980s, female gender roles were less restrictive, even in many villages, and women had more options for mobility. Schools opened to train ensemble members, and competition for acceptance into the ensembles was fierce. The singers were viewed as ambassadors of Bulgarian culture to the outside world. Many envied the ability of ensemble performers to travel, even to the West, while ordinary Bulgarians had virtually no opportunities leave the country.[24] As Gal and Kligman note, working outside the home added to the self-esteem and self-worth of professional women (*The Politics of Gender After Socialism*, 53). It is ironic that as the ensemble singers gained in prestige, the music they sang declined in popularity at home. After a short bout of curiosity in the 1950s for hearing and seeing the new ensembles, concertgoers decreased in number. By the 1970s, albums of various ensembles remained unsold for months on record store shelves as more modern fusions of jazz, rock, and folk captured the attention of young people.

An ensemble singer was supposed to be above all a socialist worker, a woman dedicated to the ensemble, the nation, and the communist path, not a woman interested in her own career. Her dedication was both ideological and practical. In structural terms, ensemble singers worked for the state and had no say in what they performed, when they performed, and where they performed. Artistic decisions were made by composers and conductors, and concert and tour decisions were made by managers and administrators, most of whom were male.[25] The lack of control over their performances was partly ameliorated by the ability of soloists to record solo songs with Radio Sofia. This way, the singers picked their own songs to record and were paid separately for them, but they still had no influence over the kind of orchestral accompaniment the recording would feature. As Stancheva narrates: "It was good that we soloists had the right to record as many solo songs as we wanted. Of course, everything had to pass a commission. We would go out and search for village songs." In addition, singers had no access to subsequent profits that the state radio and recording companies earned from their solo songs.

An ensemble singer was paid a monthly state salary, regardless of whether her songs became hits or not. This salary was secure and relatively high for the socialist period, but it was nowhere near the salary of a successful performer in the West. In 1988, the average state salary for an ensemble singer was roughly $210 a month (soloists received an extra $25 a month), plus a $15 per diem (to cover food) when visiting Western countries. Because Choir members wanted to augment their salaries by pocketing their per diem allowances, they regularly carried salamis and canned vegetables from Bulgaria in their suitcases. They viewed themselves as "crafty tricksters" or "brave victims" of the socialist state (Gal and Kligman, *The Politics of Gender After Socialism*, 53). Even if they had used their per diem allowances, the money would have never covered meal prices in major Western cites. During the same time period, the 30-person choir was charging $10,000–$25,000 for one performance in the United States. It is clear that the huge profits earned by both American producers and the Bulgarian government have rested on the exploitation of the performers. Also remember that the singers themselves received no royalties for their songs, as these went instead to composers/arrangers. Many of the chorus singers did not even own one copy of the ensemble and solo records on which they performed.

The marginalization of the performers and their alienation from the production of "The Mystery" became clear to me during the November 1, 1988, press conference introducing the Choir to the United States. The marketing director of Nonesuch introduced the Choir; then the Choir sang a few songs and fell silent, for no one was assigned to translate the proceedings for them. Not one of the singers was asked to speak; rather, Graham Nash was the spokesman for the Choir. Seeing him at the podium, the Choir members asked me, "Who is he?" "He is Graham Nash," I replied. "Who is that?" they queried. "He is a member of a popular American singing group, and he is a fan of yours," I answered. At that point they all wanted his autograph for their teenage children!

Besides not knowing what was happening around them, not knowing the

Choir's fees, and not being compensated fairly, the singers were socialized into a work culture of deference to the conductor and the directors and, by implication, of submission to the state. The most overt manifestation of this was the undercover agent who traveled with the Choir, making sure that nobody entertained the idea of defecting to the West. Katherine Verdery calls this dependence on the state "socialist paternalism. . . . Subjects were presumed to be grateful recipients—like small children in a family—of benefits their rulers decided for them" (1994, 228). Gal and Kligman similarly note how the state "infantilized" its citizens by dictating what they should say, believe, and do (*The Politics of Gender After Socialism*, 54). If singers, like other socialist workers, failed to show loyalty to the state (for example, by refusing to participate in patriotic parades), their jobs were in jeopardy. Privately, however, singers complained about financial arrangements and musical decisions.

This dual consciousness, or divided subjectivity, was a common feature of totalitarianism. Scholars have pointed out how the we/they divide revealed "a discursive opposition between the victimized 'us' and a new and powerful 'them' who ruled" (ibid., 55). For choir singers, "we" became associated with village folklore, and "they" became associated with the state that manipulated folklore. Some singers actively disliked many of the compositions they performed. Stancheva remarks: "I've sung these arrangements for forty years, but they are different from folk songs; they are not natural, not authentic. More recent arrangements tend toward classical music. When Kutev founded his ensemble, he did not allow warm-up exercises with the piano, he did not allow singers to read notes. In our songs, there are sometimes microtones, there are untempered intervals." Stancheva points to a loss of regional style in the arrangements; many singers preferred their own traditional village material, Moreover, all singers were outraged at the royalty fees which the composers collected every time they performed their compositions.[26]

The transformation of these socialist singer/workers into ethereal, exotic, "ancient" voices was artfully orchestrated by promoters, who submerged the women themselves and emphasized the female sound aspect of the music, devoid of text and context. Gender surfaced in female voices, not in real people. When asked directly by reporters during the 1988 press conference how the singers themselves experience the music and how Bulgarian audiences respond, one singer remarked, "This is normal music, it is not something special or exotic." To be sure, not one reporter used that comment! Another singer said she thought that the reason Bulgarian music was appealing was that "it is interesting, original, the mixed rhythms, the style of singing." Again, this was too mundane for reporters to quote. Women's voices, then, are a discursive trope embracing the mysterious, the old, the powerful, and the secretive; omitted are real women with real jobs, many of whom have very interesting life histories. Record and CD covers do not feature pictures of the Choir, for their stocky, conservative appearance would fly in the face of the "mystery." As Buchanan writes, "The absence of photographs and accurate information about the women's ages, training, musical competence, and repertoires in promotional materials in effect became part of the seductive 'mystery' of the musical sound, conjuring fantasies in the minds of reviewers as to how these women might appear" (1996, 197). Indeed, many audience members were surprised to find that singers were elderly and often stocky in appearance.

Buchanan further suggests that Western ideas about the authenticity and purity of pastoralism play a role the marketing of Bulgarian choral music (ibid., 197; 1997). While I agree that choir singers are often depicted by marketers as authentic villagers singing naturally (whereas actually many are school-trained and others left their villages in the 1950s), I also observe the suppression by marketers of associations with village life. The most important evidence of this is the omission of song texts from many liner notes and concert programs. More than anything else, the texts of these songs link them to village life, especially agriculture and shepherding. Depicting the life cycle, the emotions of traditional life, and the seasons in relation to the land, song texts are revealing interpretations of peasant life. Yet few reviewers devote any attention to them, and for marketers they are better left untranslated. The Choir's costumes, too, reveal the ambivalent nature of their folk roots. In most concerts of the Choir, singers wear peasant costumes during the first half and perform without a conductor. During the second half, they wear tailored black gowns and perform with a conductor. I view this transformation of costume and style as a statement that the Choir has transcended its pastoral roots and found a home in the world of the elite, high art chorus. Composers such as Kutev actively espoused this philosophy. Nonesuch promotions director Danny Kahn explained to me that Choir press kits deliberately avoided connections to folklore: "This music should be compared with Itzhak Perlman, not the Rustavi Georgian Choir." Referencing the search for universal appeal, Kahn commented that the fame of folk, ethnic, and popular artists is short lived in the record business. "We don't want to cultivate the pop music connection. Anything that is ethnic or pop is temporary. The Choir is artistically beyond that. The public wants modern things. They are interested in beautiful music, not the fact that it is Bulgarian."[27] The Choir's relationship to the pop realm, however, is a bit more ambivalent than Kahn suggests. Buchanan perceptively highlights the remaking of the choir "into cosmopolitan commodities by endowing them with attributes of sexual enticement linked more commonly to the performance of pop music" (1996, 196). Perhaps the pastoral must be suppressed because at critical times it appears asexual (daughterly or maternal) and thus interferes with the latent sexuality of the marketing imagery.[28]

The tension between the female image of the peasant and the image of the pop star was illustrated to me in 1989 when I accompanied the Trio Bulgarka to a fashion photographer's studio. The trio was to be the subject of a music article in the fashion magazine *Elle*, and Deborah Feingold was to do the photography (Dery 1989). A makeup and hair artist awaited the trio. Feingold, used to photographing avant-garde fashion and glitzy pop stars, was stymied about how to portray these robust middle-aged grandmothers glamorously. There was simply no existing visual niche in the West for the peasant pop star. Feingold finally warmed up to the Trio's folk costumes and infectious smiles, but the resulting photograph does seem somewhat anomalous in *Elle*. Moreover, the Trio Bulgarka's 1988 performance on NBC's midnight music show *Sunday Night* was designed to usher the Trio into the world of popular music.[29]

The female Bulgarian voice, then, traffics between East and West and among folk, popular, and elite levels of art. Bulgarian female village singers were first transformed into socialist ensemble singers, veritable emblems of folklore becoming high art; then they were transformed into Western pop stars. In Western marketing, the discursive trope of the female voice was not embodied; rather, female bodies were dematerialized and the resulting disembodied female voices carried meanings suggestive of power, age, and sexuality. With the removal of human bodies came the removal of context, history, life stories of performers, and economic arrangements. To understand the music, however, the economic changes of the transition period must be considered, along with their political and cultural implications.

Collaborations, Deregulation, and Capitalism

Almost as soon as Bulgarian music hit the record charts in England and the United States, there was talk of collaboration. In 1989, English pop singer Kate Bush featured the Trio Bulgarka on her album *The Sensual World*.[30] Soon after came an offer from classical composer Terry Riley to compose a piece for the Choir together with the Kronos Quartet, and in 1989 Judith Jamison used a Choir song for her choreography *Forgotten Time* for the Alvin Ailey Dance Company.[31] The effect of these collaborations was to not only to bring Bulgarian music to the attention of wider audiences but also to decontextualize it further and present it as pure sound in the service of a greater art.[32] For example, when Kate Bush sings "Deeper Understanding" in English simultaneously with the Trio Bulgarka singing in Bulgarian in the background, the Trio's text is obscured, serving as a mere backdrop for Bush's fame.[33] Whereas in village singing the text is the most important musical element to listeners, in Bulgarian choral arrangements, the text is secondary to the sound, reflecting Western polyphonic aesthetics. In many collaborations of choirs with Western artists, a further step is taken: the text itself is obliterated or rendered unintelligible, even to native speakers.

A common theme which surfaces in Bulgarian choral collaborations is meditation (Taylor 1997, 24–26). A good example is the 1996 CD *Fly, Fly, My Sadness*, a collaboration between the Tuvan throat singers[34] Huun-Huur-Tu and the choir Bulgarian Voices-Angelite (the Angels). Although space does not permit the analysis of Huun-Huur-Tu's popularity in the West or the popularity of Tibetan monk throat singers mentioned earlier, suffice it to say that throat singing is perceived by Americans to be exotic, mysterious, mystical, and sacred.[35] Perhaps it was these qualities which caused Ukrainian composer Mihail Alperin to pair Hunn-Huur-Tu with the Bulgarian Voices-Angelite in a collaboration produced by the Germany company Jaro, which also sponsored the album *From Bulgaria with Love* (see below). In the liner notes, Alperin claims there is a "common denominator of meditative structure" in Tuvan songs and in Bulgarian songs, specifically those from the Rhodope mountain region. Not coincidentally, Orpheus is supposed to have originated from this region. Alperin writes that his compositions are about distance, lack of motion, and time standing still, familiar tropes invoked for Bulgarian choral music.

The first and fourth selections of the CD feature Tuvan songs sung simultaneously with Rhodope melodies, the latter performed first as a solo, then in choral arrangement. The Tuvan and Bulgarian melodies intersect in a mass of overtones. This sound idea is repeated in all selections with a bit of rhythmic diversity, but the overtones are the central mystical, meditative symbol. The first selection is titled "Fly, Fly, My Sadness," perhaps a reference to the Tuvan text, but the Bulgarian text (which is almost, but not quite, obliterated) is about the plight of a girl who is about to enter an arranged marriage. This narrative is ignored in the liner notes, which state that it is "a song with the same mood and flying atmosphere as that Tuvan song." The Bulgarian narrative about the mundane lives of village women is sacrificed to the "mysteriously searching" Tuvan voices.

The CD liner notes underline another connection between Bulgarians and Tuvans: the Bulgars, before migrating to the Balkan peninsula and adopting a Slavic language and culture, were, like the descendants of the Tuvans, a Central Asian nomadic people speaking a Turkic-Altaic language. This grossly oversimplified history posits the two groups as possible distant cousins. In reality, there is nothing concrete shared by the two groups, musically or historically, but the notes suggest an Eastern connection. By pairing a Bulgarian choir with a Siberian group, Bulgarian music becomes more Eastern, hence more mystical and meditative (qualities associated with the East in Western views). In this collaboration, it is the Bulgarian women who are secondary to the Tuvan men. The Bulgarian mystery (as West) defers to the Tuvan mystery (as East).

Not only are texts obliterated in collaborations, but sounds are sampled and pasted into music collages, illustrating the trend toward decontextualization and commodification of the Bulgarian female voice. A good example is the 1992 CD *Le Mystère des Voix Bulgares: From Bulgaria with Love*. This CD was produced in 1992 by Jaro, a German company which has developed a scandalous reputation for unauthorized use of the name Le Mystère, misleading liner notes, misleading photographs, and mistaken performer information.[36] *From Bulgaria with Love* features a post-1990 incarnation of the Choir with Dora Hristova as conductor, but the CD mistakenly features a rival choir in photographs and mistakenly names Ivan Topalov, the director of the rival choir, as the director. Liner notes and a visual backdrop of gears and machinery boast the innovative crossover aspect: "a clandestine agreement between classical fans and punk, between sixties lovers and techno-freaks or to put it simply: between generations. . . . A musical high jump and crossover from folk music to modern music, from the Orient to the Occident, from pop song to techno, hard rock to disco, from cryptic music to the computer. This record leaves the usual separation between classical and pop far behind."

Musically, the CD features Choir songs edited into a technopop synthesized mix performed by a number of European, especially Italian, bands. In many of the CD's selections, the women's voices are sampled via loops; thus the melodic element is repeated as a musical theme in the rock genre rather than as a narrative.[37] These vocal pieces are also manipulated in terms of volume and speed. Not only is text obliterated but any semblance to Bulgarian melodies has been lost. Veit Erlmann reminds us of the ironic relationship between valorizing "difference" and selling "sameness" in world music: "An aesthetic theory of music in the global age would thus not be concerned with the truthful representation of difference per se. Instead, such a theory would examine the ways in which world music constructs the experience of global communication and authenticity through symbolic means whose very difference depends so vitally on their sameness as transnational commodities" (1996, 481). Erlmann recommends abandoning the search for posited authenticities, focusing instead on the histories of interactions of music with various technologies (ibid., 481). In Bulgaria, the fascination with loud rock-like amplified sounds has at least a 30-year history: After the 1960s, when electricity was introduced into villages, wedding bands started using amplification (in addition to Western instrumentation such as guitars and drum sets) and very loud volume; this became a mark of Westernization, of modernity, and soon developed into the "wedding music" craze (Silverman 1996).

Appropriations from and collaborations with rock music, then, are not new to Bulgarian music. Although more true for instrumental music, this was the case even of vocal music. In the 1970s, Emil Dimitrov, a Bulgarian rock star, incorporated the Sestri Kushlevi, a sextet of Bulgarian singers, into his album to great acclaim. In 1988, Janka Rupkina, a member of Trio Bulgarka and a former member of the Choir, sang with a Bulgarian rock band in arrangements by composer Dimitur Penev that combined traditional songs and a disco backup. This endeavor, however, failed to attract an audience in Bulgaria because the sound was too familiar and too formulaic. On the other hand, Gypsy rap music, another recent vocal "crossover" in which Romani lyrics are set to rap music, has achieved widespread popularity (ibid.).

From Bulgaria with Love continued to sell well in Western Europe and the United States, and its lead song, "Pipppero," was at the top of Italian radio charts in 1992 (Rule 1993). The sexual themes of "Pipppero" are displayed prominently in text and imagery. The melodic choral cuts are taken from the

Choir's arrangement of "Dilmano, Dilbero" ("Beautiful Dilmana"), a folk song with an accompanying dance which simultaneously mimes the planting of peppers and human sexual intercourse.[38] "Dilmano, Dilbero" had been used earlier in a collaboration between Emil Dimitrov and the Sestri Kushlevi that features heavy sighing and panting. The phallic imagery of the 1992 Jaro song is unmistakable—the description of planting peppers, the shape of Bulgarian peppers, and pictures of a banana and a pointed gun[39] on the CD sleeves. In "Pipppero," the Bulgarian text is not obliterated but is rather redirected and expanded into an Italian-language explication of European sexuality. The song is a dialogue between a band leader and the Choir about Bulgarian/Italian relations, both political and sexual (Buchanan 1996, 202–204). The dialogue expands the theme of sexuality, punctuated with the chorus singing "pumps, pumps, pumps." Buchanan points out that "the 'mystery' of Bulgarian voices is conflated with the erotic dance of the pepper, which again promotes the singing of these Bulgarian vocalists as sensually potent" (1996, 204). Yet the fit between peasant singers and sexual pop stars is not easy. It seems as if sexuality has become a convenient common denominator between East and West, and music is one of many forms of its dissemination.

Both within and beyond the sphere of music, female sexuality in Bulgaria has been appropriated and packaged to sell. The post-1989 explosion of pornography all over Eastern Europe has led to a proliferation of images of scantily clad women in all forms of media. Compact disk and cassette covers and music videos which contain post-1990 folk/popular music fusions (commonly known as *chalga*) regularly feature provocative female singers and sometimes nudity. Besides being a product of newfound "freedom," this phenomenon has economic, political, and discursive dimensions. As Daskalova notes, "[T]he 'feminine' woman is perhaps the most common and widespread image of women in Bulgarian society at large" (2000, 348). Bulgarian women's magazines focus on celebrities, self-care, home furnishings, fashion, love, and beauty advice. The perfect woman emerges as beautiful, sexy, and obedient to her husband (ibid., 348–349). Sexuality during the socialist period may have been suppressed, but it was barely under the surface, ready to reemerge as a capitalist commodity.

The commodification of sexuality is tied to the burgeoning prostitution industry. In Bulgaria since the transition, prostitution has gained in respectability and glamour and is touted by many young women as one of the few jobs to offer independence, good pay, and flexible hours.[40] Moreover, some upscale secretarial jobs require sexual services.[41] Scholars note the huge increase in the number of prostitutes, the growth of places where prostitution is practiced, the influx of educated women (especially those with knowledge of foreign languages), and "the existence of legal channels for recruiting prostitutes, especially through the advertisement of jobs (or training courses) for dancers, models, and 'Miss So and So' competitions" (ibid., 346). Furthermore, prostitution often starts with violence and/or rape, is propelled by poverty, and is boosted by the instability of postsocialism. As women lose their jobs and as state benefits are curtailed, pornography and prostitution become viable alternative jobs. Perhaps it is far-fetched to write about prostitution and choir singing in the same essay. But patterns of gender exploitation have deep historical roots in Bulgaria and crop up in diverse settings.

Simultaneous with the rise in sexual imagery of the 1990s is the increased visibility of the idea of domesticity embodied in the image of the devoted wife and mother. Women's magazines appeal to the devoted and sexy wife and mother. Whereas the mobilization to ban abortion is not as great in Bulgaria as it is in Croatia, Hungary, and Poland,[42] nationalist parties in Bulgaria actively advocate a return to the home and to motherhood (ibid.). This goes hand in hand with nationalist rhetoric about increasing the birthrate (of the Slavs only, not the minorities) to ensure the future of the country (Gal and Kligman, *The Politics of Gender After Socialism*, 2000b; Lampland 1994; Verdery 1994). Choir women are thus caught in a discursive bind about their image. Because they have been constructed since the 1950s by the Bulgarian state as rooted peasants (even though since the 1970s new recruits are largely young women from cities), there seems to be no easy way to modernize their image at home. In the West, on the other hand, fantasies can reign, and they can become ancient mysteries. Just as choir music has been supplanted in Bulgaria by folk/pop *chalga*, choir singers have been supplanted by sexy half-dressed *chalga* singers. Whereas choir singers lose out because their music is considered obsolete at home, their jobs are being curtailed, and they are not sexy enough, the sex stars of *chalga* are criticized because they are too loose and their music is not "really Bulgarian." Ironically, some choir members moonlight as *chalga* singers in a bid to make a living wage; other choir members are the fiercest critics of *chalga*, blaming the rise of this genre for the decline in popularity of folk music. Thus, women's bodies, including their voices, are a site of contestation about the nature and future of the family, the arts, and the nation.

The marketing of contrasting images of women (sex object, mother and wife, worker) with choir music is embedded in an economic matrix where capitalism asserts its hold over socialist holdovers. None of the musical collaborations mentioned above, for example, would have been possible in the Bulgaria of the 1970s, when no performers, not even the most famous musicians, were allowed to pursue independent economic ventures. The perestroika of the late 1980s, however, allowed for private contracts; for example, the Choir's tours and contracts with Nonesuch and Trio Bulgarka's contracts and tours with Hannibal.[43] In 1987–1988, despite the fact that Bulgarian performers were legally allowed to pursue an independent contract, one of the Trio's members faced many problems, both bureaucratic and personal, because she tried to perform simultaneously as a member of the Choir and the Trio. The deregulation of the 1990s led to a tangled mess of choir regroupings and layoffs (Buchanan 1966, 1997). The transition left everyone "free" to profit from the "Mystère" phenomenon, no matter how unscrupulously. The

Choir split into two groups, and legal battles ensued between producers over the rights to the use of the label "Le Mystère des Voix Bulgares." Five or more spin-off choirs have used this label, and various CDs, such as those of Jaro discussed above, list incorrect performers and feature incorrect photographs.

The legal battles over names and ownership rights should be viewed in the context of the fact that since 1989 the Bulgarian government has cut back tremendously on its funding of the ensembles. Concerts, tours, and festivals have been limited, and few ensemble performers can support themselves solely on their small state salaries, which often arrive late. As Stancheva narrates: "The Mystery of the Bulgarian Voices Choir is not employed anymore. Bulgarian Television decided they didn't need folklore anymore so they fired us. But we continue to rehearse with absolutely no salary. We rely on tours abroad. Nonetheless, we work hard, we learn new songs and we have many new young singers." Not only does the government have more pressing economic priorities but it also observes that choral music is unpopular in Bulgaria. This unpopularity, as noted above, in part derives from its association with the socialist past and with central planning. Today, a host of small private music companies operate in Bulgaria, but none seem interested in investing in the choirs because of the decline in the popularity of music at home, the inability of these companies to penetrate the Western market, and the increasing obligations to pay composers' royalties. Instead, various choirs are in competition with each other in their pursuit of Western financial backers; their only option is to arrange tours to the West via foreign sponsors. In 2000, the choir Angelite toured several American cities to small audiences. It is clear that the era of choir popularity has waned, even in the West. The singers also realize that neither "actually existing" socialism nor "actually existing" capitalism has benefited them in the long run. Stancheva reiterates: "We get nothing except fame. Even now it is like this. The last CD of the Mystery from October 1998 on Nonesuch label—when I received one of these CDs as a gift, I was surprised to see one of my songs on it. I hadn't authorized it; the producers didn't consult me, they hadn't asked me for permission. Well, all I have is one CD with my song on it, But we aren't refusing to sing yet. As long as we can, we'll sing."

The singers' current predicaments should be viewed within the larger economic situation; choir members recruited during the 1950s and 1960s are now retiring on pensions which are virtually worthless today. In Bulgaria, it is widely noted that the transition led to general "mass impoverishment," especially among the elderly. Currently state jobs are disappearing or provide substandard wages, and "women are less likely to find jobs in the private sphere, which tend to pay better" (Daskalova 2000, 338, 340). Discrimination against women shows up in average wage levels and in the fact that women have fewer chances to work in the areas in which they were trained (ibid., 340). Scholars note that throughout Eastern Europe, it is young men who are moving into the rapidly expanding private sector. "It is men more than women who are increasingly associated with the idealized and even romanticized private . . . capitalist sector of the economy" (Gal and Kligman, *The Politics of Gender After Socialism*, 59). Choral singers are generally absent in the sphere of capitalist entrepreneurship of their own music. Bulgarian choir promoters and agents are men. Usually they are businessmen; only rarely are they musicians. Some singers are very reluctant to embark on capitalist projects concerning music. Trained under socialism to receive funding for the arts from the state, they are resentful of the curtailing of that support. Some wait patiently for a new impresario and a new tour, but others have forged new musical careers. Kremena Stancheva, for example, teaches singing at a private university in Sofia, started a singing program for young children, and hopes to train Americans in Bulgarian folk music. Several singers have emigrated to the United States, where they work in nonmusical low-skill professions which they combine with teaching Bulgarian songs to Americans. One singer married a famous composer, and his connections led to several albums of her solo songs and her husband's arrangements with her as featured soloist. One singer formed a duet with her daughter and promotes the pair to foreign entrepreneurs. Several younger choir members have pursued careers in the more profitable "wedding music" or folk/pop *chalga* circuit.[44] In short, singers, even though they perceive themselves as victims, are not passive; they are actively engaged in ameliorating their situations. As noted by many scholars of the region, women craft together a patchwork of jobs to make ends meet. "Women's diverse strategies of combining irregular and informal employment with regular jobs in the state sector are the response to the constraints produced by postsocialist state policies" (Gal and Kligman, *The Politics of Gender After Socialism*, 81).

In 1988, Steven Feld raised the issue of clashing claims to the ownership of music in world music crossovers (1988, 31–34). Although pop stars "use" ethnic musics in their collaborations, they usually retain copyrights for themselves, in spite of the fact that some donate part of their profits to the ethnic musicians. The endorsements and even collaborations of rock stars do not alter the asymmetry of power relations in the capitalist market, where a few stars and a few companies have the power of financial backing and artistic freedom. As Feld writes, it is important not to "risk confusing the flow of musical contents and musical expansion with the flow of power relations. Even if local musicians take control in remote locales, how progressive can the world of popular music be when the practices of transnational culture industry steadfastly reproduce the forms and forces of domination that keep outsiders outside, as 'influences' and laborers in the production of pop?" (1994, 263).

Buchanan raises the question of ownership by pointing out that Bulgarian choruses and labels have been reshuffled so many times that it is not entirely clear to whom "The Mystery" belongs. In socialist Bulgaria, ownership of ensemble music was held collectively by the state, but after 1989 ownership was transferred to private foreign enterprises (Buchanan 1996, 200, 204–205). Yet the socialist and postsocialist periods evince structural similarities as well as differences in the management of vocal ensemble music. True, deregulation has erased the hegemony of the state as employer and paternalistic supplier of social benefits; true, vocal groups are free to market themselves to Western sponsors; true, singers are surviving by combining part-time jobs. But the structure of exploitation of the performers seems to have held constant despite the change in economic regimes. During socialism, the singers were treated as wage laborers in the service of the state, regardless of the fact that it was their music and their talent which was the basis of the choral sound. The composers, the choral managers, and the state enterprises benefited financially, not the singers. Now it seems that another global system, capitalism, has become an equally, if not more powerful agent of exploitation (Kurkela 1993, 81).

Feld writes that the capitalist music business is built on three pillars: record companies make the most money (approximately 93 percent of worldwide music sales is controlled by six companies); already-famous performers are given liberal contracts with artistic freedom; and, finally, musicians are "laborers who sell their services for a direct fee, and take the risk . . . that royalty percentages, spinoff jobs, tours, and recording contracts might follow from the exposure" (1988, 36; 1991, 262). The fact that Bulgarian singers still lack control of their own performances, then, is not an aberration but a normal part of the capitalist music business. Disembodied females in the form of voices are the raw materials which the former socialist East can export to the West. Prostitutes (female bodies without voices) and choral singers (female voices without bodies) are mirror images—both are gendered commodities for sale.

The free market, then, has impacted the Bulgarian choral phenomenon in multiple ways. In the economic realm, we have traced the appropriation of musical resources as sounds and singers as laborers. In the symbolic realm, we have traced the emergence of the Bulgarian female voice as a commodified vehicle for Western fantasies about sexuality and bygone eras, while at home in Bulgaria the postsocialist female is being redefined and the postsocialist singer is being fired. This gendered flow of people, images, and discourse is part of the transnational traffic that constitutes East/West interfaces.

NOTES

1. This quote is attributed to the *St. Louis Post-Dispatch* and appears as a sticker on the album *Le Mystère des Voix Bulgares*, volume 1, Elektra/Nonesuch, 1987.

2. The research on which this article is based spans 1972 to 1999. Fieldwork on the Choir's marketing began in November 1988, when I served as a translator for the first press conference of the Bulgarian Radio Television Choir and accompanied singers around New York City. In April 1991, I served as their concert liaison, lecture/ demonstration organizer, and translator in Eugene, Oregon. I also worked with the Trio Bulgarka as translator and concert liaison in 1988 in New York City and in May 1989 in Eugene. I had previously talked with many of the singers during numerous trips to

Bulgaria since the 1970s. Most recently, I interviewed Kremena Stancheva, a singer in the Bulgarian Radio Television Choir in 1999. Translations from Bulgarian are my own.

3. I use the word "invented" in the spirit of Hobsbawm and Ranger (1983), connoting the elevation of a selected part of culture to the level of national tradition, a process often involving some fundamental reworking.

4. Kutev's model was the Piatnitskii Choir of Russia (see Smith 1996); this was part of a wider pattern in which Bulgaria modeled its cultural policy after that of the USSR, its closest ally.

5. In 1951, Kutev founded the State Ensemble for Folk Songs and Dances (sometimes known as the Kutev Ensemble or the State Ensemble), composed of a female chorus, a folk orchestra, and a dance group; in 1952, Georgi Bojadzhiev founded the Ensemble for Folk Songs of Bulgarian Radio and Television (sometimes known as the Radio/Television ensemble), composed of a chorus and a folk orchestra. Herein I employ the term Choir to refer to the chorus in this ensemble. In the 1960s, many regional ensembles were formed.

6. This fee structure and exploitation was identical for instrumental ensembles, which were composed of males; see Buchanan 1995.

7. For an analysis of wedding music, see Silverman 1996.

8. For example, Bulgarian ethnomusicologist Todor Todorov said, "The polyphonic development of folk music by composers is a normal stage in its existence. This stage had to come as a natural solution to the problem of the new function of the song . . . to satisfy . . . the wider musical interests of contemporary man" (1976, 179).

9. See Buchanan 1995.

10. In the Bulgarian language, Bulgaria is a feminine noun.

11. The album, recorded by Marcel Cellier, was, in fact, first released in 1975; it received a Grande Prix in Paris but sat in obscurity until it was reissued by the British label 4AD in 1986, when it became a hit. Finally, Nonesuch/Elektra picked it up in 1987.

12. Volume 1 mistakenly attributes all songs to the Choir and mistakenly cites Kutev as its director; Kutev was never the Choir's director, but the album does feature a few selections by the Kutev ensemble. Volume 2 has more correct citations and includes a number of choirs. This confusion is discussed in detail in Kohanov 1991 and Buchanan 1997.

13. Bulgarian music is based on combinations of short and long beats in the ratio of 2:3, such as the *ruchenitsa*: 2-2-3.

14. See Rice 1989, 4–5. See below for a discussion of collaborations between Bulgarian choruses and rock groups.

15. Two articles by Donna Buchanan (1996 and 1977) perceptively analyze the marketing of the "Mystery." My article extends the analysis of marketing, public perception, and gender representation and relates it to the postsocialist economic and political transition.

16. Note that I am dating the choral arrangements to the 1950s, not the village songs on which they are based. Some of the latter may well be over a hundred years old, while others can be dated as recent creations of twentieth-century villagers. To complicate the matter, new texts are often written to older melodies and new melodies are often composed to older texts. In sum, scholars simply cannot date many songs, and they know very little about the ancient music of the Balkans. In fact, we really know very

little about vocal music of previous centuries except for liturgical music, which is a distinctly separate genre.

17. Also see Christgau 1988, who writes "this Asian/European chorus from the place the Greeks called Thrace and said Orpheus came from, is the world music/new music/new age/underground phenomenon of the past two years" (55).

18. See Lozaw 1988, who writes, "The concert was a startling mix of remarkable vocal control, medieval traditions, delicate grace, and creative flourishes that could almost be considered avant garde" (17). Also see Buchanan 1997, 149–153 for analysis of a Bulgarian quartet performing a reworked Palestrina mass.

19. See also Dery 1989, who wrote about the Trio Bulgarka: "Silhouetted against stained-glass windows, they break into a buzzing, nasal melody, punctuated by sudden yips and glisses, floating over Asian-sounding chordal drones. . . . Their tangled lines, ornamented with microtonal flourishes, are as intricate as Arabic calligraphy" (156).

20. Tom Manoff, reviewer for National Public Radio, quoted by Peter Clancy, marketing director for Nonesuch records at a press conference in New York, November 1, 1988.

21. Personal communication, October 31, 1988.

22. Graham Nash is a vocalist with the pop vocal group Crosby, Stills, Nash, and Young. He had taken a night flight to New York to officiate; he flew back to Los Angeles that afternoon. Later in 1988, he hosted a Los Angeles press conference for the choir which featured Linda Ronstadt.

23. Many of these professional singers were Roma (Gypsies). For centuries Roma have had an important place as professional musicians in the Balkans (Silverman 1999 and in press); simultaneously there has been strong discrimination and prejudice against them (Silverman 1995). Similarly, Tim Rice points out that professional male Rom musicians in Thrace were looked down upon because they played for money; their ability to play, however, was admired (1994). Also see Buchanan 1995, 386.

24. Prior to 1988, the Kutev ensemble traveled more widely than the Choir, the latter being a studio ensemble. Choir members, however, were sometimes sent as soloists or in small groups to Western countries.

25. See Buchanan 1995 for similar observations about male instrumentalists.

26. Similar observations have been reported by Donna Buchanan for instrumentalists in ensembles (1995).

27. Danny Kahn, personal communication, March 4, 1990.

28. Buchanan also suggests that the sexual may be contained within the pastoral, for in Bulgarian mythology, female nature spirits have the power to enchant men musically (1997, 134–135). Western audiences, however, would not be aware of these associations.

29. Similarly, during 1988, the Choir performed for television audiences on *The Today Show*, *The Tonight Show*, *MTV News*, VH-1's *New Visions*, and *World News Tonight with Peter Jennings* (Kohanov 1991, 71–72).

30. Trio Bulgarka is also featured on Kate Bush's 1993 CD *The Red Shoes*.

31. Buchanan discusses a collaboration in 1994 between the Bulgarka Jr., 3+1 Trio, a few male instrumentalists, and an organist in a performance of a rewritten Palestrina mass (1997, 149–153).

32. See Feld 1988, 1991, and 2000 for similar observations regarding some collaborations in other parts of the world. See below for the economic implications.

33. I do not mean to imply that Kate Bush disrespects the Trio. On the contrary,

Bush said: "I was very worried because chances were it might not work, particularly because they are so good. It might just sound like we bunged them in a Western track. I really didn't want them to be dragged down to my level. I was worried that they wouldn't want to get involved in Western music because it has a bad name" (Brown 1988, 10). My point is that the structure of collaboration is basically asymmetrical, with the West in control.

34. Throat singing is characterized by the production of two simultaneous pitches by one person; a melody is produced by emphasizing various pitches in the harmonic series above a fundamental drone note. Some Bulgarian singing employs drones, but no overtones are produced and only one pitch is produced at one time by one person.

35. For Tibetan monks, throat singing is sacred, but for Tuvans (residents of southern Siberia) it is secular.

36. Jaro's title was probably taken from the Ian Fleming spy novel *From Russia With Love*, which also became a James Bond movie. See Buchanan 1996 and 1997 for a detailed history of Jaro releases.

37. For example, in selection 5, "Jana," the word *zamraknala* (it was getting dark) is reduced to *zamrakna* and sampled via computerized loops.

38. In Bulgarian folklore, human fertility is often associated with agricultural fertility.

39. The gun also refers to selection 6, "Guns and Paprica [*sic*]," a rock version of the Bulgarian song "Pushka Pukna Gjule Moj" ("A Gun Went Off, My Love"). The gun may refer to the Italian/Bulgarian connection in the attempt to kill the pope (also see Buchanan 1996, 207).

40. Dimitrina Petrova, prominent Bulgarian feminist and human rights activist, personal communication.

41. See Perlez 1996 for comparative situation in other East European countries.

42. One reason for the anti-abortion stance in Hungary, Croatia, and Poland is that these nations are primarily Catholic; Bulgaria, on the other hand, is primarily an Eastern Orthodox nation.

43. In 1988, however, Bulgarian wedding musicians Ivo Papazov and Yuri Yunakov were denied a visa when contracted to tour for Hannibal Records. This refusal was probably linked to the fact that they are Turkish Roma (Gypsies), and the "authenticity" of their music was questioned by the government (see Silverman 1996, 1999).

44. This path is easier for women who are married to male instrumentalists, since there is still a stigma attached to women performing at weddings or in clubs without a male relative.

REFERENCES

Alarik, Scott. "Bulgarian Singers Find Fans in Unlikely Places." *Boston Globe*, November 3, 1988.

Brown, Len. "Down at the Old Bull and Bush." *New Musical Express* (London), November 12, 1988, 10.

Buchanan, Donna. "Bulgaria's Magical *Mystère* Tour: Postmodernism, World Music Marketing, and Political Change in Eastern Europe." *Ethnomusicology* 41, no. 1 (1997): 131–157.

——. "Dispelling the Mystery: The Commodification of Women and Musical Tradition in the Marketing of Le Mystère des Voix Bulgares." *Balkanistica* 9 (1996): 193–210.

——. "Metaphors of Power, Metaphors of Truth: The Politics of Music Professionalism in Bulgarian Folk Orchestras." *Ethnomusicology* 39, no. 3 (1995): 381–416.

Christgau, Robert. "Bulgarian State Female Choir." *Village Voice*, November 8, 1988.

Daskalova, Krassimira. "Women's Problems, Women's Discourses in Bulgaria." In *Reproducing Gender: Politics, Publics, and Everyday Life After Socialism*, ed. Susan Gal and Gail Kligman, 337–369. Princeton, N.J.: Princeton University Press, 2000.

De Curtis, Anthony. "The Year in Music." *Rolling Stone*, December 15–29, 1988, 13–75.

Dery, Mark. "Bulgarian Rhapsody." *Elle* IV, no. 7 (March 1989): 156 and 158.

Duncan, Amy. "Bulgarian Folk Singers Find Eager US Audience." *Christian Science Monitor*, November 21, 1988, 23.

Dyer, Richard. "Bulgarian Female Choir Is Golden." *Boston Globe*, November 4, 1988.

Erlmann, Veit. "The Aesthetics of the Global Imagination: Reflections on World Music in the 1990s." *Public Culture* 8, no. 3 (1996): 467–487.

Feld, Steven. "From Schizophonia to Schismogenesis: On the Discourses and Commodification Practices of 'World Music' and 'World Beat.'" In *Music Grooves*, ed. Charles Keil and Steven Feld, 257–289. Chicago: University of Chicago Press, 1994.

——. "Notes on World Beat." *Public Culture* 1, no. 1 (1988): 31–37.

——. "A Sweet Lullaby for World Music." *Public Culture* 12, no. 1 (2000): 145–171.

Gal, Susan, and Gail Kligman. *The Politics of Gender after Socialism*. Princeton, N.J.: Princeton University Press, 2000.

——. *Reproducing Gender: Politics, Publics, and Everyday Life after Socialism*. Princeton, N.J.: Princeton University Press, 2000.

Hobsbawm, E., and T. Ranger. *The Invention of Tradition*. New York: Columbia University Press, 1983.

Hult Center for the Performing Arts (Eugene, Oregon). *Program Brochure*, 1990–1991 season.

Kligman, Gail. *The Wedding of the Dead*. Berkeley: University of California Press, 1988.

Kohanov, Linda. "Mystery Loves Company." *Pulse* (Tower Records), March 1991, 71–74.

Kurkela, Vesa. "Deregulation of Popular Music in the European Post-Communist Countries: Business Identity and Cultural Collage." *The World of Music* 35, no. 3 (1993): 80–106.

Lampland, Martha. "Family Portraits: Gendered Images of the Nation in Nineteenth-Century Hungary." *East European Politics and Societies* 8, no. 2 (1994): 287–316.

Lozaw, Tristram. "Bulgarian Choir's Rare Vocal Depth Touches Hub." *The Boston Herald*, November 5, 1988.

Marshall, Ingram. Liner notes, *Le Mystère des Voix Bulgares*, volume 1. Elektra/ Nonesuch 9-79165-1. 1987.

Migaldi, Renaldo. "Critic's Choice: Bulgarian State Radio and Television Female Vocal Choir." *Chicago Reader*, November 4, 1988.

Miller, Jim. "Pop Takes a Global Spin." *Newsweek*, June 13, 1988, 72–74.

Moon, Tom. "They're in Bulgarian, but These Albums Sell." *The Philadelphia Inquirer*, November 4, 1988, 1D and 4D.

Pareles, Jon. "Pop from the Black Sea, Cloaked in Mystery." *New York Times*, October 30, 1988, sec 2, 27.

Parker, Andrew, Mary Russo, Doris Sommer, and Patricia Yaeger. "Introduction." In *Nationalisms and Sexualities*. New York: Routledge, 1992.

Perlez, Jane. "Central Europe Learns about Sexual Harassment." *New York Times*, October 3, 1996, A3.

Rice, Timothy. "The Magical Mystery Tour of 1988: Bulgarians on Broadway." *Ethnic Folk Art Center News*, Winter 1989, 4–5.

——. *"May It Fill Your Soul": Experiencing Bulgarian Music*. Chicago: University of Chicago Press, 1994.

Rule, Sheila. "The Pop Life: A Bulgarian Groove." *New York Times*, January 20, 1993.

Silverman, Carol. "The Gender of the Profession: Music, Dance, and Reputation among Balkan Muslim Romani (Gypsy) Women." In *Gender and Music in the Mediterranean*, ed. Tulia Magrini. Chicago: University of Chicago Press, in press.

——. "Music and Marginality: Roma (Gypsies) of Bulgaria and Macedonia." In *Retuning Culture: Musical Changes in Central and Eastern Europe*, ed. Mark Slobin, 231–253. Durham, N.C.: Duke University Press, 1996.

——. "Persecution and Politicization: Roma (Gypsies) of Eastern Europe." *Cultural Survival* 19, no. 2 (1995): 43–49. Special issue on Eastern Europe, ed. Loring Danforth.

——. "Rom (Gypsy) Music." In *Garland Encyclopedia of World Music*, Europe volume, ed. Timothy Rice, James Porter, and Christopher Goertzen, 270–293. New York: Garland, 1999.

Smith, Susannah Lockwood. "From Peasants to Professionals: The Piatnitskii Choir, Arts Policy, and the Transformation of Russian Song in the 1930's." Paper presented at the annual meeting of the Association for the Advancement of Slavic Studies, Boston, Massachusetts, November 1996.

Taylor, Timothy. *Global Pop: World Music, World Markets*. New York: Routledge, 1997.

Todorov, Todor. "Modern Life and Music Folklore." In *The Folk Arts of Bulgaria*, ed. Walter Kolar, 171–186. Pittsburgh: Duquesne University Tamburitzans Institute of Folk Arts, 1976.

Todorova, Maria. "Historical Tradition and Transformation in Bulgaria: Women's Issues or Feminist Issues?" *Journal of Women's History* 5, no. 3 (1994): 129–143.

USA Today. "Bulgaria Hysteria." *Lifeline* Section, November 2, 1988.

Verdery, Katherine. "From Parent-State to Family Patriarchs: Gender and Nation in Contemporary Eastern Europe." *East European Politics and Societies* 8, no. 2 (1994): 225–255.

Weiss, Heidi. "Bulgarian Female Choir-Becomes Pop Sensation." *Chicago Sun Times*, November 6, 1988.

Williams, Stephen. "From Bulgaria, the Art of Singing." *Newsday* (New York), November 4, 1988.

DISCOGRAPHY

n.d. (1970s). *Emil Dimitrov*. Balkanton LP BTA 1447.

1987. *Balkana: The Music of Bulgaria*. Hannibal Records LP HNBL 1335.

1987. *Le Mystère des Voix Bulgares.* Volume 1. Elektra/Nonesuch LP 9-79165-1.

1988. *Le Mystère des Voix Bulgares.* Volume 2. Elektra/Nonesuch LP 9-79201-4.

1988. *The Forest Is Crying (Lament for Indje Voivode).* Hannibal LP HNBL 1342.

1989. *The Sensual World.* Kate Bush. Columbia Records Cassette OCT 4416-4.

1992. *Le Mystère des Voix Bulgares: From Bulgaria with Love.* Jaro CD, Mesa R2 7904-0.

1993. *The Red Shoes.* Kate Bush. Columbia Records CD 5373-7.

1996. *Fly, Fly, My Sadness.* The Bulgarian Voices-Angelite and Huun-Huur-Tu. Shanachie CD 6407-1.

twelve

Four Bearings of West for the Lviv Bohema

Mark Andryczyk

Ljubyt' Ukraïnu, jak sontse, ljubyt',
Jak viter, i travy, i vody . . .
V hodinu shchaslyvu i v radosti myt',
Ljubyt' u hodinu nehody.

  —Volodymyr Sosiura, "Ljubyt' Ukraïnu" (1944)[1]

Ljubyt' Oklakhomu! Vnochi v obid,
Jak nen'ku i deddi dostotu.
Ljubyt' Indianu. J tak samo ljubyt'
Pivnichnu j Pivdennu Dakotu!

  —Oleksandr Irvanets, "Ljubyt'! . . ." (1992)[2]

In this essay, I will focus on one particular subject within the realm of post-Soviet Ukrainian culture—a loosely assembled group of intellectuals, centered on the Western Ukrainian city of Lviv, informally and occasionally referred to as Lvivs'ka Bohema (The Lviv Bohema). The people associated with this group were among the most prolific and influential creative individuals in the first decade of Ukraine's independence. After briefly placing the Lviv Bohema within the historical context of Ukrainian culture, I will point out four facets of "the West" that circumscribe the life and creativity of this group. By providing a glance into the activities of these artists during the peak of their collective existence in the mid-1990s, I will demonstrate how the presence of "the West" is reflected in their creative work.

A Century of Ukrainian Bohemians in Lviv

The Lviv Bohema is a multigenerational conglomeration of visual artists, creative writers, musicians, critics, and journalists who, together, constitute a significant segment of Lviv's and Ukraine's intellectual scene; they are a group united not only by their creative projects but also by the central role of the café in their lives. Although the lion's share of its "members" do live in Lviv, several prominent individuals associated with the Bohema do not reside in that city despite being regularly been involved with this art scene, in some fashion, in the course of their own artistic endeavors. The 1990s Lviv Bohema is the latest circle of Ukrainian bohemians in Lviv—a tradition which has had several incarnations during the twentieth century.

Throughout its history, the city of Lviv has been a home for representatives of various ethnic groups that included Ukrainians, Poles, Jews, Czechs, Armenians, and Germans; it has been ruled over by various empires. The city was founded in the mid-thirteenth century by the prince of Galicia-Volhyn, Danylo Romanovych, and named in honor of his son Lev. Lviv was under Polish rule from 1349 to 1772, at which point it became part of the Austrian Empire. At the end of the nineteenth century, the city's cultural and social life was dominated by the Poles. At that time, Ukrainian cultural institutions such as the Narodnyi Dim and the Prosvita Society did exist in the city but were shaped by the rural-oriented populist generation of Ukrainian intellectuals— first and foremost by Ivan Franko. However, at the turn of the century, a new generation of Ukrainian poets, calling themselves Moloda Muza (The Young Muse), made a determined effort to urbanize the realm of the Ukrainian intellectual. Inspired by the Młoda Polska group of Polish poets and by early modernist groupings in Western Europe, the men of the Moloda Muza formed a Ukrainian bohemian artistic circle in Lviv. Impoverished students living in cramped dormitories, the *muzyky* (the Muse-icians) spent a large part of their day sitting in Lviv cafés such as the Monopolka and Tsentral'ska.[3] There, for the modest price of a cup of coffee, these young men could read the latest newspapers and journals and learn of cultural happenings in the West. Eventually, the café became something of an office for the group's self-titled publishing firm and for their own journal *Svit* (*The World*); the Moloda Muza publishing firm was established in 1906 and produced eight books in its first year of existence, including collections by the Muza's leading poets, Petro Karmans'kyj and Vasyl' Pachovs'kyj. Having published statutes about their binding aesthetic convictions and having consistently cross-referenced themselves in their creative works, the Moloda Muza created a legend for itself in Lviv. Through these writers, decadent themes crept into Ukrainian literature, and they introduced the bohemian lifestyle of an Ukrainian intellectual in Lviv.

Attempts by the Moloda Muza to shift the balance of Ukrainian literature from social duty to art for art's sake were cut off by World War I and Ukraine's striving for and eventual achievement of independence in 1917–1919. A new generation of poets was active in Lviv (now, once again, under Polish rule) during the interwar period that included Ukrainian intellectuals who had fled Soviet eastern Ukraine, but many of them eventually emigrated to Western Europe and North America during the subsequent Soviet invasion of western Ukraine.[4] One earlier poet who became particularly influential for the 1990s Lviv Bohema was Bohdan-Ihor Antonych, who lived and wrote in Lviv until his untimely death in 1937 at the age of 28. The swirl of pagan magic, folklore, and city life presented in his poetry was banned in Ukraine until the late 1980s.

The next bohemian circle to form in Lviv was an underground group of artists that gathered in the late 1960s and early 1970s. Unlike their predecessors, these intellectuals congregated not in Lviv's cafés but in one another's apartments and studios. This was not only because of the eradication of Lviv's pre-Soviet café life but also because these men and women were gathering and creating unofficially—that is, outside the confines of Soviet cultural policy. The group of poets, musicians, and visual artists (which included Hryhorii Chubai, Mykola Riabchuk, Orest Iavors'kyi, Oleh Lysheha, and Viktor Morozov) met clandestinely to exchange their own new creations, to distribute contraband literature and music smuggled in from Poland or Western Europe, and to assemble their *samvydav* (parallel to the Russian samizdat) journal *Skrynia* (*The Chest*). This generation of Lviv bohemians was contumacious and favored hip clothes and hairstyles; although they attempted to maintain an underground creative existence, they became symbols of defiance for Lviv's free-minded youth. A 1972 crackdown brought another wave of arrests of intellectuals in Ukraine, and several of the group's members were arrested and/or thrown out of the institutions of higher learning where they had been studying. With their nerve somewhat shaken, the group was driven farther underground until the arrival of glasnost in the mid-1980s.

The abovementioned generations of Lviv bohemian circles exerted a substantial influence on forming the identity of the post-Soviet generation of Lviv intellectuals. However, the 1990s Lviv Bohema was naturally most closely tied to the group that had formed in the 1960s and 1970s and included several members of that generation in its own ranks. Young artists studying in Lviv in the 1970s and 1980s adopted the leaders of the underground 1970s generation of intellectuals as their mentors. Chubai and Riabchuk supplied this future generation of intellectuals with their knowledge of cultural achievements outside the Soviet Union. Mock exhibitions of art were held in basements and studios, where the "unofficial" work of these young artists was critiqued by their peers. In essence, a much-needed creative atmosphere was maintained in which young men and women could develop their talents outside the dictates of Soviet cultural policy. When glasnost was implemented, the "students" emerged together with their "mentors" to establish the new face of Ukrainian culture.

The 1990s Lviv intellectual circle benefited from access to a myriad of worldwide cultural achievements that had previously been prohibited. Not only could these artists finally create, present, and discuss their own ideas openly, but they could now introduce the works of previously banned intellectuals and talk about whomever they wanted as they formed their own cultural milieu. A major source for the Lviv Bohema was the multitude of volumes containing Ukrainian culture from various periods of Ukraine's history that had been banned in the Soviet years but were now being published—this flurry of literary activity included the republication of the original versions of works that had been heavily censored during Soviet times. Arriving in this wave of rehabilitation were the achievements of the earlier generations of Lviv intellectuals, including those of individuals who had eventually become part of the Ukrainian diaspora in "the West." The presence of "the West," from its role in the history of Lviv's Ukrainian intellectual-bohema to its more abrupt appearance as a result of the collapse of the Soviet Union, was a key factor that influenced the Lviv Bohema as it set out on its own artistic endeavors in the early years of Ukraine's independence.

Poland as "The West"

As a satellite of the USSR, socialist Poland enjoyed a relatively greater amount of political and artistic freedom and maintained a less-obstructed contact with the West than did nations who found themselves within Soviet borders. Thus, in a certain sense, Poland represented "the West" for many Ukrainians who observed and admired cultural happenings in Poland. This was especially true of western Ukraine, and of Lviv in particular. Today, Poland is considered to be an example of successful gradual integration into the West.

Much of Lviv's intellectual community is fluent in Polish—a language skill that grants access to Western ideas that were restricted in Soviet Ukraine. From translations of world literature to rock and jazz music, Lviv's intelligentsia gathered all they could from the closed-off "other world" of the West. Poland's own culture also attracted Lviv's freethinkers. In those days, Polish rock and jazz music was seen as something true and even radical. The idea that art and social protest could be combined had a strong influence on the Bohema. The songs of the now-legendary Lady Pank, Maanam, and other Polish punk and rock bands of the 1980s are committed to memory by many of today's Ukrainian rock stars. Lviv's bohemian circles of the 1970s, 1980s, and 1990s often felt that Polish television, radio, and newspapers provided much more informative and interesting analysis of world events than their Ukrainian counterparts. With the advent of satellite dishes in Lviv, many residents of Lviv obtained access to Polish television; Polish broadcasts, from weather forecasts to world news, are often more respected than Ukrainian sources even now.

In the early 1990s, music festivals in Poland were destination points for the rock groups in the Lviv Bohema. Although Ukrainian communities in various

Eastern European countries invited Ukraine's musicians to perform in their countries, the Ukrainian diaspora in Poland was the most active on this front. One of the first such events was the 1990 Ukraińskie Noce music festival in Gdansk, Poland. The popular Lviv rock group Mertvyi Piven' gave their first performance outside Ukraine at this event. Subsequent festivals, including the annual Iarmarok Festival in Sopot, have hosted Lviv rock stars Plach Ieremii, Mertvyi Piven', and Lazarus (who eventually moved to Poland altogether), among others. These festivals offered an opportunity for these musicians to sell and spread Ukrainian contemporary music abroad. Unlike the end of the decade, in the early 1990s, such excursions to Poland were taken up not so much for financial reasons (Poland's economy had not yet advanced much past that of Ukraine) but for reasons of prestige and even practicality. Until the mid-1990s, musicians could not buy guitar strings or drumsticks in Lviv (or anywhere else in Ukraine, for that matter); they would return from Poland with packs of strings and sticks for their colleagues back home. As people in Lviv gradually became aware of the existence of various Western products (mostly through advertisements in Western magazines and by word of mouth), a Lviv bohemian who had recently returned from Poland could often be heard remarking—"*Ta ia to bachyv u Pol'shchi!*" ("Big deal, I saw that [product] in Poland!").

Acceptance in Poland was a prestigious achievement, which often had favorable consequences upon returning to Ukraine. This was true not only for musicians but for writers and artists as well. A Lviv artist with an exhibition in Poland under his belt enjoyed more prestige back home. One of Ukraine's leading prose writers today, Yurii Andrukhovych, had some of his novels translated and published as separate volumes in Poland years before they were published in Ukraine. The Polish journals *Zustrichi* and *Vidryzhka*, which published in the Ukrainian language, provided a forum for contemporary Ukrainian literature and music. Koka, a Polish record label, recorded and distributed Ukrainian alternative music, ranging from innovators of Ukrainian folk music such as Drevo to experimental rock groups such as Foa-Khoka.

Much of the cultural exchange between Poland and western Ukraine can be attributed to the activity of the Ukrainian diaspora in Poland. Its strong ties with the Lviv Bohema were advanced not only for geographical and political reasons but also because of a similarity between the official state language (Polish) and Ukrainian, a similarity that Ukrainians in Germany, France, and North America obviously do not enjoy. Also, the southwestern dialect of the Ukrainian language shares many colloquialisms with the Polish language.

As a representative of "the West," Poland played an important role in shaping the ideas of the Lviv Bohema. Close ties with Poland's young Ukrainian diaspora community widened the scope of creative ideas and their resonance. Eventually, the prestige of a performance or exhibition in Poland waned due to the successes of contemporary Ukrainian culture in other Western countries; today, such trips to Poland are conducted primarily for financial reasons. After over ten years of independence, "the West" is accessible to Lviv's intellectuals in many more ways than it was in the late 1980s and early 1990s. However, cultural exchanges between Lviv's intellectuals and their counterparts in Poland have developed beyond what was once primarily support of home culture by the diaspora to a more general Polish interest in Ukraine. Ukraine's top two intellectual journals, *Krytyka* and *Yee*, have published several issues dealing exclusively with the topics of Polish culture and Ukrainian-Polish cultural relations.[5] Many of Ukraine's writers continue to be translated into Polish; Polish rock and jazz musicians have performed frequently in Lviv's cafés; and several conferences on Ukrainian-Polish relations have taken place. Although it is no longer viewed so much as "the West," Poland today continues to be important for Lviv's intellectuals, more as a neighbor of an independent Ukraine than as a conduit to something else. As the political integration of Poland into the West progresses, while Ukraine's remains stalled, Poland may eventually revert to its old role as "the West" for Lviv's Bohema.

The *Further* West: The North American Ukrainian Diaspora

Outside a small circle of active intellectuals, Ukrainian-Americans and Ukrainian-Canadians continue to see Ukrainian culture almost exclusively within a folkloric or patriotic frame. Frozen in the culture of the time when many of these men and women fled their homeland, the North American diaspora is reluctant to accept new experimental embodiments of Ukrainian culture. This distance from activities in contemporary Ukraine is, of course, largely the result of a generation gap—a problem also found in the aforementioned diaspora in Poland. However, lack of support from diaspora youth in North America increases this distance. Young Ukrainian-Americans who grew up and/or were born in North America may have some Ukrainian language skills but generally lack the advanced understanding of the Ukrainian language necessary to comprehend, and thus appreciate, Ukrainian high culture. They are overawed by it and ultimately respond with apathy. On the other hand, the conservative older generation has tended to react to contemporary Ukrainian culture in negative and even irascible ways. For example, when *Suchasnist'*—a leading Ukrainian intellectual journal in the West since its founding in 1961—moved its editorial offices from New York to Kyiv in 1992 and began publishing with an emphasis on contemporary Ukrainian literature, many readers in the West cancelled their subscriptions because they were appalled at the "profane" themes and language found in contemporary Ukrainian literature. Those in North America who continued to support the journal financially sent letters complaining about the journal's content and the fact that it published works written in a "Soviet-ized" Ukrainian language.[6] Although the members of the Lviv Bohema generally respect men and women of the North American diaspora for having retained their culture so far from their native land, they are repelled by the condescension they sense from these

Mark Andryczyk

Ukrainians from "the West," and they often respond to them with indifference or ridicule.

There are, however, Ukrainians in North America who are open to contemporary Ukrainian culture and who actively collaborate with today's cultural leaders in Ukraine. Among those who emigrated during World War II were many members of the Ukrainian intelligentsia, some of whom were connected directly or indirectly with previous groups of Lviv bohemians. Contemporary Ukrainian artists look to this minority of contemporary émigré artists for collaboration and support. The writings of the New York Group, made up of émigré Ukrainian poets, are well known and influential among cultural leaders in Ukraine. Subsequent cooperation among the two groups has resulted in several interesting publications, translations, recordings, and exhibits. Another example of positive exchange is found in the works of the Yara Arts Group, also located in New York City. Yara often utilizes contemporary Ukrainian culture in staging challenging, inventive interpretations of Ukrainian cultural themes. In the area of popular music, émigré rock groups such as Vapniaky (Canada), Kavune (United States) and Yeezhak (United States), who are somewhat inspired by their Polish counterparts, have collaborated with Lviv musicians in writing songs, recording, and performing both in Ukraine and in North America.

These members of the diaspora have helped to create a presence in North America for contemporary Ukrainian culture. Unfortunately, the North American diaspora lacks a substantial audience, outside an elite circle, that is capable of valuing this culture. The older generation generally rejects it, while the younger generation remains largely uninterested. A quick look at the activities of one subsection of the North American diaspora which formed a rare exception to my generalizations will help to explain my point.

The 1980s and early 1990s was a period of vibrant Ukrainian-oriented cultural activity among Toronto's Ukrainian diaspora youth. The creation of the literary journal *Terminus*, the avant-garde theater AUT, the alternative rock band Vapniaky mentioned above, and a church choir with two young conductors, each offering his own original Ukrainian Catholic liturgy, were all results of the efforts of a group of Ukrainian-Canadians living in Toronto at this time. Although the strength of the Ukrainian community in Toronto was undoubtedly a factor in educating a younger generation with a solid knowledge of Ukrainian language and culture, the major impetus for this activity was the sizable emigration of Ukrainians from Poland to Toronto in the early 1980s. Although they were born in Poland, the young people that arrived with this wave of immigration were a generation closer to Ukrainian language and culture at that time; this provided the necessary confidence and stimulus to activate Canadian-born Ukrainian youth, inspiring them to generate new ideas in Ukrainian culture. They were also able to attract an audience that could appreciate these efforts. It is not surprising that members of this group were among the first to travel to Ukraine with their productions and collabo-

244

rate with artists in Ukraine, including artists from the Lviv Bohema, as the latter conducted a cultural revolution in their native city.

"The Encroaching West" as a Topic for the Lviv Bohema

Between 1990 and 1992, the cultural scene in Lviv found itself in a favorable situation. A newfound, free, creative atmosphere and a substantial reserve of funds in Ukraine's cultural budget provided these men and women with the financial backing to realize many years' worth of creative ideas. The results of this auspicious intersection were a series of festivals that were grandiose in both scope and presentation. High points of this creative explosion were the Vy-Vykh festivals of 1990 and 1992.

The name Vy-Vykh stems from the Ukrainian word *zvykhnuty* (to twist or sprain). Organized by the Lviv Student Union, Vy-Vykh-90 was held in Lviv's Park of Culture. This three-day festival included exhibitions of music, art, and poetry along with other "twisted" sideshows. Among them: a *Leniniana*—a competition in which participants submitted portraits of Lenin (a 12-year-old's portrait took first place), *Krasa Koroleva Debiliv*—a mock beauty pageant crowning the city's "queen of the idiots," and a competition for Lviv's best joke. *Prokydannia Poezii (The Awakening of Poetry)* was a poetry-reading exhibition held at eight A.M. at which the Bu-Ba-Bu and Luhosad poetry groups, along with Kyiv's Propala Hramota and Vlodko Tsyboulko, read their works before a standing-room-only crowd. Many bands from Ukraine performed for the first time at Vy-Vykh-90, which was funded by the Ukrainian firm Plastik and the city's department of culture. In retrospect, Vy-Vykh-90 was a test of ideas and possibilities that would eventually flower two years later at Vy-Vykh-92.

The larger and more ambitious Vy-Vykh-92 was a complete takeover of Lviv by the Bohema. For three days, Lviv's citizens drank Vy-Vykh beer; ate Vy-Vykh chocolate, including the now-famous *salo v shokoladi* (fatback in chocolate, making gentle fun of the place of fatback as a delicacy in the traditional Ukrainian diet); and participated in contests such as "The Coolest Hat." Other competitions included drawing on asphalt and painting on cars. With the city at their disposal, Lviv artists painted a burned-out building and trolleys. Initially, city authorities complained about the "defacing" of its transport vehicles but later withdrew their complaint when Apple Computers decided to place their advertisement on the two "Vy-Vykh trolleys." Access to the city included use of the Lviv Opera Theater, the pride of the city. There, for three nights, the poetry-opera *Chrysler Imperial* was staged.

Chrysler Imperial, directed by Serhii Proskurnia, was loosely based on the writings of the group Bu-Ba-Bu (made up of Andrukhovych, Viktor Neborak and Oleksander Irvanets'). Inspired by an actual automobile the young poets once saw in Kyiv, the poetry-opera was a combination of ideas from the work of all three poets, with an emphasis on characters from Andrukhovych's novel *Rekreatsii (Recreations)*—including the demonic Dr. Popel, a representative of the Ukrainian diaspora in the West. The opera's staging offered live criticism from the audience (actors read actual letters published in newspapers criticizing the opera's scandalous nuances), a "TV-man" who occasionally circled the stage with a television strapped to his back (showing a popular Mexican soap opera which was playing in the weeks when the staging occurred), and a repeated warning by a long-eared troll about the coming of the Chrysler Imperial. The opera was an unrefined, muddled masterpiece, which concluded with the American automobile driving onto the stage and a choir singing Irvanets's parodic ode to Oklahoma. The obvious message was that the West is coming to save Ukraine from chaos. It was presented with typical Lviv Bohema sarcasm—a dismissive playing with serious issues in order to shield a fragile pride. This style reflects the influence of the Bu-Ba-Bu in Lviv. In their works, these writers attempt to sidestep reality and the linear progression of time by celebrating and describing life as a Rabelaisian carnival. Ideas are not concretely presented but are instead introduced buried within a multitude of concepts, all of which are exaggerated beyond customary limits. With this approach, the writers both address the problems of the real everyday world and seem to escape from their repercussions.

To this day, members of the Lviv Bohema consider Vy-Vykh-92 to be the apex of their existence. With hyperinflation approaching and a reliance on sponsorship inevitable, such a festival could only have been realized at that time. The opportunity to create freely, on such a grand scale, backed by state funds and local investors (as opposed to foreign sponsorship), has not recurred in Lviv since 1992. The organizers of Vy-Vykh-92 capitalized on the rampant enthusiasm which independence spawned and took advantage of a government willing to support anything that represented democracy and reform. A prophetic warning of imminent change, Vy-Vykh-92 and *Chrysler Imperial* will probably remain the hallmark of the leaders of the Lviv Bohema.[7]

"The West" in Post–Imperial Lviv: Your Café or Mine?

After Vy-Vykh-92, some of the festival's leaders formed the cultural cooperative Dzyga. One of Lviv's most active and successful organizations, Dzyga is headed by Markian Ivashchyshyn, former president of the Lviv Student Union. Dzyga has assembled a handful of previously unemployed musicians, artists, and journalists to develop various innovative projects. Among them is Easter Action Ie, which combines the poetry of modernist Lviv poets Karmans'kyi, Pachovs'kyi, and Antonych with contemporary music to parallel three similar periods of urban bohemian artistic life in Lviv. Through the occasional support of a successful sewing-factory side business, a talent for finding sponsors/advertisers for their events, and the creative accounting necessary to accomplish almost anything in Ukraine, Dzyga has produced hundreds of cultural events (for artists both from and outside of Ukraine) since its inception in 1993.

Dzyga is also responsible for changing the location of cultural interaction in Lviv. In the early 1990s, social gatherings for the Lviv Bohema took place as in the 1970s and 1980s—in small groups, often randomly assembled, meeting at someone's art studio or basement. With a bottle of wine or cognac, new songs were introduced, the latest poems were read, and fresh paintings were displayed in intimate domestic settings. Today, most of these people gather at one of Dzyga's three cafés: Lial'ka (The Puppet), Za Kulisamy (Backstage), and Pid Klepsydroiu (Under the Sign of the Hourglass).[8] In the mid-1990s, Lial'ka's stage replaced the kitchen as the arena for sharing new artistic creations. The rejuvenated inclination to gather socially outside the home quickly took hold. Dzyga's opening of these cafés was not a result of the import of Western restaurant culture to Ukraine, it was a conscious affirmation of the Western European traces in Lviv's pre-Soviet history and of the willingness of these bohemians to embrace the Western European style of café life as something native to their city.

As predicted in *Chrysler Imperial*, "the West" did make its presence felt in post-Vy-Vykh Lviv; it has been most obviously seen through the active participation of sponsors in the artistic lives of the members of Lviv Bohema. With the drying up of state cultural funds and minimal local sponsors, most ideas dreamed up by these intellectuals would remain dreams without the assistance of Western companies in Lviv. The most visible of those is Coca-Cola. "Zavzhdy (Always) Coca-Cola" signs dominate the city's old brownish buildings, and large red-and-white Coke umbrellas shelter almost every sidewalk café. Coke refrigerators and window decals are found in most stores, some of which don't even sell the product. For Lviv's stores, the Coca-Cola logo is more a symbol of prestige than an indication of what is actually available for purchase inside.

Coca-Cola targets young people in its advertising approach. Rock-concert stages display the familiar Coke swirl as a backdrop for performers. Sometimes free samples of Coke are distributed to fans and in backstage "green rooms." The Coca-Cola invasion began in the spring of 1995, and it has been prevalent at almost every major concert since. Coke employs locals, many from the fringes of the Lviv Bohema, to coordinate such activities. An interesting and somewhat comical display of Western corporate presence in Lviv took place at the five-year celebration of Ukrainian independence in August 1996. During an open-air rock concert attended by over 10,000 residents of Lviv, locals working for Coca-Cola and West cigarettes, the concert's two major sponsors, argued backstage over priority in advertisement placement and almost called off the concert.

Coca-Cola and other Western firms (Marlboro, Rothmans, and West cigarettes) have been rather successful in introducing the notion that their money is a necessity at cultural events. Although some members of the Lviv Bohema, such as Neborak, stubbornly resist combining art with sponsorship, most have come to terms with what *Chrysler Imperial* playfully anticipated.[9] Previously, privately funded events offered little or no financial reward for participants. Today, Western firms rarely ask artists to adjust or compromise their work, and the income they provide is appreciated. These men and women know what it was to work under a censor, and today's creative atmosphere is preferable to that of Soviet days. In fact, until the summer of 1996, there were very few sidewalk cafés in Lviv, and without Western advertising strategies they probably would not exist in such numbers as they do today. The irony of a European city obtaining a traditional symbol of European culture via North America serves to underscore Lviv's turbulent history. In past years, Lviv's bohemian intellectuals, who tended to enjoy the "European lifestyle" symbolized by the café, either fled their native city or were picked off in the various persecutions of the twentieth century. That loss, coupled with the isolation of the Soviet Union, left few to remember and appreciate such a lifestyle. Today, Europe is being introduced not to the European country of Ukraine but to Ukraine the former Soviet republic. Nonetheless, the café life of Lviv's pre-Soviet past is invoked by the Lviv Bohema. By providing cafés that attempt to avoid the commercialism of the new "Western" cafés, Dzyga tries to vault over this recently arrived product from the West and claim the café as something inherent to Lviv. In essence, they offer the Lviv Bohema an alternative to those nouveau riche–infested, Western-kitsch coffeehouses that abound in Lviv today.

While the Lviv Bohema attempts to distance itself from society in this way, befitting a bohemian subculture, society creates its own distance through indifference; the average citizen does not recognize the value of these artists' creative work. This citizen is much more interested in Western pop culture (almost exclusively imported via Moscow and thus through the Russian language) than in cultural happenings in his/her own country. Centuries of censorship and provincialization of Ukrainian culture and the persecution of its most talented leaders have managed, in the minds of its citizens, to implant the idea that Ukrainian culture is an inferior culture. Even free access to ten years of vibrant and innovative cultural activity (such as what has been produced by the Lviv Bohema) is not yet enough to regenerate recognition of this presence. Ukrainian bookstores, which were once stocked with socialist-realist literature, today sell Russian-language translations of American romance novels and horror bestsellers. These outnumber books by contemporary Ukrainian writers, which continue to be circulated in small print runs among friends. The Ukrainian government has done little to support contemporary Ukrainian culture; members of the Lviv Bohema would surely appreciate assistance from the government to help sustain their art, but considering the intrusion of various governments into Ukrainian culture throughout its history, these artists also enjoy the rare opportunity to shape Ukrainian culture freely and openly while taking in Lviv café life. Welcoming to, but wary of, today's presence of "the West" in Lviv, these men and women recognize the dangers in swapping one mass culture (Soviet) for another (Western pop culture). They are inspired by their position between "the East" and "the West"; through the art they produce and the lifestyles they choose to lead, they navigate the course of post-Soviet Ukraine as it oscillates between these two poles.

NOTES

1. This is a fragment from the poem "Liubit' Ukraïnu" ("Love Ukraine"), written in 1944 by Volodymyr Sosiura. Originally part of the 1920s VAPLITE literary group, Sosiura eventually capitulated to the demands of socialist realism. "Love Ukraine" was initially criticized for being nationalistic but eventually became a song which was popular in the Soviet Union. The following translation by Michael M. Naydan was published in *A Hundred Years of Youth: A Bilingual Anthology of 20th Century Ukrainian Poetry*, ed. O. Luchuk and M. Naydan (Lviv: Litopys, 2000), 216–219.

> Love Ukraine like the sun, o love her,
> like the wind, the grass, the water,
> in an hour of happiness, in a moment of joy,
> love her in a time of disaster.

2. This fragment is from the poem "Liubit!" ("Love Oklahoma!"), written in 1992 by Bu-Ba-Bu poet Oleksander Irvanets' and dedicated to Volodymyr Sosiura. A parody of Sosiura's popular poem, "Love Oklahoma!" pledges affection to seventeen different U.S. states. The translation of this fragment by Michael M. Naydan was published in *A Hundred Years of Youth*, 640–641.

> Love Oklahoma! At night and at supper,
> Like your mom and your dad quite equal.
> Love Indiana. And the very same way
> Love Northern and Southern Dakota!

3. A collection of Petro Karmans'kyi's memoirs on the Moloda Muza was recently published in Lviv and became quite a popular read with members of the 1990s Lviv Bohema. See Petro Karmans'kyi, *Ukrains'ka Bohema* (Lviv: Olir, 1996).

4. Memoirs of the literary scene in Lviv in the early 1940s were written by poet Ostap Tarnavs'kyi, who emigrated to Philadelphia, and were published in Lviv in 1995. See Ostap Tarnavs'kyi, *Literaturnyi Lviv: Spomyny* (Lviv: Prosvita, 1995).

5. The issues I refer to are *Krytyka* 37 (November 2000) and *Yee: nezalezhnyi kul'turolohichnyj chasopys* 10 (1997) and 14 (1998).

6. These complaints are aimed not only at Russifications in the contemporary Ukrainian language but also at the use of English words, imported through Soviet Russian, in place of existing Ukrainian words. Paradoxically, such people seem to accept borrowings from English that are made by members of the North American diaspora.

7. Viktor Neborak's book *Povernennia v Leopolis* (Lviv: Klasyka, 1998) is a collection of essays dealing with various branches of the 1990s Lviv Bohema during the peak of their existence. He has also written and produced the documentary film *Pokynuta Kaviarnia* (*The Forsaken Café*) about the Bohema and their café-hopping rituals.

8. The allusion here to Bruno Schulz's collection of short stories illustrates the Lviv Bohema's affinity for artistic achievements produced in Galicia. Schulz lived in the town of Drohobych, about two hours from Lviv. In similar fashion, the Lviv

Mark Andryczyk

Bohema sees fellow Galicians Joseph Roth and Leopold von Sacher-Masoch (born in Lviv) as part of their cultural heritage.

9. Throughout the 1990s, Viktor Neborak organized several rock concerts and evenings of poetry without relying on any sponsorship. He is convinced that if an event is timed correctly and well organized, the Lviv public will come out to support its artists and that funds earned from admission fees will be enough to pay for a hall and still allow the artists to earn money. His success has been remarkable.

WORKS CITED

Karmans'kyi, P. *Ukrains'ka Bohema.* Lviv: Olir, 1996.

Luchuk, Ol'ha, and Michael Naydan, eds. *A Hundred Years of Youth: A Bilingual Anthology of 20th Century Ukrainian Poetry.* Lviv: Litopys, 2000.

Neborak, V. *Povernennia v Leopolis.* Lviv: Klasyka, 1998.

Tarnavs'kyi, O. *Literaturnyi L'viv: Spomyny.* Lviv: Prosvita, 1995.

thirteen

"Don't Get Pricked!"

*Representation and the Politics of Sexuality
in the Czech Republic*

Věra Sokolová

Why Sexuality?

Many Czech social scientists know something about the changing ways
male and female sexualities have been understood and represented in Czech
society in the post-1989 period, but hardly anyone has written about them.[1]
This is all the more striking since sexuality is embedded in and influences
other social, political, and economic trends, such as changes in political rhetoric, cultural values, and lifestyle choices, and can thus be a fundamental lens
through which to interpret and assess the broad processes of social change that
have taken place in post-communist Central Europe. The following chapter
will attempt to fill in this gap in scholarship, analyzing representations of
sexuality in the Czech media, developments in traffic in women, and the new
political discourse on homosexuality in the Czech Republic as both integral to
and functions of the democratic and economic transition. By doing so, I show
how studies of gender politics in Central Europe can incorporate sexuality to
gain insight into a wide range of social problems that at first glance seems far
removed from questions of gender.

It is not surprising that much of the scholarship on the economic and
democratic transition after 1989 has focused on an important but restrictive set
of themes—such as changes in political culture, the development of civil

society, and privatization and the transformation of state institutions—that seek to measure or account for the various degrees of "success" or "failure" of Central and Eastern European countries in their reform policies.[2] Though these analyses have enjoyed a certain degree of primacy, they have not gone unchallenged by feminist and other writings that highlight the sometimes negative cultural consequences of policies and reforms deemed economically and democratically beneficial. These feminist scholars from both "East" and "West" consider the central role of gender in the transition process and they use a comparative history approach to understand the differences in women's experiences in the divided Europe.[3] This scholarship has been far from uncontentious. Feminists from both sides of the Iron Curtain bring different lived experiences to their work, and they also often use different theoretical approaches and empirical data. It is no surprise that by the mid-1990s their scholarship had led to sharp differences in interpretation, fueling explosive debates and disagreements about women and feminisms "East and West."[4] Thus, although they demonstrate the need to include gender analysis within the broader transition literature, these debates have also proved the need to bridge the perceived "Eastern" and "Western" experiential and theoretical gaps and tensions that characterized the feminist writings of the early 1990s in order to produce mutually acceptable and enriching frameworks of interpretation and challenge the structuralist mode of thought that is still prevalent in comparative writing on gender and sexuality in post-communist East Central Europe.

Despite these differences, feminist scholarship on post-communist East Central Europe has shared common ground by making the labor market, women in the political process, and, above all, reproductive politics the center of analysis. This is in part because feminist scholars have for some time challenged the notion of separate public and private spheres and have rightly pointed out that reproduction is by no means a private domain removed from the influences of "high" politics.[5] As Gail Kligman noted in her eye-opening study of the politics of reproduction in socialist Romania, critical inquiry into the institutionalization of social practices under communism enables us to "comprehend more fully the lived processes of social atomization and dehumanization" of totalitarian regimes and to understand "the means by which reproductive issues become embedded in social-political agendas" on both national and international levels.[6] "The politics of reproduction" analyzed by Kligman and others includes debates about abortion, child care, the use of sterilization under communism, pronatalist policies as tools for nation-building, and other political uses of ideas of family, motherhood, and womanhood. Because gender discrimination in laws is often couched in legal language, these scholars also address the rhetoric and argumentation used to institute laws regulating family and social relations. Reproductive politics, therefore, offers a way to understand how the entire political field affects the way ordinary people plan and live their private lives.

However, reproductive politics is only one dimension of gender change in the region. Another significant issue is the changing understanding of sexuality, which scholars of reproductive politics often leave out or mention only superficially. As a category of analysis, sexuality is often misunderstood and reduced to "talking about sex," a step that diminishes the category's potential for exploring continuities and changes in a society.[7] For example, new representations of sexuality in the media, causal links between prostitution and tourism, and "Western" influences on the cultural understanding of homosexuality tell us a lot about the ways economic transformation and openness to the "West" have helped redefine cultural values and models. The interactions of local practices with "global" consumer ideologies and products have dramatically altered the discourse on sexuality in the country and region.[8]

The immense growth of tabloid media, called *bulvár* in the Czech Republic, has profoundly influenced how people relate to their bodies and express their subjectivity. The sexual openness of tabloid media, which borders on outright pornography, has launched intense political and philosophical debates about professional journalistic ethics, the right to privacy, freedom of speech and expression, the social respectability and responsibilities of public figures, and so on. While these debates express the importance of ethical perspectives in the representation of sexuality, political discussions on the legalization of domestic partnerships between homosexuals show that the political imagination of homosexual behavior is still deeply embedded in biological and medical perspectives from communism that thrive due to static institutional frameworks. Thus, while some influences on the representation of sexuality, such as the consumer market and the media, have undergone rapid change, more conservative influences, such as ideas of health and biological rightness, have not. Considering the issue of sexuality from such diverse points of view, therefore, can reveal changes and continuities in post-totalitarian culture that other approaches leave hidden.

Representations of Sexuality in the Media:
Freedom without Limits

After 1989, the media in countries of the former Soviet bloc underwent a rapid and far-reaching transformation. Required for decades to write news and TV programs in dull, uniform, and politically correct ways, journalists became intoxicated with new freedoms of speech and possibilities for individual expression and creativity. As media groups competed to draw in potential audiences, using images and themes previously forbidden under communism was the most successful way to grab viewers' attention, including commercials with provocative images of women or TV programs that talked about and displayed sexual acts. In fact, almost all representations of sexuality were taken as novel and as expressions of freedom, since prior to 1989 official discussions of sexuality focused almost exclusively on reproduction and family planning (and was thus desexualized) or viewed it in terms of the criminal, socially deviant, and "medical" aspects of sexual behavior (and was thus oversexualized). Because sex under communism was either represented through officially sanctioned channels or not represented at all, the void rapidly filled with new images of sex, just as the consumer market and politics were flooded with new imported products and ideas.

Images and ideas of sexuality previously gathered from smuggled western journals and videos suddenly took on concrete shapes and colors on Czech billboards and newsstands throughout the country. Rules of "normality" and "acceptability" disappeared, and in the first years of democratic transition, few dared to challenge these trends seriously by suggesting that restrictions should be imposed on how sexuality can be represented.[9] Czech billboards in particular have been notable in their shocking, sometimes obscene depictions of female sexuality. For example, one popular commercial by Kozel, a beer company, showed a woman in luxurious underwear caressing a man with the text "Drink Your Goat" underneath. Other notable examples include *Esquire Magazine* ads where naked women sit on top of beer-filled glasses with their legs spread open (or on all fours, eating from a man's palm), a Magnum ice cream ad with women eating an ice cream bar as if performing fellatio, and so on.

What is even more shocking, however, is that these ads still regularly appear over a decade after 1989, reinforcing how the freedom to create eye-catching ads can subordinate and sexualize the female body. For example, in 2001 a popular ad by Diffusil, a producer of an insect repellant, depicts a man with mosquito wings having sex with a naked woman (visible only in her spread arms and high-heeled legs) with a warning text "Don't Let Yourself Get Pricked!"—alluding to the "naturalness" of nonconsensual sex between a suddenly appearing man and a necessarily submissive woman. Clearly, the company and presumably its targeted audience do not find depictions of female subjection (in scenarios that would be considered rape in Western countries) problematic; rather, they see them as sources of amusement and creativity.

Such ads have not been published without opposition or outcry. One of the most controversial ads of late is for Nokia's hands-free set; it came out as the Czech Parliament was debating the problem of sexual harassment in the workplace. The ad showed a laughing, excited businessman grabbing the large breasts of his female colleague, her face frozen in a comic scream, with the text: "Nokia—Dangerously Free Hands."[10] A protest immediately arose from women (and a few men) active at the Center for Gender Studies at Charles University in Prague, at Gender in Sociology, a research team at the Institute of Sociology of Academy of Sciences of the Czech Republic, and a few NGOs, indicating that public reception of representations of female sexuality has been (at least on some fronts) undergoing a process of cultural reflection and criticism. The protest was addressed to the Czech Advertisement Council, the legislative body that oversees issues of commercial ethics and legislation.

The existence of the council gives the impression that advertising ethics are monitored in some ways in the Czech Republic. However, the Advertisement Council is an advisory body that can merely suggest that a company withdraw its ad; it has no legislative authority to order an ad pulled down. After the complaint was submitted to the council, the activists inquired at Nokia head-quarters in Finland to see if they knew about the ad and to learn whether it was locally produced or internationally distributed. It turned out that Nokia had nothing to do with the production of this ad: it was a domestic product, created by Czechs.[11]

This case suggests that local perceptions of sexual representation can easily be taken for "Western imports" of obscene sexuality and notions of public acceptability. Clichés about the "American hysteria" over sexual ha-rassment add further fuel to the fire. The "West," and the United States in particular, appear in popular culture as a place where "feminists" have spiraled sexual politics to the level of absurdity. This view has been systematically created and perpetuated by well-known intellectuals and writers such as Josef Škvorecký, Lukáš Vaculík, Iva Pekárková, and the late Milan Machovec.[12] Thus, while sexuality is used to express freedom of speech, underlining the liberal values the Czech Republic shares with Western countries, it is cited at the same time to elevate and distance Czech culture from the superficial materialism and hysterical feminism of the "West," notably the United States.

One striking example of the representation of sexuality in the media comes not from private enterprise but from the Czech public TV station, which is required by law and mandated by the Czech Parliament to produce "objective, verified, comprehensive and balanced information so that viewers can freely form their opinions and attitudes."[13] Recently the station ran an hour-long documentary entitled "Sex Is Ours . . . So Harass!" about the prob-lem of sexual harassment in the country. Intentionally or not, the program's strong antifeminist biases mirrored stereotypes of female sexuality in society. The documentary took the form of a for-and-against debate, presenting only two people who defended the view that sexual harassment is a real problem but more than fourteen male "experts" and "scientists" who challenged, ridi-culed, and denied the idea that cases of sexual harassment in the Czech Republic could be substantiated. Arguments about "incidental" cases of ha-rassment involving passersby overwhelmingly supported the male challengers against the defendants, who were mostly young women who were unlikely to have had experiences of sexual harassment at work yet. While the majority of the men were introduced as having postgraduate degrees, giving the impres-sion that they were mature critical thinkers, most of the women presented were nude models, artists, or friends of the men, each of whom in some way exhibited her nudity as a part of her career and rejected the notion that sexual harassment is a problem. The choice of these young women served to reaffirm the belief that nudity and sexuality are merely expressive aspects of women's desires and thus cannot be forced upon them. In a shocking move, the document showed more than forty-two depictions of naked breasts, a revealing suggestion that only women, not men, can be used as sexual objects in this way. The program's dialogue drove home the idea that female sexuality invites men's advances and that sexual interaction is an innocent, free expression of human desire.[14]

Media images of sexuality are one of the most important ways gender inequality is produced and reproduced in the Czech Republic. Many accounts, both academic and popular, still underestimate the power of language and visual representation to cause or influence cultural trends and values over the last decade. They thus tend to ignore the fact that representation and symbolism used in popular Czech commercials and ads makes contemporary power hierarchies appear "natural" and "true."[15] In fact, the apparent "naturalness" of understanding female identity in purely sexualized terms is a consequence of the postsocialist environment, in which market forces and global images dictate trends of representation, and of liberal reactions to decades of suppression of visual images of male and female desire.

Prostitution, Traffic in Women, and Political Mobilization

The media have been able to extend significantly the limits of what can be represented sexually because they can reconcile shocking (but taken as humorous) depictions of female sexual subordination while also interpreting "the Czech woman" as someone sexually free and inviting who takes pride in her body and prowess. As these images and the concrete conditions of women's sexual lives influence each other, the question remains: Have Czech women experienced greater sexual freedom and mobility under current democratic conditions? Although such a question cannot be answered fully here, the marked rise of traffic in women and prostitution in the Czech Republic since 1989 casts a dark shadow over the consequences of democratic and economic transition for male and female sexual behavior. On the other hand, the same conditions have made political mobilization possible, a key objective for the growing number of women activists.

Freedom of movement between the perceived East and West, supported by the fact that the Czech Republic borders Germany and Austria, "gates to the West," has exacerbated the problems of trafficking and prostitution. Although in the communist period prostitution blossomed on a mostly individual basis, mainly through West German or Austrian tourists in border areas, during the 1990s prostitution became a lucrative and organized business throughout the country. Because prostitution is legal in the Czech Republic, signs announcing "Night Clubs," "Erotic Clubs," "Beautiful Girls," "Nude Girls," and "Escort Services" gleam in most Czech cities and are advertised in phone books, printed media, and on nighttime TV. Until 1989, prostitution was considered "parasitic" and was punishable according to the law, not as a sexual crime but as a crime against the socialist work ethic. In 1989, the law on the obligation to work was removed from the Czech Criminal Code, and no analogous law has replaced it.[16]

After 1989, prostitution disappeared in Czech law because it was considered neither a crime nor a "job," leaving it in the ironic position of a morally despicable but legally acceptable economic pursuit. In practice, this ambiguous legal situation has had two consequences, both of which force prostitutes into situations of economic, psychological, and physical disempowerment, vulnerability, and abuse: they are scorned by the majority of society, and their profession is not legally recognized, meaning that it lacks social provision. The absence of legal oversight of prostitution has enforced the helplessness of prostitutes in relations with their employers, where gender and coercive power dimensions are especially prominent. At the opposite extreme from social and legal misrecognition, *Peříčko*, a popular talk show about sex, celebrates and romanticizes prostitution by interviewing and presenting the "performances" of young and "sexually liberated" escorts who say that they "love" their work.[17] Situated between these social perceptions, the reality of prostitution remains one of the least understood and least regulated, as well as the most problematic, spheres of gender inequality in the Czech Republic.

As opposed to prostitution, trafficking in women is a crime in Czech Criminal Law. Paragraph §246 states that a person who "decoys, recruits or carries a woman abroad for the purpose of sexual intercourse with someone else shall be sentenced to 1–5 years of imprisonment" (or 3–8 years if committed by an organized group, if the victim is under 18 years of age, or if the crime was committed for the purpose of prostitution).[18] However, this is the only legal norm that mentions trafficking in women per se, because Czech legislation does not use the terminology of forced labor or slavery to describe or punish the subjugation of women who have already been trafficked.

According to Czech police reports, the majority of girls rescued by police from international traffickers in the Czech Republic are not Czech but come from countries of the former Soviet Union and the Balkans. Interviews carried out by the international NGO LaStrada reveal that economic factors prevail in the decisions of these women to journey westward. The Czech Republic is also considered an ideal place for trafficking in women, as a country with a high concentration of mafia gangs from Russia, Ukraine, and the Balkans and a transit country for drug-smuggling from Southeastern Europe and the Middle East. Data on trafficking in women over the last decade suggest that for traffickers, the Czech Republic combines "Western" economic opportunities and liberal values, such as freedom of movement, presumption of innocence, and the rule of law, with "Eastern" post-totalitarian cracks in the legal system, such as bribery, low manpower and finances, a confusing criminal code, and legislation that tends to follow rather than precede certain crimes.[19]

Worrisome as these trends are, they have also stimulated mobilization and grassroots activism among women. Legal challenges to prevent organized violence against women have been ineffective, so increased numbers of women have decided to create and volunteer for NGOs that help women in distress. The most visible and successful have been LaStrada, which works in the field of traffic in women; Rozkoš bez rizika (Pleasure without Risk), which covers a wide range of issues and services for prostitutes; project "Jana" in Western Bohemia, which offers women free AIDS tests and medical examinations; and Bílý kruh bezpečí (White Circle of Safety), which provides legal and psychological services for victims of rape and others. These organizations gained their understanding of prostitution and traffic in women from institutions based in the West, which provide most of their financial support.[20]

Elsewhere throughout the region of East Central Europe, abortion became the most explosive issue in gender politics following the collapse of communism. After decades of relatively easy and accessible abortion, Central European countries adopted new more restrictive laws; in Poland, for example, abortion has been illegal since the Abortion Law passed in 1994.[21] Abortion has occupied center stage in political debates which articulate claims about national and cultural morality and justice through ideas of health and national well-being. At the same time, the issue of abortion has provoked women activists to organize and learn to articulate their concerns in politically salient ways.[22] In Czechoslovakia, however, the situation was quite different, as neither the Czech Republic nor Slovakia enacted new legislation restricting access to abortion. The one significant difference was a higher fee for "non-medical" abortions, which certainly did limit access to abortions for some women but did not restrict the practice from a legal perspective. Even though topics and opinions in the media have occasionally stirred public debate, on the whole, Czech women have not had to mobilize and fight for their reproductive rights.[23]

Instead, following the pattern of West European and North American societies, Czech women's organizations and networks have centered predominantly on issues of sexual violence against women, such as rape, domestic violence, prostitution, traffic in women, and pornography. In addition to concrete assistance and counseling for victims of sexual violence, these centers engage in consciousness-raising, research, and political activities to educate the public about institutions and structures that perpetuate this kind of violence. This NGO work can be seen as an attempt to counter the influences of the media industry, such as pornography on late-night TV and in the tabloid media, which then disseminate within popular culture.[24] Unfortunately, many Czechs view prostitution and traffic in women in terms of female promiscuity and the opportunity to get foreign cash and so often blame the victims rather than seeing these phenomena in terms of the coercive practices and grave social and economic conditions that produce them.

LaStrada, for example, succeeded in making the traffic in women visible by organizing a large media-education campaign as well as ads in several major cities in East and Central Europe. The ads and commercials warn women of the frequent cases of trafficking disguised as au-pair and educational programs, ventures that are immensely popular in post-communist countries because they offer ways for young people to travel, learn new languages, and encounter new cultures. The ad campaign of LaStrada points out how these "opportunities" target young women in vulnerable situations. Given current anti-feminist sentiments in the country, such campaigns might risk backlashes against "naïve" and "adventurous" women, blaming them for walking into dangerous situations without caution. Paradoxically, then, greater freedom and mobility to travel internationally combined with increased awareness of violence against women could result in stronger pressure on women to remain dependent, fearful, and tied to home; in other words, to act according to patriarchal norms predominant in society.

Though Czech women on the whole resist attempts to organize officially for causes considered to be overly "feminist," the mutual cooperation and interconnection between these nongovernmental organizations demonstrate that women organize around issues affecting them in fundamentally different ways than men. In fact, these organizations developed alongside and because of increasing gender inequalities after communism, indicating that women's groups have been quick to perceive and respond to the changing conditions of a democratic society. However, while these activities—in content, structure, goals, and so forth—differ little from similar activities in so-called Western countries, such work is rarely understood in feminist terms in the Czech Republic. Many of the activists themselves resist that identification, revealing once more the absence of a meaningful discourse about feminist issues either under communism or today. Moreover, even though women activists could draw on a lot of support and power from joining their efforts together with homosexuals, such alliances have so far been nonexistent. Women and homosexuals (same-sex organizations and discourse are dominated by gay men) organize themselves differently in order to fight for their specific rights and to initiate serious debate in public discourse because of a mutual belief that they have little (if anything) to offer to and gain from each other. Thus, there is an absence of a meaningful discourse about homosexuality (and many Czechs still hold stereotypes and conceptions of homosexuality based on the ideological and scientific frameworks of the former regime), and feminists have been unable to connect the politics of gender with the politics of sexuality into a coherent, powerful, and productive political critique.

Homosexuality: The Issue of the 1990s

The most visible issue in the Czech Republic in the 1990s concerning gender, sexuality, and reproductive politics has been the issue of homosexuality and "homosexual marriage," better known under the term registered partnership. Immediately after 1989, the issue of homosexuality shot into public view, and it has remained a major political and cultural question ever since. The views of politicians toward homosexuality and registered partnership created unlikely alliances in Parliament and during TV debates. Homosexuality has been such a popular topic of debate that some politicians have used it to promote themselves and their programs rather than contributing to the issue itself. Through discussions in the media, the public has often learned about the sexual orientations and perspectives of political representatives and candidates; this type of information is now an integral aspect of political discourse.[25]

The way both homosexuals and heterosexuals understand homosexuality was strongly affected by the repressive apparatus of sexuality under communism. After the collapse of communism, homosexuals were among the first suppressed minorities to organize into a strong political force to fight for their rights. The categories of freedom, identity, and agency offered rhetorical tools that resonated with the concerns of the society at large. Moreover, panic about the spread of AIDS prompted government support throughout the 1990s. Given pressures from the European Union to pay attention to the treatment of all minorities, including sexual ones, and the fact that the Czech Republic is not a religiously identified country with moral prejudices against homosexuality built into its national culture, it is not surprising that the issue has attracted such a spotlight.[26]

According to a recent study by the Sexological Institute of the Czech Republic, more than half the country's population claims that they have not personally met a homosexual.[27] Though statistics suggest that Czech society is fairly open and tolerant (in fact, 70 percent of respondents replied that they would not mind if their political representative was a homosexual), other studies show that many Czechs consider homosexuality to be something "alien" that does not concern them personally. That is, Czech society tends to see homosexuality not as a natural component of society but as a problem that arose after the fall of communism and thus as a consequence of the rise of liberal democracy.[28]

During the communist regime, homosexuality was presented as a crime, a perversion, and an illness. The medicalization and criminalization of homosexuality was rightfully denounced by many writers on totalitarian regimes.[29] Until 1961, homosexuality in Czechoslovakia, as in many other East and Central European countries, was criminalized: until 1950, homosexual acts were "crimes against nature," and from 1950 to 1961, they were crimes against society that were "incompatible with the morality of a socialist society."[30] In 1961, homosexuality was decriminalized by a new law (§244 Tr.Z.) which legalized homosexual acts under specific conditions.[31] Only after the collapse of communism, in July 1990, was §241 in its entirety removed from the Criminal Code of Czechoslovakia. In 1993, when the World Health Organization officially removed homosexuality from its list of illnesses, SOHO[32] managed to ratify the removal of this item (which had been included in the Czechoslovak Medical List of Illnesses as the infamous Diagnosis 302.1) in Czechoslovakia as well.[33]

Even though charges of homosexuality as a criminal act disappeared during the last decades of communism and during the 1990s accounts of homosexuality as "unnaturalness" slowly shifted to a discourse of "difference but equality," these shifts have not transformed the understanding of sexuality from a biological and medical issue to a socially constructed and gendered category. Today, physicians no longer want to "cure" homosexuality and generally accept it as a viable alternative to heterosexuality. The medicalization of sexuality, however, especially the view that it is biologically determined, has influenced all levels of sexual and gender discourses. Most accounts, including those in periodicals, mention that "in current conceptions, homosexuality is not understood as an illness,"[34] but few authors reflect on the implications of the persistent use of medical and biological categories (rather than cultural ones) to imagine homosexuality in political and social debate.

The persistent monopoly of psychologists, psychiatrists, and sexologists on issues of sexuality to this very day, at the expense of qualified gender analysis by sociologists and historians, results in many ways from repressive communist social practices. Definitions and listed causes of homosexuality from the communist era have not changed much in the last ten years; they indicate that in the 1990s, the bases for argumentation had not progressed beyond medical discourse.[35] In 1992, experts argued that "homosexuality is a life-long, unchangeable state which is neither caused nor chosen by its carrier who, therefore, cannot be blamed for it."[36] Three years later, another influential sexologist insisted that "biological factors play the decisive role for determining sexual orientation from the prenatal stage of individual development, whether those are genetic or hormonal factors."[37] And in 2000, the author of the first original gay history written in Czech exclaimed, "Let's understand each other! This book is by no means a promotion of homosexuality. To promote homosexuality or heterosexuality is nonsense. They are simply facts."[38]

Paradoxically, however, the etiological approach—the search for the origins of homosexual desire[39]—which has characterized the medical sexological sciences and helped essentialize the biological foundations of gender and sexuality has also laid the groundwork for gay and lesbian political movements. The way scientific studies define homosexuality has clearly affected how gay and lesbian leaders articulate political claims and concerns. Many Czech homosexuals, who were represented in the early 1990s by SOHO and its president Jiří Hromada, have eagerly embraced the widespread essentialist definition of homosexuality as a "lasting and unchangeable characteristic of every individual,"[40] basing their political strategies on this view. Led by the goal of legalizing registered partnership, they have stood firmly behind sexological "experts," agreeing that "homosexuals do not choose their sexual orientation."[41] Even though some original research studies include clauses about free will and choice in their definitions of homosexuality, homosexual political representatives have so far ignored them and concentrate on arguments that "prove" biological predisposition.[42] Since 1990, Hromada (and Gay Iniciativa without and G-liga after him) has consistently argued that homosexuality is biologically determined and has gradually succeeded in convincing the public that homosexuality is an innate biological tendency. As early as 1995, on the political TV show *Aréna*, Hromada won a phone-in vote of viewers on the need to institutionally legalize registered partnership. Two-thirds of those who called said that Hromada had convinced them.[43] However, few people pause over the latent homophobia built into these debates. Why exactly do we need to know whether homosexuality is innate or a matter of choice? One of the primary ways to challenge debates on the origins of homosexuality is to question the political utility of potential answers. So far, however, most activists and academics still focus on explaining and providing answers rather than on analyzing the questions and their motivations.

Such arguments contain some contradictions that in the long run may suit various political interests. For example, Gay Iniciativa vehemently argues that homosexuality is innate, yet the crux of the conflict over legalization of registered partnership is fear of potential danger to children from inappropriate role models or the absence of "correct ones."[44] Gay Iniciativa and most studies on gay issues available in the Czech Republic argue that homosexuals and heterosexuals are "the same" with the exception of sexual preference, yet Hromada has tirelessly assured the public and Parliament that homosexuals do not want the law on registered partnership to include a clause about their ability to bear, adopt, and raise children. However, no one has provided any reasons why homosexuals should not possess the same innate desire to have children as heterosexuals. This inconsistency is especially striking given the arguments usually made by conservative Christian Democrat MPs, such as Tomáš Kvapil or Cyril Svoboda, who see the naturalness of a "maternal destiny" in all women, on the one hand, and the unnaturalness of lesbian motherhood, on the other. They have not explained who should and should not be included in their definition of "woman."[45]

So far, most analyses of gender and sexuality have been blind to a fundamentally gendered and controversial premise: that the Czech homosexual movement espouses patriarchal values and has a male orientation and Czech feminist and gender scholarship is heterosexist. Feminist analyses of gender, which focus on social relations between men and women, and analyses of sexuality, which in the Czech Republic are premised on biological difference, have not effectively critiqued or supported each other.[46] Instead, gender analysts have excluded sexuality from discussions of social relations, and analysts of sexuality have not seriously entertained the claim that sexuality is habituated through gender norms and practices. Gay representatives often reinforce gender stereotypes in their work, while feminist scholars exclude homosexuality in order to narrow gender politics to the range of their specific interests. As a result, a full account of the experiences of gays and lesbians and the politics and representations of homosexuality in the Czech Republic has yet to be written.

The contemporary history of sexuality in the Czech Republic is very much shaped by the confrontation and contestation of the ideas, institutions, and economic conditions of the socialist past and the democratic present. This confrontation produces conflicting and problematic ideas about male and female sexuality in Czech society while at the same time slowly patterning these ideas along lines common in the "West." However, whether Czech activists will also manage to instill in Czech society respect for the female body or tolerance of homosexuality is still an open question.

NOTES

1. An exception to this trend is scholarship on homosexuality, which will be discussed and cited later in the essay.

2. For example, Jiří Musil, ed., *The End of Czechoslovakia* (Budapest: Central European University Press, 1995). "Western" texts include Anders Aslund, *How Russia Became a Market Economy* (Washington, D.C.: The Brookings Institution, 1995); Jon Elster, Claus Offe, and Ulrich K. Preuss, *Institutional Design in Post-Communist Societies: Rebuilding the Ship at Sea* (New York: Cambridge University Press, 1998); Laszlo Andor and Martin Summers, *Market Failure: Eastern Europe's "Economic Miracle"* (London: Pluto Press, 1998).

3. See, for example, Renata Salecl, *The Spoils of Freedom: Psychoanalysis and Feminism after the Fall of Socialism* (New York: Routledge, 1994); Jiřina Šmejkalová, "Gender as an Analytical Category of Post-Communist Studies," in *Gender in Transition in Eastern and Central Europe Proceedings*, ed. Gabriele Jahnert, Jana Gohrisch, Daphne Hahn, Hildegard Maria Nickel, Iris Peinl, and Katrin Schäfgen (Berlin: Trafo Verlag, 2001); Nanette Funk and Magda Mueller, eds., *Gender Politics and Post-Communism: Reflections from Eastern Europe and the Former Soviet Union* (New York: Routledge, 1993); Barbara Einhorn, *Cinderella Goes to Market: Citizenship, Gender and Women's Movements in East Central Europe* (London: Verso, 1993). Another classic on gender and women in Eastern Europe, published before the collapse of communism, is Sharon L. Wolchik and Alfred G. Meyer, eds., *Women, State, and Party in Eastern Europe* (Durham, N.C.: Duke University Press, 1985).

4. The best analyses of the context of Czech gender discourse and the East-West differences include, for example, Hana Havelková, "Transitory and Persistent Differences: Feminism East and West," in *Transitions, Environments, Translations: Feminisms in International Politics*, ed. Joan Scott, Cora Kaplan, and Debra Keates (New York: Routledge, 1997), 56–64; Jiřina Šmejkalová, "Strašidlo feminismu v ženském 'porevolučním' tisku: úvaha, doufejme, historická," in *Žena a muž v médiích*, ed. Hana Havelková and Mirek Vodráčka (Praha: Nadace Gender Studies, 1998), 16–19; Hana Havelková, "Abstract Citizenship? Women and Power in the Czech Republic," *Social*

Politics (Summer/Fall 1996): 243–260; Jitka Malečková, "Gender, Nation and Scholarship: Reflections on Gender/Women's Studies in the Czech Republic," in *New Frontiers in Women's Studies: Knowledge, Identity and Nationalism*, ed. Mary Maynard and June Purvis (London: Taylor and Francis, 1995), 96–112.

5. The most comprehensive and up-to-date collection on the politics of reproduction in Eastern Europe is Susan Gal and Gail Kligman, eds., *Reproducing Gender: Politics, Publics, and Everyday Life after Socialism* (Princeton, N.J.: Princeton University Press, 2000). See also Susan Gal and Gail Kligman, *The Politics of Gender after Socialism* (Princeton, N.J.: Princeton University Press, 2000), or Hana Havelková, "Women in and after a 'Classless' Society," in *Women and Social Class: International Feminist Perspectives*, ed. Christine Zmroczek and Pat Mahony (London: UCL Press, 1999), 69–84.

6. Gail Kligman, *The Politics of Duplicity: Controlling Reproduction in Ceau-şescu's Romania* (Berkeley: University of California Press, 1998), 2.

7. For classic and introductory texts to the theories and politics of sexuality see, for example, Ann Snitow, Christine Stansell, and Sharon Thompson, eds., *Powers of Desire: The Politics of Sexuality* (New York: Monthly Review Press, 1993); and Andrew Parker, Mary Russo, Doris Summer, and Patricia Yaeger, eds., *Nationalisms and Sexualities* (New York: Routledge, 1992).

8. See, for example, Gabriele Jahnert, Jana Gohrisch, Daphne Hahn, Hildegard Maria Nickel, Iris Peinl, and Katrin Schafgen, eds., *Gender in Transition in Eastern and Central Europe Proceedings* (Berlin: Trafo Verlag, 2001); Svetlana Boym, *Common Places: Mythologies of Everyday Life in Russia* (Cambridge, Mass.: Harvard University Press, 1994); *Women 2000: An Investigation into the Status of Women's Rights on Central and South-Eastern Europe and the Newly Independent States* (Vienna: International Helsinki Federation for Human Rights, 2000).

9. For most informative and critical analyses, see, for example, Hana Havelková and Mirek Vodráčka, eds., *Žena a muž v médiích* (Praha: Nadace Gender Studies, 1998); Libora Oates-Indruchová, "Gender v médiích: nástin žíče problematiky," in *Společnost mužů a žen z aspektu gender*, ed. Eva Věšínová-Kalivodová and Hana Maříková (Prague: Open Society Fund, 1999), 131–153.

10. All Czech commercials and billboards that appeared in the 1990s are catalogued in the archive of the Czech Advertisement Council (Rada pro reklamu České republiky) in Prague.

11. This correspondence, sent in April 2001, has been filed at the archive of the NGO Gender Studies, ops, and at the archive of the Gender in Sociology, a research team of the Institute of Sociology of Academy of Sciences of the Czech Republic, both in Prague.

12. For example, Iva Pekárková, "Americké lesbičky si pěstují bradku," *Rudé právo*, January 15, 1998; Milan Machovec, "Nezhloupnout psedoaktivitou," in *Feminismus devadesátých let češkěma očima*, ed. Maria Chříbková, Eva Klimentová and Josef Chuchma (Prague: One Woman Press, 1999), 234–241.

13. *Kodex české televize*. For an insightful and informative analysis of Czech TV after 1989 see, for example, Petr Pavlík and Peter Shields, "Toward an Explanation of Television Broadcast Restructuring in the Czech Republic," *European Journal of Communication* 14, no. 4 (1999): 487–524.

14. "Sex je náš, tak haraš!" Dokumentární pořad, Česká Televize 2001. I am

indebted to my colleague Petr Pavlik, with whom I co-teach gender studies courses at the Center for Gender Studies, for our endless discussions about gender and sexuality leading to these points.

15. See, for example, Milan Machovec, "Feminismus není problém jazykový," *Mladá Fronta Dnes*, November 23, 2000. For development and discussion of these ideas from a theoretical point of view in the context of various feminist schools of thought see, for example, Pam Morris, *Literature and Feminism* (London: Blackwell, 1993).

16. *Women 2000*, 150–152, §204, Trestního zákona České republiky. See also Gender in Sociology, eds., *Relations and Changes of Gender Differences in the Czech Society in the 1990s* (Prague: Institute of Sociology of Academy of Sciences of the Czech Republic, 2000).

17. *Peříčko* (*Little Feather*) is a weekly sex-talk show on the most-watched Czech TV channel, the private TV Nova.

18. §246, Trestního zákona České republiky.

19. Statistics of the Police Presidium, 1998, and Internal documents of the NGO LaStrada CR, ops. Both cited in *Women 2000*, 151 and 153.

20. *Regionální zpráva o institucionálních mechanismech pro zlepšení postavení žen v zemích střední a všchodní Evropy—Národní zpráva České republiky* (Praha: Centrum pro Gender Studies, 1998).

21. For a survey of reproductive policies in post-communist Europe, see *Women of the World: Laws and Policies Affecting Their Reproductive Lives—East Central Europe* (New York: Center for Reproductive Law and Policy, 2000).

22. See, for example, Eva Maleck-Lewy and Myra Marx Ferree, "Talking about Women and Wombs: The Discourse of Abortion and Reproductive Rights in the G.D.R. during and after the Wende," 92–118; Krassimira Daskalova, "Women's Problems, Women's Discourses in Bulgaria," 307–337; Eleonora Zielinska, "Between Ideology, Politics and Common Sense: The Discourse of Reproductive Rights in Poland," 23–58, all in Gal and Kligman, *Reproducing Gender.*

23. Sharon L. Wolchik, "Reproductive Policies in the Czech and Slovak Republics," in Gal and Kligman, *Reproducing Gender*, 58–92.

24. Already discussed earlier, these are mainly TV talk shows *Peříčko, Sauna, Trní,* and *Ážko* and tabloids such as *Blesk, Spy, Leo, Super,* etc.

25. For example, "Hlas sexuální menšiny" *Práce*, January 10, 1991; "Homosexualové chtějí změnu zákona," *Lidové noviny*, October 20, 1994; "Názor na partnerství homoseksualů rozdělil sněmovnu," *Lidové noviny*, March 23, 1998. Marek Benda, "Nutíte nás k nebezpečněm krokěm," *Mladá Fronta Dnes*, March 24, 1998. "Tollnerův věrok o homosexuálech zaskočil i lidovce," *Mladá Fronta Dnes*, April 3, 1999. Also, in one TV debate, the leader of KDU-ČSL and the vice-chairman of ODS, two oppositional parliamentary parties, laughed about their common rejection of the need for registered partnership: "See, there are some issues we fully agree on" (Sedmička, *TV Nova*, June 2001).

26. See, for example, Pavlína Janošová, *Homosexualita v názorech současné společnosti* (Praha: Karolinum, 2000); Dřamila Stehlíková, Ivo Procházka, Jiří Hromada, *Homosexualita, společnost a AIDS v ČR* (Praha: Orbis 1995); Jaroslava Talandová, *Sociální postavení lesbických žen: alternativní rodinné modely v kontextu heterosexualní společnosti* (Praha: Alia, 1998).

Věra Sokolová

27. Cited in Vladimír Ževela, Alena Plavcová, and Eva Hlinovská, "Ve světě českých gayů," *Lidové Noviny—Pátek*, April 4, 2001, 14. Janošová claims similar results in her own research; *Homosexualita v názorech současné společnosti*, 126.

28. *Homosexualita v názorech současné společnosti*, and, for example, Jana Holíková and Gabriel Sedlák, "Homosexuálové v politice nevadí dvěma třetinám občanů," *Lidové noviny*, June 6, 1999, 7. For the best treatment so far of the struggle to legalize registered partnership, see Andrea Baršová, "Partnerství gayů a lesbiček: kdy dozraje čas pro změnu?" *Sociální studia: Sborník prací Fakulty sociálních studií brněnské univerzity* 7 (2002): 173–185.

29. For example, Antonín Brzek and Jaroslava Pondžlíčková-Mašlová, *Třetí pohlaví?* (Praha: Scientia Medica, 1992); Ivo Procházka, *Coming Out: průvodce obdobím nejistoty, kdy kluci a holky hledají sami sebe* (Praha: SAP and SOHO, 1994); Jiří Fanel, *Gay historie* (Praha: Dauphin, 2000).

30. Karel Matys a kol., *Trestní zákon—komentář*, I. část, zvláštní 2. vydání (Prague: Ministerstvo spravedlnosti ČSSR, 1980), 734. Cited in Jan Kočela, "Homosexualita a její trestnost" (M.A. thesis, Universita Jana Evangelisty Purkyně, Právnická fakulta, Brno, 1981), 31.

31. Fanel, *Gay historie*, 434.

32. SOHO = Sdružení organizací homosexuálních občanů (Association of Organizations of Homosexual Citizens), the first contemporary official organization of gays and lesbians in Czechoslovakia (and later the Czech Republic) which was formed in 1990. In January 2001 SOHO changed its name to Gay Iniciativa.

33. See interview with the president of SOHO Jiří Hromada about SOHO's accomplishments in the first half of the 1990s, "Pacient s diagnózou 302.1 je zdráv," *Nedělní Lidové Noviny*, August 12, 1995, 2–3.

34. For example, Talandová, *Sociální postavení lesbických žen*, 9.

35. Arguably, this is caused mainly by the absence of meaningful gender and feminist discourse in the country that would supply the analytical and theoretical tools to argue efficiently against biological essentialism. As the emancipatory politics of homosexuality developed in the context of Czech antifeminism that has characterized the 1990s, so far they have not been able to use feminist arguments to their advantage.

36. Brzek and Pondžlíčková-Mašlová, *Třetí pohlaví*, 19.

37. Procházka, *Coming Out*, 8.

38. Fanel, *Gay historie*, 1.

39. For comprehensive discussion of the gay gene theory see, for example, Dean Hamer and Peter Copeland, *The Science of Desire: The Search for the Gay Gene and the Biology of Behavior* (New York: Simon and Schuster, 1994).

40. Brzek and Pondžlíčková-Mašlová, *Třetí pohlaví*, 4.

41. Procházka, *Coming Out*, 5.

42. For example Štefan Dubaj, "O postoji bratislavskej verejnosti k problematike homosexuality" (M.A. Thesis, Universita Komenského, Bratislava, 1994), 82–83.

43. "Aréna pro gaye," *Lidové noviny*, November 23, 1995, 5.

44. Tomáš Kvapil, "Zákon o partnerském soužití může ohrozit rodinu," *Lidové noviny*, March 20, 1999, 3.

45. See, for example, Marek Benda, "Když jde o gaye, nezná bratr bratra—a Marek Benda zase Jana Zahradila," *Mladá fronta Dnes*, March 20, 1999, 14; or Pavel Tollner, "Zákon počkozující rodinu," *Mladá fronta Dnes*, March 3, 2001, 7.

46. Of course, there are exceptions. See, for example, Mirek Vodráčka's *Esej o politickém harémismu: kritická zpráva o stavu feminismu v Čechách* (Brno: Nakladatelství Čestmír Kocar, 1999) and "Život mezi," *Gender, rovné příležitosti, vězkum 2,* no. 3 (2001): 3–6; Marcela Linková, "Je gender transsexuální?" paper presented at the Transgender Week conference, Institute of Sociology of Academy of Sciences of the Czech Republic, Prague, March 20, 2001, unpublished; Věra Sokolová, "Representations of Homosexuality and the Separation of Gender and Sexuality in the Czech Republic before and after 1989," in *Political Systems and Definitions of Gender Roles,* ed. Ann Katherine Isaacs (Pisa, Italy: Edizione Plus, Universita di Pisa, 2001), 273–290.

Afterword: From Big Brother to Big Burger (And What's the Grand Narrative Got to Do with It?)

"Benni Goodman"

To two pairs of arthritic legs

a nashta mûka nenapisana
sama v prostranstvoto shte skita.

—Nikola Vaptsarov

We tell stories because in the last analysis human lives need and merit being narrated. This remark takes on its full force when we refer to the necessity to save the history of the defeated and the lost. The whole history of suffering cries out for vengeance and calls for narrative.

—Paul Ricoeur

[T]hose things about which we cannot theorize, we must narrate.

—Umberto Eco

First PS, November 1996:
The Muse and the Grannie; the Communist Sausage;
Bracing Writing

Today, in the era of the Small Narratives, good academic taste dictates that we must commence every great revelation with a jazzy personal confession. For instance, if you want to coddle your reader, begin with something pure and innocent like your earliest memories of the Eucharist, describe the crumb quivering on the moustache of Uncle Ben, and then make an elegant transition toward your topic—*Hamlet* as a leftover tragedy. But if you scheme to scandalize the reader (you adore Dada and Derridada and suspect that the reader might be a prudish hypocrite), start by revealing your secret agony when you discovered the inevitability of pubic hair when you were barely eight, intertwine this pubic-cubic hair with nudity in Braque and Picasso, and launch a retributive attack à la Orlando Furioso at depilation as a misogynist construct. I presume that a paper whose theme is the invincibility of the Grand (Anti)Communist Narrative should also open with a series of touching and highly instructive Small Narratives that . . .

Ooops! I hear My Western Reader: "Define Small and Grand Narrative!"

"Do you remember Augustine? 'There are few things, in fact, which we state accurately; far more we express loosely, but what we mean is understood.' Isn't this odorous?"

"Jeez, I want to understand you really well! Dialogue, my friend, let's keep up our dialogue!"

First Small Narrative: In 1949, the first collection of poems by Valeri Petrov appeared, *Stikhotvoreniia (Poems)*. It ranks among the best in Bulgarian post–World War II poetry. But the book was castigated by the pseudo-Marxist critics for its lack of correct ideological views, intellectual individualism, petty-bourgeois and decadent sentiments, and formalism. At one point Petrov, an ardent communist himself, thought that he might really have been wrong and that his mentors might have been right. The poet's next two collections (1952 and 1954) testified to his honest efforts to conform to the literary standards of the time. In the first of these books, in the poem "Prosveta" ("Enlightenment"), he contrived the following memorable quatrain:

> Uchat redom baba s vnuche,
> uchi shloser mlad,
> i Chervenkov sûshto uchi
> Stalinov doklad.

> The grannie and her grandchild study side by side,
> A young mechanic studies,
> And Chervenkov also studies
> Stalin's report.

In 1952, Vûlko Chervenkov was the good guy—the general secretary of the Bulgarian Communist Party from 1952 to 1956; after that he became the bad guy—the initiator of a personality cult. Petrov masterfully suggests (I'd rather skip the close reading) that the grannie, the grandchild, and the mechanic study the same text as Comrade Chervenkov—the Grand Communist Narrative of *tovarishch* Stalin. (Poor Valeri! He satisfied his critics but not his Muse. He paid for the compromise with several years of artistic silence, restoring his artistic self-confidence.) The moral of this Small Communist Narrative is that the Grand Communist Narrative is protean and omnipresent, and even the best minds of the time are not immune from it. Therefore, rejoicings at the death of the Grand Communist Narrative along with the death of communism may turn out to be premature. Verily, verily, Valeri, Iosif Vissarionovich is dead, but his deeds live on!

Ooops, the Western Reader again: "In an anthology about the post-1989 era you speak of the post-1949 times?"

"Yeah, our Anthology:

> *Commu Nismo sat on the Wall,*
> *Commu Nismo had a great fall;*
> *And all Ph.D. experts, all the Ph.D. men*
> *Couldn't construe past/post Commu. Again.*

In November 1989, intoxicated by freedom and red wine in the center of Sofia, I thought that 1989 was a beginning. It took me years to realize, lulled on amber waves of grain, swinging like a rusty gate, that 1989 and post-1989 were but a continuation of 1949 and post-1949. To speak of the present is to remember the past. I'm an assiduous student of history, but I can't remember a single successful revolution. Revolutions explode in euphoria but expire in despair. I know, I know—the cadaver of the Grand Communist Narrative is very handy for scholarly dissection and makes fantastic fat-free, cholesterol-free, speech-free academic sausages. I'm nostalgic, though; I feel like resurrecting it. Isn't this odious?"

Second Small Narrative: In Bulgaria, immediately before the collapse of communism, the Grand Communist Narrative was seriously challenged by the Small Narratives in the spring of 1989, when some young intellectuals, through samizdat, started publishing their own magazines. The challenge, in spite of—or thanks to—its halo of heroism and martyrdom both in the eyes of the authors and their closest friends and only readers (besides the guys from the secret police, of course), seems downright comic today. Most of the good poems and articles published there had already appeared in the official literary journals, which in the years of glasnost opened their doors wide to innovative texts. The other contributions in the samizdat magazines were either by people suffering from graphorrhea or else by illustrious thinkers with Bulgarian names who had settled in Western Europe decades before. On the pages of the samizdat magazines, as if in a fool's paradise, Mr. Nobody Nobodev danced cheek to cheek with M. Tzvetan Todorov in a carnivalesque embrace. What made the samizdat magazines a cultural phenomenon was not their content but their mere existence. Freedom of speech in Bulgaria started not as freedom of saying but as freedom of speaking. The first moral of this second Small Narrative is that the Grand Communist Narrative, if we judge from the energy spent by the secret police in hunting down the authors and readers of the samizdat periodicals, when challenged for the first time, could be scared to death by the Small Narratives. However, the second moral, which will be disclosed in the final postscript, is that the Grand Narrative, in its wise adulthood, is not afraid of Small Narratives but lovingly proliferates them.

"I'm starting to enjoy your bracing writing . . ."

"When the secret police invited me to report on some samizdat colleagues of mine I went absolutely berserk: in a democratic paroxysm I explained to them that all men were born free and equal, and . . . and shitted in my pants. That was not fear, oh no, that was protest! 'Open the window, we need some bracing air,' said somebody in the room. Isn't this obstreperous?"

Third Small Narrative: Shortly before and shortly after the breakdown of the dirty communist system, everything in Bulgaria was political. Wives were leaving their husbands after forty years of happy marriage because they suddenly discovered that he was "red"—a communist and antidemocrat, whereas she was bluish if not absolutely "blue"—democratish and anticommunistish. (Bye-bye, Auntie Bonka! Uncle Petko gets drunk every evening, weeps, and swears at our sweet dawning democracy . . .) Immediately after 1989, public space was crammed with vociferous political commentators swarming into the media. Their divinations were in the genre of the Small Narrative and were short lived like the daily papers, which they inspired and where they expired. But on a beautiful day in 1994, as unexpectedly as they had fallen from power before, the communists unexpectedly came back to power as socialists who, in just a few years, had evolved into the biggest capitalists in the country. Why did the majority vote for the communists-socialists-capitalists—and not only in Bulgaria but also in the rest of the ex-communist countries? The Small Narratives of the political commentators (and the rococo-like diagrams of the Western experts on Eastern Europe that I later contemplated awestruck and soon after that started drawing myself) helplessly shrugged when they encountered the suicidal electoral preferences of the population.

In literature and culture, a similar paradox took shape. Post-communist literature started to be analyzed within the framework of postmodernism [sic] and postcolonialism [sick]—ah, this Latin prefix "post"! In the West, such scholarly ruminations became marketable (cf. "From Big Brother to Big Burger" by one Penny Goodman, Ph.D., a political swinging single and expert on postisms, baloneyisms, jive, jazz, and all that jazz). Nevertheless, within this paradigm, it is difficult to explain how the pauperized 80–95 percent of the population of the post-1989 Eastern European countries, struggling on a daily basis with the abdominal-visceral void, embraced the postmodern void (which is literally void) after living for decades within the communist void (modeled after the Platonic-Christian-romantic-modernist void, which presupposes a second, true Being either in the form of a "bright communist future" or a transcendental hyperouranic domain). The moral of the third Small Narrative is that the epistemological potential of the Small Narratives—in politics as well as in literary and cultural studies—is often small, and other approaches to post-communist realities must also be explored.

Second PS, December 1995:
Svetlana and Sauvignon; Hadj to Theory; *Die Geburt der Limerick*

In anno domini nineteen and ninety-one, on the thirtieth day of the merry month of May, around 5:37 P.M., while strolling with Svetlana in Sofia (at that time there was still no shooting in the streets, a glass of white wine was an affordable pleasure, and, what was most important, this was Svetlana's birthday), I concocted a naïve analogy between mythical cosmogony and communism. I improvised a jocular alternative to the limited epistemological capacity of the Small Narratives of the political and cultural analysts. (I like it when Svetlana laughs, you know, and she likes my fantastic fantasies, fantasias, and phantasmagorias, which are her birthday presents.) I felt that the miniatures of these experts were daubs lacking historical perspective and depth. The political soap opera of Auntie Bonka and Uncle Petko, the suicidal electoral choices, the meontic character of communist culture, even my hoax that you are reading now—all these pieces had to fit into the mosaic of the Grand Communist Narrative, we thought, fishing the fictitious bits of cork out of our fictitious glasses of Sauvignon.

I unfolded my argument as a sort of a footnote to Nietzsche, who, in *The Birth of Tragedy*, thinks that even the state does not know more powerful unwritten laws than the mythical foundation that guarantees its connections with religion, its growth on mythical notions. In this endeavor I was encouraged by Hayden White, who writes, "The very notions of explanation and enplotment [in Nietzsche] are dissolved; they give place to the notion of historical representation as pure story, fabulation, myth conceived as the verbal equivalent of the spirit of music." Between 5:37 and 8:12 P.M. on the thirtieth day of the merry month of May in the year of our Lord's Incarnation nineteen and ninety-one, the parallel between the communist state and the realm of myth, suggested by the German thinker, was so palpable, so much in the fragrant spring air and Svetlana's perfume, that I never bothered to ask myself about the methodological footing for viewing reality as a narrative. Unconsciously, I was following a major principle of phenomenological narratology, which, through Paul Ricoeur, pleads for "the precedence of narrative understanding over narratological rationality." Today, on the thirtieth day of the merry month of May in the Year of Grace nineteen and ninety-seven, at 11:34 A.M., the possibility of a relation between reality and narrative can be based, as the French philosopher suggests, on three theoretical premises. The first is mastery of the conceptual network of action, which means the achievement of practical understanding. The second anchorage of narrative composition in the practical understanding is the symbolism in the practical field. "If . . . human action can be narrated, it is because it is always already articulated by signs, rules, and norms. It is always already symbolically mediated."

The third feature of a preunderstanding of action is the temporal elements onto which narrative time bases its configuration: "in action [there are] temporal structures that call for narration."

Nietzsche and Ricoeur, therefore, provide a theoretical framework for interlacing narrative and praxis. The German philosopher suggests that practical reality grows on the basis of archetypal mythic narratives, whereas the French thinker argues that our praxis provides prefigured narrative patterns, which, through writing, become configured narratives, and finally, by means of reading, are transfigured into enriched praxis.

Once I have completed my hadj to the Kaaba of Theory, I feel free to return to my unenlightened groping on the thirtieth day of the merry month of May in the year of the Word made Incarnate nineteen and ninety-one, toward the Grand Communist Narrative and my half-empty glass of Sauvignon. (Sorry for the touch of dialectic, which may enrage the adherents of the Small Narratives but, good Lord, how can one discuss the Grand Narrative without dialectic?)

"Your subtitles are postscripts. Why?"

"We tell the biography of our ideas in the genre of the postscript. We don't rewrite an old text—we add a new one to it. The latter explains the former. Prospective traveling as a retrospective journey. Phenomenological Rückfrage, *if you like. Isn't this odysseyous?"*

But before continuing, I must define some of my main terms, you're right. (*My Western Reader pats me on the back.*) This explanation is true to the classics of Marxism-Leninism:

There lived a Reader in the West,
For whom communism
Meant both communism
And socialism.
But for me, one who has been barbecued in the hell of socialism,
Socialism
Is not communism.
Socialism
Is the first phase of communism,
Whereas communism
Is the second and true phase of communism.
Before falling, socialism
(i.e., communism, part I)
Had only reached the stage of "ripe" socialism,
Or, in other words, the phase of gradual transition from socialism
To communism.
The party that guides the building of socialism
Calls itself communist,
After the final goal of its destination—communism.

Logically, the party that buried Bulgarian socialism
Calls itself socialist
Because its final aim is civilized capitalism
Achieved through jungle capitalism.
Oh, poor Reader in the West!

Third PS, May 1991–May 1997:
Telescopes and Microscopes; the Non-Aristotelian Lizard's Plot;
Tears in the Ink; Is There Communism in This Anticommunism?

Succeeding in a single country, as Lenin predicted, socialism and the Communist Party that identifies itself with it and its state in reality takes on the role of the mythical culture hero and demiurge, a role which socialism and the Party before that have had only in potential—in the theories of the proletariat as a class-in-itself, which will become a class-for-itself. The culture hero and demiurge has two major functions: (i) that of a Supernatural Being and, (ii) that of a *Deus/Dea faber*.

(i) The culture hero is an omnipotent Supernatural Being who wrenches the cosmos, the universe, order from chaos, nothingness, and the primal void. He divides the firmament from the waters, orders the celestial bodies and the seasons, and creates the first men and women. With these cosmic activities the culture hero, historically and semantically, develops toward God as a creator (in the case of the undeveloped socialist countries, God who creates ex nihilo). (ii) The culture hero also teaches humans of crafts, hunting, and the arts, presents them with fire, the tools of labor, and cultivated plants; he or she regulates matrimonial rules, rituals, and holidays. With these craftsmanly and practical activities the culture hero acquires features of the epic hero. The Communist Party, when in power, and the socialist state proceed and mythologize themselves in the same two fashions. The first is ideal and changes reality by creating meanings. The second is material and transforms reality practically.

(i) The divine meanings in the cosmogony of the Communist Party are most perspicuous in the humanities. In philosophy and ideology, unsophisticated rationalism takes the upper hand and starts preaching social progress—in other words, changing reality according to a plan. In mythical terms, this means creating cosmos from chaos. Socialist realism as an artistic method stressing "the presentation of reality in its revolutionary development" (to refer to the famous definition coined at the First Congress of Soviet Writers in 1934—or thereabout; with age memory starts to fail me) is the aesthetic analogue of philosophical rationalism. The "positive hero" in Bulgarian socialist prose fiction and the narrative arts (cinema, theater, TV serials) exists in several variants emulating the roles of the Party as a culture hero. The character of the Party secretary and, later, in the 1970s and 1980s, of the intellectual who thinks about how "to mend the shortcomings and deformities of the System" (as the official criticism used to put it), are closest to the mythical god as an abstract force that creates in a magical way—ex nihilo or by word. The character of the engineer, the leader of a big socialist construction site, resembles the mythical craftsman. The socialist twins of Agent 007 remind one of the ingenious epic heroes who kill the chthonic—capitalist—monsters.

The generation of Bulgarian poets born around 1925–1935 is called the "April generation." This critical label connects these poets with the post-Chervenkovian era of Bulgarian socialism, which parallels the Soviet post-Stalinist "thaw": the Party plenum at which Chervenkov was replaced by Todor Zhivkov as a Party leader took place on April 4–6, 1956—or thereabout—did I mention supra that with age memory starts to fail me? See supra. Through these poets, the ordering spirit of the Party culminates in the domain of literature. They are the ones who, from the late 1940s to the mid 1960s, imposed the excavator and the hoist as the main lyrical heroes in Bulgarian poetry and who invented the entrancing rhyme, "concrete—ferroconcrete."

"Ha! Ha! Ha!"

"Well, this picture of socialist art is a caricature illustrating my thesis of the omnipotence of the Grand Communist Narrative. But isn't this thesis also yours?"

"???"

"Don't you equate socialist art with socialist realism? Don't you impose the Soviet model of socialist art and realism over the rest of the socialist cultures—the cultures of the 'Soviet satellites,' as you astronomically express yourself? Don't you comfortably live with works that fit in the paradigm of socialist realism in Western culture but condescendingly mock the same paradigm in non-Western art? Don't you think that in cultural studies one needs not only telescopes but also microscopes? Does the Big Bomb mean Big Culture?"

The paradox of the Grand Communist Narrative in art is that its consolidation is its disintegration. The supremacy of the Grand Narrative consists in its ontological priority to the Small Narratives: they need it in order to exist themselves. In this sense, the culture of "ripe" socialism (1970s–1980s) is split: the Small Narratives try to outwit the Grand Narrative. The outmaneuvering is allegorically coded: the work says "apple," but the reader or viewer understands "orange." The culture of "ripe" socialism is a secret alliance of the Author and the Perceiver against the Censor. This alliance presents itself as a collaboration with the Censor. The Small Narratives try to pass for the Grand Narrative. This hide-and-seek strategy provides the existential content of this art, the exhilarating blessedness of always living on the edge between being silenced by the censor and being heard by the clandestine ally. The fact that the Small Narratives live in the guise of the Grand Narrative explains why after 1989 Bulgarian art did not produce the Great Dissident Oeuvre out of the drawer: this Oeuvre had already been publicized as allegorical Small Narratives. The Eastern freedom of allegorical speech is the counterpart of the Western freedom of speech. Bulgarian poetry, prose fiction, drama, and cinema during socialism are not solely different expressions of the Grand Communist Narrative but also allegorical Small Narratives. Here, however, I want to illustrate my point by bestowing voice on the silent art of the visual images.

During early socialism in Bulgaria—from the mid-1940s to the mid-1960s—in painting, the still life and landscape, genres that follow nature too closely, are superseded by the industrial landscape where the struggle with nature is underscored. Still, in the 1960s and 1970s, socialist art, which is hostile to modernism in principle, sub rosa reinvents some of the tenets of Bauhaus in the architecture of Bulgarian Black Sea resorts, while the monuments of the national heroes and revolutionaries of that time remind one of the corpulent figures of Fernand Leger. In the 1970s and 1980s, the most resourceful and successful painters develop a style that is a hybrid of socialist themes and Western modernist modes of representation. The workers and peasants, for instance, are depicted in the fashion of Picasso's classical period from the early 1920s, or the industrial sites are painted with American abstract expressionism in mind. In the 1960s through the 1980s, the still life, the landscape, and private interiors are reintroduced under the guise of "chamber" art, a critical term of the time denoting more personal, even intimate, works using smaller canvas formats. The artist who wants to be officially noticed and praised executes a state commission and paints for the sanctioned exhibitions in the grand socialist style (the recognizable heroic typage and topic are a must), whereas at his one-man or smaller shows he exhibits "personal" views in the form of landscapes, still-life paintings, and female nudes in interior settings.

The syndrome of the late socialist artist as his own *Doppelgänger* culminated in the summer of 1989 in the case of Svetlin Rusev. Rusev started his career in the 1960s with impressive big-format works on historical and revolutionary subjects treated introspectively. By the 1980s, he had established himself as the most powerful figure in Bulgarian painting—not only through the quality of his art oriented both to official expectations (the large-scale paintings on heroic topics) and to connoisseurs ("chamber" art) but also through his key positions in the artistic and political hierarchy. In spite of that, in spring and summer of 1989, this pillar of the artistic orthodoxy confronted the communist dignitaries. A national campaign against Rusev was organized, he was kicked out of the Party, he lost most of his positions, and he fell into such disgrace that his colleagues were forced "from above" to convoke meetings and ostracize him unanimously. But his colleagues who feared him when he was on the top defended him when he fell to the bottom. Svetlin (this name means "light") began to shine with the halo of an anticommunist martyr. Question: How can this paradox of the tyrant who becomes a martyr be explained? Answer: by the double nature of late socialist culture. In the culture where the Grand Communist Narrative is pregnant with Small Communist Narratives, the Tyrants and paragons of socialist art are also the Martyrs and paragons of antisocialist art.

It is only a small step from the "ripe" socialist culture to post-communist culture—the Artist must contumeliously pretend or unfeignedly believe that he (or she or we or you or they or I) has never made Orthodox Art by his own will, that he was coerced for decades to paint or write this Bad Bad Bad Socialist Art, that he had been dragooned into holding cardinal artistic and political positions, that he was pressured to take the money for the state commissions and to indulge in the privileges of power. The plot of the triumphal birth of the Great Post-Communist Artist from the Great Late-Socialist Artist would have baffled Aristotle: the Martyr murders the Tyrant. The Small Narrative slays the Grand Communist Narrative. This plot was followed by most of the first-tier Bulgarian intellectuals who, by 1989, had established solid artistic and institutional résumés. Like lizards they bade their communist tails adieu and with dignity crawled into postcommunism.

"What about the younger intellectuals born from the 1940s to the 1960s?"

"I'm going to publish a separate article on that. I need publications for my vita, I need a job and tenure, you know. I'm wondering why I have put so many ideas in one single article instead of peddling them postscript by postscript . . ."

"Because you, the East-European intellectual, rave about the social mission of the writer. You write and cry; you mix the ink with tears. You put all your 35 years on 35 double-spaced pages, courier, and rise them in the sky as a holy gonfalon. You think that you'll be seen and heard. Wrong, buddy! Forget your mawkish East European naïveté and write not to be read but to be published. And, by the way, shorten your paper to 7,527 words and add a bibliography of some 40–50 titles."

By now even the apprentice in semiotic symbolism should have figured out that the difference between late communism and early postcommunism is one of nuances, not of essence, because the mentality and culture of these two allegedly polar eras are both forms of allegorical signification. (*Waiter, another bottle of wine, please, and no bits of cork this time! In Sauvignon veritas!*)

(ii) The second role of the Party, *Deus/Dea faber*—the creator in his form as a craftsman or artist—can be seen most clearly in the practical field. In the Party programs—the fairy-tale version of the Grand Communist Narrative—the economy is always thought of as developing at an accelerated pace and on a huge scale. In Bulgaria, Party leaders dream of building "the largest plant in the Balkan peninsula," while their Soviet magisters build industrial complexes that are "the biggest in the world." During socialism every city in Bulgaria acquires a badge of practical creativity, which, as a rule, is an industrial construction. In the ideal case, the human settlement is a workshop. Nikola Vaptsarov, a great poet who was shot by the fascists in 1943, by drawing on some modernist ideas, expresses this notion in the following way: "*Shte stroim zavod za zhivota!*" ("We will build a factory for life!"). In the 1950s, his poetic dream became a reality:

the industrial city of Dimitrovgrad (the City of Dimitrov) was built in the middle of the fertile Thrace Valley. In this unique case, the human settlement, industry, and the sacred name of Georgi Dimitrov, the hero from Leipzig in 1933 and the country's first communist leader, coincided.

Now, once we are done with the two major roles of the Party and the socialist state, let us turn to four bagatelles (*To your health, Svetlana! My God, time flies so fast when we're together . . .*): (i) the socialist cosmogony; (ii) the socialist organization of time; (iii) the socialist organization of space; and (iv) the post-communist peripeteia of (i), (ii), and (iii).

(i) Every myth tells how something came into existence. Cosmogony, which tells how the cosmos came into existence, enjoys particular prestige because the creation of the world precedes all others. This is why cosmogony is a model for all myths of origin. The major function of the myth is to provide exemplary models for all rites and all meaningful human activities. Hindu ritualists in "Sápatha Bra-hmana," for instance, say, "We must do what the gods did in the beginning." The "thaw" in the Soviet Union and Bulgaria in the late 1950s and the early 1960s and, later on, perestroika in the late 1980s, can be viewed as Marxism-Leninism forced to return to its origins, to repeat the exemplary creation of the "true and pure Marxism-Leninism." By reciting myths or, as in the case of perestroika, by incessantly quoting Marx, Engels, and Lenin as *tovarishch*/Mr. Gorbachev did, one in a way becomes "contemporary" with the events that are evoked, shares in the presence of Gods and Heroes—that is, of the "classics of scientific communism."

(ii) The sacred time of myth is the time when the Event—the creation of cosmos—took place for the first time. Socialism invents its own calendar. The axial moment in it, the moment in reference to which every other event is dated, is the point when the Communist Party comes to power. This is also the sacred temporal point in the new calendar and the new national holiday. This holiday is a ritual repetition, a relearning of the creation myth of socialism.

(iii) The center of mythical space is the Temple, the man-made cosmic mountain, the navel of the world from which creation started; the Temple stands for the life principle in its fundamental level. The axial point in the socialist space is the Party House or the Party Palace in the center of the capital. It imitates and supersedes the former national center: the national cathedral. In the exemplary case, the new sacred center coincides with the traditional one—the Palace of Congresses in the midst of the Kremlin churches in Moscow. The urban architecture of socialism in many respects rests on this spatial narrative. The Party House in Sofia epitomizing the urban thinking of early socialism emulates the basic characteristics of the national cathedral St. Alexandûr Nevski, which stands five or six hundred yards from it: the orientation East-West, the tripartite vertical structure symbolizing the three dimensions of the cosmic mountain—the chthonic, the human, and the divine—and a "face" that, when one nears it, rises as a cosmic mountain. The organization of the whole public space follows similar principles. Every city and village, every office and classroom have their own sacred centers: the local Party House, the monument of the local communist heroes, and the portrait of the Party Leader.

In late or "ripe" socialism (*Svetlana: "Ripe for rape! . . ."*), the second urban center of Sofia became the People's Palace of Culture (opened in 1981), based on opposite architectural principles: open straight-line park spaces in the central part (implying continuity with the straight Party line) but closed curved-line park spaces on several levels in the periphery (implying the Party's maneuvers in deferring the arrival of communism; the recognition of a certain privacy and opacity in the lives of the socialist subjects). The building lacks a "face"; it does not rise like a cosmic mountain but respects the mountain of Vitosha behind it (one of the initial projects was for a high edifice that would have hidden Vitosha). The interior is subdivided into numerous seemingly disorderly scattered secluded spaces (cf. the "chamber" art). The walls are covered with frescoes and tapestry, and they revive the Romantic spirit of empathy through art (cf. the intimate interiors).

(cccxxxviii) (*Svetlana, we're running out of time, and I jazzed my story up. I must have skipped some numbers. . . . Can you follow me?*) Without bearing in mind the cosmogonical and the temporal-spatial aspects of the Grand Communist Narrative, it is impossible to understand what happened after 1989. The most notable and noticeable change in the temporal sphere is the return of the precommunist national holiday, March 3rd, the day on which the third Bulgarian state was officially born in 1878 after the liberation from the Ottoman yoke (1396–1878). September 9th, the day when Bulgaria overthrew fascism under the "leadership of the Communist Party and with the decisive help of the Red Army"—to employ the formula of pre-1989 history textbooks—which during socialism was the national holiday now remains a holiday solely for leftists (who, in recent years, are more and more ashamed to celebrate their victory over fascism).

The most grandiose expression of the temporal shifts is the resurgence of old—and often obsolete—values immediately after 1989. In the early 1990s, politicians emerged with speeches spelled as if the orthographic reform in 1945 had never taken place. After a short spell of political sentimentalism, these jazzbos sank back into oblivion. But before that their ideas, smelling of mothballs, fueled the initial triumph and collapse of the newly hatched Bulgarian democracy. When the first democratic and anticommunist Parliament and government of the SDS (the Union of the Democratic Forces) took power in 1991, its activity was guided by nostalgic appetites. Their main exploit was restitution for property lost under socialism by a small bunch of former real-estate owners. The hopes for a large-scale positive change were dashed and the SDS ignobly lost power, while the socialists (the former communists) took over.

The Socialist/Communist Party itself was torn apart between the past and the future. The first act of its rejuvenation was a reverential excursion in its own past. The Party excoriated its communist skin and started radiating the primal beauty of socialist—even social-democratic!—ideals as they were (ostensibly) formulated at its founding congress in 1891. Between 1990 and 1994, several factions existed in the Party, which veiled the struggle for power within the Party with the democratic principle of "free debate." Early in 1994, the three major factions published drafts for a new Party program that was to be compiled from the best of every draft (*Svetlana: "How?"*). That was the unmistakable syndrome of the nostalgia for the Grand Communist Narrative that now, the socialists thought, could be created not autocratically "from above" but democratically "from below" (*Svetlana: "Yeah, right!"*). The project of the first faction, the pragmatic majority of seasoned aparatchiks, was a highbrow rigmarole of leftist slogans spelled out with rightist phraseology borrowed from the West. Its authors were scholars in the Party's Center for Strategic Research. (No wonder; the head of the Center was the same *sapientisimus vir* who authored the Party program documents before 1989. His transition from "ripe" socialism to postcommunism also followed the plot of the lizard.) In the first draft, the catchword was "relative." The document "scientifically" predicted that Bulgarian capitalism would have a human socialist face—another Party limerick. The second faction, the minority of idealistic intellectuals attracted to politics by the noble cause of instructing and leading the nation in times of trouble, offered a draft whose pivot was "dialectic." It enacted *post factum* the spirit of Soviet perestroika. (Zhivkov ruled from 1956 to 1989, and this explains why in Bulgaria there was no perestroika in the Soviet sense—perestroika presupposes a change of Leader. In Bulgaria, the plot of the lizard was the rule. Zhivkov erected his own monument in the early 1980s as well as a monument to *tovarishch* Brezhnev, but when Gorbachov came to power the sly Bulgarian leader dismounted his and Brezhnev's monuments. The monuments, like the lizard's tail and tale, were guilty for the "aberrations" from the "true" principles of communism. Cut off the tail, retell the tale, destroy the monument, and rule as a reborn post-communist leader! In memoirs published in 1997, shortly before he passed away in 1998, Zhivkov reveals that from the very start of his rule he knew that Marxism was nonsense but had no other choice but to keep silent. Thus, the epiphany of the venerable fighter for the ultimate triumph of communism all over the globe illuminates the peculiarity of Bulgarian Marxism: it was not of the ilk of Karl, but of Groucho!) The third faction, a cohort still living in the olden days, stuck to the formula of "class struggle." This draft prophesied that the future battle against Bulgarian capitalism and world imperialism would be a resplendent repetition of the past victories of the proletariat. The drafts were Small Narratives, and no amount of spunk under the sun was able to lump them together in a new Grand Party Narrative. When the first faction regained power in 1994, the program project was abandoned.

During socialism and immediately after 1989, the past was also yearned for as the time of true spirituality—only in times of atheism does religion have a virtual numinous aura. The Patriarch was condemned as a communist collaborator, and a group of high clergy proclaimed themselves the new Holy Synod unmarred by the communist leprosy. For the first time in more than eleven centuries of Christianity, Bulgaria had two Orthodox churches. By that time industrial output had decreased by 50 percent compared with 1989 but the number of the Patriarchs had increased by 100 percent—an optimistic index of spiritual growth. The battle for the true faith took place in the center of Sofia. The holy fathers of Synod A, with white beards flying in the air, led a gang of (brandy-) intoxicated believers against their opponents barricaded in their headquarters across the square. Half an hour later, the holy fathers from Synod B, with white beards flying in the air, counterattacked and dragged the loot (inkpots, candles, saucepans, etc.) back into their fortress. (The precious icons and goblets were smuggled out of the country by naughty parishioners for hard currency.)

"*And I stood in the middle of the square, but I beheld no seven angels with seven trumpets, only seven paparazzi from seven tabloids. And no mountain or island was moved out of their places, only an hundred and forty and four thousand children were dancing with the Californian missionaries, and were singing with a loud voice: 'O Lord, I love you, ye-e-e-e-e-e-eah!'* "

In the spatial domain, the battle with the Grand Communist Narrative was even more spectacular. First, the sacred urban center of Sofia was switched from Ninth of September Square, which is in front of Dimitrov's mausoleum, back to the square around the national cathedral, St. Alexandûr Nevski—the meetings of the SDS started and still take place there, whereas the socialists prefer to meet in the park of the People's (now renamed National) Palace of Culture, the epitome of "ripe" socialism.

Next, in August 1990, the Party House was set on fire in mysterious circumstances. In the mutual accusations between the socialists/communists and the anticommunists/democrats ("red" references to the fire in the Reichstag in 1933 and "blue" retorts alluding to the Molotov-Ribentrop pact in 1939), nobody perceived that this was a symbolic incineration of the previous temple of national life. Soon after that the Party House, the People's Palace of Culture, and the mausoleum lost their sacred status. The armed guards—together with Dimitrov's mummy—disappeared. The white limestone walls of the mausoleum were covered with motley inscriptions, the wittiest of which read, "This is the largest public shitter [*kenef*] in the Balkan peninsula." In the late 1990s, the mausoleum was blown up: Boom! BOOOMM! BOOOOOMMMM!!!! The Party House, a phoenix bearing the scars of the fire, became a place where grannies and their grandchildren watched Disney movies and drank Pepsi. The Palace of Culture, in good biblical tradition, was flooded by merchants of suspicious goods from the neighboring Balkan countries. Ninth of September Square, a pedestrian mall until 1989, was turned into a parking lot by the first SDS mayor of Sofia. The portraits of the forever-young frowning Party Leaders were superseded by posters of forever-healthy macho cowboys smoking "ONLY MARLBORO" and forever-happy negligée gals who "NEVER SUFFER CONSTIPATION, WOW!" From Big Brother to Big Burger!

Third, all monuments—socialist and presocialist—were also profaned. Memorials were ruined by angry democrats, by smart gypsies earning a buck by selling the head or the arm of a bronze hero for recycling, or by studious teenagers exercising their English by writing with spray cans on the granite, "FUCK OFF!!!!"

"BLEEP!!!!"

"In the beginning of postcommunism was the English Word, and the English Word was not the To-Be-or-Not-to-Be Word or the Declaration-of-Independence Word, but the Four-Letter Word. I, the English Tutor, am guilty for the fact that my Bulgarian students learned what a Big Mac is but didn't learn what teamwork is; I am guilty for the fact that my students learned where Palm Beach is but didn't learn where Silicon Valley is; I am guilty for the fact that my students learned who Michael Jackson is but didn't learn who Abraham Lincoln is. All farces of History are my fault!"

The Grand Communist Narrative struck back as a Grand Anticommunist Narrative. As Marx (Karl, but why not Groucho as well?) used to say, atheism is a negative repetition of religion.

Fourth PS, May 1992–April 1997:
The Dinosaur as the Doubting Thomas; the Empty Glass;
Everlasting Camaraderie

It would have been wonderful if the cosmogony of the Communist Party and the socialist state had perished together with the social and political reality that gave birth to it and to which, reciprocally, it gave birth. Alas, the postcommunist man continues to be a captive of this myth even when the socialist reality is no longer real. This man cannot distinguish between the cosmos of the Communist Party and the cosmos in general. The principle of his thinking is *pars pro toto*—he believes that the Part(y) is the whole. For the socialist man, the Party is the cosmos and the cosmos is the Party. That is why when the Good Party Leader passes away, the tears of his socialist subjects give birth to rivers deeper than the Nile. And, conversely, when the Bad Party Leader falls from power—like Stalin, Brezhnev, or Ceauşescu—this automatically becomes a social revolution. In both cases, what passes away is not the concrete person but the Party, its order, its cosmos. This explains why the socialist man has an apocalyptic vision of social change: the fall from power of the Communist Party is not thought of as a catastrophe solely of the Party's cosmos—which is one of the many possible cosmoses—but the end of the cosmos as such, *the* Apocalypse.

The myth of the Communist Party as a culture hero sanctifies the triangle Leader-Party-Cosmos, and it turns its three constituents into complete synonyms. This tripartite unity is the last, but most powerful, lever through which the communist or the reformed Socialist Party controls the ex-socialist man. In Bulgaria, immediately after the fall of Zhivkov on November 10, 1989, the general secretary of the Party and chairman of the State Council—while the communists were still in power, however—Party propaganda threatened that if the Party fell from power, there would inevitably be a civil war.

The myth of the Party as a culture hero, when taken as "true," is the dinosaur decease of the ex-socialist man. But this man is also a doubting Thomas: he must see with his own eyes the new nonsocialist cosmos in order to be convinced that, besides the cosmos of the Communist Party and state, there are other possible cosmoses. The problem with the new cosmoses in the ex-socialist countries is that they are carnivalesque, reversed, oxymoronic, and unconvincing qua cosmoses. (The German term for the transition from socialism to postcommunism and from DDR to DBR—*die Wende*—is an excellent expression of this new carnivalesque cosmos.) Because of this the socialist parties, which generously promise "capitalism with a human face"—the ideological counterpart of the perestroika slogans of "socialism with a human face"—are back in power after a short spell of democratic rule in the early 1990s. (*Svetlana: "These dudes swing both ways!"*) The nostalgia for the communist cosmogony is a hermeneutic paradox: in his future, the ex-socialist man sees only his prejudices from the past, that is to say he perceives his new capitalist cosmos as his old socialist cosmos. The outcome of this dinosaur schizophrenia is a dinosaur outcome.

"I emptied my glass, Svetlana paid the bill, and we rushed to her place. Our flesh shivered under the burden of urgent questions. . . ."

"Jeez, now I understand you really well! Dialogue, my friend, let's keep up our dialogue! So you were jazzed to jazz him?"

"Uh . . . Svetlana is . . . is a woman, you know . . ."

"Oh, I missed that. . . . Sorry . . ."

The Grand Communist Narrative struck back. As they say, to repeat is to negate oneself. From 1994 to 1997, the socialists/communists irrevocably ruined Bulgaria and their backers, the good old doubting Thomases, started to die of malnutrition, exhaustion, lack of affordable medical help, and despair. Why do the scientists still iterate that they have but hypotheses about the extinction of the dinosaurs?

"Hello, Svetlana. . . . No, I'm not in Sofia . . . from Swingville . . . America, America . . . And how are your parents? . . . Yes, I sent them the medicine . . . of course I remember the faded ink inscription on the yellowish inch-square photograph that we, in our indecent curiosity, discovered in the wallet of your father: 'To comrade Rasho—a sign of everlasting camaraderie. His comrade Liuba. September 9, 1944.' Kiss Auntie Liuba and Uncle Rasho for me! . . . No, not "miss" but "kiss"! . . . Yes, yes, I sent you Songs for Swingin' Lovers. . . . Svetlana, dear, Slûnchitse . . . Operator! Operator!! Damn it! . . ."

Fifth PS, March 1997:
The Russian Renaissance; Divine and Demoniacal
Commercials; 100,001 Dalmocratians

Soliloquy of the pious and holy Maximus the Greek on his deathbed written down by his humble pupil Big Bando of Clarinetburgh, a wretched sinner and a man of little understanding: "And when I, as a young man, arrived in Muscovy from Constantinople that had fallen to the pagan Turks for its sins, the Grand Prince Ivan III invited me to his palace. And he asked me, 'What is going on in the world?' And I told him, 'The earth is round, and a man named Columbus has discovered America.' The Grand Prince didn't believe me, and Metropolitan Macarius condemned me as a heretic. And I was chained and exiled to the Volokolam Monastery. And I wrote a letter of repentance, and Macarius allowed me to return to Moscow. The Russians wore animal skins and didn't know Greek. And I decided to enlighten them, and I learned Church Slavonic and wrote many books in their own language. And Macarius said to me, 'You have trans-lated the Psalms from Greek into Church Slavonic wrongly!' And he condemned me. And they put fetters on my ankles and sent me to Tver'. And I again repented in a letter and was allowed to come back to Moscow. And there I wrote many books on Slavic grammar. The Russians didn't know anything about pleophony, and used to say gorod *and* golova *instead of* grad *and* glava. *And Macarius blamed me, 'You don't know South Slavic. The South Slavs write* gorod *and* golova *just as the Russians do.' And this time I was exiled farther North. And I repented and returned to Moscow. And there I organized the first press in Russia, and when Macarius saw the first printed book he sniffed it in horror and said, 'This thing smells of sulfur, it is the work of Satan!' And the machines were burned down, and they put shackles on me again, and sent me still farther North where there were no men but only wild beasts and the things and places didn't have names. And I ate bark from the trees. And one day I was very lucky and killed a beast for food and in its belly I found a piece of parchment, and it read, ' "Recite in the name of Thy Lord who created." He heard this and ran to Khadija crying in horror, "Cover me, hold me, hide me—" ' What was this? For the first time in my life I didn't know something. And I scraped the strange words off the parchment. And the ink was frozen and I wrote a letter to Macarius with my blood on the piece of parchment. And he pardoned me, and I came back to Moscow, and this time I organized the first Censorship for the Grand Prince. (And later the sons of the censors became the first Oprichniks of the great tsar Ivan the Terrible, God bless him!) And then Macarius and I collected in the twelve books of the Great Menology all the knowledge of the world and wrote that the earth was flat. And then we wrote* The Book of Degrees, *and portrayed all Muscovite Princes as men full of 'virtues pleasing the Lord.' And we burned the heretic books that stated otherwise and ordered the tongues of the unbelievers to be cut off and thrown to the dogs. And the chronicler of the Grand Prince wrote, 'And the Renaissance commenced in Russia. Maximus the Greek brought it from Florence where he burnt Girolamo Savonarola at the stake.' And my letters of repentance were collected, and I became the inventor of the epistolary genre in Russian literature. And at the top was the letter I wrote on the strange parchment. And I said to myself, beating my golova against the wall: 'Maximus, Maximus, why don't you forget your ornate and convoluted hypotaxis? This is the speech of Satan! Start expressing yourself simply and in parataxis as in* The Primary Chronicle*!' And I stopped dreaming of the iridescent firmament of Athos, and the gray sky of Moscow became much sweeter to my heart. And the epiphany of old age enlightened the blindness of my youth. And I'm so grateful to die here praising the Lord. Glory be to God. Into Thy hands, oh Lord, I commit my spirit. Amen."*

Recently I showed my American students a Bulgarian film about a sculptor in the 1960s whose artistic career and personal life were ruined by a political joke. During our discussion, quite predictably, the students reiterated that the central issue in the movie was the lack of freedom of speech and expression under communism. I asked them whether they had seen any TV commercials. The answer, predictably again, was affirmative. We sketched the communicative models in a society where freedom of speech reigns and in a society where censorship reigns. On the right half of the blackboard we drew people with mouths but no ears. On the left we portrayed people with ears but no mouths. Freedom of speech versus freedom of hearing. In my pedagogic inexperience, I started pleading that if in the beginning was the Word, and the Word was with God, and the Word was God, this might have happened only on the left side of the blackboard. Had the Word been with God on the right side, in the next commercial Satan would have appeared with Another Word, most probably about the Deluge, promising to amend God's Imperfect Creation from the previous commercial—in a mere forty days, guaranteed!

The Small Narrative is a narrative born in the milieu of freedom of speech. Its final goal is to be heard and recognized among a multitude of other competitive Small Narratives. This is why its slogan is "political correctness." Every Small Narrative is centripetally oriented—it is obsessed only with itself, and thus it does not threaten the status quo. Conversely, the Grand Narrative exists in the realm of freedom of hearing. Its ultimate aim is not to hear another Grand Narrative, because this is the end of both Grand Narratives. This is why its slogan is "political erectness." The Grand Narrative is centrifugal, it envelops in its network the whole of social reality, and in this way it constitutes the status quo.

But the Grand Narrative and the Small Narratives are not absolute opposites. In both the postindustrial and the post-communist world, the Grand Narrative and the Small Narratives live in peaceful symbiosis. In the postindustrial world, the Small Narratives seem not to frighten the Grand Narrative of those in whose safes and computers the real power resides. The Small

Narratives—through committees, institutions, foundations, departments, publishing houses, TV stations—are bred, multiplied, reproduced, propagated, procreated, proliferated, spawned, cloned, and clowned. In my third postscript, I suggested that the Small Narratives in "ripe" socialism try to pass for the Grand Communist Narrative by means of elaborate allegorical techniques. Conversely, the Grand Postindustrial Narrative tries to pass for Small Narratives through intricate sponsoring techniques.

When one enters a postindustrial country, he or she is kindly invited to fill out a special form at the airport. Side A explains that everybody—no matter what one's racial, sexual, ethnic, gender, etc. characteristics (i.e., no matter what one's Small Narrative)—is welcome. On side B the visitor is warned that the entrance of members of a Communist Party is forbidden (no smugglers of a Second Grand Narrative, please!).

One hot-blooded Bulgarian democrat visited the postindustrial world in order to specialize in social and political sciences. As a studious novice, he began his education at the airport by carefully reading the aforementioned form and taking copious notes. After his specialization, the democrat returned to Bulgaria and applied his Western expertise there. Through certain complicated legal procedures he proved that the Socialist/Communist Party was, in fact, illegal because it had never been properly founded in 1891. Therefore, this Party had never existed at all. Alas, the enthusiastic apprentice of democracy and analytic philosophy was too late in his struggle against the Grand Communist Narrative. In the post-communist world, the Grand (Anti)Communist Narrative, nurtured by the deep social practices and traditions and hidden by multitudinous bubbly Small Narratives, was already ruling in the guise of a socialist-capitalist-criminal-democratic social order. The fellowship of the Bulgarian democrat was for only two years of foreign study—a period too short to learn that a Grand Narrative cannot be superseded by Small Narratives but only by Another Grand Narrative (*hélas*, professeur Jean François!).

"*So what has been going on in Bulgaria since 1989?*"

"*I'd like someone to ask me what's been going on in the Bulgarians since 1989. Kierkegaard used to say that in Hegel's system there was a place for everything but the individual. Sartre, following in Kierkegaard's wake, grafted existentialism onto Marxism to make the latter truly human. Vaptsarov, in the early 1940s, addressed History in this way:*

> Shte khvanesh konturite samo,
> a vûtre, znam, shte bûde prazno
> i niama nikoi da razkazva
> za prostata choveshka drama. . . .
> a nashta mûka nenapisana
> sama v prostranstvoto shte skita.

> You will sketch only the contours
> But inside, I know, will be empty

"Benni Goodman"

> And nobody will narrate
> The simple human drama. . . .
> And our unwritten suffering
> Will wander alone in space.

One day in January 1997, the major American papers had stories about Bulgaria on their front pages: the streets of Sofia were filled with hungry and angry people clattering pots and pans, the socialist/communist rulers were agonizing, democracy was advancing with flying banners, history was being made in this Balkan and Balkanized corner of the Earth. A week later I received a short letter from my parents, with no jazz. 'Dear son,' they wrote, 'today we were at the meeting in Alexandûr Nevski Square. There were many beautiful speeches. At the end, the leader of the democratic opposition said, "Those of you who refuse to jump are communists!" And 100,000 people started jumping for five minutes. We didn't jump. We are well and hope that you are well, too. And don't write too much, spare your eyes. Kisses, Mom and Dad.' I'm sure that had my old-fashioned parents known what performance art meant, they too would have jumped like two young gazelles on their arthritic legs. What would you do, my Western Reader, my democratic Bruder *who swing impeccably in all sort of performances and jog five miles a day, if you were in the square?"*

Swingville, 1990–1997

NOTE

"Benni Goodman" is Tisskett Yellowbasskett Professor in the Humanities at Swingville University. He is author of *Sing, Sing, Sing: Bulgarian Wines in the Wake of Deconstruction* (1993), *And the Angels Sing: A Hermeneutics of Shopski Salad and Slivovica* (1996), and *The King of Swing: Feta Cheese Metaphysics in South-Eastern Europe* (2000). He is now editing a major international project, entitled *Eastern Europe from a Sheraton Window: The Institution of the Expert from Plato to Derrida.*

Selected Bibliography

Akhavan, Payam, and Robert Howse, eds. *Yugoslavia, the Former and Future: Reflections by Scholars from the Region.* Washington, D.C.: The Brookings Insitution, 1995.

Aleksievich, Svetlana. *Voices from Chernobyl: Chronicle of the Future.* London: Aurum Press, 1999.

———. *Zinky Boys: Soviet Voices from the Afghanistan War* New York: W.W. Norton & Co., 1992.

Allain, Paul. "Coming Home: The New Ecology of the Gardzienice Theatre Association of Poland." *The Drama Review* 39, no. 1 (Spring 1995): 93–121.

Åman, Anders. *Architecture and Ideology in Eastern Europe during the Stalin Era: An Aspect of Cold War History.* New York: The Architectural History Foundation, and Cambridge, Mass., and London: MIT Press, 1992.

Andor, Laszlo, and Martin Summers. *Market Failure: Easter Europe's "Economic Miracle."* London: Pluto Press, 1998.

Anzulovic, Branimir. *Heavenly Serbia: From Myth to Genocide.* New York: New York University Press, 1999.

Applebaum, Anne. *Between East and West: Across the Borderlands of Europe.* New York: Pantheon Books, 1994.

Apter, Emily. "Balkan Babel: Translation Zones, Military Zones." *Public Culture* 13, no. 1 (2001).

Ash, Timothy Garton, Ralf Dahrendorf, Richard Davy, and Elizabeth Winter, eds. *Freedom for Publishing, Publishing for Freedom: The Central and East European Publishing Project.* Budapest: Central European University Press, 1996.

Aslund, Anders. *How Russia Became a Market Economy.* Washington, D.C.: The Brookings Institution, 1995.

Babb, Roger. Review of *Metamorphoses, or the Golden Ass,* by Gardzienice. *Theatre Journal* 53, no. 4 (December 2001): 657–659.

Bach, Jonathan. " 'The Taste Remains': Consumption, (N)ostalgia, and the Production of East Germany." *Public Culture* 14, no. 3 (2002).

Baniewicz, Elżbieta. "Theatre's Lean Years in Free Poland." Trans. Joanna Dutkiewicz. *Theatre Journal* 48, no. 4 (December 1996): 461–478.

Barker, Adele Marie, ed. *Consuming Russia: Popular Culture, Sex, and Society since Gorbachev.* Durham, N.C.: Duke University Press, 1999.

Baldwin, James. "Notes for a Hypothetical Novel." In *Nobody Knows My Name: More Notes of a Native Son.* New York: Dell, 1961.

———. "Princes and Powers." In *Nobody Knows My Name: More Notes of a Native Son.* New York: Dell, 1961.

Baršová, Andrea. "Partnerství gayů a lesbiček: kdy dozraje čas pro změnu?" *Sociální studia: Sborník prací Fakulty sociálních studií brněnské univerzity* 7 (2002): 173–185.

Barthes, Roland. *Empire of Signs.* Trans. Richard Howard. London: Jonathan Cape, 1982.

Bartlett, Roger, and Karen Schönwälder, eds. *The German Lands and Eastern Europe.* New York: St. Martin's Press, 1999.

Bartosiewicz, Dariusz. "Nadwiślański cud biblioteczny." *Magazyn Budowalny* (July 1999): 16–21

Baudrillard, Jean. *The Illusion of the End.* Trans. Chris Turner. Stanford, Calif.: Stanford University Press, 1994.

Bell, David Scott, ed. *Western European Communists and the Collapse of Communism.* New York and London: Berg Publishers, 1993.

Bell, John D. *Bulgaria in Transition: Politics, Economics, Society, and Culture after Communism.* Boulder, Colo.: Westview Press, 1998.

Benda, Marek. "Nutíte nás k nebezpečněm krokěm." *Mladá Fronta Dnes*, March 24, 1998.

Berdahl, Daphne. *Where the World Ended: Re-unification and Identity in the German Borderland.* Berkeley: University of California Press, 1999.

Berns, M. "The Role of English in Europe: EIL or EFL?" Paper presented at the Conference on World Englishes Today, Urbana, Ill., April 1992.

Bergquist, William H, ed. *Freedom! Narratives of Change in Hungary and Estonia.* San Francisco: Jossey-Bass Publishers, 1994.

Bernhard, Michael H., and Henryk Szlajfer, eds. *From the Polish Underground: Selections from Krytyka, 1978–1993.* Trans. Chmiliewska Szlajfer. University Park: Pennsylvania State University Press, 1995.

Berry, Ellen E., and Anesa Miller-Pogacar, eds. *Re-entering the Sign: Articulating New Russian Culture.* Ann Arbor: University of Michigan Press, 1995.

Bhabha, Homi K. *The Location of Culture.* London and New York: Routledge, 1994.

——, ed. *Nation and Narration.* New York: Routledge, 1991.

Bianchini, Stefano, and George Schöpflin, eds. *State Building in the Balkans: Dilemmas on the Eve of the 21st Century.* Ravenna: Longo Editore, 1998.

Blaut, J. M. *The Colonizer's Model of the World: Geographical Diffusionism and Eurocentric History.* New York: Guilford Press, 1993.

Błoński, Jan. "The Poor Poles Look at the Ghetto." 1987. Reprinted in *Four Decades of Polish Essays,* ed. Jan Kott, 222–235. Evanston: Northwestern University Press, 1990.

Bobinski, Christopher. "Warsaw Is Acknowledging Its Jewish Past." *The Financial Times London*, September 27, 1997, 22.

Bollerup, Soren Rinder, ed. *Nationalism in Eastern Europe: Causes and Consequences of the National Revivals and Conflicts in Late 20th-Century Eastern Europe.* New York: St Martin's Press, 1997.

Bonnell, Victoria E., ed. *Identities in Transition: Eastern Europe and Russia after the Collapse of Communism.* Berkeley: University of California Regents, 1996.

Boone, Peter, Stanislaw Gomulka, and Richard Layard, eds. *Emerging from Communism: Lessons from Russia, China, and Eastern Europe.* Boston: MIT Press, 1998.

Borenstein, Eliot. "About That: Deploying and Deploring Sex in Postsoviet Russia." *Studies in XX Century Literature* (Winter 2000).

——. *Men without Women: Masculinity and Revolution in Russian Fiction, 1917–1929.* Durham, N.C., and London: Duke University Press, 2000.

——. "Was It Sexy or Just Soviet? The Post-Communist Expat Safari Novel Has Its Day." *The Nation*, February 3, 2003, 33–36.

Borkowska, Grażyna, Małgorzata Czermińska, and Ursula Phillips. *Pisarki polskie od średniowiecza do współczesności: Przewodnik.* Gdańsk: słowo/obraz terytoria, 2000.

Boym, Svetlana, *Common Places: Mythologies of Everyday Life in Russia.* Cambridge, Mass.: Harvard University Press, 1995.

———. *The Future of Nostalgia.* New York: Basic Books, 2001.

Bozóki, András. *Intellectuals and Politics in Central Europe.* Budapest: Central European University Press, 1999.

Braidotti, Rosi. *Nomadic Subjects: Embodiment and Sexual Difference in Contemporary Feminist Theory.* New York: Columbia University Press, 1994.

"The Brand Is a Piece of East Germany." *Horizont. Zeitung für Marketing, Werbung und Medien* 44 (November 1, 1991).

Braun, Kazimierz. *A History of Polish Theater, 1939–1989: Spheres of Captivity and Freedom.* Westport, Conn.: Greenwood Press, 1996.

Bringa, Tone. *Being Muslim the Bosnian Way: Identity and Community in a Central Bosnian Village.* Princeton, N.J.: Princeton University Press, 1996.

Bronner, Stephen Eric. *Rosa Luxemburg: A Revolutionary for Our Times.* University Park: Pennsylvania State University Press, 1997.

Brydon, Diana, ed. *Postcolonialism: Critical Concepts in Literary and Cultural Studies.* New York: Routledge, 2000

Buchanan, Donna. "Bulgaria's Magical *Mystère* Tour: Postmodernism, World Music Marketing, and Political Change in Eastern Europe." *Ethnomusicology* 41, no. 1 (1997): 131–157.

———. "Dispelling the Mystery: The Commodification of Women and Musical Tradition in the Marketing of Le Mystère des Voix Bulgares." *Balkanistica* 9 (1996): 193–210.

———. "Metaphors of Power, Metaphors of Truth: The Politics of Music Professionalism in Bulgarian Folk Orchestras." *Ethnomusicology* 39, no. 3 (1995): 381–416.

Buchli, Victor. *An Archaeology of Socialism.* Oxford: Oxford University Press, 1999.

Bunce, Valerie. *Subversive Institutions: The Design and the Destruction of Socialism and the State.* Cambridge: Cambridge University Press, 1999.

Burawoy, Michael, and Katherine Verdery, eds. *Uncertain Transition: Ethnographies of Change in the Postsocialist World.* Lanham, Md.: Rowman & Littlefield Publishers, 1999.

Burgess, Adam. *Dividing Europe: The Culture of Moral Superiority.* London: Pluto Press, 1998.

Busheikin, Laura. "Is Sisterhood Really Global? Western Feminism in Eastern Europe." In *Ana's Land: Sisterhood in Eastern Europe,* ed. Tanya Renne, 12–21. Boulder, Colo.: Westview Press, 1997.

Campbell, David. *National Deconstruction.* Minneapolis: University of Minnesota Press, 1998.

Chambers, Ian. *Border Dialogues: Journeys in Postmodernity.* New York: Routledge, 1990.

Chatterjee, Partha. *The Nation and Its Fragments: Colonial and Postcolonial Histories.* Princeton, N.J.: Princeton University Press, 1993.

Chernetsky, Vitaly. "Opening the Floodgates: The New Ukrainian Writing." *The Slavic and East European Journal* 41, no. 4 (Winter 1997): 674–677.

Chester, Pamela, and Sibelan Forrester, eds. *Engendering Slavic Literatures.* Bloomington: Indiana University Press, 1996.

Selected Bibliography

Cioffi, Kathleen M. *Alternative Theatre in Poland, 1954–1989*. Amsterdam: Harwood Academic Publishers, 1996.

Cohen, Israel. *Vilna*. Jewish Communities Series. Philadelphia: Jewish Publication Society, 1992.

Colton, Timothy J., and Robert Legvold, eds. *After the Soviet Union: From Empire to Nations*. New York: W.W. Norton & Co., 1992.

Condee, Nancy, Evgeny Dobrenko, and Marina Balina, eds. *Endquote: Sots-Art and the Dilemma of Post-Soviet Literature*. Evanston, Ill.: Northwestern University Press, 2000.

Condee, Nancy, ed. *Soviet Hieroglyphics: Visual Culture in Late Twentieth-Century Russia*. Bloomington: Indiana University Press, 1995.

Corrin, Chris, ed. *Gender and Identity in Central and Eastern Europe*. London and Portland, Ore.: Frank Cass, 1999.

Cote, Kevin. "East Germans Return to Familiar Brands." *Advertising Age*, September 30, 1991.

Crawley, David. "People's Warsaw, Popular Warsaw." *Journal of Design History* 10, no. 2 (1997): 206.

Crowley, D., and S. E. Reid, eds. *Socialist Spaces: Sites of Everyday Life in the Eastern Bloc*. Oxford: Oxford University Press, 2001.

Cushman, Thomas. *Notes from the Underground: Rock Music Counterculture in Russia*. New York: State University of New York Press, 1995.

Cubilié, Anne. "Cosmopolitanism as Resistance: Fragmented Identities, Women's Testimonials and the War in Yugoslavia." In *Critical Ethics: Text, Theory, Responsibility*, ed. Dominic Rainsford and Tim Woods. London and New York: Macmillan and St. Martin's Press, 1999.

Czerny, Jochen, ed. *Wer war Wer—DDR. Ein biographisches Lexikon*. Berlin: Ch. Links Verlag, 1992.

Daskalova, Krassimira. "Women's Problems, Women's Discourses in Bulgaria." In *Reproducing Gender: Politics, Publics, and Everyday Life after Socialism*, ed. Susan Gal and Gail Kligman, 337–369. Princeton, N.J.: Princeton University Press, 2000.

Dawidowicz, Lucy S., ed. *The Golden Tradition: Jewish Life and Thought in Eastern Europe*. Syracuse: Syracuse University Press, 1996.

Deleuze, Gilles, and Félix Guattari. *Kafka: Toward a Minor Literature*. Trans. Dana Polan. Minneapolis: University of Minnesota Press, 1986.

Demetz, Peter. *Prague in Black and Gold: Scenes from the Life of a European City*. New York: Hill & Wang Publishing, 1998.

Diesener, Gerald, and Rainer Gries, eds. *Propaganda in Deutschland. Politische Massenbeeinflussung im 20. Jahrhundert*. Darmstadt: Wissenschaftliche Buchgesellschaft, 1996.

Dionne, Claude, Silvestra Mariniello, and Walter Moser. *Recyclages: Économies de l'appropriation culturelle*. Montréal: L'Univers des discours, 1996.

Domanski, Henryk. *On the Verge of Convergence: Social Stratification in Eastern Europe*. New York: Central European University Press, 2000.

Domizlaff, Hans. *Die Gewinnung des öffentlichen Vertrauens. Ein Lehrbuch der Markentechnik. Neu zusammengestellte Ausgabe*. 1939/1940; reprint, Hamburg: Verlag Marketing Journal, 1992.

Draitser, Emil A. *Taking Penguins to the Movies: Ethnic Humor in Russia.* Detroit: Wayne State University Press, 1998.

Drakulić, Slavenka. *Café Europa: Life after Communism.* New York: Penguin, 1996.

———. *How We Survived Communism and Even Laughed.* New York: Harper Perennial, 1993.

Drury, J. "Pre-service English Teacher Training in Poland: The Need, the Demand and the Supply." In *Directions towards 2000: Guidelines for the Teaching of English in Poland,* ed. C. Gough & A. Jankowska, 39–45. Poznań: Instytut Filologii Angielskiej, UAM, 1993.

Dubaj, Štefan. "O postoji bratislavskej verejnosti k problematike homosexuality." M.A. thesis, Universita Komenského, Bratislava, 1994.

Edelman, Marek. "The Ghetto Fights." In *The Warsaw Ghetto: Das Warschauer Ghetto,* designed and produced by Bożena and Marek Potyralscy. Warsaw: Drukarnia Naukowo-Techniczna, n.d.

Edwards, Ivana. "Constructing a New Czech Republic," *Metropolis* 15 (May 1996): 109–109, 113, 115, 117.

Einhorn, Barbara. *Cinderella Goes to Market: Citizenship, Gender and Women's Movements in East Central Europe.* London: Verso, 1993.

Elias, Norbert. *Studien ueber die Deutschen.* Frankfurt/Main: Suhrkamp Verlag, 1989.

Elster, Jon, ed. *The Roundtable Talks and the Breakdown of Communism.* Chicago: University of Chicago Press, 1996.

Elster, Jon, Claus Offe, and Ulrich K. Preuss. *Institutional Design in Post-communist Societies: Rebuilding the Ship at Sea.* Cambridge: Cambridge University Press, 1998.

Engelstein, Laura. "Culture, Culture Everywhere: Interpretations of Modern Russia, across the 1991 Divide." *Kritika* 2, no. 2 (2001): 363–393.

Enloe, Cynthia. *The Morning After: Sexual Politics at the End of the Cold War.* Berkeley: University of California Press, 1993.

Erlmann, Veit. "The Aesthetics of the Global Imagination: Reflections on World Music in the 1990s." *Public Culture* 8, no. 3 (1996): 467–487.

Epstein, Mikhail, Aleksandr Genis, and Slobodanka Vladiv-Glover. *Russian Postmodernism: New Perspectives on Post-Soviet Culture.* New York: Berghahn Books, 1999.

Esbenshade, Richard S. "Remembering to Forget: Memory, History, National Identity in Postwar East-Central Europe." *Representations* (Winter 1995): 72–90.

Eyal, Gil, Ivan Szelenyi, and Eleanor R. Yownsley. *Making Capitalism without Capitalists: The New Ruling Elites in Eastern Europe.* London: Verso Books, 1999.

Fanel, Jiří. *Gay historie.* Praha: Dauphin, 2000.

Fanon, Franz. *Black Skin, White Masks.* Trans. Charles Lam Markmann. New York: Pluto Press, 1986.

Faraday, George. *Revolt of the Filmmakers.* University Park: Pennsylvania State University Press, 2000.

Feld, Steven. "From Schizophonia to Schismogenesis: On the Discourses and Commodification Practices of 'World Music' and 'World Beat.'" In *Music Grooves,* ed. Charles Keil and Steven Feld, 257–289. Chicago: University of Chicago Press, 1994.

Feldman, Jan. *Lubavitchers as Citizens: A Paradox of Liberal Democracy.* Ithaca, N.Y.: Cornell University Press, 2003.

Ferguson, Russell, Marthe Gever, Trinh T. Minh-ha, and Cornel West, eds. *Marginalization and Contemporary Cultures*. New York and Cambridge, Mass.: The New Museum of Contemporary Art and MIT Press, 1990.

Filipowicz, Halina. "Expedition into Culture: The Gardzienice (Poland)." *The Drama Review* 27, no. 1 (Spring 1983): 54–71.

———. "Gardzienice: A Polish Expedition to Baltimore." *The Drama Review* 31, no. 1 (Spring 1987): 137–163.

———. *A Laboratory of Impure Forms: The Plays of Tadeusz Różewicz*. New York: Greenwood Press, 1991

———. "Othering the Kościuszko Uprising: Women as Problem in Polish Insurgent Discourse." In *Studies in Language, Literature, and Cultural Mythology in Poland: Investigating "The Other,"* ed. Elwira M. Grossman, 55–83. Lewiston, Maine: Edwin Mellen Press, 2002.

———. "Polish Theatre after Solidarity: A Challenging Text." *TDR: The Drama Review—A Journal of Performance Studies* 36, no. 1 (Spring 1992): 70–89.

Fink, Hermann, and Liane Fijas. *America and Her Influence upon the Language and Culture of Post-Socialist Countries*. Frankfurt am Main and New York: Peter Lang, 1998.

Fisiak, J. "Training English Language Teachers in Poland: Recent Reform and Its Future Prospects." In *Directions towards 2000: Guidelines for the Teaching of English in Poland*, ed. C. Gough & A. Jankowska, 7–15. Poznan: Instytut Filologii Angielskiej, UAM, 1994.

FitzGerald, Nora. "In Warsaw, a Jewish Street Reborn." *The Washington Post*, July 13, 1999, C1, C8.

Friedman, Susan Stanford. "'Beyond' Gynocriticism and Gynesis: The Geographics of Identity and the Future of Feminist Criticism." *Tulsa Studies in Women's Literature* 15, no. 1 (Spring 1996): 13–40.

Fritze, Lothar. "Identifikation mit dem gelebten Leben—Gibt es DDR-Nostalgie in den neuen Bundesländern?" In *Das wiedervereinigte Deutschland. Zwischenbilanz und Perspektiven*, ed. Ralf Altenhof and Eckard Jesse. Munich: Bayerische Landeszentrale für politische Bildungsarbeit, 1995.

Frojimovics, Kinga, and Geza Komoroczy, eds. *Jewish Budapest: Memories, Rites, History*. Budapest: Central European University Press, 1999.

Funk, Nanette, and Magda Mueller, eds. *Gender Politics and Post-Communism: Reflections from Eastern Europe and the Former Soviet Union*. New York: Routledge, 1993.

Fuszara, Małgorzata. "New Gender Relations in Poland in the 1990s." In *Reproducing Gender: Politics, Publics, and Everyday Life after Socialism*, ed. Susan Gal and Gail Kligman, 259–285. Princeton, N.J.: Princeton University Press, 2000.

Gaddis, John Lewis. *The United States and the End of the Cold War: Implications, Reconsiderations, Provocations*. New York and Oxford: Oxford University Press, 1992.

Gal, Susan, and Gail Kligman. *The Politics of Gender after Socialism*. Princeton, N.J.: Princeton University Press, 2000.

———. *Reproducing Gender: Politics, Publics, and Everyday Life after Socialism*. Princeton, N.J.: Princeton University Press, 2000.

Gapova, Elena. "On Nation, Gender and Class Formation in Belarus . . . and Elsewhere in the Post-Soviet World." *Nationalities Papers* 30, no. 4 (2002): 639–662.

Gates, Henry Louis, Jr. "Good-Bye Columbus? Notes on the Culture of Criticism." In *Multiculturalism: A Critical Reader*, ed. David Theo Goldberg. Oxford: Basil Blackwell, 1994.

Gates, Henry Louis, Jr., ed. *"Race," Writing, and Difference*. Chicago: University of Chicago Press, 1986.

Gender in Sociology, eds. *Relations and Changes of Gender Differences in the Czech Society in the 1990s*. Prague: Institute of Sociology of the Academy of Sciences of the Czech Republic, 2000.

Gensicke, Thomas. *Mentalitätsentwicklung im Osten Deutschlands seit den 70er Jahren. Vorstellung und Erläuterung von Ergebnissen einiger empirischer Untersuchungen in der DDR und in den neuen Bundesländern von 1977 bis 1991*. Speyer: Forschungsinstitut für Öffentliche Verwaltung bei der Hochschule für Verwaltungswissenschaften, 1992.

Gerzova, Jana. *Ladislav Carny: Pictures Objects Installations*. Zilina: Museum of Art, 1995.

Geyer-Ryan, Helga. "Imaginary Identity: Space, Gender, Nation." In *Vision in Context: Historical and Contemporary Perspectives on Sight*, ed. Teresa Brennan and Martin Jay, 117–126. New York: Routledge, 1996.

Gibas, Monika, and Rainer Gries. "'Vorschlag für den Ersten Mai: die Führung zieht am Volk vorbei!' Überlegungen zur Geschichte der Tribüne in der DDR." *Deutschland Archiv* 5 (1995): 481–494.

Gibas, Monika, Rainer Gries, Barbara Jakoby, and Doris Mueller, eds. *Wiedergeburten. Zur Geschichte des runden Jahrstage der DDR*. Leipzig: Leipziger Universitätsverlag, 1999.

Gilman, Sander L. "Ethnicity-Ethnicities-Literature-Literatures." *PMLA* 113, no. 1 (January 1998): 19–27.

Gilroy, Paul. *Against Race: Imagining Political Culture beyond the Color Line*. Cambridge, Mass.: The Belknap Press of Harvard University Press, 2000.

———. *The Black Atlantic: Modernity and Double Consciousness*. Cambridge, Mass.: Harvard University Press, 1993.

———. *"There Ain't No Black in the Union Jack": The Cultural Politics of Race and Nation*. Chicago: University of Chicago Press, 1991.

Gizycki, Marcin. "Splendid Artists: Central and East-European Women Animators." *Animation World Magazine* 1, no. 2 (1996).

Gladsky, Thomas, and Rita Gladsky, ed. *Something of My Very Own to Say: American Women Writers of Polish Descent*. New York: Columbia University Press, 1997.

Glenn, Charles L. *Educational Freedom in Eastern Europe*. Washington, D.C.: Cato Institute, 1995.

Gołaczyńska, Magdalena. "The Alternative Theatre in Poland since 1989." Trans. Marcin Wąsiel. *New Theatre Quarterly* 17, no. 2 (May 2001): 186–194.

Goldberg, David Theo, ed. "Multicultural Conditions." In *Multiculturalism: A Critical Reader*, 1–44. Oxford: Basil Blackwell, 1994.

Goldfarb, Jeffrey. *After the Fall: The Pursuit of Democracy in Central Europe*. New York: Basic Books, 1992.

———. *Beyond Glasnost: The Post-Totalitarian Mind*. Chicago: University of Chicago Press, 1989.

———. *Civility and Subversion: The Intellectual in Democratic Society*. London and New York: Cambridge University Press, 1998.

———. *On Cultural Freedom: An Exploration of Public Life in Poland and America.* Chicago: University of Chicago Press, 1982.

Goldsworthy, Vesna. *Inventing Ruritania: The Imperialism of the Imagination.* New Haven, Conn.: Yale University Press, 1998.

Goldzamt, Edmund. *Architektura zespołów śródmiejskich i problemy dziedzictwa.* Warszawa: Panstwowe Wydawnictwo Naukowe, 1956.

Goodman, Walter. "Upheaval in the East: TV Critic's Notebook; Television Has Become a Weapon in Panama and Romania." *New York Times,* December 26, 1989, A18.

Gordiejew, Paul Benjamin. *Voices of Yugoslav Jewry.* New York: State University of New York Press, 1998.

Gorsuch, Anne E. "Women's Autobiographical Narratives: Soviet Presentations of Self." *Kritika* 2, no. 4 (Fall 2001).

Goscilo, Helena. *Dehexing Sex: Russian Womanhood during and after Glasnost.* Ann Arbor: University of Michigan Press, 1996.

Goujon, Alexandra. "Language, Nationalism, and Populism in Belarus." *Nationalities Papers* 27, no. 4 (1999): 661–677.

Grant, Bruce. "New Moscow Monuments, or, States of Innocence." *American Ethnologist* 28, no. 2 (2001): 332–362.

Gray, Rockwell. "Travel." In *Temperamental Journeys: Essays on the Modern Literature of Travel,* ed. Michael Kowalewski, 33–52. Athens and London: University of Georgia Press, 1992.

Greskovits, Béla. *The Political Economy of Protest and Patience.* Budapest: Central European University Press, 1998.

Gries, Rainer. "Der Geschmack der Heimat. Bausteine zu einer Mentalitätsgeschichte der Ostprodukte nach der Wende." *Deutschland Archiv* 10 (1994): 1041–1058.

———. "Nostalgie—Legende—Zukunft? Geschichtskultur und Produktkultur in Ostdeutschland." *Universitas. Zeitschrift für interdisziplinäre Wissenschaft* 51, no. 2 (1996): 102–115.

Gries, Rainer, Volker Ilgen, and Dirk Schindelbeck. *Gestylte Geschichte. Vom alltäglichen Umgang mit Geschichtsbildern.* Münster: Verlag Westfälisches Dampfboot, 1989.

Gries, Rainer, and Silke Satjukow, eds. *Sozialistische Helden. Eine Kulturgeschichte von Propagandafiguren in Osteuropa und der DDR.* Berlin: Ch. Links Verlag, 2002.

Grois, Boris. *The Total Art of Stalinism: Avant-Garde, Aesthetic Dictatorship, and Beyond.* Princeton, N.J.: Princeton University Press, 1992.

Gross, Jan Tomasz. *Neighbors: The Destruction of the Jewish Community in Jedwabne, Poland.* Princeton, N.J.: Princeton University Press, 2001.

Grossman, Elwira M., ed. *Examining the "Other" in Polish Culture: Studies in Language, Literature, and Cultural Mythology.* Ceredigion, UK: Edwin Mellen Press, 2000.

Grosz, Elizabeth. "Bodies-Cities." In *Sexuality and Space,* ed. Beatriz Colomina, 242–243. New York: Princeton Architectural Press, 1992.

Gruber, Ruth Ellen. *Upon the Doorposts of Thy House: Jewish Life in East-Central Europe, Yesterday and Today.* New York: John Wiley and Sons, 1994.

Grynberg, Henryk. *Children of Zion.* Trans. by Jacqueline Mitchell. Evanston, Ill.: Northwestern University Press, 1998.

Gueorguieva, Tsvetana. "Bulgarians between East and West." In *The Balkans: National Identities in a Historical Perspective*, ed. Stafano Bianchini e Marco Dogo. Ravenna: Longo Editore, 1998.

Günther, Cordula. "'Praesent 20.' Der Stoff aus dem die Träume sind." *Universitas. Zeitschrift für interdisziplinäre Wissenschaft* 51, no. 2 (1999): 116–126.

Gutschow, Niels, and Barbara Klain. *Zagłada i utopia. Urbanistyka Warszawy w latach 1939–1945. Vernichtung und Utopie. Stadtplanung Warschau 1938–1945.* Frankfurt/Main and Warsaw: Deutscher Werkbund e.V., Muzeum Historyczne m.st. Warszawy, 1995.

Hadas, Miklos, and Miklos Voros, eds. *Replika* Special Issue—*Colonization or Partnership? Eastern Europe and Western Social Science.* Budapest, 1996.

Hall, Stuart, David Morley, and Kuan-Hsing Chen, eds. *Critical Dialogues in Cultural Studies.* London and New York: Routledge, 1996.

———. "Cultural Studies and Its Theoretical Legacies." In *Cultural Studies*, ed. Lawrence Grossberg, Cary Nelson, Paula A. Treichler, 277–94. New York: Routledge, 1992.

Hann, Chris. "Nationalism and Civil Society in Central Europe: From Ruritania to the Carpathian Euroregion." In *The State of the Nation: Ernest Gellner and the Theory of Nationalism*, ed. John Hall. Cambridge: Cambridge University Press, 1998.

Harasym, Sarah, ed. *Gayatri Chakravorty Spivak: The Post-Colonial Critic—Interviews, Strategies, Dialogues.* New York: Routledge, 1990.

Hardtwig, Wolfgang. *Geschichtskultur und Wissenschaft.* Munich: dtv, 1990.

Haug, W. F. *Critique of Commodity Aesthetics.* Minneapolis: University of Minnesota Press, 1986.

Havelková, Hana. "Abstract Citizenship? Women and Power in the Czech Republic." *Social Politics* (Summer/Fall 1996): 243–260.

———. "Transitory and Persistent Differences: Feminism East and West." In *Transitions, Environments, Translations: Feminisms in International Politics*, ed. Joan Scott, Cora Kaplan, and Debra Keates, 56–64. New York: Routledge, 1997.

———. "Women in and after a 'Classless' Society." In *Women and Social Class: International Feminist Perspectives*, ed. Christine Zmroczek and Pat Mahony, 69–84. London: UCL Press, 1999.

Havelková, Hana, and Mirek Vodráčka, eds. *Žena a muž v médiích.* Praha: Nadace Gender Studies, 1998.

Hawkesworth, Celia, ed. *A History of Central European Women's Writing.* Basingstoke and New York: Palgrave, 2001.

Herling-Grudzinski, Gustaw. *Dziennik pisany nocą, 1989–1992 (Daybook Written at Night, 1989–1992).* Warszawa: Czytelnik, 1993.

Heschel, Abraham Joshua. *The Earth Is the Lord's: The Inner World of the Jew in Eastern Europe.* Woodstock, Vt.: Jewish Lights Publications, 1995.

Higley, John, Jan Pakulski, and Wlodzimir Wesolowski, eds. *Postcommunist Elites and Democracy in Eastern Europe.* New York: St. Martin's Press, 1998.

Hodge, R., and G. Kress. *Language as Ideology.* 2nd ed. London: Routledge, 1993.

Hoffman, Eva. *Exit into History: A Journey through the New Eastern Europe.* London: Minerva, 1994.

———. *Lost in Translation: A Life in a New Language.* New York: Penguin, 1989.

———. *Shtetl: The Life and Death of a Small Town and the World of Polish Jews.* New York: Houghton-Mifflin, 1997.

Selected Bibliography

Holíková, Jana, and Gabriel Sedlák. "Homosexuálové v politice nevadí dvěma třetinám občanů." *Lidové noviny,* June 6, 1999.

Holmes, Leslie. *Post-Communism: An Introduction.* Durham, N.C.: Duke University Press, 1997.

Holy, Ladislav. *The Little Czech and the Great Czech Nation: National Identity and the Post-Communist Transformation of Society.* Cambridge and New York: Cambridge University Press, 1996.

hooks, bell. *Outlaw Culture: Resisting Representations.* New York: Routledge, 1994.

Hoptman, Laura J. *Beyond Belief: Contemporary Art from East Central Europe.* Chicago: Museum of Contemporary Art, 1995.

———. "Seeing Is Believing." In *Beyond Belief: Contemporary Art from East Central Europe,* 1–15. Chicago: Chicago Museum of Contemporary Art, 1995.

Hroch, Jaroslav, David Hollan, and George F. McLean, eds. *National, Cultural, and Ethnic Identities: Harmony beyond Conflict.* Washington, D.C.: Council for Research in Values and Philosophy, 1998.

Huggan, Graham. "Decolonizing the Map." In *The Post-Colonial Studies Reader,* ed. Bill Ashcroft, Gareth Griffiths, and Helen Tifflin. New York: Routledge, 1995.

Iordanova, Dina. *Cinema of Flames: Balkan Film, Culture and the Media.* London: British Film Institute, 2001.

Jahnert, Gabriele, Jana Gohrisch, Daphne Hahn, Hildegard Maria Nickel, Iris Peinl, and Katrin Schafgen, eds. *Gender in Transition in Eastern and Central Europe Proceedings.* Berlin: Trafo Verlag, 2001.

Jameson, Frederic. *Postmodernism; or, The Cultural Logic of Late Capitalism.* Durham, N.C.: Duke University Press, 1991.

Janos, Andrew C. *East Central Europe in the Modern World: The Politics of the Borderlands from Pre- to Postcommunism.* Stanford, Calif.: Stanford University Press, 2000.

Janošová, Pavlína. *Homosexualita v názorech současné společnosti.* Praha: Karolinum, 2000.

Jaquette, Jane S., and Sharon L. Wolchik, eds. *Women and Democracy: Latin America and Central and Eastern Europe.* Baltimore: Johns Hopkins University Press, 1998.

Johnston, Bill. "The Expatriate Teacher as Postmodern Paladin." *Research in the Teaching of English* 34 (1999): 255–280.

Judah, Timothy. *The Serbs: History, Myth and the Destruction of Yugoslavia.* New Haven, Conn.: Yale University Press, 1997.

Kaplan, Robert D. *Balkan Ghosts: A Journey through History.* New York: Vintage Books, 1994.

———. "The Fulcrum of Europe." *The Atlantic Monthly,* September 1998, 28–36.

Kaufman, Jonathan. *A Hole in the Heart of the World: Being Jewish in Eastern Europe.* New York: Viking Penguin, 1997.

Keefer, Janice Kulyk. *Honey and Ashes: A Story of Family.* Toronto: Harpercollins Canada, 1998.

Keen, Sam. *Faces of the Enemy: Reflections of the Hostile Imagination.* San Francisco: Harper, 1986.

Kelly, Catriona, and David Shepherd, eds. *Russian Cultural Studies: An Introduction.* Oxford and New York: Oxford University Press, 1998.

Kennedy, Michael D. *Cultural Formations of Postcommunism: Emancipation, Transition, Nation, and War.* Minneapolis: University of Minnesota Press, 2002.

———. *Envisioning Eastern Europe: Postcommunist Cultural Studies.* Ann Arbor: University of Michigan Press, 1994.

Kinzer, Stephen. "In 'East Germany,' Bad Ol' Days Now Look Good." *The New York Times,* August 27, 1994.

Kirschbaum, Stanislav J., ed. *Historical Reflections on Central Europe: Selected Papers from the Fifth World Congress of Central and East European Studies, Warsaw, 1995.* New York: St. Martin's Press, 1999.

Kisielewski, Stefan. *Wołanie na puszczy. Pisma wybrane.* Warszawa: Iskry, 1997.

Kligman, Gail. *The Politics of Duplicity: Controlling Reproduction in Ceauşescu's Romania.* Berkeley: University of California Press, 1998.

———. *The Wedding of the Dead.* Berkeley: University of California Press, 1988.

Klíma, Ivan. "The Spirit of Prague." In *The Spirit of Prague and Other Essays.* New York: Granta, 1994.

Kočela, Jan. "Homosexualita a její trestnost." M.A. thesis, Universita Jana Evangelisty Purkyňů, Právnická fakulta, Brno, 1981.

Kohrt, Wolfgang. "A Personal Sip." *Die Zeit Magazin* 31 (July 30, 1993): 22–25.

Konrad, Gyorgy. *The Melancholy of Rebirth: Essays from Post-Communist Central Europe, 1989–1994.* New York: Harcourt Brace, 1995.

Kopecky, Petr, and Cas Mudde, eds. *Uncivil Society? Contentious Politics in Post-Communist Europe.* London: Routledge, 2002.

Kott, Jan. *Still Alive: An Autobiographical Essay.* Trans. Jadwiga Kosicka. New Haven, Conn.: Yale University Press, 1994.

Krainak, Paul. "Siting Slavs at the Factory." *New Art Examiner,* March 1996.

Krajewski, Stanislaw. *Żydzi, Judaizm, Polska (Jews, Judaism, Poland).* Warszawa: Oficyna Wydawnicza "Vocatio," 1997.

Kristeva, Julia. "Bulgaria, My Suffering." In Julia Kristeva, *Crisis of the European Subject.* Trans. Susan Fairfield. New York: Other Press, 2000.

———. *Nations without Nationalism.* Trans. Leon S. Roudiez. New York: Columbia University Press, 1993.

———. *New Maladies of the Soul.* Trans. Ross Guberman. New York: Columbia University Press, 1995.

———. *Possessions: A Novel.* Trans. Barbara Bray. New York: Columbia University Press, 1998.

———. *Strangers to Ourselves.* Trans. Leon S. Roudiez. New York: Columbia University Press, 1991.

Kritika: Explorations in Russian and Eurasian History. Special issue: *Negotiating Cultural Upheavals: Cultural Politics and Memory in 20th-Century Russia.* 2, no. 3 (Summer 2001).

Kuncewicz, Maria. Letter to Hugh McLean, April 4, 1969. Private collection.

Kuncewiczowa, Maria. *Dyliżans warszawski (Warsaw Stagecoach).* Warszawa: Instytut Wydawniczy Pax, 1997.

Kundera, Milan. "The Tragedy of Central Europe." *New York Review of Books,* April 26, 1984.

Kuperhand, Miriam, Saul Kuperhand, and Alan Adelson. *Shadows of Treblinka.* Champaign: University of Illinois Press, 1998.

Kurkela, Vesa. "Deregulation of Popular Music in the European Post-Communist Countries: Business Identity and Cultural Collage." *The World of Music* 35, no. 3 (1993): 80–106.

Kurti, Laszlo, and Juliet Langman, eds. *Beyond Borders: Remaking Cultural Identities in the New East and Central Europe.* Boulder, Colo.: Westview Press, 1997.

Kvapil, Tomáš. "Zákon o partnerském soužití může ohrozit rodinu." *Lidové noviny,* March 20, 1999.

Laitin, David D. *Identity in Formation: The Russian-Speaking Populations in the Near Abroad.* Ithaca, N.Y.: Cornell University Press, 1998.

Larsen, Susan. "Melodramatic Masculinity, National Identity, and the Stalinist Past in Postsoviet Cinema." *Studies in XX Century Literature* (Winter 2000).

Lazari, Andrzei. "Contemporary Russian Nationalism and the Idea of a Rule-of-Law State." *Vostochnaia Evropa: politicheskii i socio-kul'turny vybor* 3–4 (1994).

Ledeneva, Alena. *Russia's Economy of Favors: Blat, Networking and Informal Exchange.* New York and London: Cambridge University Press, 1998.

Lederhandler, Eli. *Jewish Responses to Modernity: New Voices in America and Eastern Europe.* New York: New York University Press, 1997.

Like Water, Like Fire: An Anthology of Byelorussian Poetry from 1828 to the Present Day. Trans. Vera Rich. London: George Allen & Unwin, 1971.

Linková, Marcela. "Je gender transsexuální?" Paper presented at the Transgender Week conference, Institute of Sociology of Academy of Sciences of the Czech Republic, Prague, March 20, 2001.

Lipsitz, George. *The Possessive Investment in Whiteness: How White People Profit from Identity Politics.* Philadelphia: Temple University Press, 1998.

Longworth, Philip. *The Making of Eastern Europe: From Prehistory to Postcommunism.* New York: St. Martin's Press, 1997.

Lubachko, Ivan. *Belorussia under Soviet Rule.* Lexington: University Press of Kentucky, 1972.

Lukić, Jasmina. "Media Representations of Men and Women in Times of War and Crisis: The Case of Serbia." In *Reproducing Gender: Politics, Publics and Everyday Life after Socialism,* ed. Susan Gal and Gail Kligman, 393–423. Princeton, N.J.: Princeton University Press, 2000.

——. "Women-Centered Narratives in Contemporary Serbian and Croat Literatures." In *Engendering Slavic Literatures,* ed. Pamela Chester and Sibelan Forrester, 223–243. Bloomington: Indiana University Press, 1996.

Lynes, Robert. *Teaching English in Eastern and Central Europe.* Los Angeles: NTC Publishing Group, 1995.

Lytle, Douglas. *Pink Tanks and Velvet Hangovers: An American in Prague.* Berkeley, Calif.: Frog, 1995.

Machovec, Milan. "Feminismus není problém jazykový." *Mladá Fronta Dnes,* November 23, 2000.

Mack, Arien, ed. "Privacy in Post-Communist Europe." *Social Research* 69, no. 1 (Spring 2002).

Mack, Arien, and Elżbieta Matynia, eds. "Civil Society Revisited." *Social Research* 68, no. 4 (Winter 2001).

Maleck-Lewy, Eva, and Myra Marx Ferree, "Talking about Women and Wombs: The Discourse of Abortion and Reproductive Rights in the G.D.R. during and after the Wende." In *Reproducing Gender: Politics, Publics, and Everyday Life after Social-*

ism, ed. Susan Gal and Gail Kligman, 92–118. Princeton, N.J.: Princeton University Press, 2000.

Malečková, Jitka. "Gender, Nation and Scholarship: Reflections on Gender/Women's Studies in the Czech Republic." In *New Frontiers in Women's Studies: Knowledge, Identity and Nationalism*, ed. Mary Maynard and June Purvis, 96–112. London: Taylor and Francis, 1995.

Malmborg, Mikael, and Bo Ströth, eds. *The Meaning of Europe: Variety and Contention Within and Among Nations*. Oxford and New York: Berg, 2002.

Mandel, Ruth, and Caroline Humphrey, eds. *Markets and Moralities: Ethnographies of Postsocialism*. Oxford and New York: Berg, 2002.

March, Michael. *Description of a Struggle: The Vintage Book of Contemporary Eastern European Writing*. Introduction by Ivan Klíma. New York: Vintage Books, 1994.

Marples, David R. *Belarus: Denationalized Nation*. Amsterdam: Harwood Academic, 1999.

———. *Belarus: From Soviet Rule to Nuclear Catastrophe*. New York: St. Martin's Press, 1996.

Masek, Miroslav. "Six Years after the Velvet Revolution." *Architectural Design* 60, no. 1 (January/February 1996).

Maurer, Jadwiga. "Q i pensjonarka" ("Q and the Boarding-School Girl"). *Tygodnik Powszechny*, no. 21 (May 24, 1998): 9.

Mayhew, Alan. *Recreating Europe: The European Union's Policy towards Central and Eastern Europe*. London and New York: Cambridge University Press, 1998.

Mazierska, Ewa. "The Exclusive Pleasures of Being a Second Generation *Inteligent*: Representation of Social Class in the Films of Andrzej Wajda." *Canadian Slavonic Papers* XLIV, nos. 3–4 (September–December 2002): 233–249.

McBride, William Leon, and Yvanka Raynova. *Philosophical Reflections on the Changes in Eastern Europe*. New York: Rowman & Littlefield, 1999.

McLuhan, Marshall. *The Mechanical Bride: Folklore of Industrial Man*. London: Routledge & Kegan Paul, 1967.

Meltzer, Milton. *History of Jewish Life from Eastern Europe to America: The Lost World and the Discovered World*. Northvale, N.J.: Jason Aronson, 1996.

Mertus, Julie, Jasmina Tesanovic, Habiba Metikos, and Rada Boric, eds. *The Suitcase: Refugee Voices from Bosnia and Croatia*. Berkeley: University of California Press, 1997.

Meuschel, Sigrid. *Legitimation und Parteiherrschaft in der DDR*. Frankfurt: Suhrkamp Verlag, 1992.

Michnik, Adam. *The Church and the Left*. Ed. David Ost. Chicago: University of Chicago Press, 1993.

———. *Polskie Pytania* (Polish Questions). Warszawa: Niezalezna Oficyna Wydawnicza, 1993.

Michnik, Adam, Irena Grudzinska Gross, and Jane Cave, eds. *Letters from Freedom: Post–Cold War Realities and Perspectives*. Berkeley: University of California Press, 1998.

Miłosz, Czesław. *Poezje Wybrane: Selected Poems*. Trans. David Brooks et al. Krakow: Wydawnictwo Literackie, 1996.

Moi, Toril. "Feminist Literary Criticism." In *Modern Literary Theory: A Comparative Introduction*, ed. Ann Jefferson and David Robery, 204–221. Totowa, N.J.: Barnes and Noble Books, 1986.

Selected Bibliography

Moore, John Hampton. *Legacies of the Collapse of Marxism.* Fairfax, Va.: George Mason University Press, 1995.

Morris, Pam. *Literature and Feminism.* London: Blackwell, 1993.

Morrison, Toni. *Playing in the Dark: Whiteness and the Literary Imagination.* New York: Vintage Books, 1992.

Mrożek, Slawomir. *Dom na granicy (House on the Border).* Dialog 5 (1967): 5–18.

Mummendey, Amelie. "Verhalten zwischen sozialen Gruppen: Die Theorie der sozialen Identität," in *Theorien der Sozialpsychologie,* vol. II: *Gruppen-und Lerntheorien,* ed. Dieter Frey and Martin Irle, 185–216. Bern/Stuttgart/Toronto: Huber, 1985.

Musil, Jiří. ed. *The End of Czechoslovakia.* Budapest: Central European University Press, 1995.

Nagorski, Andrew. "The Polish-Russian Gap," *Newsweek,* July 17, 2000, 4.

———. "The Return of the Reds." *Newsweek,* December 4, 1995, 47ff.

Nicholls, Ana, Theresa Agovino, Joe Cook, Florian Gimbel, Francis Harris, and Peggy Simpson. "Fighting Corporate Flab: A Survey of Capital Markets." In *Business Central Europe,* April 1997, 41–56.

Niethammer, Lutz. "Konjunkturen und Konkurrenzen kollektiver Identität. Ideologie, Infrastruktur und Gedächtnis in der Zeitgeschichte." Commencement Address, Friedrich Schiller University, Jena, 1994. *Prokla: Zeitschrift für kritische Sozialwissenschaft* 96 (1994): 378–399.

Nikolchina, Miglena. "The Seminar: Mode d'emploi. Impure Space in the Light of Late Totalitarianism." *Differences* 13, no. 1 (2002).

Novikova, Irina. "Gender, Ethnicity and Identity Politics in Latvia." In *From Gender to Nation,* ed. Rada Iveković and Julie Mostov. Ravenna: Longo Editore, 2002.

Nowakowski, Marek. *Notatki z codziennosci (grudzien 1982–lipiec 1983) (Notes from the Everyday, December 1982–July 1983).* Warszawa: Czytelnik, 1993.

Oates-Indruchová, Libora. "Gender v médiích: nástin žíče problematiky." In *Společnost mužů a žen z aspektu gender,* ed. Eva Věšínová-Kalivodová and Hana Mažíková. Prague: Open Society Fund, 1999.

Offe, Claus. *Varieties of Transition: The East European and East German Experience.* Cambridge, Mass.: MIT Press, 1996.

O'Grady, Desmond, and Andrew M. Greeley. *The Turned Card: Christianity before and after the Wall.* Chicago: Loyola Press, 1997.

Orlovsky, Daniel, ed. *Beyond Soviet Studies.* Washington, D.C.: Woodrow Wilson Center, 1996.

Ostrowski, Jan K. *Land of the Winged Horsemen: Art in Poland, 1572–1764.* New Haven, Conn.: Yale University Press, 1999.

Ottaway, Marina. *Democratization and Ethnic Nationalism: African and Eastern European Experiences.* Policy Essay, no. 14. Washington, D.C.: Overseas Development Council, 1994.

Oushakine, Serguei. "The Fatal Splitting: Symbolizing Anxiety in Post-Soviet Russia." *Ethnos: Journal of Anthropology* (National Museum Of Ethnography, Stockholm) 66, no. 3 (2001): 291–319.

———. "In the State of Post-Soviet Aphasia: Symbolic Development in Contemporary Russia." *Europe-Asia Studies* 52, no. 6 (2000): 994.

———. "The Terrifying Mimicry of Samizdat." *Public Culture* 13, no. 2 (2001): 191–214.

Ozick, Cynthia. "Save My Child!" *The New Yorker*, June 24 and July 1, 1996, 134–147.

Paul, Barbara Dotts, comp. *The Polish-German Borderlands*. Westport, Conn.: Greenwood Publishing Group, 1994.

Paletz, David and Karol Jakubowicz. *Glasnost and After: Media and Change in Central and Eastern Europe*. Cresskill, N.J.: Hampton Press, 1995.

Parker, Andrew, Mary Russo, Doris Summer, and Patricia Yaeger, eds. *Nationalisms and Sexualities*. New York: Routledge, 1992.

Patterson, Patrick Hyder. "On the Edge of Reason: The Boundaries of Balkanism in Slovenian, Austrian, and Italian Discourse." *Slavic Review* 62, no. 1 (Spring 2003): 110–141.

Pavis, Patrice, ed. *The Intercultural Performance Reader*. New York: Routledge, 1996.

Pavlík, Petr, and Peter Shields. "Toward an Explanation of Television Broadcast Restructuring in the Czech Republic." *European Journal of Communication* 14, no. 4 (1999): 487–524.

Pavlović, Tatjana. "Remembering/Dismembering the Nation: the Archeology of Lost Knowledge." In *From Gender to Nation*, ed. Rada Iveković and Julie Mostov. Ravenna: Longo Editore, 2002.

Pejić, Bojana, and David Elliott eds. *After the Wall: Art and Culture in Post-Communist Europe*. Stockholm: Moderna Museet, 1999.

Pekárková, Iva. "Americké lesbičky si pěstují bradku." *Rudé právo*, January 15, 1998.

Pennycook, A. *The Cultural Politics of English as an International Language*. London: Longman, 1994.

Peteri, Gyorgy. *Academia under State Socialism*. New York: Columbia University Press, 1999.

Petrie, Ruth. *The Fall of Communism and the Rise of Nationalism: The Index Reader*. London: Cassell Academic Press, 1997.

Pfeil, Fred. *White Guys: Studies in Postmodern Domination and Difference*. London: Verso, 1995.

Pieterse, Jan Nederveen, and Bhikhu Parekh. *The Decolonization of Imagination: Culture, Knowledge and Power*. London: Zed Books, 1995.

Pietrasik, Zdzisław. "Odkurzony Peerel." *Polityka*, no. 30 (22 lipca 2000): 3–9.

Peterson, Dale E. *Up from Bondage: The Literatures of Russian and African American Soul*. Durham, N.C., and London: Duke University Press, 2000.

Phillipson, R. *Linguistic Imperialism*. Oxford: Oxford University Press, 1992.

Piirainen, Timo. *Towards a New Social Order in Russia: Transforming Structures and Everyday Life*. Hanover, N.H.: Dartmouth University Press, 1997.

Podgórska, Joanna. "Powrócić tu" ("To Return Here"). *Polityka*, 20, no. 2350 (May 18, 2002): 70–72.

Pogonowski, Iwo, and Richard Pipes. *Jews in Poland: A Documentary History*. New York: Hippocrene Books, 1997.

Pondžlíčková-Mašlová, Jaroslava, and Antonín Brzek. *Třetí pohlaví?* Praha: Scientia Medica, 1992.

Pratt, Mary Louise. *Imperial Eyes: Travel Writing and Transculturation*. New York: Routledge, 1992.

Procházka, Ivo. *Coming Out: převodce obdobím nejistoty, kdy kluci a holky hledají sami sebe*. Praha: SAP and SOHO, 1994.

Quinlan, Paul D., and Anthony DeLuca, eds. *Romania, Culture and Nationalism: A Tribute to Radu Florescu*. New York: East European Monographs, 1998.

Rabasa, José. "Allegories of Atlas." In *The Post-Colonial Studies Reader*, ed. Bill Ash-croft, Gareth Griffiths, and Helen Tiffin. New York: Routledge, 1995.

Radel, Nicholas F. "The Transnational Ga(y)ze: Constructing the East European Ob-ject of Desire in Gay Film and Pornography after the Fall of the Wall." *Cinema Journal* 41, no. 1 (2001): 40–62.

Ramet, Sabrina P. *Nihil Obstat: Religion, Politics, and Social Change in East-Central Europe and Russia*. Durham, N.C.: Duke University Press, 1998.

———. *Whose Democracy? Nationalism, Religion, and the Doctrine of Collective Rights in Post-1989 Eastern Europe*. Lanham, Md.: Rowman & Littlefield, 1997.

Ramet, Sabrina P., ed. *Eastern Europe: Politics, Culture, and Society since 1939*. Bloom-ington & Indianapolis: Indiana University Press, 1999.

———. *Rocking the State: Rock Music and Politics in Eastern Europe and Russia*. Boul-der, Colo.: Westview Press, 1994.

Ramet, Sabrina P., and Ivo Banac. *Balkan Babel: The Disintegration of Yugoslavia from the Death of Tito to Ethnic War*. Boulder, Colo.: Westview Press, 1996.

Regionální zpráva o institucionálních mechanismech pro zlepšení postavení žen v zemích střední a všchodní Evropy—Národní zpráva České republiky. Praha: Centrum pro Gender Studies, 1998.

Reid S. E., and D. Crowley, eds. *Style and Socialism: Modernity and Material Culture in Post-War Eastern Europe*. Oxford and New York: Oxford University Press, 2000.

Rév, István, et al. "Identifying Histories: Eastern Europe before and after 1989." Intro-duction to *Representations* (Winter 1995).

Rice, Timothy. *"May It Fill Your Soul": Experiencing Bulgarian Music*. Chicago: Uni-versity of Chicago Press, 1994.

Richie, Alexandra. *Faust's Metropolis: A History of Berlin*. New York: Carroll & Graf, 1998.

Ries, Nancy. *Russian Talk: Culture and Conversation during Perestroika*. Ithaca, N.Y.: Cornell University Press, 1997.

Rogoff, Irit. "'Other's Others': Spectatorship and Difference." In *Vision in Context: Historical and Contemporary Perspectives on Sight*, ed. Teresa Brennan and Mar-tin Jay. New York: Routledge, 1996.

Roman, Denise. *Fragmented Identities: Popular Culture, Sex, and Everyday Life in Postcommunist Romania*. Lanham. Md.: Lexington Books/Rowman & Littlefield, 2003.

Roskin, Michael. *The Rebirth of East Europe*. Upper Saddle River, N.J.: Prentice Hall, 1997.

Rouse, John. "Comment." *Theatre Journal* 48, no. 4 (December 1996): 404.

Rozwadowska, Ewa. "Soc-land, sosland—Czy powstanie muzeum komunizmu w War-szawie?" *Architektura/Murator* 1, no. 64 (styczeń 2000): 51–55.

Said, Edward W. *Culture and Imperialism*. 1978; reprint, London: Chatto and Windus, 1993.

———. *Orientalism: Western Conceptions of the Orient*. New York: Penguin, 1995.

———. *The World, the Text, and the Critic*. London: Vintage, 1983.

———. "Yeats and Decolonization." In *The Edward Said Reader*. New York: Vintage Books, 2000.

Salecl, Renata. *(Per)Versions of Love and Hate*. London: Verso, 1998.

———. *The Spoils of Freedom: Psychoanalysis and Feminism after the Fall of Socialism*. New York: Routledge, 1994.

Sandi, Ioana. "Ethics for and Architecture of Another Europe." *Architectural Design* 60, no. 1 (January/February 1996).

Sayer, Derek. *The Coasts of Bohemia: A Czech History*. Princeton, N.J.: Princeton University Press, 1998.

Schechner, Richard. "Preface." In *The Grotowski Sourcebook*, ed. Lisa Wolford and Richard Schechner, xxv–xxviii. London and New York: Routledge, 200.

Schindelbeck, Dirk. "Stilgedanken zur Macht. 'Lerne wirken ohne zu handeln!': Hans Domizlaff, eines Werbeberaters Geschichte." In *"Ins Gehirn der Masse kriechen!" Werbung und Mentalitätsgeschichte*, ed. Rainer Gries, Volker Ilgen, and Dirk Schindelbeck. Wissenschaftliche Buchgesellschaft Darmstadt, 1995.

Schulte-Sasse, Jochen. *Literarischer Kitsch*. Tübingen: Max Niemeyer Verlag, 1979.

Segel, Harold. *Columbia Guide to the Literatures of Eastern Europe since 1945*. New York: Columbia University Press, 2003.

Schierup, Carl-Ulrik, ed. *Scramble for the Balkans: Nationalism, Globalism and the Political Economy of Reconstruction*. New York: St. Martin's Press, 1999.

Scott, Joan W., Cora Kaplan, and Debra Keates, eds. *Transitions, Environments, Translations: Feminisms in International Politics*. New York: Routledge, 1997.

Shallcross, Bożena, ed. *Framing the Polish Home*. Athens, Ohio: Ohio University Press, 2002.

———. *Through the Poet's Eye: The Travels of Zagajewski, Herbert, and Brodsky*. Evanston, Ill.: Northwestern University Press, 2002.

Shohat, Ella, and Robert Stam. *Unthinking Eurocentrism: Multiculturalism and the Media*. New York: Routledge, 1994.

Sierakowiak, Dawid. *The Diary of Dawid Sierakowiak: Five Notebooks from the Lodz Ghetto*. Trans. Kamil Turowski. Ed. Alan Adelson. Oxford and New York: Oxford University Press, 1998.

Siklová, Jirina. "Feminism and the Roots of Apathy in the Czech Republic." *Social Research* 64, no. 2 (Summer 1997).

Silber, Laura, ed. *Yugoslavia: Death of a Nation*. New York: Penguin USA, 1997.

Silverman, Carol. "The Gender of the Profession: Music, Dance, and Reputation among Balkan Muslim Romani (Gypsy) Women." In *Gender and Music in the Mediterranean*, ed. Tulia Magrini. Chicago: University of Chicago Press, forthcoming.

———. "Music and Marginality: Roma (Gypsies) of Bulgaria and Macedonia." In *Retuning Culture: Musical Changes in Central and Eastern Europe*, ed. Mark Slobin, 231–253. Durham, N.C.: Duke University Press, 1996.

———. "Persecution and Politicization: Roma (Gypsies) of Eastern Europe." *Cultural Survival*, 19, no. 2 (1995): 43–49. Special issue on Eastern Europe, ed. Loring Danforth.

———. "Rom (Gypsy) Music." In *Garland Encyclopedia of World Music*, Europe volume, ed. Timothy Rice, James Porter, and Christopher Goertzen, 270–293. New York: Garland, 1999.

Silverman, Kaja. *The Threshold of the Visible World*. New York: Routledge, 1996.

Simon, Ted. *The Gypsy in Me: From Germany to Romania in Search of Youth, Truth, and Dad*. New York: Random House, 1997.

Slobin, Mark, ed. *Retuning Culture: Musical Changes in Central and Eastern Europe*. Durham, N.C.: Duke University Press, 1997.

Šmejkalová, Jiřina. "Gender as an Analytical Category of Post-Communist Studies." In

Gender in Transition in Eastern and Central Europe Proceedings, ed. Gabriele Jahnert, Jana Gohrisch, Daphne Hahn, Hildegard Maria Nickel, Iris Peinl, and Katrin Schafgen. Berlin: Trafo Verlag, 2001.

——. "Strašidlo feminismu v ženském 'porevolučním' tisku: úvaha, doufejme, historická." In *Žena a muž v médiích*, ed. Hana Havelková and Mirek Vodráčka, 16–19. Praha: Nadace Gender Studies, 1998.

Smith, Graham, Vivien Law, Andrew Wilson, Annette Bohr and Edward Allworth. *Nation-Building in the Post-Soviet Borderlands: The Politics of National Identities.* Cambridge and New York: Cambridge University Press, 1998.

Smith, Karen E. *The Making of EU Foreign Policy: The Case of Eastern Europe.* New York: St. Martin's Press, 1999.

Smith, Patricia J., ed. *After the Wall: Eastern Germany since 1989.* Boulder, Colo.: Westview Press, 1998.

Szmit-Zawierucha, Danuta. *Opowieści o Warszawie.* Warszawa: Wydawnictwo DiG, 2000.

Snitow, Ann, Christine Stansell, and Sharon Thompson, eds. *Powers of Desire: The Politics of Sexuality.* New York: Monthly Review Press, 1993.

Softic, Elma. *Sarajevo Days, Sarajevo Nights.* Trans. Nada Conic. St. Paul, Minn.: Hungry Mind Publishers, 1996.

Sokolová, Věra. "Representations of Homosexuality and the Separation of Gender and Sexuality in the Czech Republic before and after 1989." In *Political Systems and Definitions of Gender Roles*, ed. Ann Katherine Isaacs, 273–290. Pisa, Italy: Edizione Plus, Universita di Pisa, 2001.

Sontag, Susan. Comments in "Symposium on Kitsch." *Salmagundi* (Winter/Spring 1990).

——. "A Lament for Bosnia." *The Nation* 261, no. 22 (December 25, 1995): 818–821.

Soto, Hermine G. de, and Nora Dudwick, eds. *Fieldwork Dilemmas: Anthropologists in Postsocialist States.* Madison: University of Wisconsin Press, 2000.

South End Press Collective, eds. *Talking about a Revolution: Interviews with Noam Chomsky, Howard Zinn, Barbara Ehrenreich, bell hooks, Winona Laduke, Manning Marable, Urvashi Vaid, and Michael Albert.* Boston: South End Press, 1998.

Spiegelman, Art. *Maus: A Survivor's Tale. Part I: My Father Bleeds History.* New York: Pantheon Books, 1986.

——. *Maus: A Survivor's Tale. Part II: And Here My Troubles Began.* New York: Pantheon Books, 1991.

Splichal, Slavko, and John A. Lent, eds. *Media beyond Socialism: Theory and Practice in East-Central Europe.* Boulder, Colo.: Westview Press, 1995.

Staar, Richard F., ed. *Transition to Democracy in Poland.* New York: St. Martin's Press, 1998.

Stefanova, Kalina, ed. *Eastern European Theater after the Iron Curtain.* Amsterdam: Harwood Academic Publishers, 2000.

Stehlíková, Dřamila, Ivo Procházka, Jiří Hromada. *Homosexualita, společnost a AIDS v ČR.* Praha: Orbis 1995.

Stiglmayer, Alexandra, ed. *Mass Rape: The War against Women in Bosnia-Herzegovina.* Trans. Marion Faber. Lincoln: University of Nebraska Press, 1994.

Sujecki, Janusz. "Druga śmierć miasta. Przyczyny i konsekwencje." In *Historyczne centrum Warszawy: Urbanistyka, architektura, problemy konserwatorskie*, ed. Bożena Wierzbicka. Warszawa: Biblioteka Towarzystwa Opieki nad Zabytkami, 1998.

Suleiman, Susan Rubin. *Budapest Diary: In Search of the Motherbook*. Lincoln: University of Nebraska Press, 1996.

———. *Risking Who One Is: Encounters with Contemporary Art and Literature*. Cambridge, Mass.: Harvard University Press, 1994.

Suny, Ronald, and Michael D. Kennedy, eds. *Intellectuals and the Articulation of the Nation*. Ann Arbor: University of Michigan Press, 1999.

Sutherland, Jeanne. *Schooling in the New Russia: Innovation and Change, 1984–95*. New York: St Martin's Press, 1999.

Svacha, Rostisav, ed. *Devetsil: Czech Avant-Garde of the 1920s and 30s* (Oxford: Museum of Modern Art, and London: Design Museum, 1990.

Symynkywicz, Jeffrey B. *1989: The Year the World Changed*. Parsippany, N.J.: Dillon Press, 1995.

Szymborska, Wisława. *Miracle Fair: Selected Poems of Wisława Szymborska*. Trans. Joanna Trzeciak. New York and London: W.W. Norton & Co., 2001.

———. *Nic dwa razy. Nothing Twice: Selected Poems*. Selected and trans. Stanisław Barańczak and Clare Cavanagh. Krakow: Wydawnictwo Literackie, 1997.

———. *View with a Grain of Sand: Selected Poems*. Trans. Stanisław Barańczak and Clare Cavanagh. New York: Harcourt Brace, 1995.

Szalai, Wendelin. "Wie 'funktionierte' Identitätsbildung in der DDR?" In *Identitätsbildung und Geschichtsbewusstsein nach der Vereinigung Deutschlands*, ed. Uwe Uffelmann, 58–108. Weinheim: Beltz Fachverlag, 1993.

Szpilman, Władysław. *Pianista*. Kraków: Wydawnictwo Znak, 2002.

Tagliabue, John. "A Year after Fall of Wall, Some Nostalgia." *The New York Times*, November 9, 1990.

Talandová, Jaroslava. *Sociální postavení lesbických žen: alternativní rodinné modely v kontextu heterosexuální společnosti*. Praha: Alia, 1998.

Talbot, Margaret. "Back to the Future: Pining for the Good Old Days in Germany." *New Republic*, July 18, 1994.

Taras, Ray, ed. *National Identities and Ethnic Minorities in Eastern Europe: Selected Papers from the Fifth World Congress of Central and East European Studies, Warsaw, 1995*. New York: St. Martin's Press, 1998.

Tayler, Jeffrey. "This Side of Ultima Thule." *The Atlantic Monthly*, April 1997, 24–41.

Taylor, Timothy. *Global Pop: World Music, World Markets*. New York: Routledge, 1997.

Tismeanu, Vladimir. *Fantasies of Salvation: Democracy, Nationalism, and Myth in Post-Communist Europe*. Princeton, N.J.: Princeton University Press, 1998.

Titkow, Anna. "On the Appreciated Role of Women." Trans. Paweł Cichawa. In *Women on the Polish Labor Market*, ed. Mike Ingham, Hilary Ingham, and Henryk Domanski, 21–40. Budapest and New York: Central European University Press, 2001.

Todorov, Tzvetan. *On Human Diversity: Nationalism, Racism, and Exoticism in French Thought*. Trans. Catherine Porter. Cambridge, Mass.: Harvard University Press, 1993.

———. *The Morals of History*. Trans. Alyson Waters. Minneapolis: University of Minnesota Press, 1995.

Todorova, Maria. "Historical Tradition and Transformation in Bulgaria: Women's Issues or Feminist Issues?" *Journal of Women's History* 5, no. 3 (1994): 129–143.

———. *Imagining the Balkans*. Oxford and New York: Oxford University Press, 1997.

Selected Bibliography

Tollner, Pavel. "Zákon počkozující rodinu." *Mladá fronta Dnes*, March 3, 2001.

Torgovnick, Marianna. *Gone Primitive: Savage Intellects, Modern Lives.* Chicago: University of Chicago Press, 1990.

Tuszynska, Agata. *Singer: Pejzarze pamieci (Singer: Landscapes of Memory).* Gdańsk: Wydawnictwo Marabut, 1996.

Tyszka, Juliusz. "Polish Alternative Theatre during the Period of Transition, 1989–94." Trans. Jolanta Cynkutis and Tom Randolph. *New Theatre Quarterly* 12, no. 1 (February 1996): 71–78.

Ugrešić, Dubravka. *The Culture of Lies: Antipolitical Essays.* Trans. Celia Hawkesworth. University Park: Pennsylvania State University Press, 1998.

Updike, John. "Licks of Love in the Heart of the Cold War." *The Atlantic Monthly,* May 1998, 81–90.

Veenis, Milena. "Consumption in East Germany: The Seduction and Betrayal of Things." *Journal of Material Culture* 4, no. 1 (1999): 79–112.

Verdery, Katherine. "From Parent-State to Family Patriarchs: Gender and Nation in Contemporary Eastern Europe." *East European Politics and Societies* 8, no. 2 (1994): 225–255.

———. *The Political Lives of Dead Bodies: Exhumation, Reburial, and Postsocialist Change.* New York: Columbia University Press, 1999.

———. *What Was Socialism, and What Comes Next?* Princeton, N.J.: Princeton University Press, 1996.

Vianu, Lidia. *Censorship in Romania.* Budapest: Central European University Press, 1998.

Vickers, Miranda. *Albania: From Anarchy to a Balkan Identity.* New York: New York University Press, 1997.

Vodráčka, Mirek. *Esej o politickém harémismu: kritická zpráva o stavu feminismu v Čechách.* Brno: Nakladatelství Čestmír Kocar, 1999.

Wachtel, Andrew. *Making a Nation, Breaking a Nation: Literature and Cultural Politics in Yugoslavia.* Stanford, Calif.: Stanford University Press, 1998.

———. "Translation, Imperialism, and National Self-Definition in Russia." *Public Culture* 11, no. 1 (1999).

Walicki, Andrzej. *Marxism and the Leap to the Kingdom of Freedom: The Rise and Fall of the Communist Utopia.* Stanford, Calif.: Stanford University Press, 1997.

———. *Philosophy and Romantic Nationalism: The Case of Poland.* Oxford: Clarendon Press, 1982.

Wallace, Claire, and Sijka Kovatcheva. *Youth in Society: The Construction and Deconstruction of Youth in East and West Europe.* New York: St. Martin's Press, 1998.

Wanner, Catherine. *Burden of Dreams: History and Identity in Post-Soviet Ukraine.* University Park: Pennsylvania State University Press, 1998.

Wark, McKenzie. *Virtual Geography: Living with Global Media Events.* Bloomington: Indiana University Press, 1994.

Wedel, Janine R. *Collision and Collusion: The Strange Case of Western Aid to Eastern Europe.* New York: St. Martin's Press, 1998.

Wejnert, Barbara ed. *Transition to Democracy in Eastern Europe and Russia: Impact on Politics, Economy, and Culture.* Westport, Conn.: Praeger, 2002.

West, Cornel. *Prophetic Reflections: Notes on Race and Power in America.* Vol. 2. Monroe, Maine: Common Courage Press, 1993.

———. *Prophetic Thought in Postmodern Times Beyond Eurocentrism and Multicultural-ism.* Vol. 1. Monroe, Maine: Common Courage Press, 1993.

Wiącek, Taddeusz. *Zabic Żyda!: Kulisy i tajemnice pogromu kieleckiego 1946 [To Kill a Jew: Background and Secrets of the Kielce Pogram 1946].* Kraków: Telemax, 1992.

Wierzbicka, A. "Antitotalitarian Language in Poland: Some Mechanisms of Linguistic Self-Defense." *Language in Society* 19 (1990): 1–59.

Williams, Raymond. *Keywords: A Vocabulary of Culture and Society.* New York: Oxford University Press, 1983.

Wilson, Andrew. "National History and National Identity in Ukraine and Belarus." In *Nation-Building in the Post-Soviet Borderlands,* ed. Graham Smith, Vivien Law, Andrew Wilson, Annette Bohr, and Edward Allworth, 23–47. Cambridge and New York: Cambridge University Press, 1998.

Wilson, Elizabeth. *The Sphinx and the City: Urban Life, the Control of Disorder, and Women.* Berkeley: University of California Press, 1991.

Wislocki, Peter. "Warsaw's Identity Crisis." *World Architecture* 86 (May 2000): 35.

Wolchik, Sharon L. "Reproductive Policies in the Czech and Slovak Republics." In *Reproducing Gender: Politics, Publics, and Everyday Life after Socialism,* ed. Susan Gal and Gail Kligman, 58–92. Princeton, N.J.: Princeton University Press, 2000.

Wolchik, Sharon L., and Alfred G. Meyer, eds. *Women, State, and Party in Eastern Europe.* Durham, N.C.: Duke University Press, 1985.

Wolff, Larry. *Inventing Eastern Europe: The Map of Civilization on the Mind of the Enlightenment.* Stanford, Conn.: Stanford University Press, 1996.

Women 2000: An Investigation into the Status of Women's Rights on Central and South-Eastern Europe and the Newly Independent States. Vienna: International Helsinki Federation for Human Rights, 2000.

Women of the World: Laws and Policies Affecting Their Reproductive Lives—East Central Europe. New York: Center for Reproductive Law and Policy, 2000.

Woysznis-Terlikowska, Grażyna. *Wczoraj-dziś-jutro Warszawy.* Warszawa: Książka i Wiedza, 1950.

Yezierska, Anzia. "How I Found America." In *How I Found America: Collected Stories of Anzia Yezierska.* New York, Persea Books, 1991.

Young, Robert. *White Mythologies: Writing History and the West.* New York: Routledge, 1990.

Yuval-Davis, Nira. *Gender and Nation.* London: Sage Publications, 1997.

Zaborowska, Magdalena. "The Best View Is from the Top: Autobiographical Snapshots, Communist Monuments, and Some Thoughts on (Post)Totalitarian Homeless-ness." In *Framing the Polish Home,* ed. Bożena Shallcross, 179–215. Athens, Ohio: Ohio University Press, 2002.

———. "Ethnicity in Exile in Maria Kuncewicz's Writings." In *Something of My Very Own to Say: American Women Writers of Polish Descent,* ed. Thomas S. and Rita Gladsky, 170–190. New York: Columbia University Press, 1997.

———. "The Height of (Architectural) Seduction: Reading the 'Changes' through Sta-lin's Palace of Culture in Warsaw, Poland." *Journal of Architectural Education* 54, no. 4 (May 2001): 205–217. Special issue "Political Change and Physical Change," ed. Jeffrey M. Chusid.

———. *How We Found America: Reading Gender through East European Immigrant Narratives.* Chapel Hill: University of North Carolina Press, 1995.

———. "Lire l'esprit post-totalitaire." ("Engendrer l'autre de l'Europe de l'ouest"). In *La Memoire des Dechets—essais sur la culture et la valeur du passe* (*Memory of Waste: Objects and Images in the Economy of the Past*), ed. Claude Dionne, Brian Neville, and Johanne Villeneuve. Trans. Johanne Villeneuve. Quebec: Nuit Blanche Editeur, 1988.

———. "Three Passages through (In)Visible Warsaw." *Harvard Design Magazine* 13 (Winter/Spring 2001): 52–59.

Zagajewski, Adam. "Changes in the East" In *Two Cities: On Exile, History, and the Imagination.* Trans. Lillian Vallee. New York: Farrar, Straus, Giroux, 1995.

———. *Solidarity, Solitude: Essays by Adam Zagajewski.* Trans. Lillian Vallee. New York: Ecco Press, 1990.

Zagańczyk, Marek. "Between the East and the West: *Carmina Burana* by Włodzimierz Staniewski at the Gardzienice Theatre Association." *The Theatre in Poland,* May 1991, 6–8.

Zepetnek, Steven T. de, ed. *Comparative Central European Culture.* West Lafayette, Ind.: Purdue University Press, 2002.

Zaremba, Marcin. "Urzad zapomnienia." *Polityka* 41, no. 2319 (13 October 2001).

Ževela, Vladimír, Alena Plavcová, and Eva Hlinovská. "Ve světě českých gayů." *Lidové Noviny—Pátek,* April 4, 2001.

Zherebkin, Sergei, and Barbara Wejnert. "The Politics of Architecture and the Architecture of Politics." In *Transition to Democracy in Eastern Europe and Russia: Impact on Politics, Economy, and Culture,* ed. Barbara Wejnert, ed. Westport, Conn.: Praeger, 2002.

Zielińska, Eleonora. "Between Ideology, Politics, and Common Sense: The Discourse of Reproductive Rights in Poland." In *Reproducing Gender: Politics, Publics, and Everyday Life after Socialism,* ed. Susan Gal and Gail Kligman, 23–57. Princeton, N.J.: Princeton University Press, 2000.

Zielińska, Marta. *Warszawa-dziwne miasto.* Warszawa: Instytut Badań Literackich, 1995.

Zinn, Howard. *Marx in Soho: A Play on History.* Boston: South End Press, 1999.

Žižek, Slavoj. "Caught in Another's Dream in Bosnia." In *Why Bosnia: Writings on the Balkan War,* ed. Rabia Ali and Lawrence Lifschutz, 233–241. Stony Creek, Conn.: The Pamphleteer's Press, 1993.

———. *Did Somebody Say Totalitarianism? Five Interventions in the (Mis)use of a Notion.* New York and London: Verso, 2001.

———. *The Metastases of Enjoyment: Six Essays on Women and Causality.* London: Verso, 1994.

———. "Multiculturalism; or, The Cultural Logic of Multinational Capitalism." *New Left Review* 225 (September/October, 1995): 28–52.

———. *Tarrying with the Negative: Kant, Hegel, and the Critique of Ideology.* Durham, N.C.: Duke University Press, 1993.

Contributors

Mark Andryczyk is a Ph.D. candidate in Ukrainian Literature at the University of Toronto.

Andaluna Borcila teaches Humanities, Culture, and Writing at James Madison College, Michigan State University.

Halina Filipowicz teaches at the University of Wisconsin-Madison. Her books include *The Great Tradition and Its Legacy: The Evolution of Dramatic and Musical Theater in Austria and Central Europe* (co-edited with Michael Cherlin and Richard L. Rudolph).

Sibelan Forrester is Associate Professor of Russian at Swarthmore College, where she also teaches Eastern European Literature in Translation and a Translation Workshop. She is co-editor (with Pamela Chester) of *Engendering Slavic Literature* and translator of Irena Vrkljan's *The Silk, the Shears*.

Elena Gapova is Associate Professor and Director of the Centre for Gender Studies at European Humanities University in Minsk. She is editor of the books *Zhenshchiny na krayu Evropy* (*Women at the Edge of Europe*); and (with Almira Ousmanova) *Gendernye istorii Vostochnoi Evropy* (*Gendered (Hi)stories from Eastern Europe*) and *Antologiya gendernoi teorii* (*Anthology of Gender Theory*).

Rainer Gries is a Doctor Habil. of Philosophy, guest Professor at the Institut für Publizistik-und Kommunikationswissenschaft der Universität Wien (University of Vienna, Austria), and Privatdozent at the Historischen Institut der Friedrich-Schiller-Universität Jena (Germany). His recent publications include *Sozialistische Helden. Eine Kulturgeschichte von Propagandafiguren in Osteuropa und der DDR* (co-edited with Silke Satjukow); *Produkte als Medien. Kulturgeschichte der Produktkommunikation in der Bundesrepublik und der DDR;* and *Die Mark der DDR. Eine Kommunikationsgeschichte der sozialistischen deutschen Währung.*

David Houston is Director of the Rudolph E. Lee Gallery and Lecturer in Art and Architectural History at the College of Architecture, Arts and Humanities, Clemson University.

Contributors

Bill Johnston is Director of the Polish Studies Center at Indiana University. His most recent publications are *Values in English Language Teaching* and a translation of Magdalena Tulli's *Dreams and Stones*.

Paul Krainak is an artist, critic, and Professor of Painting at West Virginia University. He is a contributing editor to *Artpapers Magazine* and has published numerous essays in exhibition catalogs and magazines such as *Sculpture, Afterimage,* the *New Art Examiner,* and *Inland Architect.*

Willard Pate is a teacher of American Literature at Furman University by profession and a photographer by avocation. Her photographs have won numerous awards in juried shows and are in several private collections.

Anca Rosu is Chair of Composition and Communications at the DeVry College of Technology in North Brunswick, New Jersey, and is author of *The Metaphysics of Sound in Wallace Stevens.*

Carol Silverman, Associate Professor of Anthropology and Folklore at the University of Oregon, is involved with East European culture and music as a researcher, performer, and teacher and has investigated the relationships among politics, music, identity, and gender.

Věra Sokolová is Assistant Professor of History and Gender Studies at the School of Humanities of Charles University in Prague, Czech Republic.

Wisława Szymborska is one of the most prominent living poets. Born in Bnin, Poland, she has lived in Kraków since 1931. In 1996 she won the Nobel Prize for Literature.

Joanna Trzeciak is Visiting Assistant Professor of Russian at Reed College and has published work on Vladimir Nabokov as well as translations of Szymborska.

Lisa Whitmore, Ph.D., has published various articles and completed a dissertation on fringe poets in the GDR at Stanford University.

Magdalena J. Zaborowska is Associate Professor in the Program in American Culture and the Center for Afroamerican and African Studies at the University of Michigan. She is author of *How We Found America: Reading Gender through East-European Immigrant Narratives* and editor of *Other Americans, Other Americas: The Politics and Poetics of Multiculturalism* and (with Nicholas F. Radel and Tracy Fessenden) *The Puritan Origins of American Sex: Religion, Sexuality and National Identity in American Literature.*

Index

Index

Index

Hall, Willis, 175
Hamer, Dean, 266n39
Hampel, Angela, 95
Hardtwig, Wolfgang, 198n30
Harris, Francis, 14
Hartley, John, 43, 63n12
Harwood, Ronald, 102
Havel, Václav, 78, 120, 121
Havelková, Hana, 263n4, 264nn5,9
Hawkesworth, Celia, 178n4
Hennecke, Adolf, 192, 198n25
Hensel, Kerstin, 91, 92–93
Heterosexism, 262, 262
Heterosexuality, 259, 260
Hitler, Adolf, 100, 101, 116, 151, 155, 174
Hlinovská, Eva, 266n27
Hobsbawm, E., 232n3
Hodge, R., 133
Hoffman, Eva, 10, 22–23, 44, 47, 54–58
Höge, Helmut, 90
Holíková, Jana, 266n28
Holliday, A., 134
Holocaust, 19, 98, 99, 100, 156, 174, 210
Homosexuality, 32n22, 251, 253, 259–263,
    263n1, 265n25, 267n46
Honecker, Erich, 92, 183, 193
hooks, bell, 2
Hoptman, Laura J., 43, 59
Horbatski, Uladislau, 86n11
Hromada, Jiří, 261–262, 265n26, 266n33
Huggan, Graham, 6
Humor, 5, 6, 26, 194
Hungary, 11, 12, 55, 75, 142, 228, 234n42
Huun-Huur-Tu, 224–225
Hymes, Dell, 138

Iavors'kyi, Orest, 240
Ilgen, Volker, 199n33
Intellectual, 5, 68, 72, 75, 78–80, 82, 84–85,
    164, 239, 241, 244, 271, 275–276, 278, 281
Irvanets', Oleksandr, 238, 245, 249n2
Ivashchyshyn, Markian, 246

Jähn, Sigmund, 192, 194, 198n27
Jahnert, Gabriele, 264n8
Jakoby, Barbara, 196n4
Jamison, Janis, 224
Janion, Maria, 164
Janošová, Pavlína, 265n26, 266n27
Jarocki, Jerzy, 169
Jarzebski, Jerzy, 166
Jewish culture and experience, 3, 7, 18–19,

33n29, 40, 41, 75, 78, 81, 98, 99–107, 116,
    152, 155, 156, 165, 174, 210
Jewish Renaissance Foundation (Warsaw), 105
John Paul II, Pope, 114, 115, 177, 234n39
Johnson, K., 138
Johnston, Bill, 131, 135, 137
Jong, Erica, 81
Jung, Franz, 93

Kahn, Danny, 218, 223, 233n27
Kant, Hermann, 92
Kantor, Tadeusz, 168–169
Kaplan, Robert, 12, 40, 146–158
Karmans'kyj, Petro, 239, 246, 249n3
Kennedy, Michael, 10
King, Stephen, 78
Kisielewski, Stefan, 108, 118n32
Klain, Barbara, 100, 110, 117n11, 118nn14,16
Klamerus, Wojciech, 104, 105, 118n21
Kligman, Gail, 216, 219, 220, 221, 222, 228,
    229–230, 252, 264nn5,6
Klíma, Ivan, 124, 125n9
Kočela, Jan, 266n30
Kohanov, Linda, 232n12
Kohrt, Wolfgang, 197n6
Konwicki, Tadeusz, 117n7
Kowalewski, Michael, 146, 154
Krainak, Paul, 211n2
Krajewski, Stanisław, 19
Krasel, Christine, 197n8
Krauss, M., 134
Kress, G., 133
Kristeva, Julia, 6, 13, 17, 26, 32n21, 34n31,
    34–35n40, 82, 87n33
Kronenfeld, D. B., 132
Krytyka, 243, 249n5
Kuhn, Thomas, 149, 153
Kuncewicz, Maria, 8, 97, 117n2
Kundera, Milan, 73, 78, 86n25, 124, 125n10
Kupala, Yanka, 82–83
Kurkela, Vesa, 231
Kutev, Filip, 213, 214, 219, 220, 222, 223,
    232nn4,5,12
Kuteva, Maria, 214
Kvapil, Tomáš, 266n44
Kwaśniewski, Aleksander, 128
Kyiv (Kiev), 73, 243, 245

Labuda, Barbara, 15
Labor camp, 155. See also Concentration
    camps
Lampland, Martha, 216, 228

316

Index

Index